ARDEN
OF FAVERSHAM

ARDEN EARLY MODERN DRAMA

ARDEN EARLY MODERN DRAMA

ARDEN OF FAVERSHAM

Edited by
CATHERINE RICHARDSON

THE ARDEN SHAKESPEARE
LONDON · NEW YORK · OXFORD · NEW DELHI · SYDNEY

THE ARDEN SHAKESPEARE
Bloomsbury Publishing Plc
50 Bedford Square, London, WC1B 3DP, UK
1385 Broadway, New York, NY 10018, USA
29 Earlsfort Terrace, Dublin 2, Ireland

BLOOMSBURY, THE ARDEN SHAKESPEARE and the Arden Shakespeare logo are
trademarks of Bloomsbury Publishing Plc

First published in Great Britain 2022

Cover design by Charlotte Daniels
Cover images: Texture © Caracter Design / iStock; Bottles © Jill Ferry / Trevillion Images

A catalogue record for this book is available from the British Library.

A catalog record for this book is available from the Library of Congress.

ISBN: HB: 978-1-4742-8930-6
          PB: 978-1-4742-8929-0
          ePDF: 978-1-4742-8932-0
          eBook: 978-1-4742-8931-3

Series: Arden Early Modern Drama

Typeset by RefineCatch Limited, Bungay, Suffolk
Printed and bound in India

To find out more about our authors and books visit www.bloomsbury.com
and sign up for our newsletters.

The Editor

Catherine Richardson is Professor of Early Modern Studies at the University of Kent, UK. She is author of *Domestic Life and Domestic Tragedy in Early Modern England: The Material Life of the Household* (2006), *Shakespeare and Material Culture* (2011) and (with Tara Hamling) *A Day at Home in Early Modern England: Material Culture and Domestic Life 1500–1700*. She is editor of *Clothing Culture 1350–1650* (2004), with Tara Hamling, *Everyday Objects: Medieval and Early Modern Material Culture and its Meanings* (2010), and with Tara Hamling and David Gaimster, *The Routledge Handbook of Material Culture in Early Modern Europe* (2016).

For Genevieve, who has grown up on the marsh, in sight of the Ferry

CONTENTS

LIST OF
ILLUSTRATIONS

GENERAL EDITORS' PREFACE

Arden Early Modern Drama (AEMD) is an expansion of the acclaimed Arden Shakespeare to include the plays of other dramatists of the early modern period. The series publishes dramatic texts from the early modern period in the established tradition of the Arden Shakespeare, using a similar style of presentation and offering the same depth of information and high standards of scholarship. We define 'early modern drama' broadly, to encompass plays written and performed at any time from the late fifteenth to the late seventeenth century. The attractive and accessible format and well-informed editorial content are designed with particular regard to the needs of students studying literature and drama in the final years of secondary school and in colleges and universities. Texts are presented in modern spelling and punctuation; stage directions are expanded to clarify theatrical requirements and possibilities; and speech prefixes (the markers of identity at the beginning of each new speech) are regularized. Each volume contains illustrations both from the period and from later performance history; a full discussion of the current state of criticism of the play; and information about the textual and performance contexts from which the play first emerged. The goal of the series is to make these wonderful but sometimes neglected plays as intelligible as those of Shakespeare to twenty-first-century readers.

AEMD editors bring a high level of critical engagement and textual sophistication to their work. They provide guidance in assessing critical approaches to their play, developing arguments from the best scholarly work to date and generating new perspectives. A particular focus of an AEMD edition is the play as it was first performed in the theatre. The title-page of each volume displays the name of the company for which the play was written and the theatre at which it was first staged: in the Introduction the play is discussed as part of a company repertory as well as of an authorial canon. Finally, each edition presents a full scholarly discussion of the base text and other relevant materials as physical and social documents, and the Introduction describes issues arising in the early history of the publication and reception of the text.

Commentary notes, printed immediately below the playtext, offer compact but detailed exposition of the language, historical context and theatrical significance of the play. They explain textual ambiguities and, when an action may be interpreted in different ways, they summarize the arguments. Where appropriate they point the reader to fuller discussions in the Introduction.

CONVENTIONS

AEMD editions always include illustrations of pages from the early texts on which they are based. Comparison between these illustrations and the edited text immediately enables the reader to see clearly what a critical edition is and does. In summary, the main changes to the base text – that is, the early text, most often a quarto, that serves as the copy from which the editor works – are these: certain and probable errors in the base text are corrected; typography and spelling are brought into line with current usage; and speech prefixes and stage directions are modified to assist the reader in imagining the play in performance.

Significant changes introduced by editors are recorded in the textual notes at the foot of the page. These are an important cache of information, presented in as compact a form as is possible without forfeiting intelligibility. The standard form can be seen in the following example:

31 doing of]   *Coxeter; of doing Q; doing Rawl*

The line reference ('31') and the reading quoted from the present editor's text ('doing of') are printed before the closing square bracket. After the bracket, the source of the reading, often the name of the editor who first made the change to the base text (*'Coxeter'*), appears, and then other readings are given, followed by their source ('of doing *Q;* doing *Rawl'*). Where there is more than one alternative reading, they are listed in chronological order; hence in the example the base text Q (= Quarto) is given first. Abbreviations used to identify early texts and later editions are listed in the Abbreviations and References section towards the end of the volume. Editorial emendations to the text are discussed in the main commentary, where notes on emendations are highlighted with an asterisk.

Emendation necessarily takes account of early texts other than the base text, as well as of the editorial tradition. The amount of attention paid to other texts depends on the editor's assessment of their origin and importance. Emendation aims to correct errors while respecting the integrity of different versions as they might have emerged through revision and adaptation.

Modernization of spelling and punctuation in AEMD texts is thorough, avoiding the kind of partial modernization that produces language from no known period of English. Generally modernization is routine, involving thousands of alterations of letters. As original grammar is preserved in AEMD editions, most modernizations are as trivial as altering 'booke' to 'book', and are unworthy of record. But where the modernization is unexpected or ambiguous the change is noted in the textual notes, using the following format:

102 trolls]   *(*trowles*)*

Speech prefixes are sometimes idiosyncratic and variable in the base texts, and almost always abbreviated. AEMD editions expand contractions, avoiding confusion of names that might be similarly abbreviated, such as Alonzo/Alsemero/Alibius from *The Changeling*. Preference is given to the verbal form that prevails in the base text, even if it identifies the role by type, such as 'Lady' or 'Clown', rather than by personal name. When an effect of standardization is to repress significant variations in the way that a role is conceptualized (in *Philaster*, for example, one text refers to a cross-dressed page as *Boy*, while another uses the character's assumed name), the issue is discussed in the Introduction.

Stage directions in early modern texts are often inconsistent, incomplete or unclear. They are preserved in the edition as far as is possible, but are expanded where necessary to ensure that the dramatic action is coherent and self-consistent. Square brackets are used to indicate editorial additions to stage directions. Directions that lend themselves to multiple staging possibilities, as well as the performance tradition of particular moments, may be discussed in the commentary.

Verse lineation sometimes goes astray in early modern play-texts, as does the distinction between verse and prose, especially where a wide manuscript layout has been transferred to the narrower measure of a printed page. AEMD editions correct such mistakes. Where a verse line is shared between more than one speaker, this series follows the usual modern practice of indenting the second and subsequent part-lines to make it clear that they belong to the same verse line.

The textual notes allow the reader to keep track of all these interventions. The notes use variations on the basic format described above to reflect the changes. In notes, '31 SD' indicates a stage direction in or immediately after line 31. Where there is more than one stage direction, they are identified as, for example, '31 SD1', '31 SD2'. The second line of a stage direction will be identified as, for instance, '31.2'. A forward slash / indicates a line-break in verse.

We hope that these conventions make as clear as possible the editor's engagement with and interventions in the text: our aim is to keep the reader fully informed of the editor's role without intruding unnecessarily on the flow of reading. Equally, we hope – since one of our aims is to encourage the performance of more plays from the early modern period beyond the Shakespeare canon – to provide texts which materially assist performers, as well as readers, of these plays.

PREFACE

I first read this play as an undergraduate, on a course called Early Drama, taught by Marion O'Connor, and writing this preface marks thirty years since that first encounter with it. The module set a trajectory for me that I'm still following – I worked on *Arden* again for my PhD, also with Marion; it featured prominently in my first monograph, *Domestic Life and Domestic Tragedy in Early Modern England*, and has appeared in several subsequent books and articles. Firstly then, profound thanks to Marion for that first encounter, and for so much more since then. Marion also introduced me to Lena Orlin, who has inspired me throughout about domestic drama and the rich materiality of its practice.

During the majority of those thirty years, I've been lucky enough to inhabit the play's geography, and that has been a significant element in the shaping of this edition, not least in the solace that it has given in a time of coronavirus during lockdown walks by the water. The town of Faversham reserves a special place in its heart for *Arden*, and I have been helped at every stage by people keen to tell the entwined stories of town and play. The Faversham Society members have been incredibly generous with thoughts, time and delving into their archives, in particular Clive Foreman, who was enthusiastic from the outset. Thanks also to Mark Gardner and John Coulter for help with local productions, to Norma Pleasance for telling me wonderful stories of Arden's House and the various performances it has witnessed, to David Shaw for advice about eighteenth-century printers and to Justin Croft for sharing his expertise about Faversham publications.

When I wasn't living in Kent, I was at the Shakespeare Institute in Stratford-upon-Avon, the other great shaping force on this edition. Working with Martin Wiggins taught me more about early modern drama than I ever thought I'd know, and everything I publish on it (as well as much more besides) has been improved by his wisdom and kindness. Working with John Jowett on *Arden* since I left the Institute has been a fascinating journey further into the exacting world of play editing. My thanks to him for his generosity, his infinite patience and his firm commitment to getting it right.

At a crucial point in the process, I was saved from putting off properly getting started by an invitation from Gary Taylor and Terri Bourus to join their *Arden* seminar at the 2016 annual meeting of the Shakespeare Association of America in New Orleans. Apart from being a wonderful setting, it was also an introduction to a generous group of scholars who helped me to see the play in the round. Especial thanks to Gary and Terri for organizing, welcoming and sharing their work on the play then and since. My thanks also to Cassie Ash for the images of *Arden*'s eighteenth-century life which are still pasted on the back of my office door, to Laurie Maguire for helping me think about Franklin, and to Mac Jackson for invaluable feedback on my paper and leads into the play's puppet life. Thanks also to Gerald Baker for sharing his research into *Arden*, and to Brian Vickers for sharing his on the Kyd connections.

Staff at the Huntington Library and the Folger Library have answered many queries and sent over many images (Abbie Weinberg at the Folger was especially helpful on D.a.6), and Hannah Lilley kindly got to grips with the Southouse MS for me in the course of her Huntington fellowship. Rebecca Duffeix at the Musées Gadagne, Heather Rowland at the Society of Antiquaries and Eleni Bide at the Goldsmiths' Company all helped with specific queries. I spent an inspiring week at the Shakespeare Birthplace Trust in Stratford-upon-Avon, rooting through the performance archive for the play, and then, when they were closed, back at the Institute Library. The warm glow of peaceful scholarship and interest in helping it to flourish was much appreciated at both.

I have had many revelatory talks with colleagues about the play and the issues surrounding it – thanks to John McCormick, Iman Sheeha, Clare Wright, Rebekah Higgitt, Tiffany Stern, Elly Lowe and Holger Syme. It has also been enormously useful (not to mention enjoyable) to talk through questions of status in the play with the Middling Culture team. In the latter stages, brave people were prepared to read the introduction – thanks to Mark Merry, Callan Davies, Andy Kesson and Sarah Dustagheer. In addition to taking on that task, Rory Loughnane has debated finer points of editorial practice with me on many occasions, and I'm looking forward to carrying on those discussions with him in future projects. Margaret Bartley at Arden has shepherded the edition through with calm grace, and Jane Armstrong has been a meticulous and thoughtful copy editor, furnished with good suggestions and even maps of the landscape.

Personally, I've been working on the edition through a period of great familial change, during which we have lost our most senior lady, the strongest, most loving woman and most profound influence on my life. Others have grown and thrived in that time, despite the strange circumstances of lockdown, and we have shared unexpected, precious time together as a family. This edition is dedicated our most junior lady, now much more and more wonderfully grown-up than I could ever have imagined when I started – *Arden* is certainly not a narrative that lends itself as a pattern of behaviour for women, but it is a piece of theatre that shows what substantial roles there are for them to play . . .

Catherine Richardson
University of Kent

xviii

INTRODUCTION

POWERFUL PLAY

Welcome inside the earliest surviving household tragedy. You have just opened one of the most powerful and quietly influential texts emanating from the late-sixteenth-century theatre. At the time of its writing, around 1588, *Arden of Faversham* was at the centre of new currents in both drama and history writing, currents that shaped many different genres and ideas to come. As described by a variety of critics from the eighteenth century to the present, not only is it the first extant domestic tragedy and the first true crime play and detective story, but it has also become known as the first of William Shakespeare's collaborations and his first drama in print, and the first play with a woman's part that exceeds in size and emotional scope those of the male characters.[1] *Arden* is clearly rooted in similar concerns to the other texts that surround it, and it grows out of the practices of around two decades of experimentation in commercial drama in London. But its theatrically bold and still-shocking engagement with the lived experience of relatively ordinary men and women – the social and sexual context of murder within their daily lives, the significance of political unrest in the provinces and the weight and consequence of what happens in the household – make it strikingly different. In many ways, *Arden*'s angle on these issues has never seemed anything other than daring. And, in the twenty-first century, with ferment over its authorship and a developing scholarly investment in the lived experience of the past, its interests are centre stage once again.

1   Andrew Power's 'Roles and Requirements' chart in B&T (*CRE*) (19–20) gives Alice's contribution as 24.7 per cent against Arden's at 12.5 per cent. For caveats see below, p. 53. Frances Dolan states, 'Only two dramatizations of actual husband murders, committed by non-noble women and set in England, survive', the other being the anonymous *Warning for Fair Women* (1599) (51).

This introduction explores *Arden*'s genre, its authorship, its staging and its text. It investigates the play's engagement with the troubled early modern relationship between the private and the public, the moral and the political, the provincial and the national. *Arden* gets to the very heart of what societies think 'counts' as both history and tragedy, and the form that both should take. The play is based on a true crime – a scandalous murder that took place in 1551 and was widely reported in the forty or so years before it became the subject of a play. The story of Alice, her lover Mosby and the group of conspirators they recruit to murder her husband Arden was a powerful one that had a deep impact on the English imagination. Raphael Holinshed, in his 1577 *Chronicles*, described the story of Thomas Arden's murder as 'impertinent' (meaning something like 'inappropriate') to his wider history of the British Isles (see p. 290). It is such a strikingly early modern use of the word that critics have become entranced by it, and it has set the tone for many of our responses to a play that seems to stand out from its surroundings in similarly impertinent ways. The aim of this introduction is to think through the various contexts within which Arden's story first appeared, in order to establish just how 'impertinent' it really was – where and how it must have struck people as unusual, and conversely in what contexts it must have seemed familiar and at home.

'PLAIN CLUES' AND 'PROTRACTED TIME': MURDEROUS MATERIAL FOR *ARDEN OF FAVERSHAM*

Who told stories about murders in the 1550s, and how did those stories circulate? Arden was finally dispatched on Valentine's Day 1551. Exactly a month later his wife's lover Mosby, and Mosby's sister, were hanged at Smithfield in London. Henry Machyn, a London merchant tailor, recorded the event in his manuscript diary: 'The fourteenth day of March was hanged, in

Smithfield, one John Mosbe and his sister, for the death of a gentleman of Feyversham, one Master Arden the customer [collector of taxes], and his own wife was ... burned at Canterbury, and her servant hanged there, and two at Feyversham and one at Hospryng, and another in the high way to Canterbury, for the death of Master Arden of Feyversham.'[1] At a later date, in a different ink, he added that 'at Flusshyng was burned Blake Tome [Black Tom] for the same death of Master Arden', completing the story as the final punishment was meted out. If we want to know why this play was written, we need to try to understand why Arden's contemporaries found it so shockingly noteworthy – why Machyn wrote it into his diary, and what company the story eventually kept in the printed sources from which the drama was written. The most direct source for the play was Holinshed's *Chronicles*. But Arden's story was notorious by then – Holinshed did not make it famous, he included it because it already was so – and the tale travelled, rolling into itself moral and political significance on the way, from Faversham, through London to England at large, and eventually beyond.

Two interests come across most strongly in the various other events Machyn notes in his diary: the display of the power and authority of the rich, in details such as 'triumphs' (tournaments) at Greenwich, and the appropriate punishment of those who threaten social disorder, such as the hanging and drawing at his own door of 'a grett ryche man' involved in an insurrection in Norfolk in 1551. Arden's story fits neatly into the latter category. We can compare the context of the murder's very first appearance in print, in the *Breviat Chronicle* of 1552 (see p. 4): in the *Breviat*'s passage through history from 1066 to 1551, coronations, noble marriages and deaths, battles and great affairs of state are gradually supplemented with news of

---

1   Machyn, 3–13.

insurrections and 'commotions' and then, from the 1530s, individual punishments for murder and the start of religiously motivated executions as the Reformation bites: 'The holy maid of kent & her companyone put to deathe' (sig. L2^r), for example. From 1540, the list of executions grows to include more secular cases. Three gentlemen are put to death for 'a murdre of a symple man, and an unlawful assemble made in Sussex', for example, or 'a maide boyled in Smithfelde, for poysoninge of divers honest persons that she had dwelled with, in the Citie of london' (sig. L6^v). Regnal and religious changes made it ever more important to advertise the quelling of rebellions domestic and urban, and in this context Arden's story is a particularly horrifying example of a wider issue.

After relating national events, including the handing back of Boulogne to the French in 1550 (an event that casts a long shadow over the play), the *Breviat* features two incidents in Kent, the county in which Faversham is situated: 'Joan of Kent' was burned at Smithfield for heresy, with a sermon given at her death by a Canterbury preacher 'shewinge vnto the people her abhomynable opinions, warnyng al men to beware of them'; and then the apprehension of 'certaine lighte personnes' for a commotion in Kent, two of whom were hanged in Ashford and one in Canterbury (sig. N3^r). Arden's murder follows these stories, in a run interrupted only by an earthquake in Middlesex: 'This yeare on. S. Valentines daye at feuersham in Kent was comytted a shamefull mourther for one Arden a gentilman was by the consente of hys wyfe mourthered wherfore she was brent at Canterbury, and there was one hanged in Chaynes for that mourther, and at Feuersham was .ii. hanged in chaynes, and a woman brente, and in smithfelde was hanged one Mosby and his syster for the same murther also' (sig. N3^r). It is Alice's 'consent' that leads the story, and her punishment that comes first. Regional and national events mix in these histories in the interests of demonstrating the reinstatement of secular and religious order. Kent, it is worth emphasizing, was a crucial county for national defence, being nearest to France, and it contained the most important English cathedral at Canterbury. Faversham was a prosperous and well-known town: although frequently referred to in scholarship on the play as a village, it was known across the country throughout the medieval and early modern periods for its prominent abbey (a royal burial place) and its port (a corporate member of the Cinque Ports trading with the Baltics and Netherlands).

At the start of the unstable reign of the young King Edward VI, any kind of potential political instability had to be stamped on. The years leading up to Arden's death were beset with commotions and insurrections, and Kent was a particularly troublesome county. The political situation in the county in the decade before the murder gives a yet more worrying context to the list of Kentish crises in the *Breviat*: the Prebendaries' Plot against the Archbishop of Canterbury of 1543; war with France in the 1540s, leading to an influx of sick and deserting soldiers into Kent, often unable to work because maimed and destitute; in June 1550 a rising of around 10,000 peasants who gathered at Sittingbourne (just outside Faversham), and were eventually dispersed by Sir Thomas Cheyne with cavalry; at Christmas, concerns about Anabaptists in Kent and Essex joining forces and, less than two weeks before Arden's murder took place, the appearance of several of their number before the Privy Council.[1] As this context makes clear, Arden's murder isn't at all 'impertinent' in either Machyn's or the *Breviat*'s records of the period. Its status is, however, raised by having conspirators put to death in both metropolitan and provincial locations, a complex punishment usually reserved for insurrectionists.[2] Such novelty as it has in these records is linked to the breadth

---

1 Hyde, 11.
2 See, e.g., the 'preestes and laye men' put to death 'in dyverse places, one Leghte, and two other ... at London ... sir John Nevel knight draune, hanged, and quartered, at Yorke on corpus Christie even' for an uprising (*Breviat*, sig. L5ʳ).

of its ramifications, affecting both provincial and national justice and detailing the long list of murderers, the different locations of their demise and the nature of the bonds that bound victim and attackers.

Arden's murder is identically described in the *Breviat* in its nine editions between 1552 and 1561. Smaller in format and cheaper than the larger and more expensive chronicles, *Breviats* were very popular volumes. Unlike the later editions, which were printed in London (by John King or Thomas Marsh), the first three editions were 'Imprinted at Canterbury, in Saint Paul's Parish' by John Mychel, *'cum privflegio ad imprimendum solum'* ('with the exclusive right to print'), Mychel reminding readers of the proud Kentish tradition of history-writing by mentioning 'our worshipfull conty manne mayster Beade' (Dedication). This is very unusual, as the vast majority of books were printed in London at the time.[1] Mychel, apparently trained in London, was lured back to Canterbury to print monastic books, and the *Breviats* were his only secular titles. It is probably the town in which he was born, and he was certainly living there (in St Paul's parish) in the 1530s and 1540s.[2]

Mychel may, then, have known about the hanging of Mosby and his sister, but he will definitely have known of the burning of Alice and may even have witnessed it. The initial editions of

---

1 EEBO-TCP lists only eighteen titles with Canterbury as their place of publication up to 1600, all printed by John Mychel; thirteen of them in the 1550s. His other contemporary publications were of spiritually inspiring texts or visitation articles (questions set in advance of an inspection by the diocesan bishop), although he did also print some radical material (see Palmer for a full discussion of his output). Mychel claims to have 'by my poore laboure somwhat augmented' a previous chronicle (apparently that of John Byddell, 1542), enlarging it with 'more matter'. He dedicates his labours to Sir Anthony Aucher (see 1.294), and pleads with his 'frendes and brothers of the occupacyon of printing to suffer me quietlye to enioye the benefite of these mine owne labours, and to haue the aduantage of myne owne inuencion'. The plea apparently fell on deaf ears.

2 He was the only Canterbury printer until 1717 (Freeman; see also Blayney, and Palmer).

the book that launched Arden's story into English print set the story of the murder firmly on the boundaries of metropolitan and provincial life. The inclusion of the story in the *Breviat* underscored and guaranteed the fame of both its local and national significance.

Arden's story had already circulated in over twenty editions of various types of chronicle before its first outing in Holinshed. Not all of them follow exactly the same wording, but they all offer their readers the same key facts: name of victim, status, geographical location and punishment in several places of named murderers, one identified as his wife. The *Breviat* epitomized the crime, packing it small and making it famous in Kent and London, if not further afield, and in this way the story became distributed like a contemporary urban legend, some of its details appearing more or less faithfully to the earliest accounts in many different places, as though it was perpetually on writers' minds. The Oxford scholar John Rainolds, for instance, in a learned tract on divorce that takes its examples mainly from classical, biblical and continental humanist sources, draws attention to only three relatively recent events: the assassination of the French king in 1589, the defeat of the Spanish Armada in 1588 and Arden's murder.[1]

But if these texts record the justice done, showing the uniqueness of the crime through the number and social range of the murderers, then Holinshed's importance to the story as it appears in the play is as describer of the event of the murder itself. He gives a lengthy, detailed description of the circumstances of Arden's death and the key players in it – a full narrative where action and explanation are built into their material and social location. Expanding the earlier writers' focus on the sheer number of conspirators and their multiple

---

1 Rainolds. See also full discussion of contemporary mentions of the crime in Orlin, *Private*, 62–78.

punishments, Holinshed also adds to the sense of horrific excess by enumerating the roll-call of unsuccessful murder attempts. As Orlin argues, it is this aspect that shapes the play, 'which finds its structure, locates its tone, and builds its suspense in this sequence of frustrations' (Orlin, *Private*, 67).

Holinshed had informants for his expanded account. 'The history of a moste horrible murder commytyd at Fevershame in Kent', a manuscript account of the murder by John Stowe, now in the British Library, gathers together the reports of at least two witnesses whose evidence was collected directly or indirectly from the trial of the murderers and during their time in prison.[1] There are very close parallels throughout between the Stowe manuscript and Holinshed's account. Key, striking verbs are by and large copied verbatim – Alice's being 'inflamed' with love for Mosby leading to her 'loathing' of Arden, or the way she 'tilted over' the broth, for instance. But there are also clues to how early modern stories change from manuscript to print: Stowe's report is much closer than Holinshed's to linear memorial recall, and changes occur in the latter to the structure of sentences, but also in the introduction of a tighter cadence and more arresting punctuation. There are places where Holinshed has apparently made his text more 'polite' for the print market. In the distinction between Stowe's 'before the dede doynge' and Holinshed's 'before the murder was committed' we can see a movement away from provincial or demotic forms. And compare Stowe's Black Will, who 'marvelowsly chafed and vexyd . . . swore wounds and blowd that where he met Arden's man he will kyll hym first', with Holinshed's, who 'with manie terrible oths threatened to kill maister Ardens man first, wheresoeuer he met him'.

---

1   Stowe. Hyde investigates the biography of Robert Cole, likely to have been one of the contributors, suggesting as a result that 'the information on which Stowe's account is based is even earlier than that in the wardmote book' (13).

The rapid pace of linguistic change in these decades, which will be significant for the play's history in print, can be seen here too. Stowe was apparently writing (or his witnesses recounting) before 1577 when his account was included in the *Chronicles*, but after the return and execution of Greene 'certyene yeres aftar' the murder, and far enough after that it makes sense to say that witnesses were 'at this day' alive who remembered the print of Arden's body in the grass. Holinshed updates some rather old-fashioned language as he writes the story up, swapping, for example, 'said' for 'quod', 'burned' for 'brent'. But he also reshapes the overtly Protestant take on the story offered by Stowe's reporters, who say that various members of the guard 'beynge papistis and hatynge Adam Fowle for the gospell' arrested him and took him to the Marshalsea prison: this context of religio-political rivalries is cut. Political concerns, as well as the London print market exerting an influence on provincial dialect and detail, shape Holinshed's telling.

But there were other changes taking place in this period too. Richard Helgerson claims that the whole idea of history was shifting like sand underneath Holinshed's feet as he wrote. He argues that the way Holinshed introduces Arden's story shows that he was caught between 'conflicting notions of historical selection: one that still valued horribleness, wherever it might be found; but another that considered "private matters," however prodigious, impertinent'.[1] And Helgerson points to the gap that 'opened between a world of state politics, of calculation and contingency, of human action and human effect, on the one hand, and a very different world of commoners and women, of

---

1 Helgerson, 134. See also Catherine Belsey's point that, 'in a period when liberty [from marriage] is glimpsed but not authorized . . . in a struggle larger than her chroniclers recognize', 'it may be the political significance of Arden's assassination which causes Holinshed to identify Alice Arden's crime as marking the border between private and public, pamphlet and history' (98).

crimes and prodigies, of the local, domestic, social, and economic, on the other. Only the former belonged to history. The latter had its place in poetry, religion, and similar old wives' tales' (151). The words Helgerson uses to describe those ultimately victorious forms of history's views of such material – 'trivial, trashy, and vulgar' (135) – suggest that stories of 'ordinary' life such as Arden's become associated not only with the demotic but also with the provincial. Arden's story has always teetered on the balance between local trash and national importance.

In many ways, *Arden* is building on a tradition of murder pamphlets and broadside ballads about murders that germinated in the late 1570s. Anonymous lost plays from this period, such as *The Cruelty of a Stepmother* (Wiggins 653) and *Murderous Michael* (Wiggins 661), may well have offered models for ways of making drama out of such material. But Helgerson notes that 'the murder play, the crime pamphlet, and the collection of wonders – all got going in the decade and a half following the publication of Holinshed's first edition and may owe something to the fascination exercised by its account of the Arden murder' (137). So, the story may have shaped the genres of history, as well as being shaped by them. And to Helgerson's list we can add the story's impact in the later early modern period and beyond; we will see this below in its performance history, but it is also present in the historical narratives of the events in question. From the thick trunk of Holinshed's narrative, the story grew a canopy of smaller branches, reaching out to touch the representation of Faversham over the coming centuries. The murder, in addition to its continued iteration in both editions of Holinshed's chronicles and numerous of Stowe's well into the seventeenth century, also appeared in editions of the *Newgate Calendar*, a lurid account of justice meted out to the sinful, whose enormous popularity from the mid-eighteenth to mid-nineteenth centuries ensured it a place in the majority of homes. From here, the story made its way into other models of notoriety, including reports in newspapers of the 'On this day in history . . .' type in the nineteenth century.[1] It stretched as far, at the turn of the twentieth century, as lurid publications such as Arthur Vincent's *Lives of Twelve Bad Women: Illustrations and Reviews of Feminine Turpitude Set Forth by Impartial Hands*,[2] novels such as Diane Davidson's 1969 *Feversham, a Story of Murder and Satanic Love* and other plays like Don Nigro's *Ardy Fafirsin* (1993), set in 'Mythological Tudor England' with a 'set of broken Elizabethan architecture, suggesting the fragmented insides and outsides of houses'.

Arden's story appeared time and again in annals of crime and punishment, but also featured in the placemaking work of histories of English towns. Alongside the history of Faversham's abbey and the arrest of James II, caught as he was trying to sneak away in a boat up its creek in 1688, the famous murder formed one of the key moments when aspects of the town's history reached national importance. The shadow of the murder was a constant moral and admonitory presence there for at least three hundred years after its judicial conclusions.[3] The way the publication traditions described here built incrementally on past works, along with their interaction with local knowledge and memory kept fresh in print and public consciousness, ensured that the story Mychel told in 1552 continued in almost unbroken line along several different paths to the present day. It remained for many readers and writers a touchstone of depravity from the moment Alice put down her knife, because of the way

---

1   See for instance *Reynold's Newspaper* for 1869, or the *Bucks Herald* for 1888.
2   The 1897 volume was a companion to Thomas Seccombe's *Lives of Twelve Bad Men* (1894), described by the *Daily Telegraph* as 'A very storehouse of useful information'. Both the *Men* and the *Women* were reprinted in 1911.
3   A. H. Bullen reports speaking to a Mr Charles Smith of the Market Place, who told him that an annual sermon in memory of Arden and his philanthropy was paid for by the corporation until 1836 (iv).

early modern stories spread, in circular form: from oral to written and back, and from province to capital and return.

'LAMENTABLE AND TRUE TRAGEDIE': *ARDEN*'S GENRE

By 1577, then, we have an enduringly popular, shocking story, fully realized by Holinshed with many dramatic elements, but we are still a good way off the play of *Arden* that was written sometime between 1588 and 1592.[1] And if the murder story fits relatively easily into the narrative history genre's focus on aberrant behaviour and its unrelenting punishment in this period, it nevertheless raises significant issues in relation to theatrical genre in these first twenty years or so of commercial playing – issues that are connected to those questions about the place of lower-status sensational crime in history. With a predominantly socially 'middling' cast of characters, is Arden's story a tragedy, a history, or a kind of black comedy?

Two strands of the relationship between narrative histories and theatrical genre are especially relevant to our understanding of *Arden*. First, there were narratives with tragic endings that, as the stories of the past falls of great men, had a lot in common with histories. *The Mirror for Magistrates* was a very popular collaboratively written collection of poems, its last and largest edition of seventy-three disastrous downfalls, published in 1587, standing out because of the direct address through which 'a succession of tragic English princes and noblemen . . . were made to tell their sorry stories in their own ghostly persons'.[2] There were links here to the morality tradition of early Tudor drama, in which a central character traced a pattern of moral development or degeneration through interaction with personified attributes

---

1 For arguments about precise dating between 1588 and 1592, see Wine, xliv–xlv, and Taylor and Loughnane, 487–8.
2 Pincombe, 5.

with which they entered into dialogues both serious and scurrilous, drawing out the implications of their actions for the audience's moral edification.[1] Another narrative genre was that of the 'tragical tale', a sensational story in which events are motivated by sexual desire. In William Painter's *Palace of Pleasure* (1566), for example, a very popular source of plots for commercial plays containing over a hundred stories by its 1575 edition, historical events and lurid, sexualized sensationalism shared the narrative form of tragic downfall. *Arden* combines these strands, weaving them together to explore historical downfall through sexual motivation.

Stage tragedy's most influential model was the classical one of Seneca – translations of his tragedies had been published together, as *Seneca His Ten Tragedies*, for the first time in 1581. In these plays the characters delivered a range of clamorous outcries in which they insisted upon the terrible significance of the events to which they gave rise or bore witness. As Mike Pincombe puts it, 'the Elizabethans were clearly very much in tune with the idea that tragedy required the fall of a great man and a lot of shouting to go with it' (9). The issue for *Arden*, however, is the social background of the shouters. Taking its lead from classical theories, sixteenth-century drama had a clear-cut sense of appropriate characters: tragedies showed the deeds of kings and matters of state, but tales of 'little streets and unimportant households' properly belonged to the genre of stage comedy.[2] The former treated issues of public importance, the latter things of only private interest. Although these theories were famously warped out of shape by the innovative nature of early modern playwrighting practice, they speak quite clearly to *Arden*'s novelty as drama, and also to Helgerson's points about Arden's story: wrapped up in these theories of generic form are assumptions about status, gender and location.

---

1   See, for instance, the late-fifteenth-century plays *Everyman* and *Mankind*.
2   Diomedes, *Ars Grammatica*, quoted in Orlin, *Private*, 75.

In its early modern form, the story of Arden's murder occupies a space somewhere between public history and a private, familial story, shifting its emphasis slightly in its different retellings. The situation is complicated by the way Elizabethan and Jacobean society understood the relationship between the two. Early modern political thought saw the stability of rule as guaranteed by a series of overlapping circles of authority – states were governed by kings, towns by mayors, congregations by priests, parishes by churchwardens and houses by householders. These roles were both administrative and authoritative, and only the effective execution of every single one would ensure political stability in the nation as a whole – one household head who failed to govern his dependants (wife, children, apprentices, servants and lodgers) could potentially bring the whole edifice crumbling down. As Queen Elizabeth expanded the roles and responsibilities of her government out into the provinces, however, insisting on the recording of a greatly expanded set of information about her people, so a whole new class of individuals invested with responsibility for the nation's peace and efficient operation was founded: an extended list of offices of provincial civic and religious authority.[1] In this context, the class of men (and they were nearly all men) whose domestic lives mattered to the state, because their power was microcosmically analogous to the monarch's, was considerably expanded, far below the level of the elite, down to those of the 'middling sort' (from 'independent trading households', manual, mercantile or professional) who were its churchwardens, vestrymen, overseers of the poor, aldermen or mayors.[2] These changes might make Arden's position at the centre of a stage tragedy more secure – he was a householder, 'customer' of the port of Faversham and former

---

1   For further discussion of the rise of Tudor administration see Hindle, *State*; for its relation to domestic tragedy, see Richardson, *Domestic*, 84–6.
2   Barry and Brooks, 2; see also Middling Culture.

mayor of the town itself, after all, so his life had political consequence. When historical narrative becomes drama, however, as Orlin has noted, the focus of the play itself on Arden's 'vexed and irregular private life', to the exclusion of those other roles, is striking. She calls it a purging.[1]

SOCIAL STATUS AND TRAGIC FORM

The role that the play foregrounds for Arden is only one aspect of its engagement with materials befitting tragedy, though – it is part of the plot rather than the mode of its delivery. Early modern England was a very hierarchical society, in which the evidence of all the senses was used to determine an individual's rank. If we want to think through how a play maps out the communities of status of its characters, then we have to consider how they look and how they speak, as well as their roles and occupations. Early modern audiences' first view of the characters' clothing and accessories (types of cloth worn, colours and amounts of it, plus jewellery, swords, gloves and spurs, etc.) would have given them an immediate hierarchy, stretching from Lord Cheyne (knight) to Arden and Alice, Franklin, Mosby and the Mayor (various lower ranks of gentry), to Greene (decayed gentry), Clarke, Bradshaw, Dick Reede and Adam Fowle (artisans/shopkeepers), Susan and Michael (servants in a gentry house) and Black Will and Shakebag (former soldiers/vagabonds). Early modern audiences would have appreciated a much finer set of gradations of status within and between these groups than we do now, and the play's repeated drawing of attention to many of its characters' social positions (both as they are and have been, and as they would like them to be) makes this issue a key part of the context for the murder.

1   Orlin, *Private*, 71, 39.

Michael Neill's work on the play's use of the language of status gives us insight into how the distinctions between the characters might have been heard. He argues that 'it is above all through the characters' minutely inflected language of deference and abuse that issues of rank are constantly negotiated and a ferocious competition for status played out' (80). He concentrates on the terms of address between one character and another, showing how the supposedly bald facts of status become live, fundamentally contested issues in the moment-by-moment development of the interaction between characters, as, for instance, Reede fails to call Arden 'Master' Arden after he is himself referred to derisively as 'Sirrah' (13.21), and then addresses him as 'thou', a form only used from more to less elevated individuals (Neill, 87).

Characterization is another aspect of *Arden*'s investigation of status. Some features of these social groups map, at least for part of the play, onto equivalent theatrical types that shape their presentation. Michael, for instance, as he appears in Holinshed, is obviously a servant with a good deal of responsibility, useful to and relied upon by Arden: the latter sends him to Lord Cheyne's house on his behalf, and his repeated excuses (especially having lost his purse near the broom close) lead him to be denigrated by his master as acting 'like a knaue' partly because they are out of character (see below, p. 296). At many points in the play, however, Michael becomes the stage servant from comedy, unable to write and misunderstanding the nature of justice.[1] The knock-about scene in which he fights with Clarke over Susan is a part of this comic role – 'Such another word will cost you a cuff or a knock' (10.73–4), Clarke tells him. But behind that comedic aspect of his part opens up a

---

[1] For links between the ignorant servant figure and the *zanni* of the *commedia dell'arte*, see Marrapodi. Lance in *Two Gentlemen of Verona* (*c.* 1594) provides an interesting parallel (Wiggins 970). For more on the meanings of mastery and service in the play, see Sheeha, ch. 1.

richer emotional life of conflicted loyalties that makes him a much more complex character.

The popularity of some of the characters also apparently influenced later plays. Black Will and Shakebag are most easily categorized as types of the low-status professional murderer.[1] Will in particular was apparently a notorious figure, with a life beyond *Arden*. Haunting chronicle histories of brutal murder as one of those left to guard the princes in the tower, he also appears in the anonymous play *The True Tragedy of Richard the Third* (Wiggins 839; entered in the Stationers' Register two years after *Arden* in 1594), where he is introduced as one of two 'pittilesse villaines, that all London cannot match them for their villanie', and he enters swearing, 'Zownes sir'. In *When You See Me You Know Me* (Wiggins 1441), a loosely historical play about Henry VIII printed in 1605, the disguised monarch meets Black Will in London. Will enters, having committed murder, stating, 'I must withdraw a while till the heat be o'er, remove my lodging, and live upon dark nights and misty mornings'. In other words he begins here roughly where he left off in *Arden* – setting aside the reports of his death! Here too, he swears 'S'blood',[2] talks about his sword and buckler, and boasts, 'I am chief commander of all the Stewes, there's not a whore shifts a smock [takes off her clothes] but by my privilege, nor opens her shop, before I have my weekly tribute'; 'I'll teach ye to stand upon interrogatories'. Fighting the King, he is inevitably wounded, but gives his majesty the advice that 'when thou shouldst have born thy buckler here, thou letst it fall to thy knee'. These reappearances, here possibly linked to a revival of

---

1   See Wiggins, *Journeymen*.
2   In Richard West's *The Court of Conscience*, he is one of the versified list of 'Prophane Swearers': 'Naay here come they that I haue long expected / *Shakebag* of *Kent*, and Ruffianly *Dick Coomes:* / Swearing *Black-Will*, the diuels cheefe elected, / The seeds and flowers that *Pluto* sheds & bloomes. / Hels cheefe supporters and her royall states, / The very hookes and hinges of her gates' (sig. E3ʳ).

Arden itself around the time of Q2 in 1599, suggest that Will was a stock rogue character, seen as an epitome of lawless threat, but also maintaining the capacity for humour as a part of his stage presence.

If the lower-status roles' representations are shaped to an extent by the character typologies of comedy, then pitching the higher-status characters in relation to more fitting tragic roles is a harder task because their concerns are simply not high enough. However significant to the state, men like Arden simply did not display elite qualities. In *Arden*, rather than the arguments of the nobility about blood lines, we see the testing of varied ways of achieving middling identity. 'So, sirrah, you may not wear a sword', Arden says to Mosby, 'The statute makes against artificers' (1.309–10), calling into question his rival's new-found gentry identity. Their ensuing competitions are not courtly trials of hierarchy within a social group, but rather the efforts of one member of a group to keep another out. As a result, they are very patronizing and harshly hierarchized, offering the audience a level of contempt normally only seen between nobility and 'ordinary' men, where there should be no argument about superiority and no non-fantasy chance of anything but the obvious outcome. The exchange between Greene, Black Will and Michael in Sc. 7 is similarly complicated in its power dynamic: Greene is a decayed gentleman, Michael a servant with attitude and opinion and Black Will a powerfully physical adversary; as such, they are able to threaten one another more intimately, face to face, in a greater range of ways that balance physical strength against status, than can the nobility of more traditional staged stories of elite power struggles. This gives *Arden*'s brand of tragedy a particular social complexity and its events a firm context in community-specific rivalry. As a result, their appeal to an audience is a more direct one of familiar, empathetic experience, as the social mix of the play is closer to that of the audience.

Tragedy and the household

Understanding how the play mixes features of tragedy with the domestic concerns that should in strictly classical generic terms belong to comedy is crucial to comprehending its power.[1] The opening of the first scene is decisive in establishing *Arden*'s ambitious agenda. It begins with a great deal of information, economically conveyed – Arden is drooping with sadness, but is expected to be revived by the grant of the lands of Faversham Abbey. Within the first seven-line speech Franklin mentions the Duke of Somerset (thereby setting the period of the play by naming the young King Edward VI's Protector),[2] letters patent (documents usually emanating from a monarch) and the Abbey of Faversham (one of the largest and most important monastic houses within a day's travel of London, and the twelfth-century burial place of King Stephen and Queen Matilda). We are firmly within a national political scene, and an audience is invited to join Franklin in presupposing that such important news, accompanied by the documents themselves that have presumably just arrived from London, will lift Arden's mood. In his reply, of course, and perhaps also through his demeanour as Franklin speaks, we find out that this is not the case, and we are dragged away from letters patent to the deep pain caused by the love letters that have passed between his wife and her lover.

By any standards this is a strikingly raw and honest pairing of personal and state business, facilitated by the character of Franklin, a social equal for Arden whom the play adds to Holinshed's list of those involved at least partly to permit just this type of confidential discussion. Such an intimate revelation, apparently news to

1 For cautions about the operation of generic categories in this period, see Kesson, 'Comedy'.
2 Edward Seymour was the first holder of the title of Duke of Somerset in its new creation of 1547, reinventing it for himself in his capacity as Lord Protector. The previous holder was Henry Fitzroy, illegitimate son of Henry VIII, who died in 1536.

Franklin, so early on in the play unsettles both characters and audience. As an opening, it instantly sets up the relationship between the local and the national, the political and the domestic, tossing the two together and insisting on their inseparable connection, not as political causation but as the complex lot of one individual. *Arden*'s subject-matter is both national and domestic, because its perspective is one of individual experience.

At the start of the play the audience are exposed not only to the twinned subject-matter but also to an insistent variety of registers of language. Within the first 100 lines we hear the legal language of grant and deed, the ranting bombast of revenge tragedy ('that injurious ribald . . . / Shall on the bed which he thinks to defile / See his dissevered joints and sinews torn' (36–40)), and the lyrical love talk of Ovid ('we two, Ovid-like, / Have often chid the morning when it 'gan to peep, / And often wished that Night's purblind steeds / Would pull her by the purple mantle back' (59–62)). We witness intimate and heart-felt emotional exchanges between two men, and between a man and a woman, situated within the dual contexts explored above (see pp. 12–15). Seen with the hindsight of later tragedy, this might look like a rather bumpy and uneven linguistic register, a hedging of bets; viewed in the context of the period in which it was written, it is boldly exciting and experimental writing: a show of skill. It conveys and contextualizes the power of emotion, both positive and negative, and defines both the pitch at which *Arden* will be played and the generic take it will offer on tragedy itself.

Throughout the play we hear the high tenor of oaths, tears and railing, and the majority of the interactions between the central characters are loud and intense. The introduction of the plotters in Scs 1 and 2 gives them all an opportunity to swear their dedication to the task in different languages of excess: 'Now fie upon him, churl, / And if he live a day, he lives too long!', says Greene (1.508–9); 'Give me the money, and I'll stab him as he stands pissing against a wall, but I'll kill him', Black Will vows (2.100–2); and such dedication through excessive language is also heard in the lovers' protestations: 'Thine overthrow? First let the world dissolve!', insists Mosby (1.216).

But there is also a less febrile atmosphere of emotional intensity, achieved largely through introspective discussion of feelings, beginning with Arden in the love-lines quoted above, but then stretching to Alice, Mosby, Greene and even Arden's servant Michael. The latter's speech beginning 'Thus feeds the lamb securely on the down' (3.197–215) is elevated in its mood and subject-matter, exploring the tension between his loyalty to his master and his desire to save himself from the wrath of Arden's murderers if he does not fulfil his promise to them to give his master up. The audience witness and share his thought-process and the emotions it entails directly through soliloquy, in a way that became very familiar in later tragedy but was still relatively new and super-exciting at this point.[1] Such calm and reflective speeches that explore mental process develop the heightened emotional tone of the play – its high stakes – and the mood of doubt and conflict that grows in the dark. They also develop our sense of Michael's character, but they do not aim to give a mimetic feeling of a servant's thought-process. Michael has already told the audience that he needs help to write a convincing letter, but his speech here is as rhetorically sophisticated as those of his betters; in Sc. 4 his speech beginning 'Conflicting thoughts . . .' (58ff.) is implicitly paired with Franklin's 'Ah, what a hell is fretful jealousy!'(39ff.) as a couple of anguished night-time ruminations. The patterning

---

1   For similarities and differences, see e.g., Phao in Lyly's *Sapho and Phao*, who opens scenes with interior musings, but ones in which he addresses himself directly. *Arden* is part of a group of extant plays probably written 1587–90 that developed new types of stage presentation. Wiggins gives 'best guess' dates for, for instance, Kyd's *Spanish Tragedy* and the two parts of Marlowe's *Tamburlaine* of 1587, the latter's *Doctor Faustus* and *Dido, Queen of Carthage* of 1588 and *The Jew of Malta* of 1589, and *Arden* of 1590, but uncertainty remains about the order in which they were written and performed: wider possible date ranges for this group in the years 1585–92 indicate their close relationship and, doubtless, mutual influence.

insists on an equal emotional capacity for these men of divergent status.

The peculiar type of revenge that the characters pledge, and the 'tragic interiority' that it develops in some of them, is by and large not driven by the strictures of a high political system. We will consider shortly the extent to which such an analysis might apply to Alice, but characters like Michael and Greene are entirely differently motivated. Partly, this reflects the distinctively middling, urban social focus of the play: Lord Cheyne, its most socially elevated character, has only the authority over the plot of a bit-part who watches action from the sidelines without any awareness that he is nearly involved in lethal events. The lofty verse echoes out, not from castles, palaces or settings of state but from the houses and community of a provincial town. Anguish is born of social condition and competition, and of personal emotion and loyalties.

Staging the household

Attention is drawn to this focus by the play's staging. *Arden* is rightly famous for the mimetic nature of its dramaturgy, with its interest in establishing a realistic domestic logic to the way the scenes are configured – not necessarily as highly realized domestic interiors, although more of *Arden*'s action probably takes place in front of the key domestic furniture of table, stools and chair than is the case for any play written in the decade 1585–95 – but with a full engagement with the type of actions and activities that characterize domestic life.[1] In structuring its action around such props, *Arden* was reflecting the centrality of

---

1 For more on the role of props in domestic tragedy more generally, see Richardson, *Domestic*; Richardson, 'Properties'. Of the seventy plays and entertainments listed by Wiggins for the decade 1585–95, around half require a table or seating as a prop, but only eleven demand the use of both together in the same scene. Beginning in 1588, this latter category suggests the increasing importance of props and staging in managing the social representation of groups of characters and articulating questions around hospitality.

this kind of heavy wooden furniture to the home. Often designated 'standards', long dining tables in particular were intended to stay with the house, seen as an essential part of its furniture and fittings, without which it could not function. Fig. 1 shows both the type of furniture envisioned, with its inbuilt status distinctions between chair and stools, and the context within which early modern audiences would have imagined it, the parlour – often the most highly and lavishly decorated room in the house. Key furniture in guild-halls and inns as well as domestic households, this range of objects would be available to be used in touring performances of the play as well as London productions. A brief comparative example clarifies the nature of *Arden*'s engagement with the domestic. In Sc. 17 (4.5) of *2 Henry VI* (1591) (Wiggins 888), Lord Scales enters '*upon the Tower walking*' and converses with several citizens below, in a way that gives dignity to public buildings and displays of elite authority. In *Arden*, domestic spaces have insides but not upper parts. The lack of use of the balcony space for such elevated places tells us something visually about the nature of its scale and the concentration of its action, as well as the spaces within which it may have been performed.

If we consider how the play is plotted in more detail, we cannot fail to notice the two very long scenes, 1 and 14, the main ones set in or about the Ardens' Faversham house.[1] In both cases the location apparently determines the scenic structure. In Sc. 1, the opening interaction between Arden and Franklin might have been a separate scene, had they not called Alice in for their breakfast (55). It is as though the Faversham house exerts a strong pull on the plotting as a location, one that makes it impossible to think of the action that takes place there

---

1   In the 2016 Hoosier Bard production, for example, the opening scene played at just over a quarter of the total running length (https://www.youtube.com/watch?v= OXQD3H4zYWA).

1 The parlour, Avebury Manor, showing the scale and decoration of the room that the play's audiences might imagine for the Ardens' house

in separable units, but rather encourages a sense of its coherence as a way of situating the murder attempts.[1]

At key moments this concentration has a considerable impact on the interaction between the characters. For example, Mosby and Alice's exchange ending 'No, let our love be rocks of adamant / Which time, nor place, nor tempest can asunder' (10.84–103) is spoken in front of Greene, who begs the couple to 'leave protestations now, / And let us bethink us what we have to do' (104–5). Like a break-up on social media, their relationship, bounded by the house and community, is luridly public; they are apparently increasingly used to having an audience whom they are forced to disregard, and it leads in the end to their total misjudgement of the permeability of the house

---

1 Tom Lockwood, commenting on *Arden*'s relationship to its sources, argues that the play 'is constructed with the special kind of artfulness that can look like apparent artlessness' (p. x).

in Sc. 14. While the playwright's point is one about tragic circumstance, it maps neatly onto a credible representation of the relatively permeable, multiply occupied· spaces of the upper-middling household.[1]

In contrast, the 'London scenes' (3–7) are broken up into small units that offer the audience views of the same space from different perspectives, and pattern inside and outside in their plotting of action. As Franklin and Arden leave the fray in Sc. 3, the fractured focus represents a city anonymity contrasted sharply with their provincial experience: lives do not impact on one another – do not rub up and rub off in terms of consequence or cause and effect – they slide past in the night. The next four scenes, patterning inside and outside Franklin's London house, extend this sense of proximate but divided lives. An essential part of this play's domestic feel, therefore, comes from its layering of action over a range of imagined spaces in palimpsestic fashion. In Sc. 16, when the party step outside the house to 'See, Mistress Arden, where your husband lies' (1), the claustrophobia of the focus on the interior is finally broken. The 2014 RSC production, in which snow fell on Alice as she looked at Arden's body (see Fig. 2), captured the potential of this scene to underline both Arden's own exposed and unprotected (literally unhoused) resting place and the murderers' precarious position on the edge of the play's society.

In *Arden*, then, there is a remarkable consonance between the physical features of an early modern urban property and the staging practices of the contemporary theatre. The playwright uses the frequent entrances and exits of the first scene in particular to establish the nature of such a household, its constant business pressures determining the way the building is situated in relation to the town, and even to the rhythm of the tides, as Arden goes to the quay to unload goods (1.89). When

1   On which see Hamling and Richardson.

2 RSC 2014 production, Swan Theatre, dir. Polly Findlay, designer Merle Hensel, with Sharon Small as Alice

Mosby asks, of Greene, 'what's he that comes yonder?' (446), the audience have a clear sense of the distance of perspective given by the provincial urban street (the important houses linked in, thanks to their prominent position), that is palpably different to the shifting spaces of London, where you cannot be sure that a man will walk one way rather than another.

Community

These scenic structures are an important part of the play's representation of community. The focus of a significant strand of scholarship on Arden's ownership of land tends to obscure the extent to which this is an inherently urban play. Rather than representing a kingdom with its political structures, domestic tragedies usually present a neighbourhood, and what *Arden* offers is a geographical, rather than a social, slice of life. This is partly a consequence of its non-elite plot. Aristocratic living conditions are not situated within diverse neighbourhoods; social groups are kept apart, within the house and between its grounds and the communities that surround it. Faversham and London, in contrast, arc represented by located dwellings such as Arden's and Franklin's houses, or the Fleur-de-Lis and Salutation inns. When the characters are left onstage to expand to the audience their deepest fears in soliloquy, they often find themselves isolated in and by a clearly articulated social and material context. This is most obviously seen when Michael has his doubts about leaving Franklin's doors open – the space of his poetic passion is not one of mental anguish, it is the quotidian material one of a servant sleeping on the threshold. Domestic tragedy shapes emotion and tragic subjectivity through social space as well as character.

Arden offers the earliest, and arguably also the fullest, representation of the relationship between households and communities, private and public action around murder. Scholarship on the play has explored it in fascinating detail. Orlin's study of privacy in early modern England underpins much of this work, as she unpicks the moral threat that the invisibility of private action posed to communities, and the clear connection that was mapped between its policing and the maintenance of social order.[1] Emma Whipday has considered how such concepts affect the audience's engagement with the drama, pointing out that as Alice 'becomes ever more indiscriminate in her hospitality, the private spaces of her home are increasingly visible to the offstage audience'; she argues, focusing on London performance, that they are 'rendered part of the onstage community' through the conditions of universal lighting and thrust stage which might be expected in this type of playing.[2]

The long opening scene, with its characters sequentially presented, establishes that a substantial part of the town knows

---

1   Orlin, *Locating*.
2   Whipday, 100.

about the lovers' business. Within the time between Alice's revelations of her plot and Arden's eventual death – a 'fleeting fantasy in which desire can be given its own social space'[1] – the lovers' manipulation of their surrounding community takes shape. With the spreading knowledge of their intentions, the importance of Alice and Mosby's skill in using the information at their disposal is key. Clarke, for instance, enters Arden's house to try his luck with Alice's maid, saying to Mosby, 'if fair Susan and I can make a gree, / You shall command me' to use his skills in poisons (1.546–7). Some domestic tragedies offer their audiences an intellectual proposition for debate – in Thomas Heywood's *A Woman Killed with Kindness*, for example, such a proposition might be: 'If a respectable gentleman offered an apparent social equal the free rein of his house, what might go wrong?' But neither the relationships nor their consequences are of this type in *Arden*; rather, this play gives us a deep investigation of 'why' and 'how' that explores the motivations of lust and the drivers of local communities: 'Who would do what, for whom, for what reward?'

That premise necessitates a realistic social context. The plotting is carefully arranged to offer us a series of small mentions of actions we have not seen, in order to build a sense of Faversham's offstage life. 'Had we no talk of Mosby yesternight?' (1.76), asks Alice, trying to explain calling out his name in the night; in doing so, she plunges the audience into the social and domestic situation of the Arden household and Franklin's role within it. 'Oh, you are an honest man of your word', Mosby says to Clarke (246), without making the audience party to the context in which his word has been given, and thereby situating the action in pre-existing social relations. It is from the precision of these shared experiences, the careful weighings of characters' mutual beholdenness and the proximities rendered by loyalty that Mosby and Alice construct their plots at the start of the play.

1   Schutzman, 308.

These informal elements of social interaction play both with and against more formal connections. From the very start, there is a narrative and poetic focus on the ties that bind: on documents of ownership, vows, swearing and mandates. 'Tush,' says Black Will, 'I have broken five hundred oaths!' (3.93), bringing back to the audience's attention Alice's assertions that 'marriage is but words, / And therefore Mosby's title is the best' (1.100–1). The simultaneously dense but fragile texture of Faversham society – so many spiders' webs of allegiances and bonds – provides the context against which Alice rebels. The long and ironic passage of pledging in Sc. 14 (170–224) reminds us just how important, and yet how ineffectual, allegiance has been to the characters when all is exploded by murder.[1]

The play takes as its setting the competitive communal space of defamation and slander and the suppression of disorder. Legally, defamation was the speaking of words (true or untrue) in front of witnesses that affected an individual's reputation, and its prosecution was increasing sharply in the sixteenth century.[2] In Sc. 1, Alice rages at her husband after her poisoned broth has failed to have the desired effect, using the breakfast table as her diagram of social positions, pointing to Mosby, 'Here's he that you cast in my teeth so oft', and insisting 'Now will I be convinced, or purge myself' (371–2). In doing so, she opens herself up to the kind of trial that one gets in a court of law, either to establish her guilt or to find her innocent once and for all. In a comic echo of her feigned outrage, Black Will in Sc. 9 appeals to Greene about the wrong done him by Shakebag's accusations: 'It is not for mine honour to bear this!' (23). Both characters appeal outwards to audiences onstage and off, suggesting that they have been slandered. Similar language is used by Arden when he denies Dick Reede's claim to the land behind his house in Sc. 13, referring to the latter's 'clamorous

---

1   For more on oaths, see Kerrigan.
2   See Gowing; Ingram, 13–15.

impeaching tongue' (22). The play keeps slipping into the register of slander – bad words spoken loudly, railingly, in front of an audience who are therefore liable to be convinced of the victim's poor credit, with disastrous consequences.

Accusations of slander bring with them an automatic focus on the audience for the spoken word, and here again *Arden*'s social mix is distinctive. The community of onstage bystanders that can be influenced by these words is largely made up of the middling sort of urban characters and is, therefore, more malleable and unpredictable because it is not based on blood lines or allegiances built up over generations, but on a live and shifting notion of credit that is only ever as good as the last performance.[1] The period's social precarity invited a close policing of reputation. *Arden* represents a community under severe threat from poor domestic governance (Arden over Alice, Alice and Mosby over Susan and Michael) and from the inherent lawlessness of men like Black Will and Shakebag. Faversham is threatened from inside and outside.

What the audience see is also important to our sense of the structure of Faversham's community. Key objects, prominently staged, keep this community before the audience's eyes. Some things are obvious – the prominently placed table, stools and chair have already been mentioned, and to them can be added the objects with which their social uses are articulated, the cups, jugs, bowls and playing tables of hospitable dining. Use of these things enjoins a series of gestures around pledging and swearing that includes kissing and shaking hands, especially in the symbolically loaded Sc. 1. Fig. 3 gives an example of a cup used for such symbolic actions, its polished surface elevating their status.

There are also less textually obvious props that nevertheless play an important role in performance. Arden mentions in his first speech seeing the ring, put on Alice's finger on her wedding day, on Mosby's hand; readers tend to forget it, but onstage it

1   On early modern credit, see Muldrew.

3 Turned pewter wine beaker, *c*. 1590–1610, rose stamp on base with maker's mark 'HI' and 6 fluid ounce capacity

can shine out prominently, providing a clear image of vows abandoned throughout the play. Fig. 4 shows the very distinctive and personal form that early modern rings could take (before specifically designed marriage bands were common). Some props are submerged – not seen, but thought about and talked on. When Alice states, having ripped the pages from her prayer-book in a moment whose power and shock value may have rivalled Arden's murder for early modern audiences, 'in this golden cover / Shall thy sweet phrases and thy letters dwell' (8.119–20), she is referring to the love letters from Mosby with

4 Gold 'fede' ring with bezel composed of two clasped hands, shoulders shaped to resemble ornate cuffs. The inscription on the inside reads 'MY * HART * YOU * HAVE'. Sixteenth–seventeenth century, found in Somerset

which, along with his protestations, she will replace the prayers. The bold assertion takes us back once again to Arden's opening anguish about the letters that he has apparently seen, as though all material circulations in Faversham were somehow partially visible to him. The letters are a submerged property that forms evidential proof of Alice and Mosby's relationship but which we do not actually see: always represented by other texts, of the letters patents or the prayers, both of which are staged almost in their stead, the intimate love letters are written out, culturally, by these higher-status, national words.

This well-realized community, within which *Arden*'s action has meaning, shapes the play's character types by setting up a key question for an early modern playwright: is it really possible to have a tragic hero whose actions only count – only have an impact – within one community? As has been noted frequently, the shift from chronicle narrative to stage play is also one from straightforward moralizing to ambiguity and complexity, one in which Arden's responsibility for his wife's behaviour becomes comparatively under-written. But how are early modern audiences likely to have read this complexity?

Arden – a 'gentle gentleman'?

In some ways, the play's portrait of Arden is clear-cut. The intense emotion already noted in his opening speech, coupled with his admission that he knows about Alice's affair and the implication that he has not acted, would ring loud alarums for the play's first audiences. There was a special word for men who turned a blind eye to their wife's adultery, 'wittol', and it was not a flattering one. As well as being the butt of endless jokes and loud public shamings, such men were less than men: unable to exercise appropriate authority, their domestic disorder threatened a wider breakdown in communal behaviour. We have already considered Arden's rapid movement from melancholy to extreme anger in the first scene. It is possible to add the condescension and bitterness of his descriptions of Mosby as having 'Crept into service' through 'servile flattery' (1.26–7), and the way he attacks him socially when he takes away his sword. Randall Martin argues that the play characterizes Arden 'as a victim of his own extreme emotions'.[1] Beyond these clear social responses, however, the play offers a multitude of moral subtleties in its portrayal of Arden.

His unevenness of mood is partly a reflection of Arden's slightly-less-than-elite status. Important scholarship has considered in detail the foundations of that status, and its effect on the narrative, trying to pin him down to early modern social types. This is especially hard because, both as a historical figure and as a theatrical character, Arden was one of those men of chameleon, rapidly ascending rank in the years that followed the Reformation. Although the character calls himself 'by birth a gentleman of blood' (1.35), his actions suggest that he is not secure in his position, and still inhabits the fluid space between middling and elite known as 'mere gentlemen' – a group whose fortunes were profoundly affected by the economic changes of

1   Martin, 15.

the middle and late sixteenth century: the periods of Arden's social rise and death, and of the play's initial staging.[1] His authority has been linked to the types of property ownership available to an aspirant man in a period of change.[2] Garrett A. Sullivan points to 'an Elizabethan struggle over the cultural function of land', a shift from a 'conception of property as social office' towards an agrarian capitalism in which land was increasingly regarded as commodity, from 'the beneficent, fatherly landlord' to 'a more unabashedly economic relationship between lord and tenant'.[3] While all of this is certainly in play on the stage, Arden is not straightforwardly represented as an elite landowner, settled and self-confident in his status. Ann Christensen's work on Arden's business obligations, and the interplay of settled domesticity and itinerant working identities, offers an important balance to views of him as elite landowner, stressing his less secure, mercantile identity.

If we assess Arden's characterization against the protagonists in contemporary plays, his embittered rhetoric does not compare flatteringly with valiant and chivalrous (if sometimes truth-stretching) statements from other plays, for instance Suffolk's assertion, in *2 Henry VI*, that

> I wear no knife to slaughter sleeping men,
> But here's a vengeful sword, rusted with ease,
> That shall be scoured in his rancorous heart
> That slanders me with murder's crimson badge.
>
> (3.2.197–200)

The confidence with which personal qualities are asserted, rather than others' being denigrated, is obvious here; Arden's gory speeches smack of frustration, rather than valour: 'the

---

1   For more on the relationship between the gentry and the middling sort, see Middling Culture.

2   See Whigham, 63–120, on the post-dissolution redistribution of monastic property; Attwell; Sullivan, 'Arden'.

3   Sullivan, 'Arden', 242, 231, 235.

over-anxious prickliness of an *arriviste*', not 'the wounded amour propre of a true "gentleman of blood"'', as Neill describes his behaviour.[1] Arden's interaction with Dick Reede is even more damning. Here it is not his domestic authority, or even his emotional bond, that is under threat, it is his coffers. The scene is set up with a big oath that takes on the tenor of Holinshed's judgements of Arden's acquisitiveness: Arden's actions will leave Reede's wife and children 'Needy and bare. For Christ's sake let them have it [the land]!' (13.17). Arden comes across as petty, ungenerous and lacking the self-confidence to demonstrate true elite qualities. The playwright here treads a delicate line between showing Arden's lack of elite fortitude and maintaining a tragic register.

Arden is also likely to have been seen as emotionally unstable, his grip sliding away at crucial moments. He shifts emotional ground like a sprinter in Sc. 13, going from his suggestion to Franklin that they hurry up 'And take her unawares playing the cook; / For I believe she'll strive to mend our cheer' (73–4), to 'Injurious strumpet, and thou, ribald knave' (78) when he sees Alice and Mosby together. The instant change and inability to bridle his temper while in public suggests volatility. This is particularly true when his behaviour towards Alice is taken into account. As they make up after he has accepted his 'fault' (116) of mistrusting her, he asks for forgiveness: 'For in thy discontent I find a death, / A death tormenting more than death itself' (119–20). As Franklin points out at the end of the scene, Arden has lost all perspective. In a period in which advice literature insisted that women should fit themselves to the moods of their husbands, reflecting them as a mirror does one's face, this role reversal, where a woman's discontent causes a man's symbolic death, begins to sound rather like the world turned upside down. With a murderous Alice now firmly in charge, these scenes are worryingly

1   Neill, 82.

redolent of disorder. Husband and wife are both unpredictable and inappropriately violent (Arden chiefly linguistically); Arden is feebly dependent on a woman.

In performance, these weaknesses can be played up or down, and with our own generally more positive view of excessive love of one's wife, even to the point of blindness to her wrongs, in many ways the balance between admiration for Alice's strength of character and Arden's uxoriousness is more even than it would have been for the play's first audiences. In practice, a few fairly small points tip the scales away from Arden in the audience's sympathies. First a brief line which fascinates students of the play in the classroom: Franklin's gnomic reply to Arden's assurance, after Reede's curse, that 'I ne'er did him wrong': 'I think so, Master Arden' (13.57–8). Although it is more likely than not that early modern phrasing makes this sound a much more qualified endorsement to modern ears than would originally have been the case, its complexity and brevity nevertheless makes it possible that it includes a significant hesitancy from Arden's greatest onstage fan.

Differently complex is Arden's response to the curious little tale that Franklin tells on their way home from London in Sc. 9. The story is about a woman who has been 'reprehended for the fact, / Witness produced that took her with the deed, / Her glove brought in, which there she left behind', and Franklin is forced to break off his tale at the point where 'the gentleman did check [stop or rebuke] his wife' (73–6). Although we are never told what her crime was, the way the story is laid out and the context given strongly suggest that this was a sexual misdemeanour, and that it is being told or being received as of interest for the model it offers of male accusation and chastisement and female response. Arden is curious: referring to the point where 'Her husband asked her whether it were not so', a familiar moment in ecclesiastical court depositions, he presses Franklin for 'Her answer then? I wonder how she looked, / Having forsworn it with such vehement oaths, / And at the instant so approved upon her' (78–81). He appears to

36

be engaging imaginatively with the story. The way we read this speech is central to our understanding of what Arden thinks he is doing about Alice's behaviour. Is his very obvious interest prurient, amused, nervous? Like Franklin's 'I think so', the language is opaque and full of possibilities for different deliveries and inflections. These complex stagings of potential culpability are subtly and skilfully managed by a talented writer, or writers.

AUTHORSHIP

Arden's authorship has been a bitterly fought area of scholarship on the play in recent years. In some ways, readers or audiences may feel that it does not matter to them who wrote the play – they might consider that it should not alter their sense of its intrinsic merits. There are, however, three primary ways in which it concerns us here: first in terms of the way it could bear signs of a process of collaboration, second in relation to how we understand its place alongside other contemporary, earlier and later works, and third how that process of comparison of practice sharpens our sense of what is happening, linguistically and dramaturgically, in this play. Thinking through who wrote it further clarifies our sense of *Arden*'s novel contribution to early modern drama.

Top candidates for single or collaborative authorship have been Christopher Marlowe, Thomas Kyd and Shakespeare. Marlowe's hand as collaborator was first suggested by E. H. C. Oliphant in 1926.[1] The attribution was based on textual parallels, followed by interest in his birth and childhood in Canterbury in relation to the local details of the plot, although such suggestions misunderstand both the levels of migration and knowledge of provincial life circulating in London at the time. The argument for Kyd's authorship was first made in 1891, by F. G. Fleay,[2] and has recently been revisited by Brian Vickers

---

1   Oliphant, 'Hand'; White, xv.
2   White, xiii.

in the *TLS* as part of his expansion of the Kyd canon.[1] There are clearly some interesting parallels of language choice between Kyd's works (which are, however, themselves hard to establish as a canon) and *Arden*. Kyd's potential authorship of the play currently lacks the large number of rigorous multi-author statistical studies undertaken for other writers, however, and the multi-author work that has included both Marlowe and Kyd as candidates has cast doubt on the contribution of either to *Arden*.[2] About Shakespeare's possible contribution more will be said below. For now, it is worth saying that, given Shakespeare's extraordinary cultural status, this attribution above all others will undoubtedly continue to matter most to the play's fortunes.

Collaboration

In 1739 Henry Collyer, the puppet-master who was responsible for what was probably the most popular version of the play in performance at the time, authored a pamphlet on the subject of *Arden* and the history of its characters. '*A Short Account of Lord* Cheyne, *Lord* Shorland *and Mr.* Thomas Arden' was printed in Canterbury 'for the Author', and sold at the cost of three pence.[3] 'As to the Play of Arden', Collyer wrote, 'as it is acted by the Men of Feversham, it is supposed to have been writ a Hundred and Fifty Years; and when it was wrote, it was done by several mean Hands, for the lowest ruffianly Parts speaks in the same Stile as the best Characters' ('To the Reader'). As far as we know, this is the first printed identification of *Arden* as a collaboratively written play. In the twentieth century, scholars of early modern drama began to express

---

1 Vickers, 'Kyd'; see also Freebury Jones.
2 Hugh Craig and Arthur Kinney suggest, for instance, that 'the quest to find Shakespeare's partner or partners in the *Arden* enterprise must look beyond' both Kyd and Marlowe (99).
3 I am extremely grateful to MacDonald P. Jackson for his help in tracking this pamphlet down.

similar opinions, often on similarly pejorative stylistic grounds. Oliphant suggested it in 1926, and stated in 1931 that 'The play is not in a single style. In the case of an anonymous play, the chances are always greater of its being a joint work than the work of a single writer'.[1]

Collaborative authorship need come as no surprise: estimates suggest that 'as many as half the plays of professional dramatists' between 1590 and 1642 'incorporated the writing at some date of more than one man.'[2] Playwrights tended to work within an apprenticeship system, where younger writers learned from more experienced craftsmen with significant professional experience by working on a play together, just as an apprentice goldsmith might have created a piece of goldsmithing work conceived by their master, imitating, and with the benefit of, his skills. The 'plot', detailing the narrative ground to be covered in each scene, would be prepared in advance, in order to show it to theatre companies and to divide the work between collaborating authors.[3]

Full understanding of the conditions under which early modern plays were produced depends, therefore, on attention to the particular qualities of collaborative writing – to the logistics and the pragmatics of poetic inspiration within the busy world of the early modern commercial theatre. It necessitates an appreciation of playwrights' skills acquisition, and the impact on the text of the pressure to produce work at scale for a repertory system. Such an understanding insists that we see a relationship between writers playing out across a drama that we are predisposed, as audiences witnessing characters embodied by an actor or readers of a typographically cohesive text, to see as a single unified whole. Unpicking who may have written what gives us access to individual writers' approaches to characterization, poetry and

1 Oliphant, 'Hand'; *Dramatists*, 297.
2 Bentley, 119.
3 Stern, 8–35.

plot, for instance, and to the processes of producing a holistic set of ideas, voices and concerns.

In the twenty-first century, extensive computer-aided identifications of authorship have enabled studies to move beyond the so-called 'disintegration' of texts based on subjective judgements ('this is not what I consider good writing, so it could not be by my favoured authorial candidate'), and added considerably to the evidence for *Arden*, in relation both to the presence of markers of co-authorship and to the identification of potential candidates. The most recent work is largely agreed on the identification of Shakespeare as one of the authors of the central scenes of the play: Sc. 8 most certainly, but arguments have also been made in relation to as much of *Arden* as Scs 4–9.[1] These arguments seem clear and convincing as far as they go at the present moment, but it is important to set out some of the reasons why they cannot be utterly conclusive.

Predicated on the idea that different authors have distinctive patterns of word choice and organization and peculiar ways of approaching the development of imagery that separate them out from one another, this attribution work is neither uncontroversial nor incontrovertible for any drama, but for plays produced during this first phase of commercial theatrical practice it offers some particular challenges. First, it is harder to identify the unique style of a particular writer as there is a paucity of securely attributed work for comparative material: Jack Elliott and Brett Greatley-Hirsch state that 'only 29 printed plays that were certainly or probably first performed between 1580 and 1592 can be confidently assigned to a single playwright' (140); 63 per cent of the playbooks that Rory Loughnane and Andrew

---

1   Craig and Kinney 'hazard that Shakespeare's portion lies within the sequence beginning at Scene iv in the modern division of the play and ending with Scene ix' (99); both the *Arden* part of Jackson's book-length study of authorship, *Determining*, and Taylor and Loughnane come to similar conclusions (Jackson also considers Sc. 3 and parts of Sc. 2; Taylor and Loughnane identify 'all or most of scenes 4–8' (454).

Power classify as early do not identify their authors. In addition, Loughnane remarks that 'it is clear that many more plays were lost from the 1580s than survive'.[1] Authorial samples from this period that have made their way down to us are likely to be unrepresentatively small.

In addition, the period itself was one of especially swift and powerful ferment in the quality of spoken and written English. Within this shifting sea of language, the nature of genre was also, as we have seen, morphing fast. Any type of authorship test will be less conclusive in such circumstances, when there are fewer reliable markers by which to navigate and much passing traffic. Our play, probably written around 1588 and obviously before 1592, has fewer still securely authored texts for comparison.

Then there are the problems with the scrappy nature of parts of the first quarto (Q1). The opening scenes in particular were originally seen as bearing the marks of memorial reconstruction by actors: significant repetitions, metrical irregularity and omissions. Although such theories of reconstruction, and especially the term 'bad quarto' with which they were associated, have been called into question, these features raise significant questions that make identification of authorship even more problematic. The features are clustered at the start and end of the play, and ensure the opening and closing sections sound different from the central passages, either artificially (because of error) or because of distinct authorship patterns, or perhaps both. Marina Tarlinskaja has observed, for instance, 'that whereas in *Arden*, Scs. 4–8, 4.3 per cent of iambic pentameter lines have "omitted syllables", from Sc. 9 to the end the figure is 13.5 per cent.'[2] But is this as a result of the distinctive verse style of two playwrights, one 'given to such metrical irregularity' (or working, we might add, before a

---

1 Loughnane, 23. In fact this is likely to be true of later decades as well.
2 Tarlinskaja, *Versification*, 107.

concept of metrical regularity was firmly set), or because of the corrupt nature of the text as it has come down to us – 'the products of scribal carelessness or memorial error' as MacDonald P. Jackson puts it?[1] Tarlinskaja concludes that 'scenes 1–3, and in particular scene 1, show signs of a more archaic style, as though composed by an older author'.[2]

There are further issues associated with identifying the output of a youthful author, because people's writing styles change as they age. What the various types of analysis seek to identify would be a writing profile that adapts and develops, in relation to maturity and to the environment of other writing, other speaking and the generic development of the medium. The 'print' of a youthful author is made increasingly dim by such high levels of interference from the stable patterns of more mature work.

Finally, some of the authorship tests are less reliable on domestic tragedies. Such plays tend to pick up large numbers of parallel phrases and collocations based on what Jackson calls 'the "everyday life" context, in which a demotic linguistic register prevails', or 'the small change of domestic conversation'.[3] As with all the authorship work, this should give us pause for thought about what is really being tested – here a poetic language far removed from everyday registers of speech would clearly suit the method better, and that not only tells us something about the analysis, but something fundamental about the balance between high poetry and earthy pragmatics that is closer to Collyer the puppet-master's complaints about its 'mean hands'.

Nevertheless, despite all those caveats and notwithstanding the possibility of future revelations, as things stand the play does appear to show two distinct patterns of writing. And they

---

1   Jackson, '*Lover's*', 135.
2   Tarlinskaja, 'Additions', 188.
3   Jackson, *Determining*, 75, 22.

are ones that relate in interesting ways to its dramaturgical shape, and approach to character development and interaction, as explored above (see pp. 22–6). Textual and dramaturgical patterns appear to map onto one another, and the breakdown of the very different dramaturgies and ways of conceiving place and action, with the alternative modes of geographical precision and their scenic structure, can be seen in productive relation to the stylistic differences noted by the attribution scholars.

The print of Shakespeare?

So, if these two distinct patterns suggest two writers, who were they? Edward Jacob, the play's eighteenth-century editor, was the first to propose Shakespeare as author of *Arden*, expanding his 1770 transcription of the Q1 title-page thus: 'With a Preface; in which some Reasons are offered, in favour of its being the earliest dramatic Work of Shakespeare now remaining'. In that preface, Jacob quotes Nicholas Rowe, from the Preface to the latter's edition of Shakespeare's plays: 'it would be without Doubt a Pleasure to any Man curious in Things of this Kind, to see and know what was the first Essay of a Fancy like his'. It is in relation to Rowe's challenge that Jacob offers his own edition, 'submitted to the discerning Critics to determine, whether this anonymous Tragedy of Arden is not the Thing so long wished for'. Similarly, later on, having established reasons why the play might not have been included in the First Folio, he states, 'No Wonder is it then, that it should so long escape the critical Observations of the professed Admirers of the unparalleled Shakespear, to whose Judgment, it is now most willingly submitted either to be approved as his, or to be rejected.' Unseen by recent editors, Jacob's argument runs, the play cannot seriously be considered as a contender for inclusion in a Shakespeare *Works*, and it is clear what important work Jacob did in publicizing the by-then rare quarto text, ensuring that knowledge of it remained to be included in the lists that preserved a canon of sorts of perhaps-Shakespearean drama.[1] Although few rushed to agree with Jacob, A. C. Swinburne was an enthusiastic convert: 'Considering the various and marvellous gifts displayed for the first time on our stage by the great poet . . . I cannot but finally take heart to say, even in the absence of all external or traditional testimony, that it seems to me not pardonable merely or permissible, but simply logical and reasonable, to set down this poem, a young man's work on the face of it, as the possible work of no man's youthful hand but Shakespeare's.'[2]

The field of attribution studies has moved at considerable speed in the last decade or so, and looks set to continue to develop rapidly as computer-aided techniques become more sophisticated. *Arden* has been subjected to computational stylistics tests of various types, identifying authorial fingerprints in prosodic form, word strings and the use of function words, but also more sophisticated versions of the type of imagery analysis undertaken in previous centuries. The weight of the evidence demonstrates close parallels between the central scenes of *Arden* and the work of a young Shakespeare. More precision is not forthcoming: Jackson states that it is within Scs 4–9 that Shakespeare's contribution is 'concentrated', but that it is also the case that Sc. 3 is a borderline anomaly, offering an 'overlap' of results that 'may indicate mixed authorship'.[3] The very language used indicates a kind of osmosis, a spilling over of influence, or a smoothing of the edges from one writer to another, and such 'border scenes' might be expected to be especially open to revision by the second dramatist. It is

1   For more on Apocrypha see Kirwan; Jowett.
2   *Study of Shakespeare*, quoted in Bayne, iv.
3   Jackson, *Determining*, 81. See also Gary Taylor who, identifying Sc. 11 as 'a classic Elizabethan question-and-answer gentleman-and-underling clown scene, like those featuring Speed or Lance in what was probably Shakespeare's earliest surviving play, *The Two Gentlemen of Verona*', suggests that this too deserves a closer look (894).

currently impossible to tell to what early modern process of co-writing or editorial practice such results might point.

Arden was included in the 2016 *New Oxford Shakespeare: The Complete Works* (B&T), with Sc. 8 also being included in Eric Rasmussen and Jonathan Bate's *RSC Shakespeare and Others: Collaborative Plays* (2013). Taylor and Loughnane justified its full inclusion for the first time in a *Works* edition by stating that 'The hypothesis of collaborative professional authorship, and the identification of Shakespeare as the junior collaborator, are now supported by extensive, independent, interlocking evidence' (490). The range of tests is so broad and the results they give so regular as to suggest that there cannot be this level of smoke without some kind of fire.

About the play's more experienced collaborator, less certainty has emerged. Here, the problems associated with identifying early authorship, outlined above, are exacerbated: not only must this author be writing in a comparatively early period, but they are also likely to be one whose career is well advanced at this point in time. The play is located on yet another watershed, what Loughnane and Power refer to as a 'generational shift', with the first generation of commercial playwrights 'retiring' in various more or less shocking ways, including murder, only a few years after *Arden* was published.[1] Thomas Dekker's reference to contemporary writers, in *Knight's Conjuring* (1607), divides them into two groups – an older group made up of Thomas Watson, Kyd and Thomas Achelley, and a younger one of Marlowe, Robert Greene, George Peele, Thomas Nashe and Henry Chettle (sigs K4^v–L1^v). Michael J. Hirrel argues that Watson was 'among the first to intermix comedy and tragedy in single plays' and that he 'substantially

---

1 Loughnane and Power, 4; Dalya Alberge, 'Shakespeare's secret co-writer finally takes a bow . . . 430 years late', *Guardian*, 5 April 2020. Available online:https://www.theguardian.com/stage/2020/apr/05/shakespeares-secret-co-writer-finally-takes-a-bow-430-years-late.

contributed' to the drama that 'had been developing for almost a decade' by the time of *Arden*, although he has now 'almost been forgotten as a playwright'.[1] This is in no small part due to the fact that none of his plays is currently known to survive – his *ODNB* entry describes him as 'poet and translator', although it does also quote William Cornwallis, Watson's employer, as stating that 'devising "twenty fictions and knaveryes in a play" was his "daily practyse and his living"' (Chatterley). Gary Taylor's selection of Watson as the most likely candidate for the more experienced author of *Arden* involved a method that aimed to circumvent some of the problems of early attribution by including non-dramatic as well as dramatic works. In a wide-ranging analysis of eighteen separate aspects of Watson's work and the play itself, including linguistic and generic features, source use and historical details, he identifies 'evidence for Watson in scenes 1–3, 9–10, and 12–Epilogue: all the scenes (except 11) that seem least likely to have been written by Shakespeare'.[2] The connections he highlights include Watson's status as an original and wide-ranging writer with a 'relentlessly experimental ambition' (894), helping us to think further about *Arden*'s generic novelty, and his 'exceptional command of contemporary Italian literature and poetics' (879): Taylor points out that Watson was perhaps the best-known Ovid-inspired poet before the English translation of the *Elegies* was published (15), one who frequently alluded to the *Amores* and knew well the *Remedia Amoris*, a text that may have influenced the development of the character of Franklin (881). Thinking of Watson as part-author of *Arden* helps to highlight the way a play with a relentlessly provincial English setting and characters

---

1 Hirrel, 201, 204. In Francis Meres's *Palladis Tamia* (1598), Watson is again in the 'older' group of playwrights: 'As Italy had *Dante, Boccace, Petrarch, Tasso, Celiano* and *Ariosto:* so England had *Mathew Roydon, Thomas Atchelow, Thomas Watson, Thomas Kid, Robert Greene* & *George Peele*' (sig. Oo2ᵛ).
2 Taylor, 894. For reservations, see Vickers, 'Authorship'.

nevertheless interweaves a significant strand of classical views on love.

Collaborative thinking

For many of the scholars undertaking the studies outlined above, the exciting thing about their findings is the insight they can offer into the nature of Shakespeare's writing at an early stage in his career – tracing a nascent poetic style and exploring his response to the task of collaboration as the subservient partner. As Ronald Bayne, a nineteenth-century editor of *Arden*, said, 'If Shakespeare wrote *Arden* it is the most interesting fact in his literary development' (Preface). Although he didn't elaborate, we might suppose that this was both because it is so different and yet so similar to aspects of his later work – Alice similar to Lady Macbeth, perhaps, but the play as a whole different in its portrayal of the social, material and emotional structures of domestic misery. The interests of an introduction to this play, however, must be rather different to those of the Shakespeare editor: we can learn from the way critics have seen *Arden* as fitting into Shakespeare's later style, as we come to identify what makes this play unique, but then we must go further and explore what co-authorship means for this play in particular.

The part of *Arden* attributed to Shakespeare is almost exclusively in verse: 'Less than 1 per cent of Shakespeare's share of *Arden* is prose, in contrast with 15 per cent in the rest of the play', and that tiny percentage is entirely made up of the letter from Greene in Sc. 8.[1] But it is the distinctive style of this verse that is important. Jackson argues that 'The most persistent feature of Shakespeare's language is its concreteness – its tendency to tie abstractions to physical phenomena, to express thoughts and feelings through images of

---

1   Taylor and Loughnane, 454.

objects and actions', and he finds this feature in numerous places in the centre of *Arden*.[1] This concreteness works in interesting ways within a geographically specific play with a historically precise narrative, where 'reality' is a large part of its power as engaging and moralizing theatrical experience. It offers an imagistic specificity of imaginative thinking that works entirely differently from the identifications of place names and features of the landscape – contrast, for example, Mosby's image of his tree-top nest with the scene in Paul's Yard with the apprentice and his stall. We might find an inverse relationship in the majority of Shakespeare's later writing between the prominence given to the geographical location of his plots and this feature of his language – location is more nebulously conveyed and imagery more concretely realized – but here, in a domestic tragedy, things are necessarily different as place is always relatively specific, and the two ways of representing it are in much closer dialogue with one another.

And we can examine that question of how the play works out its ideas across the whole canvas more fully. First, there is the shape of the plotting. We have considered above the connections made between the two long scenes set in and around Arden's house, 1 and 14, but the patterning of the material is equally strong in other places. Two scenes are set on the road towards and back from London (2 and 9); two short scenes of prophetic dreaming at and around Franklin's house (4 and 6) are interspersed with two other short ones of threat from the murderers (5 and 7); back in Kent, 11 and 12 are paired scenes set at Harty Ferry, coming between two scenes of fighting (10 and 13), the first over Susan and the second over Alice; following the murder in 14, four short scenes and the Epilogue show the dissipation of the murderers and the disintegration of their common purpose once the deed is done. There are unifying

1 *Determining*, 86.

thematic echoes, such as Arden's offer to take Alice with him in both Scs 1 and 10, or Michael and Greene's excuses to avoid witnessing the murder attempts in Scs 3, 9 and 10. Other patterns, for instance of close engagement of one group of characters in violence or emotion, followed by the intervention of others, permit the demonstration of authority. Seeing the play in this way also suggests a rather different configuration of characters across the whole piece: analysis of distribution of groups of characters across the different scenes sees the largest numbers in Scs 14 (13 characters), 1 and 13 (9 characters), 3 and 9 (8 characters) and 10 and 18 (7 characters), in other words mainly at either end of the play. Of these, only Sc. 9, the attempt on Arden's life on Rainham Down, lies inside the section tentatively attributed to Shakespeare, and it is on the very edge of it. If 4–9 are by a different author from that of either end of the play, then they tend towards the same aims, but with the really complex interaction between multiple characters handled by the more experienced playwright.[1]

Whoever was responsible for setting out the plot of *Arden* clearly had a strong sense that the frustration of repeated failed attempts at murder could be built up partly by having victims and aggressors occupy the same space sequentially, set-up and failure mirroring one another in ironic repetition. Groups of scenes are imagined not just for their narrative content and verse structure, but also for their physical location, clustering around Franklin's London house, and later on around the marshes at Harty Ferry. The patterns of separate action in the same imagined geographical spaces represent a part of the play's definition of tragedy through its consideration of, for instance, fate in dreams and the intervention of fog. By and large, then, the coherence of the plotting and the working out

---

1   See Stanley Wells's analysis of *TGV*: he finds that scenes with more than four
    characters 'betray an uncertainty of technique suggestive of inexperience' (1).

of ideas across the piece is impressive.[1] Seeing the play in this way allows us to formulate arguments about how distinct styles might relate to common preoccupations and a shared sense of plot and purpose in this period, at the end of the first generation of commercial playwrights' work, when co-writing was likely being worked out in collaboration with the next generation. It tells us something about the creative potential of co-authorship.

In addition to its links to the chronicle sources with which it shared both material and intention (see above, pp. 2–12), we can look at *Arden* in connection with canonical early Shakespeare. Loughnane suggests that it expands our sense of the playwright's early ambition as it shows him demonstrating 'an ability to write in each of the major genres', and that this 'ability to write across genre and form, to cater for the various needs of different companies and audiences, can be seen as a mark of, or harbinger for, success'; he characterizes early Shakespeare as a 'study in ambition'.[2] We can see *Arden* as

---

1 The main area of confusion, either editorial or compositorial, is over getting the actor playing Michael on and off the stage. He is onstage in what appears to be a deliberate pattern that lies outside the plotting structures of paired scenes and locations explored here, and may be linked to the demands put on the actor – in Scs 1, 3–4, 6–7, 9–10, 13–14 and 18. In Sc. 1, for instance, Michael's first entrance and exit are straightforward, but then he is addressed again by Arden at 362, 'Sirrah Michael, see our horse be ready', without his entrance having been signalled. Wine's edition brings him on with Arden, presumably using the logic that, as his man, they will enter together, at 288; B&T with Alice at 358, to help with the breakfast. Does he then go out to ready the horses and return, or does he remain onstage? He is to exit again at 415 with Arden and Franklin, but has no stage directions during the intervening action. In Sc. 13 the opposite happens, as he is brought on with Franklin and Arden at 8 but plays no part whatsoever in the scene's various arguments. In Sc. 14 his first two appearances are straightforward, but when he exits at 172 to fetch the tables he is given no re-entry before his speech at 202, at which point he is asked to fetch wine but not taken off or on to do so. While both of these anomalies might be explained by the tables and wine being very close to the exit, he is also caught up in the confusion over how to get Arden's body and those who remove it on- and offstage again. These confusions may suggest that the role was expanded during *Arden*'s writing.

2 Loughnane, 46; Loughnane and Power, 7; Loughane, 48.

precocious in this way too – it drives new generic models as part of the early work of a playwright determined to experiment, particularly around the representation of emotion and emotional interaction. Whereas, as Loughnane and Power are at pains to point out, a writer's early work is often seen in pejorative terms, carrying 'connotations of reduced worth, under-development, and immaturity',[1] we could see central *Arden* as part of a different concept of youth and creativity, of a vibrant, inventive, energetic liveliness that is perfectly played off against the constraints of a developing generic and dramaturgical context and the contrasting styles of writing that surround it locally. While one of the play's writers may not have been as confident or technically proficient as he would later become, we might entertain the idea that here he was bold, daring and audacious in the particular way that getting older and more used to 'how things are usually done' can make it harder to be.

So we can analyse *Arden* in relation to other early plays by Shakespeare. Jackson identifies a thematic panoply within whose context we can understand some of the choices made around the characterization and poetic construction of our play: 'Adulterous liaisons (Alice and Mosby, Queen Margaret and Suffolk, Tamora and Aaron), kings as seducers or would-be seducers (Edward III, Edward IV), strongly portrayed women (the Countess of Salisbury, Lady Gray), including three who are fiercely passionate and complicit in murder (Alice Arden, Queen Margaret, Tamora), men revealing their ambitions in soliloquies (Mosby, the Duke of York, Richard Gloucester) – all in scenes of some psychological and emotional complexity'.[2] Loughnane suggests that 'Shakespeare's earliest surviving plays are typified by their tendency towards sensation and controversy.'[3]

---

1 Loughnane and Power, 6.
2 Jackson, *Determining*, 125.
3 Loughnane, 4.

Alice – murderous strength

We can put together all the different types of information and analysis considered so far here to look in particular at the crucial role of Alice. If we are seeking a tragic hero in this domestic play, one who is destroyed 'by some version of this confrontation between the desiring personal imagination and the relentless machinery of power',[1] and whose subjectivity comes into being through their struggles with and against the constraints of the social system under which they live, then we need to look, not at Arden himself, but at the figure of Alice.

Alice's has long been recognized as one of the most remarkable tragic female roles written for the early modern commercial theatre. It is enormously demanding, both in terms of its size and its emotional range. Its length is unusual in relation to other roles for boy apprentices[2] and in relation to the male roles in *Arden*. Alice speaks 4,840 words (24.7% of the text), twice as many as both Arden (12.5%) and Mosby (11.9%),[3] and the 'combination – of (a) amount of memorization required, (b) dominance of the play, and (c) sustained female performance – makes Alice unique'.[4] Holger Syme has done some initial work on a broader set of statistics, starting with the fact that the average 1590s lead was around 3,700 words: 'out of 24 plays written in the 1590s that have a woman among the three biggest roles, *thirteen* are by Shakespeare'. On average, he says, Shakespeare's leads (male and female) have around 4,700 words in the 1590s, whereas everyone else's are over a thousand words shorter.[5]

---

1 Sullivan, 'Tragic', 75.
2 Wiggins, 285.
3 Power.
4 Bourus.
5 Syme; the revised figures presented here have been updated since the post, and communicated in personal correspondence. Syme points out how specific this pattern was to adult companies: 'In the 1580s . . . the boys' companies performed a remarkably different repertory than their adult colleagues. 33% of their plays had

Alice fits well into this pattern: she is one of very few 1590s female leads with more than 4,000 words not currently regularly attributed to Shakespeare (Syme), and hers is the second longest female role of the decade (after Rosalind). On the other hand, Terri Bourus picks up on Jackson's identification of the distribution of the part – the majority of the lines lie in the two long scenes at the start and end of the play. This would suggest that its size was not the result of a young Shakespeare's desire to write such a part. On the contrary, she suggests that Scs 2–7 provide a rest for the actor, lasting 600 lines, leading up to the concentration of Alice's part as written by Shakespeare in Sc. 8. She also notes the straightforward nature of the cues the actor had to take note of: he was given every alternate speech in Sc. 8, and interacts with a single character for the majority of Sc. 1.[1] Martin Wiggins argues that the length of the part 'aligns it with a sequence of very long parts for apprentices that appear periodically in the repertory of the Lord Chamberlain's/King's Men, at intervals of roughly eighteen months to two years, and which seem to be graduation pieces for successive senior apprentices'.[2] Alice's role too may well have been what Wiggins terms 'a graduation piece', although we cannot be certain for what company, and therefore what actor.[3]

As a role, Alice has a clear kinship with characters from earlier tragedies, like Clytemnestra in John Pickering's *Horestes*

female leads, and only a third of them did not have at least one female character among the top three. By contrast, there's not a single female lead in any play written for an adult company in the 1580s, and even secondary and tertiary female leads are a rarity.' The allegorical female roles in Lyly's plays compare well (e.g. Pandora, who speaks *c.* 30 per cent of the lines in *Woman in the Moon*). See also Kesson, 'Woman', who argues that in Lyly's plays, 'female characters often predominate and are almost always central' (33).

1   Bourus.
2   He gives the examples of Juliet, Portia, Beatrice, Rosalind, Viola, Isabella, Helena, Cleopatra, possibly Arethusa, Imogen. Wiggins, personal correspondence.
3   Bourus therefore proposes that the most likely actor for such an advanced apprentice role was Richard Burbage, 'near his peak as a female impersonator' by 1588.

(1567; Wiggins 451). When Horestes is said to have arrived to invade Mycoene, Clytemnestra declares, 'The walles be strong and for his forse, I sure set not a pyn' (C4^v). Such statements characterize the strength of these women's will, a force inherent in the static rhetorical style of classical tragedy and its direct address to the audience. Alice shows a similar tragic pattern of statement and explication, exhibiting the 'characteristics of an archetypical "bold" woman', as she has been described,[1] offering decisive summaries of opinion and exposition spoken in the first person, packed with imperatives. She speaks on a grand scale, rising above the everyday world of Faversham to embrace life and death: 'Look on me, Mosby, or I'll kill myself!' (8.112). And, in keeping both with a play obsessed with contracts and a genre preoccupied with grand pronouncement, she states her purpose boldly: 'As surely shall he [Arden] die / As I abhor him and love only thee [Mosby]' (1.139–40). Later in Sc. 1 she says, 'seeing I cannot, therefore let him die' (275): her summaries are brutally straightforward; utterly black and white and open, but still part of a recognizable social fabric of close ties that makes their familial, as well as their political, impact clear. The social world turned upside down that she allows the audience to glimpse in these few lines, and their mode of delivery, sets her up as bold, daring and opinionated.

But Alice's direct addresses are less stately, and less 'statementy', than Clytemnestra's. She shares ideas and opinions with the audience rather than simply imparting information. Already, early in the first scene, she addresses them directly but confidentially, left alone on stage to muse – 'Ere noon he means to take horse and away. / Sweet news is this!' (92–3) – when Arden and Franklin have departed for the quay to attend to business. In the next ten lines she explains her

---

1   Mary Floyd-Wilson, '*Arden of Faversham*: tragic action at a distance', in Smith and Sullivan, 188–99, 195.

position, caught between love and marriage, in the language of land ownership, suggesting that 'Mosby's title is the best' because 'Love is a god, and marriage is but words' (100–1). These are clearly very dangerous ideas, taking the audience back to Arden's pairing of letters patent and love letters as different types of authority, but extending it to the setting up of idols and the denigration of verbal contract.

The character of Alice exhibits two further noteworthy divergences from the basic model of the tragic woman. First, her passion is at points very high-pitched and unsympathetic. The speech 'Was ever silly woman so tormented?' (1.388ff.), for example, has the potential to be played as a type of railing – the speech exhibited by 'unquiet women' who often find themselves in court for the disruptive nature of their behaviour. In Terry Hands's 1982/3 production of the play this speech was cut, leading Jenny Agutter's Alice to seem calmer and more in control of her emotions and situation. Again in the opening scene, her statement that Arden should return 'Within a day or two, or else I die!' (85) demonstrates an excessive emotion that could be read as moving towards melodrama, and the playwright seems to be trying out a way of registering middling emotion for Alice, as for her husband (see above, pp. 33–7), that is only partly controlled. The role of Adam Fowle, a rather minor character who one might think had been needlessly imported from Holinshed's account of the murder, has the important task of giving an audience their one opportunity to assess how Alice's behaviour seems to those outside her direct circle of influence. In response to her excessive 'And were thy house of force / These hands of mine should raze it to the ground, / Unless that thou wouldst bring me to my love', he replies, 'Nay, an you be so impatient, I'll be gone' (116–19) – the passage functions as the double of Arden and Franklin's exchange at the opening of the play, the one character trying to calm the other, but in this case by shutting down Alice's outburst, as befits dealing with a woman.

Alice is, however, in control of the emotions of her fellow townsfolk. We see her thinking on her feet with Greene, telling him to 'hire some cutters' rather than do the job himself (1.520). Frances Dolan describes her as 'a skilful performer who manipulates possible versions of the murderous wife narrative' (52), but suggests she is presented as desiring 'the liberty to *elect* her governor' (54) rather than any more radical self-government. Alice's great skill is getting people to act for her by employing their passions. As she later explains the encounter with Greene to Mosby, 'he stormed amain, / And swore he would cry quittance with the churl', and it was when she 'saw his choler thus to rise' that she suggested the cutters (1.557–8, 561). Carol Mejia Laperle argues that 'Alice asserts a sense of self that depends upon the improvised and limited manipulation of external forces', as she 'articulates her agency within and through a world that is perpetually situational and thus fundamentally unstable'.[1] In other types of tragedy, as in histories, she would be managing emotion within a structure of national, rather than domestic, politics; in this play she is able to manipulate, up to a point, the social and communal structures instead.

When Alice challenges Mosby to tell the 'truth' of his interaction with her, the power of her language is palpable: 'I charge thee speak … Thou … thou … thou' (1.373–4). In addition to her use of the derogatory 'thou' that elevates her in relation to Mosby, the phrase 'I charge thee', with 'charge' meaning command (it had not yet acquired its modern meaning of legal accusation), suggests a verbal challenge or showdown equivalent to the duel – it is a bold move on the part of a woman to shift the discussion between men up a gear; to change its focus and direction. 'I charge thee before God', or 'on pain of death I charge thee' are familiar versions of the saying, with

---

1 Carol Mejia Laperle, 'Rhetorical situationality: Alice Arden's kairotic effect in *The Tragedy of Master Arden of Faversham*', *Women's Studies: An Interdisciplinary Journal,* 39.3 (2010), 175–93, 191.

formal moral consequences. But this type of speech resonates in a very particular way in the hall or parlour of a domestic house, as opposed to a civic space. It is a public type of behaviour that has many echoes of a semi-judicial context within it, where everything is formal and noted. Using this type of semi-public speech, hyper-sensitive to its audience in its offstage manifestations as we saw above, enables the writer to elevate this domestic interaction towards a tragic register.

But there are losses and gains for Alice's authority within Faversham, and for her force as a character, in this resiting of powerful speech. The domestic location complicates matters, confusing a stage model of declamatory classical rhetoric with a type of female behaviour familiar from the local courts. Dolan shows that representations of murderous wives in general 'present violent resistance as one means by which women could be constituted and recognised as subjects' in this period (57), but Alice has been called a 'bourgeois Clytemnestra' for murdering her husband in his own home, as Clytemnestra did Agamemnon.[1] This suggests a less valid, or less powerful register. It is possible rather to see such qualities as making her threat greater, not less real or vital, to the household, community and state, and such a view gives her a greater agency, if a destructive one. Alice's emotional composure comes later, after the murder. When she declares to Arden's corpse, 'In heaven I love thee, though on earth I did not' (16.11) she is dignified emotionally (if spiritually delusional), suggesting that the emotionally punishing tenor of her earlier outbursts is the embodiment of her sexualized passion and determination to indulge it.

Another important aspect of Alice's character is the way it is developed for the audience through her interaction with men. As

---

1 A description first used by John Addington Symonds, its history traced by Orlin (*Private*, 69). See also Kate McLuskie, who argues that the authenticity of Alice's character 'is created by interweaving the roles of the whore, the misunderstood wife and the lover into the same theatrical persona' (36).

we have seen, she has an almost visceral effect on her husband's mood. She apparently has a very similar effect on her lover, who calls her 'Ungentle Alice', claiming a similar direct, pervasive connection: 'thy sorrow is my sore' (8.54) – a contagion that breeds in him and makes him dependent upon her for his life and happiness. We see the direct impact that she has on both men as changes in their behaviour and the impairment of Arden's decision-making capacity in particular, but it is the development of her liaison with Mosby that forms the main emotional subject of the play. The reciprocity of Alice and Mosby's relationship ensures it unfolds before the audience, rather than being stated as part of the pre-existing emotional architecture of the play – their love is mutable, and much of the fascination of *Arden* is the audience's appreciation of its ebb and flow in relation to the murder attempts. The couple argue twice, in Scs 1 and 8. In Sc. 8, Alice's excessive emotional power figures rather differently to its impact at the breakfast table (as explored above, see pp. 29–30). The barrage is close-up; the emotion directed towards Mosby gains velocity as it bounces back and forth between them without awareness of an audience.

It is interesting to consider Alice's character in relation to the very different feel of the central scenes of *Arden*. Scholars have suggested that the role of the junior dramatist was often centred in the heart of the play. In *2 Henry VI*, for example, also thought to be a collaboration involving Shakespeare,[1] this central passage marks both an emotional crescendo for the plot, in which prominent deaths intensify the atmosphere of dangerous political intrigue, and the dilation of the narrative as the first wave of plotters against the Crown come to sticky ends. These scenes are imagistically vivid, emotionally intense and powerful. The Cardinal's vision of Gloucester is a study in

---

1 See Jackson, *Determining*, 66; Taylor and Loughnane, 494–6. More work is needed on Shakespeare's specific contribution to the play.

mental disintegration: 'Comb down his hair; look, look, it stands upright, / Like lime twigs set to catch my winged soul' (3.3.15–16). The action of the opening scenes, with their laying out of policy and the shifting patterns of allegiance in scenes of rapid dialogue, gives way in the middle to a grand arc of emotional process.

In *Arden* too, the central passages show a marked move towards longer speeches that explore emotional states and set a mood of dark, threatening confusion. Michael shifts up a register, from a comic character in a faintly ridiculous situation to one who offers a speech that makes tragic his conflicted loyalties: 'My master's kindness pleads to me for life' (4.62). The writing in this section is especially effective at evoking the imagination of scenes within space – we hear about the time when 'Franklin left his napkin where he sat' (7.10), and see Franklin's house as Michael treasonously describes the way in 'Over the threshold to the inner court, / . . . on your left hand you shall see the stairs' (3.187–8) – rather than setting the events out with action. In the opening scene in particular, events are staged, whereas here they are reported, coloured with memory and imagination.

The scenes of *Arden* said to have been written by Shakespeare, then, are the emotional core of the play – the places where action stops for its motivating emotions to be bodied forth in front of the audience. They give a different pace and texture to the play's journey towards murder, and they show a relationship in development, rather than a politico-moral premise up for debate. They suggest that the playwright was employing a different concept of how language and gesture combine to advance characterization in performance, and that he was interested, in these sections, in the creation of atmosphere. These have often seemed to critics to be the most impressive scenes, as they engage fully and openly with the emotional impact of characters' decisions, laying them bare before us on the stage. If our ideas about collaborative playwriting and the evidence of the attribution scholars are right, however, these might have been seen, in plotting terms at least, as the easier bits, requiring fewer skills in dealing with large numbers of characters at once, and less need to convey the narrative complexities of the characters' allegiance to one another or the development of the plot.

Seeing the character of Alice in this context, we can argue that *Arden*'s central relationship, between her and Mosby, is significantly developed in the play's central passage. One small section of Sc. 1 serves for contrast: 'I did it for the best', Alice says, disappointed that Mosby does not share her sense that her news of Greene's involvement in the plot is positive. 'Well, seeing 'tis done, cheerly let it pass' is his reply (582–3). There is much potential in the space between these lines, but nothing scripted – in these early scenes the playwright appears to leave more gaps for subtle exploration of power dynamics through actors' gesture. In the centre of the play, the focus on long exploratory speeches that plumb the depths of the heart and soul represents a very different interaction between the lovers, more linguistically focused. Mosby's famous speech at the start of Sc. 8, beginning 'Disturbed thoughts drives me from company' (1–43), picks up or keeps in play the atmosphere of introspection from the night scenes, extending their eerie metropolitan isolation (characters alone and conflicted in the dark) to Faversham. But it is also part of an arc of emotional action that extends for 149 lines. This includes substantial speeches for Alice and Mosby that reply to one another while at the same time developing interior thought and representing the groundswell of emotion: 'Nay, if thou ban, let me breathe curses forth . . .' (80) is balanced by 'Ay, now I see, and too soon find it true . . .' (106); the rhetorical poise of the antiphonal statement and response in tension with the uncontrolled emotion of its content. The whole exchange is fairly static physically, but covers a massive amount of ground emotionally; it is intense and gripping in a totally different way to the action-focused Scs 1 and 14. Alice emerges from these central scenes as the emotionally powerful and linguistically articulate desiring subject of her own tragedy.

TRAGEDY AND COMEDY

Whilst the focus of these central scenes is on the development of emotion that tends towards tragic events, on the page and perhaps more strongly in performance, *Arden* is, for most of its length, a very funny play. It is not alone in such generic complexity. In 1569/70, Thomas Preston's *Cambises* (Wiggins 480), for instance, was named as a 'lamentable tragedy mixed full of pleasant mirth', and that might serve as a fairly apt description of *Arden* too. This bothered both early modern and modern commentators on drama – Sir Philip Sidney famously talked about reforming the clowns out of tragedy,[1] for instance – and in more modern times the critic from the *Daily News* wrote, for example, that many of the lines 'sounded humorous enough to modern ears', although he assumed the play 'evidently was not intended to be comic' (7 December 1925). In the context of the work of contemporary film directors the Coen brothers and Quentin Tarantino, however, the mixture of the tragic and the blackly comic is once more looking less impertinent.

Spending a little time thinking about where the comedy arises in *Arden* contributes both to our sense of its generic contributions and to our reading of the possible divisions of the play around authorship. The main comic characters in *Arden*, Black Will and Shakebag, are also the murderers, and that immediately gives us a clue about how they work in generic terms. The irony of the comedy arising from their inability to complete their task is both part of *Arden*'s structure and the way

1 Sidney, 136.

it knits its genres into one powerful strand. The villains are amusing not because they are incompetent – description of their skills is always left to their own speeches, ensuring that the audience are essentially unsure whether to believe them or not, depending on the way they are played – but because they represent a threat that, while deadly, is held off for most of the play. Sc. 2 introduces an audience already unsettled by a worrying disorder amongst the supposedly respectable households of Faversham to a pair of masterless men who live outside all community. Their representation is excessive, and the violence they promise both terrifying and overblown. The world of the play is in many ways determined by their propensities – the 'cockshut light' (5.47) in which they prosper benights most of *Arden*'s action; scenes are set at crepuscular moments as dawn breaks or night falls, and unnatural weather dims the skies and obscures the sun. Playing to audiences as part of a post-1580s repertory familiar with Robert Greene's cony-catching pamphlets (books purporting to uncover a secret underworld of criminal gangs who functioned like networks of professionals with their own training systems and language – six different titles were published in 1591–2), in episodes such as the plate stealing in Sc. 2 *Arden* maximizes the appeal of a safely bounded lawlessness.

At points the action is explicitly comic, for instance when Will talks about murder becoming an occupation like any other, and gives himself the most important job, the highest status within his trade: 'I should be Warden of the Company!' (2.115). But at other times the combination of terror and laughter is apparent only in performance: 'Seest thou this gore that cleaveth to my face?', Will asks; 'From hence ne'er will I wash this bloody stain / Till Arden's heart be panting in my hand' (3.108–10). This is big bombast, whose threat of violence saves it from pure mocking humour. In the Hoosier Bard production in Indianapolis in 2016, the lines are spoken with a low and intimate menace that unsettles Greene, ending as they do with

Will's hand outstretched, ready to hold Arden's heart. The moment raised uncertain laughter.[1]

If we look at the scenes in which Black Will and Shakebag are most prominent, the majority of the humour comes out in Scs 9 and 14. Both scenes begin with the energy and speed of the comedy of the pair's frustrated efforts and competition with one another:

SHAKEBAG

> Come, Will, see thy tools be in a readiness:
> Is not thy powder dank, or will thy flint strike fire?

BLACK WILL

> Then ask me if my nose be on my face,
> Or whether my tongue be frozen in my mouth.
> Zounds, here's a coil!

(9.1–5)

Although there is threat, there is also the rivalry for superior skills and firepower, patterned against the serious introspection, doubt and fear of the other characters. Comedy relieves the tension of silent waiting. As Cheyne leaves the stage in Sc. 9, Black Will makes his presence known with my favourite line in the whole play, 'His Lordship chops me in' (130). Even the phrase itself is telling – 'chops me in' combines the prosaic sense of 'interrupts me' with the violence of a potential bodily dismemberment. It has to raise a laugh, after the preceding tensions of the imminent murder. Sc. 13 ends with Franklin's bitter speech of rejection as Arden leaves with Alice, having gone against his advice, but Sc. 14 opens with Will's comic frustration: 'Sirrah Greene, when was I so long in killing a man?' Such comic openings mark the changing of scenes, bringing the audience up to date with the frustration of a job not yet done.

1 https://www.youtube.com/watch?v=OXQD3H4zYWA.

This is not, however, the only register in which the villains speak. They have relatively long speeches in scenes across the play, but towards the end in particular these are descriptions of past villainies, either chances missed or misdeeds stacked up as proof of valour, that are not essential to the plot. These descriptions read a lot like the clown's digressive part – the space left to expand with improvisation in response to an audience – and offer actors a chance to give local and topical texture to the scenes in performance. But Black Will and Shakebag also express their feelings about the murder in richly evocative verse, and we can make a division of sorts here: their language in Scs 4–8 is heavily weighted towards setting the mood of menace rather than towards their comic interaction, whereas their contribution to the beginning and end of the play is characterized by a richer mixture of deadly and amusing frustration. The comedy runs alongside their sense that Alice and Mosby's love might find a way, but the vicious, self-serving edge it had from the start is laid bare as soon as Arden is dead. It is only towards the end that their energetic comedy opens scenes, leaving the middle and the moments after the murder as the most monotone in generic terms. If we consider this pattern in terms of co-authorship, we find the author of the centre of the play less likely to combine humour and horror, and less focused on comic interaction between characters than the writer of the opening and closing scenes, either by inclination or through a mutual decision to vary the play's effects.

ARDEN ON THE STAGE

Early modern Arden

As is the case for many plays of the period, the title-page of *Arden* does not give any details of its early performances – neither specifics of company, venue or event, nor general phrases about being 'recently played upon the stage' are included. There is no direct evidence to suggest the company to which *Arden* belonged, although Roslyn Knutson has argued that it moved from the ownership of Pembroke's Men in the early 1590s and into the repertory of the Chamberlain's Men after 1594. In the absence of certainty, we can make some general assumptions about the play's early staging. First, as noted above (pp. 22–6), while *Arden* does not use the upper space, it does use a discovery space and makes a feature of the stage doors, using them in several scenes to represent both the inside and the outside of houses. It apparently also uses a trap door for Shakebag's fall into the ditch in Sc. 12. The doors are the key requirement, and work-arounds could be found for the other features in a touring situation. The dialogue calls, as a minimum, for swords, pistols, knives, a buckler, money, drinking vessels, silver dice, letters, a prayer-book, a key, a set of playing tables (like a backgammon board), a towel (long piece of linen), a table with chair and stools, and a way of representing a stall from which to sell items, either as part of the set or a free-standing barrow-type prop. Although these requirements are not inconsiderable, they do not involve objects that would be difficult to source in either a playhouse or guild-hall/inn environment – the main challenge in performance is likely to be the prayer-book whose leaves are torn out (see below, pp. 87–8). *Arden* is a fairly flexible play, then, capable of being staged in a metropolitan or provincial location.

As there is no direct evidence of any performances before the eighteenth century, we have to consider carefully the evidence offered by the various texts that survive, from between the sixteenth and the eighteenth century, printed and in manuscript, if we are to understand this play on the stage. By doing so we can piece together a shadowy performance culture that stretches from London stages to provincial pubs, historic houses and the puppet-booths of the fairground. It shows us a play seen first as a cautionary tale about murder and then as a story of intense domestic sexuality and demotic everyday life, but at all points powerful and truly shocking.[1]

We can start with the first three quartos, of 1592 (Q1), 1599 (Q2) and 1633 (Q3). These suggest an enduring interest in *Arden*, and their appearance may well indicate moments of revived stage popularity. The play is a good candidate for performance by travelling players visiting the provinces, where its levels of provincial realism might have been expected to speak to an audience constituted similarly to its list of characters. It would seem to be an obvious candidate for touring in Kent, where the story was well known. Whilst we do not have direct evidence of its performance in any location, the Records of Early English Drama for Kent (Gibson) do show the amount of traffic on the south-eastern touring circuit, indicating the range of players who might have brought *Arden* with them: between 1587 and 1592 (Wiggins's date limits for the writing of *Arden*), seven different companies played in Faversham alone: the Queen's Men, the Earl of Essex's, Earl of Leicester's, Earl of Worcester's, Lord Admiral's, Lord Strange's and the Earl of Hertford's (Baron Beauchamp's) men.[2]

In the eighteenth century, *Arden* was still being performed by professional travelling companies who worked the circuit of east Kent theatres, fairs and races from the Medway towns (near to the play's Rainham Down) to Margate, Sandwich and Dover on the coast, and sometimes back through west Kent.[3] It was also being put on by amateur theatrical groups – as the

1 Knutson, 349. Wiggins's analysis of the role of Alice (see p. 53 above), suggests to him that *Arden* 'serves a specific company need and so was procured at company instigation, rather than offered on spec', and that it 'had limited transferability between companies and could only be revived when a company had an apprentice at the top of his game'. It may well be that it is this aspect of the play that caused its relatively early appearance in print and is linked to the gaps between the revivals that may be associated with its second and third quartos (Wiggins, personal correspondence).

2 Gibson, vol. 2, 559–61. See also B&T, who calculate that between 1577 and 1592 thirteen different acting companies travelled through the county from London (3).

3 Rosenfeld, chs 11 and 12.

local newspaper for 1729 states, the editors 'hear from Feversham, that a Company of their Townsmen design to Act the Tragedy of ARDEN, at the Roe-buck joining to that Place; and to begin next Friday'.[1] This is the earliest direct record so far found of a tradition discussed by Edward Jacob, who edited the play later in the eighteenth century. In the Preface to his 1770 edition of *Arden*, he states that some of Faversham's 'Inhabitants have till of late, at a few Years interval, doubly murdered it, by the excessive bad Manuscript Copies they used, and their more injudicious acting; to the no small Discredit of this valuable Tragedy'.[2]

But the play was performed in other media too. It was a very popular marionette show, put on in the mid-eighteenth century by troupes like Collyer's and Middleton's, and in the nineteenth century by Clunn Lewis.[3] Middleton's claimed to be able to trace their puppet performances back to 1711, and eighteenth-century marionettes of the *Arden* story may well still have been in use in the early twentieth century.[4] Clunn Lewis bought Middleton's marionettes, and ones identified with performances of *Arden* are currently part of the collection of the Musées Gadagne in Lyon. Fig. 5 suggests the expressive possibilities of the puppets' eyes and fine gestures for sensational drama, and the significance of their dress for making sense of the play's social stratifications. Before the advent of cheap copies of early modern texts in the nineteenth century, it is possible that *Arden* was kept on the stage through the relationship between travelling theatre companies

---

1 *Kentish Post*, Saturday 20 December–Wednesday 24 December 1729, no. 1179, p. 1, col. 2. For a useful comparison, see Kim Gilchrist's work on Mucedorus and its provincial performances.

2 Jacob, iv. An anonymous letter in the *Sunday Times*, 14 April 1935, asserts the play's performance in thirty-five Kentish theatres from the early eighteenth century to 1825.

3 For more on the early history of the puppet play, see Richardson, 'Scene'.

4 McCormick, 18. Clunn Lewis was still playing *Arden* when he was interviewed in 1911.

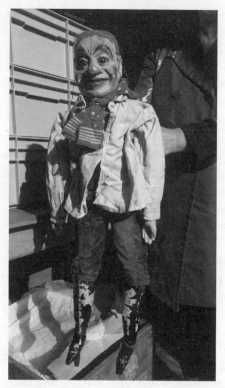

5 Clunn Lewis puppet, 71cm high, wood with oil paint, glass eyes

and marionette troupes who both depended at least partly upon it. John McCormick suggests that 'It is probable that puppeteers used an old and unpublished text, passed down through companies' (114), and describes a number of surviving 'notebooks with complete scripts, parts of scripts, or short sequences of dialogue' for other plays: 'They are often written in pencil, tightly spaced, and clearly of little use during a performance' (112).

Two eighteenth-century manuscripts of *Arden* shed light here. Folger D.a.6 begins with a part-copy of 'A Short Account of Lord *Cheyne* and Ld. *Shorland*' (see above, p. 38) and other printed and manuscript materials.[1] These are followed by a densely written manuscript copy of the play without verse line-breaks, plus extracts from *Hamlet*, *The Unhappy Marriage* (likely Thomas Otway's 1680 play *The Orphan*) and *Cato* (probably Joseph Addison's 1712 version), suggesting that it was linked to amateur or puppet performances.[2] An example of the layout, and the added Epilogue, can be seen in Fig. 6. We can compare this text with the Huntington Library's Southouse manuscript, a neatly presented transcription of the quarto text that aims at accurate representation,[3] but also contains much other historical material (referring mainly to the events and institutions of medieval and early modern Faversham) besides *Arden*; it was named after the author of its most substantial source text (the 1671 *Monasticon Favershamiense in Agro Cantiano*), the antiquary Thomas Southouse.[4] The date 1716 is written after a prologue which is added to the play, a prologue that indicates local amateur performance: 'Its Ardens Tradgedy,

---

1 For the differences between this copy of 'Short Account' and the one discussed on p. 38, see Richardson, 'Scene'. The manuscript sections include a magic square and scale of chords.

2 Interestingly, the extracts from *Hamlet*, *Unhappy Marriage* and *Cato* (the first two of which come halfway through *Arden*, before 'Castrophe! or the tragic Part of Mr Arden continued', and the latter at the end) retain their line breaks in the transcription. This perhaps suggests that they were played in a different style.

3 J. M. Nosworthy analyses the borrowings from the quartos, finding that 'Unique readings from all three quartos are, in fact, represented in this MS., and at this point it must be confessed that light thickens' (115). In an article caught between its writer's desire to find modern standards of scholarly transcription and his awareness that something rather different was in fact going on, Nosworthy finally throws up his hands at the 'so numerous, and often strange' readings with 'no Q backing' (117), and posits a source in 'prompt copy used by provincial or local players', making reference to an older manuscript compiled 'apparently, no later than about 1650' (122). The level of error in the rest of his analysis calls this suggestion into question.

4 Little work has been done on the text, and what has been done is confusing – Nosworthy states, for instance, that Southouse was the writer of the manuscript in 1716, despite the fact that he had died in 1667. See Richardson, 'Scene', and Marino for corrections of some of Nosworthy's greater errors and a fuller account of the manuscript writer's aims.

6 William Cook, miscellaneous material chiefly relating to Thomas Arden and his murder, including a manuscript copy of the play, *c.* 1750–70, showing the Prologue (Folger D.a.6)

a Story sad / Nothing is worse, the Actters are as bad' (105). Both texts, then, begin with substantial historical accounts of the murder, the individuals involved and the town as a whole, seeing it as key to a full understanding of the play – their compilers' response to its historical and geographical specificity perhaps.[1]

1 But see also, with many thanks to Gerald Baker for drawing my attention to it, the possibility that the *Short Account* has links back as far as Robert Armin. Richard Schoch (126–7) notes that William Oldys annotated a copy of Langbaine's *Account of the English Dramatick Poets* (1691), probably in the 1730s (so around the time of this pamphlet), thus: 'Mr. Jn Campbell tells me this Armin wrote some historical account also of Arden of Feversham to explain the Tragical Play of that name & promises me some further account of it.' Armin was playing in Faversham and Dover with Lord Chandos's Men in the mid- to late 1590s, just before his move to

In many ways, the texts could not be more different: the hand in D.a.6 could in no way be called one of 'exceptional neatness and regularity'[1] like the Southouse scribe's – it is better described as erratic. Radically cut down, the Folger version also includes imaginative alterations and additions: at the start of the play, for instance, 'Franklyn! thy Love prolongs my weary days'[2] is followed by these lines before it rejoins the rest of the speech from the original play:

> Thy tender Love I say, and friendly care:
> 'Livens my heart, and burries all Despair,
> For whil'st on Earth our painfull Lives we spend,
> How happy's he that finds a faithfull friend!

Even the much 'cleaner' Southouse manuscript makes similar moves: Will exits for the final time to the lines 'Now for Flushing, I know tis me they seek / Let happen what will, I dare to stay and speak. / Being thus armed no danger Can I see / No Ile make danger stand in fear of me'[3] (see Fig. 7). Despite their differences, both suggest cross-fertilization from amateur or puppet performance traditions with other verse forms. However distant from Q1 they might be, though, they establish a clear respect for early modern verse and suggest the writers' interest in an authentic transmission from the original quartos, even as the sixteenth-century verse intermingles with other modes of telling Arden's story. Performing and watching these texts was

---

the Chamberlain's Men in 1599; Chandos is also connected with a troupe of puppet players appearing in 1590 in Gloucester (Speaight, 62); 1599 was, of course, the year of Q2 *Arden*. The notion of a historical account 'to explain the play' may therefore have a longer history.

1 Nosworthy, 113.

2 The writer clearly knows *Hamlet* well (he writes out 'The Heads of it' in two pages (fol .37^{r-v}) after Sc. 12), so may be thinking of Hamlet's 'This physic but prolongs thy sickly days!' (10.31, Q1).

3 SMS, 226.

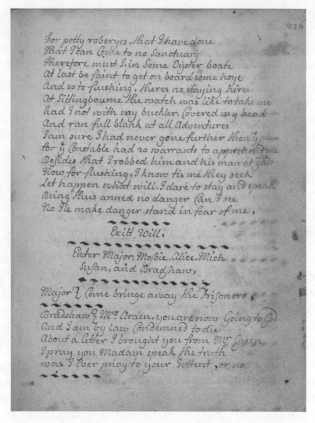

For petty roberyes, that I have done
That I can come to no Sanctuary
Therefore must I in Some Oyster boate
At last be faint to get on board some hoye
And so to flushing, Heres no staying here
At Sittingbourne the watch was like to take me
had I not with my buckler, Covered my head
And ran full blank at all Adventures
I am sure I had never gone further then ye place
for ye Constable had no warrants to apprehend me
Besides that I robbed him and his man at gold
Now for flushing, I know tis me they seek
Let happen what will, I dare to stay and speak
Being thus armed no danger Can I see
No Ile make danger stand in fear of me,

Exitt Will,

Enter Major, Mossie, Alice, Mich
Susan, and Bradshaw,

Major} Come bringe away the Prisoners,

Bradshaw} Mrs Arden, you are now Going to God
And I am by law Condemned to die
About a letter I brought you from Mr Green
I pray you Madam speak the truth
was I ever privy to your Intent, or no

7 Southouse manuscript, *c.* 1717, p. 226, showing the shift in tone from quarto to doggerel

apparently intended to make a direct, audible link to the sixteenth-century quarto, even while it revelled in connections to very different stage traditions.

In the middle of the eighteenth century, however, *Arden*'s history was rewritten in a contemporary idiom when the story was picked up by the playwright George Lillo. Lillo had a particular interest in early modern stories: his *London Merchant* (pub. 1731), the play that made his name, was a story of moral downfall ending in murder that he based on a seventeenth-century ballad and that became one of the most popular plays of the century.[1] Like his later *Fatal Curiosity*, it explored the tragedy of men and women of middling status. He subtitled his 1761 *Arden of Faversham*, 'An Historical Tragedy: taken from Holingshead's Chronicle, in the reign of King Edward VI', like other eighteenth-century writers showing an interest in the interplay between the story as play and as history. Lillo's version, which makes Alice into a largely innocent victim of Mosby's plotting and opens after three attempts on Arden's life have already taken place, offers a radically different take on both the characterization of the original and its episodic move towards climax – it is overtly eighteenth-, as opposed to sixteenth-, century. Mosby opens the play with a speech that includes the assertion that Alicia (as Alice is renamed) 'must, she shall comply: when to my arms / Her honour she resign'd, her fond reluctance whisper'd, / She cou'd deny me nothing.' (pp. 5–6). Arden's initial rage is shared with Alice, not Franklin, but he relents from killing her at the last moment, leading her to exclaim, 'I see your cruel purpose: I must live, / To see your hand and honour stain'd with blood. / Your ample fortune seiz'd on by the state, / Your life a forfeit to the cruel laws. / O *Arden*, blend compassion with your rage, / And kindly kill me first' (p. 7).

Although Lillo's version held sway on the London stages, in the provinces at least a contest was staged between 'original' and 'modern' *Arden*s. In 1765 the play was given in Canterbury by Smith's Company 'as originally written', as a rival attraction to the Chatham Company, who advertised that they were acting

---

1   'An excellent BALLAD of GEORGE BARNWELL, an Apprentice in the City of LONDON, who was Undone by a STRUMPET, who caused him thrice to Rob his Master, and to Murder his Uncle in Ludlow, etc. To the Tune of, The Merchant, etc.' (n.d.), English Broadside Ballad Archive (EBBA 32718).

Lillo's version. Both were clearly popular. In 1770, when the local antiquarian Edward Jacob produced his edition of the quarto text, he rebalanced the market by ensuring that there were copies of the original in print for players to work from, alongside its later incarnation. He made explicit reference to Lillo: 'It may not be amis to inform them [his readers], that a Play lately written by Mr. Lillo, with the Title Arden of Feversham, contains many Sentiments, Expressions, and even whole Speeches taken from this very Performance' (Preface), and there is a suggestion that he produces his edition as a counter to this now more readily available text.[1] Each time this play was staged, it must have been received by its audience as one version among several simultaneously circulating, in ways that drew their attention to the mode (puppet/actor) and the style (eighteenth-century London 'emotional'/sixteenth-century Kent 'moral') of the one attended. Such a sense of choice and product differentiation suggests a rich local performance culture through which the visceral event of murder could be experienced in different modes.

From today's perspective, three bold images of *Arden* epitomize our sense of the intertwined histories of the play as text and performance. The 1633 quarto is accompanied by the woodcut in Fig. 14 (see p. 100), which shows the moment of Arden's murder. The cover of the pamphlet written by the puppet-master Henry Collyer, in which he advertises the closeness of his text to the original material of the play (giving the opening speeches in both the original and his puppet version; see Fig. 8), shows figures that were perhaps intended to depict his puppets, dressed in eighteenth-century costume

---

1   The Folger's D.a.6 copy of the play includes a page headed 'A Preface to this Tragedy it being ye earliest dramatic work of Shakespear now remaining. Mr. Lille has written many Sentiments, Expressions, & even whole speeches, from this play.' In recording this information, it makes clear its debt to Jacob's edition, from which the information is copied, but also its sense of the importance of the fact that Lillo had himself been interested enough in the story to rewrite it.

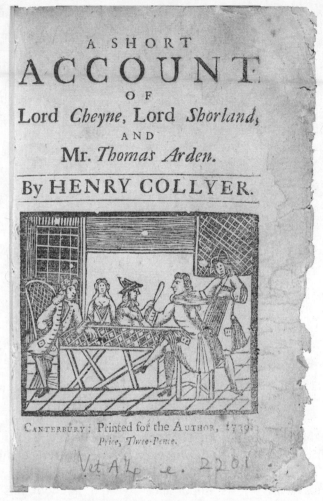

8 Front cover of Henry Collyer's '*A Short Account of Lord* Cheyne, *Lord* Shorland, *and Mr.* Thomas Arden' (Canterbury, 1739)

but recognizably referencing the third quarto's accompanying woodcut in the grouping of the figures around the game of tables. Finally, Fig. 9 shows a similar scene, underdrawn in pencil with watercolour over, from the Southouse manuscript.

9 Eighteenth-century watercolour rendering of the moment of Arden's murder, *c.* 1717, Southouse MS, facing p. 103

Here the dice are prominent on the table, and the scene is almost theatrically lit. All these texts epitomize the play by imagining the same moment, and in doing so they link their publisher or scribe's sense of its importance to both its book history (appreciation of the 1633 woodcut) and its power in performance (this moment as the peak of any production's crescendo).

Arden *in the twentieth century*

Around the turn of the twentieth century the original quarto text (or versions advertising their connections to this, rather than to

Lillo's rewriting) was again being staged in London. William Poel's first staging was of a heavily truncated one-act version of the play, called *Lilies That Fester*, for the Elizabethan Stage Society in 1897.[1] It was a brevity necessitated by his feeling that 'unity or design is wanting' in early modern plays, 'as well as continuity of action leading directly to climax',[2] but his text was nevertheless constructed out of the original verse. When Poel staged the play again, this time for Renaissance Theatre at the Scala in Charlotte Street in 1925, it was in an expanded form much closer to the original, his confidence in the latter apparently having grown. Between these two productions lay C. F. Tucker Brooke's influential edition of *The Shakespeare Apocrypha* (1908), a collection of fourteen plays previously ascribed to Shakespeare, which opened with *Arden of Faversham*.

But it was in the 1950s that *Arden* began to come into its own again as the mother of all domestic plays, with its demotic subjects and gritty, sexually motivated murder, in a theatrical climate that was more open to both Elizabethan and Kitchen Sink drama. Reviews of Joan Littlewood's 1955 production for Theatre Workshop mention a set dominated by three giant trees that were thought to represent the love triangle at the centre of the play.[3] But *Arden*'s opening and closing static focus on the household, its regional settings and its realism, spoke to the period in which, for instance, John Osborne's *Look Back in Anger* (1956) played out its own love triangle in a one-room provincial English flat; in 1958 Littlewood also brought *A Taste of Honey*, Shelagh Delaney's story of working-class north-west England households, to the stage.

Littlewood's production of *Arden* went to the Paris Theatre Festival following its London staging; the play was 'already

---

1 It was staged with scenes from *King Edward III* titled *Love's Constancy*; see Poel, v.
2 Poel, v.
3 *The Times*, review, 29 September 1955.

familiar to French audiences, having been given there in French in recent years'.[1] In fact there was a very lively continental tradition of both translation and performance of *Arden*. It had first been translated from the original text as part of the works of Shakespeare, in the last volume of the fifteen-volume set by François-Victor Hugo, son of the novelist Victor Hugo, published between 1859 and 1867.[2] The play became popular again in André Gide's 1933 translation from which, in *The First Manifesto of the Theatre of Cruelty*, published the previous year, Antonin Artaud stated his intention to perform it.[3] He had hoped to stage it, 'intensifying its madness, brusqueness, and spasmodic qualities that he believed were somewhat deficient in its present manifestation', not by changing Gide's text, but by, as he said, pushing 'the *interpretation* in whatever direction I find necessary', and adding 'any formal inventions inspired by the text, and thus not opposed to its spirit, but developed to the furthest degree, that I deem indispensable'.[4]

Out of this European tradition of performing the intense, bourgeois power of *Arden* grew a small number of twentieth-

1   '"Arden Of Faversham" In Paris', *The Times*, 25 May 1955. It was staged at Théâtre Hébertot. Wine (lii) mentions H.-R. Lenormand's 'reconstituted' *Arden*, staged at Théâtre Montparnasse in 1938 as a prologue and ten tableaux. Littlewood's production subsequently went on tour to Scandinavia.

2   The edition familiarised French audiences with the plot, turning it into comparative cultural information: Frances Parthenope, Lady Verney, sister to Florence Nightingale and author of *Peasant Properties, and other selected Essays*, notes, in her description of her 1882 tour of the Auvergne, 'I looked through the French newspapers every day; they were singularly jejune. There was very little about the war in Egypt, but much about the theatres and the last horrid (Fenayrou) murder, which was being dramatised "as", said the learned critic, "was done by Shakespeare in his *puissante ebauche*, 'A Yorkshire Tragedy!' and again in 'Arden of Feversham,' also by him, *singulierement puissante*"!!!' (vol. 1 (1885), 128–9).

3   Esslin, 87.

4   Quoted in Di Ponio, 160–1. A well-informed scholarly edition, *Arden de Faversham*, was published in 1950, translated and with a full introduction by Félix Carrère, who argued for Kyd's authorship.

century conceptual takes on the play. In 1970 *Arden* was directed by the Romanian Andrei Serban at Ellen Stewart's La MaMa Experimental Theatre Club in New York, in an Artaud-inspired production (with a cast including Billy Crystal) which brought Serban to the notice of director Peter Brook. The latter invited him to the International Centre of Theatre Research in Paris. When the production toured in Europe, its emphasis on 'primarily visual' modes of communication helped with the language barriers[1] – Clarke was played as a toad and Arden was castrated.[2] It was seen by critics as expressing a world view 'so savage in its necessities that survival itself becomes the solitary virtue', but also as a 'confused, blood-boltered mess'.[3]

Perhaps the most intensely political reworking of the story was the opera *Arden muss Sterben*, with music by Alexander Goehr and libretto by Erich Fried, first performed at the Hamburg State Opera in 1967. Fried wrote in *The Listener* in the year of the opera's London premiere about how his trip to Faversham with Goehr had changed the focus of the piece, highlighting as it did Arden's enemies: 'the action shows up the viciousness, also, of those who regard themselves as good'. He described his approach in the programme notes, explaining that he exploited the sense of communal hypocrisy by inventing the character of Mrs Bradshaw, who 'keeps protesting that she is against the murderous deed, but at the same time becomes increasingly a party to the guilt'.[4] She is the 'typical by-stander', and the production as a whole was seen by some as a comment on German politics.[5] The role played by the

---

1   Fliotos and Vierow, 388.
2   B. A. Young, *Financial Times*, Friday 22 May 1970, 3.
3   Clive Barnes, *New York Times*, 17 February 1970; Michael Billington, in his review of the RSC Goodbody production in *The Times*, 6 November 1970.
4   Quoted in Jansohn, 65.
5   Jansohn, 65.

hired killers, 'who try to "conquer their past" by offering to execute their former accomplices', was considered by the Hamburg audience a clear allusion to Nazi history, and the music intensified that impression: the love duet Alice and Mosby sang while Arden was killed was based on a Nazi song. While many applauded on the opening night, 'some booed and defiantly sang Deutschland, Deutschland uber Alles'.[1] After the war, *Arden*'s strong emotion, and its domestic focus and provincialism, ironically gave it an international appeal and reputation.

Staging the everyday

The majority of later twentieth-century productions of *Arden*, in the UK at least, have, however, responded to the realism they saw in the historical veracity and plain, straightforward verse and storytelling of the play. With their set and props they establish the normality that the murder violates, and indicate, simultaneously, the status of the Arden household. Most productions imagine the play as anchored by a central living space of some kind, usually represented by the key furniture of table, stools/benches and a chair. Seeing the groups of actors seated around such a table gives a sense of stability and rootedness, and also of hospitality, both of which are radically undercut by the action. Katie Mitchell's 1990 production, in the 'oppressive, darkened intimacy of the Old Red Lion Theatre' in Islington,[2] used a trestle-table and stools. In this smaller space, however, reviewers noted both domesticity and claustrophobia, where the 'thick carpet of earth' on the stage developed a mood 'at once homely and sinister'.[3]

---

1 Erich Fried, *The Listener*, Thursday 18 April 1974, vol. 91, issue 2351, 501–2.
2 Sarah Eltis, *TLS*, 24 August 1990.
3 Paul Taylor, *Independent*, Saturday 11 August 1990.

Reviewers read the space as a kitchen, the modern equivalent of the early modern hall or parlour space in the sense that it is central to domestic life as a hub for food preparation and consumption.[1]

The furniture focuses the attention of both actors and audience, organizing them into a group facing one another in a way that makes credible Black Will's invisibility to Arden as he focuses on the game in Sc. 14. But it also gives productions a chance to develop contrasting domestic themes of ease and formality. In Hands's 1982/3 production, Michael sprawled across the table talking to his mistress (see Fig. 10), and Mosby sat on the back of the chair in Sc. 1, talking to Alice about the painter. Mosby also left his hat on the table, where it remained

10 RSC 1982 production, dir. Terry Hands, designer Kandis Cook, with Jenny Agutter as Alice and Mark Rylance as Michael

1   Eltis.

on Arden's entrance, marking his sense of partial ownership, and Arden, entering for the game of tables in Sc. 14, left his cloak there to be cleared by Michael, and later laid his belt and purse down as an ironic sign of his relaxation. In contrast, the first scene of Polly Findlay's much more commodity-obsessed production of 2014 for the RSC was centred around an office desk with swivel chair (mainly swivelled by Mosby as he 'interviewed' potential murderers), explicitly contrasted against the mahogany dining room table and matching chairs of the murder scene. A wall of floor-to-ceiling waving cats, the Japanese lucky *maneki-neko*, formed a gold backdrop suggestive of both Arden's acquisitiveness and his initial good fortune. When Alice and Mosby exited at the end of Sc. 1 – 'He well may be the master of the house' – they apparently entered a domestic space for the first time, but in doing so they forced the audience to question modern lives lived in offices and refocused around business success.

In the twentieth century performances, household furniture was often given context by sets involving wooden structures that alluded to the timber framing used in Elizabethan domestic architecture. The set for Buzz Goodbody's 1970 RSC production, for example, featured a series of uprights at the back of the stage, one acting as a general exit and one as the counting house (with trussing to indicate their weight-bearing capacity), over which the upper stage area ran. In designer Merle Hensel's staging for the RSC in 2014, the boundaries of domesticity were set up in different ways. When the detritus of the factory in which the office table and swivel chair sat was cleared, yellow lines like car park markings were revealed on the floor. The production archive indicates both director and designer's interest in the questions of scale and familial life this suggests. Photographs and emails kept with the rehearsal notes, one of the latter sent, for instance, to the team of Deborah Meaden (a successful businesswoman and star of the UK entrepreneurs' show *Dragons' Den*), reveal the production's desire to understand and reflect global distribution systems, enormous packing warehouses and the extra-human scale of commodity culture.[1]

Such staging affects the way the play demonstrates the claustrophobia of the Faversham community. When Alice referred to her 'prying neighbours' in the 2014 production she gestured towards a factory operative working an electric hoist on the side of the stage. The Mayor was abandoned as a character part-way through rehearsals and replaced with Scene of Crime Officers. And the role of Susan was silently expanded, by adding an extensive mime of cleaning that connected both work and home locations with the fastidiousness of her intimate dusting of furniture, adjusting of objects and cleaning up of mess and then blood. Her overall and trolley of cleaning products connected her with Mrs Reede, substituted for her husband in Sc. 13 and played as a dispossessed woman, also wearing an overall with big pockets. Together, they deftly suggested the gender politics of invisible low-status work, zero-hours contracts and precarious financial lives that took away both women's agency, making Susan invisible as she moved with eerie slowness around kissing lovers and dead bodies, restoring the material appearance of domestic life even as its morality tumbled out of the characters' hands.[2] In more recent productions, then, the domestic is more likely to be seen as a place of threat, and directors like Mitchell and Findlay have brought out the bizarre in everyday life.

Provincially, in the twentieth century the tradition of local amateur performance was revived in Faversham, where it was

---

1 Meaden, on tour with the hit television ballroom show *Strictly Come Dancing*, was unable to help. RSC 2014 rehearsal notes also include, 'Ms Findlay has requested to meet a Poundland or Amazon distributor to come and talk to the Company during the early stages of rehearsals'.
2 Ian Shuttleworth, for the *Financial Times*, described her 'wealth of wordless drudgery that is by turns comical and exquisitely agonising' (7 May 2014).

Arden's private and domestic story that resonated. Instead of being staged at inns and fairs, productions started to map onto the specific buildings and spaces that Arden knew. In 1952 Faversham celebrated the 700th anniversary of its charter with a production of *Arden* at Davington Priory, produced by John Spalding. The producer's note in the programme describes the significance of the setting. Although admitting that 'the incidents of the play had no relationship whatever with Davington Priory', he does point out a historical connection: 'the house was given by Henry VIII to Sir Thomas Cheyne', the play's most socially elite character. A further assertion, rendered curious by the admission that the house was not a setting for any of the play's events, gets to the heart of the site-specificity of this type of production: 'It has nevertheless been felt essential to arrange the action of the play so that the players coming from local places such as Sheppey, Rochester, Rainham, or even Faversham itself should appear to be coming from the directions one would expect at Davington.' The mapping of the play onto the resonant historical spaces of Faversham had given the story a particular frisson. Students from RADA, who came to perform the play at the town's Queen Elizabeth's Grammar School in 1975, also spent time in the grounds of Davington Priory (see Fig. 11). Performers began to be aware of and to exploit the power of the site-specificity possible with a play that re-enacted a murder whose original location was still standing.[1] More recently, productions have taken place mainly in and around the historical Arden's still extant house (see Fig. 12), where he can be murdered again and again very close to the spot where he was originally dispatched. In staging the play in such a space, *Arden* becomes a domestic drama in a different sense – one whose mapping of imagined and located spaces onto one another has a clear resonance at a personal, as opposed to communal, level.

1 For more on site-specific practices, see Bennett and Polito.

11 RADA students pictured in the grounds of Davington Priory, just outside Faversham, in June 1975, preparing to perform the play at Queen Elizabeth's Grammar School in the town, dir. Geoff Bullen

Significant props

Within this context of relatively uniform levels of domestic realization, if very different styles, the significance of certain props to the play's articulation of 'household' becomes especially clear in performance. Some of these important objects – the dining goods, prayer-book and ring – have been explored above for their contribution to the definition of community (see

12 Arden's House as it stands today

pp. 30–2). Thinking specifically about those with a domestic function, we can see them as indicating the guests' levels of comfort and discomfort with the hospitality on offer in Arden's house, and influencing the audience's response to that offer as either conventional hospitality perverted by lust and murder, or a social configuration uncomfortable from the start in a more structural way. Contrast, for instance, two sets of instructions: first, in 1970, 'On Round wooden tray three pewter Tankards and the rubber Tankard. On the silver tray the five silver cups and two napkins', a standard offer of sustenance and pledge that allows Arden to demonstrate his status and his guests to respond according to their own; and second, the assertion, in the rehearsal notes for the RSC 2014 production, that 'Bradshaw requires a small potted plant to bring to dinner in 13.2' (27 February). In a production with a wicked eye for telling detail that played up the comic in the horrific, the awkward Bradshaw aimed at social niceties, ending up alone at the dinner table, wiggling to music while Arden's blood dripped onto the stage out of the bottom of the packing box into which his body was shoved.[1] Here, notions of hospitality were approached ironically as hollow and inadequate. These props deftly articulate our changing sense of the relationship between a household and its neighbours.

Seeing the play in performance, one realizes the extent to which props structure *Arden*'s action more generally – a relatively small number of objects whose visual presence in key scenes and verbal echoes in others gives coherence through recurrence and aids characterization. Alice's prayer-book is given prominence in the majority of productions, forming a key element through which her identity is interpreted to the audience. It has made most complex meaning in productions with a well-realized sense of the spiritual stakes of the murder: in her analysis of Mitchell's 1990 production, Elizabeth Schafer notes that Alice's desecration of the prayer-book 'was a key section, and linked up with other moments in the play that explore penance, a concept Alice engages with thoroughly after Arden's murder' (263). Agutter's Alice read throughout her lover's speech, tearing out pages without histrionics but with a quiet passion, kneeling at his feet when she was done. The stage manager's notes on the difficulties encountered with the need for such a renewable prop include the suggestion that it could 'get "The Prop of the Production" award'.[2] Elizabeth Williamson has argued that the material ephemerality of prayer-books posed a problem for their function as carriers of an immutable Word in general, and that in Alice's hands the book becomes symbolic of a rift 'between the ideal of an immaterial faith and the realities of daily life', a troubling fracture that is

---

1   The Coen brothers' films sprang to the minds of several critics, see, e.g., Dominic Maxwell in *The Times*, 8 May 2014.
2   17 February 1983, RSC/SM/2/1982/91–5 Pit rehearsal notes (RSC 1982/3).

echoed in the audience's response to its material destruction (372). Fig. 13, in contrast, gives a material sense of the way the early modern care and attention that could be lavished on such items was tied up with gendered practices and behavioural norms, and the books' essentially non-disposable nature.

Many productions include the silver dice that link Alice and Mosby across the troubled waxing and waning of their relationship. These too are open to a symbolic reading, suggesting fate and the gamble with eternal life in which Alice and Mosby are engaged, for instance. For Hands in 1982/3 they were a part of a small group of props personal to Alice, including a comb and mirror in a box, and were kept in a small drawstring purse in her dressing gown pocket – concealed close to the body they underlined her intimate sexual appeal. In RSC 2014, in contrast, the onstage props list included both a box of silver dice keyrings and one separate dice keyring used as the dice referred to in the text (1.122): personal objects here were part of a non-specific commodity culture, and could simply be borrowed from mass-produced stock and put back.

Arden is a play whose props shade into environment – domestic tables large and solid enough to virtually constitute scenery, or factory walls made of lucky cats. Seen together, these objects serve to build up the play's sense of domestic and communal life. But the way productions negotiate the distinctions between the relative atmospheres and threats of inside and outside, province and capital, is also a vital part of their meaning-making and the play's changing impact over time. In Goodbody's production, the lack of 'scenic distinction between London streets and the Kentish countryside' either did or did not matter depending on your point of view, but was certainly noticeable.[1] The music cues for the production

---

1   Billington, *The Times*, 6 November 1970; Kenneth Hurren for *The Spectator* found that 'there is no great disadvantage in the lack of evocative scenery' (14 November 1970).

13 Bible and Book of Common Prayer, *c*. 1607, with front and back covers depicting Adam and Eve in the Garden of Eden, standing by the Tree of Knowledge. Often worked by women, such imagery reflected moral themes, here around marriage and obedience. 34.3 x 23.5 cm, satin worked with silk and metal thread, spangles

suggest that some of this work was done aurally, through the cries of marsh birds.

The most rurally invested production was perhaps Hands's in 1982/3. Advice was sought on the nature of the canopy and a visit taken to English Woodlands,[1] resulting in a set that included branches overhead, hanging 'below eye level of front row gallery', but 'high enough so as not to be lit during interior scenes'.[2] In exterior scenes, then, they formed a pattern of intersecting foliage on the stage floor that was both natural and faintly sinister. Costs were also incurred for the purchase of a dead crow (artificial), presumably to add to the mood, but this was later apparently abandoned.[3] The effect of the branches was particularly seen in Sc. 7, as the loudly threatening fight between the four men took place in eerie light cast through their shadow, obscuring the detail of the struggle. The rushes strewn on the floor of Arden's house, laid 'at feet of front row', were particularly effective in defining the area between the actors and audience. For this purpose, a considerable investment was made in the type of marsh reeds used for thatching (£135.47, plus an extra £20 for their emergency redelivery to the right theatre in time for press night); a part of one has been archived with the production files.[4]

Findlay's 2014 production was considerably more urban: sprayed-out security cameras and fire extinguishers were initially considered as part of the villains' arsenal, and a massive crowbar and a sniper's rifle, both inexpertly wielded, featured in the eventual performance. Here, distinctions between inside and outside were treated both less romantically and with more

---

1   The company, founded in 1919, is based in Heathfield in East Sussex.
2   RSC/SM/2/1982/91–5 Pit rehearsal notes; set design (RSC 1982/3).
3   RSC/OP/1/1/11 Production costs, 1982 (RSC 1982/3).
4   Excess note from Wilkinson Transport for redirected delivery of rushes from the Aldwych to the Royal Shakespeare Theatre in Stratford-upon-Avon on 23/3/82, RSC/OP/1/1/11 (RSC 1982/3).

of a sense of wonder. The murderers paused with Arden's body as the snow came down over the stage, in a tableau static as though entering a snow globe. Then Alice, tart turned domestic, cleared a black space in the snow around the dining room table, deftly making the space inside again. As Scene of Crime Officers put evidence into plastic bags and Alice cried stridently to be brought to her husband, snow once again filled the rectangle of floor that she had cleared, transporting her into a very intimate outside space with the body, a location in which she talked to him closely and touchingly.

The very different modes of separation and connection of interiors and exteriors, of rural and urban settings, that the productions employ all preserve the play's essential early modern flexibility, even, in Findlay's case, in a modern environment. In doing so, they use props and staging to create the contrasts which highlight those moments of intense intimacy that shape *Arden* as tragedy.

THE TEXT: NOVELTY, MOULDY TALES AND STRANGE BEDFELLOWS

Thinking about the earliest versions of the text of *Arden* offers us another way of understanding its novelty as a play, within, in this case, the print culture of the late sixteenth and early seventeenth centuries. There is no surviving manuscript of *Arden*, so the text as we know it comes from the first quarto, Q1 (printed by Edward Allde for the publisher Edward White, STC 733) in 1592, and two substantially similar reprints: Q2 (James Roberts for White, STC 734) in 1599 and Q3 (Elizabeth Allde, STC 735) in 1633. Although relatively few plays from the public theatres were published in the early 1590s, White did also publish *Soliman and Perseda* and *The Spanish Tragedy* in the same year as Q1. In this context, *Arden* was a modestly popular play in early modern print, with three editions; *Soliman and*

Perseda had just two pre-Restoration editions, while *The Spanish Tragedy* had eleven. The list of editions is swiftly brought up to the nineteenth century by adding Edward Jacob's 1770 version of the first quarto, 're-printed verbatim by J. & J. March, for Stephen Doorne, bookseller at Feversham: and sold by Mess. Hawes & Co., London; and by all the booksellers in Kent'; *Arden* arrived back with London printers in 1851 with its inclusion in Henry Tyrrell's *The Doubtful Plays of Shakespere.*

Arden was entered into the Stationers' Register to Edward White on 3 April 1592, as 'The tragedie of Arden of Feuersham & blackwill', and the play was printed by Edward Allde. White was apprenticed as a printer in 1565, and had been admitted to the livery of the Stationers' Company in 1588, by which time he was a mature and experienced professional, his success indicating 'hard work, canny business sense and close working relationships with fellow stationers'.[1] Nadia Bishai, who has analysed his output in detail, points to the 'consistent sale of literature of crime at the Gun' (White's shop sign), in all sorts of formats – mainly popular literature such as pamphlets and ballads, often concerned with current affairs, and plays focused on 'treason, traitors, heresy, heretics, murder and murderers' (15). She suggests that around a quarter of White's catalogue is classifiable as literature of crime, but there was also a good deal of 'cheap print' type material – acts of God and the weather, for instance, such as a book on 'the second earthquake in Kent', entered on 16 May 1580.

White's admittance to the livery of his company did not mean that his activities always met with his fellows' approval. We get some sense of how saleable cheap print was when we look at the regular fines he received for illegal printing of ballads, presumably to make a quick buck. *Arden* itself was the

---

1   Bishai, 13.

subject of a dispute between White and Abel Jeffes – the men were both fined on 18 December 1592, White for publishing *The Spanish Tragedy*, which belonged to Jeffes, and Jeffes for pirating White's *Arden*. Wine dates Jeffes's illegal (and now lost) *Arden* to between 3 April and 7 August (xx). Its publication is evidence that both men saw a market for the play that was immediate and pressing, and worth risking a fine over, especially in the context of *Spanish Tragedy*, which we know was very popular on the stage. White evidently had a strong sense of the market and moved quickly to cash in on popular stories and books; his familiarity with the market in newsworthy crimes and other current affairs must have made him an ideal seller of *Arden* and his shop a perfect context for its lurid title-page.

In editorial terms the relationship between the quartos is quite straightforward, and this edition, like all others before it, is based on Q1. Q2 does not deal with any of the key textual cruxes of Q1 (e.g. 'gentle stary gaile', 'fence of trouble' (8.17, 133)), and corrects some lesser errors while introducing others. Printed from Q2, Q3 clears up some of these latter problems while continuing to modernize spelling and grammatical forms, in a process begun in Q2. Three copies of Q1 survive: Edmond Malone's, now at the Bodleian Library, Oxford; Alexander Dyce's, at the Victoria and Albert Museum in London; and the Mostyn-Perry copy, at the Huntington Library, California. The Malone copy lacks the blank leaf K2, and the Dyce lacks I4–K2 (from the end of Sc. 14 to the end of the play).

Wine studied the type, spelling and punctuation use throughout Q1, and suggested that it pointed to a single compositor.[1] Scholars have found few corrections between the

---

1   Wine adds, 'It is not possible to discover clearly whether type was set by formes or *seriatim*', although he assembles some evidence in favour of the latter: unsystematic resetting of headlines and ending on signature K which wastes paper (xxxii).

three copies of Q1. They occur on six formes (i.e. single sides of the printed sheet). Bourus and Taylor point out that they are concentrated mainly in two of them: F outer (with nine variants on three pages) and I inner (with seven variants on three pages)'.[1] Even in the formes with the heaviest concentrations of corrections, however, obvious mistakes remain. This is not to say that Allde was an incompetent printer, rather that the type of printing for which he was known did not require the highest of standards – he produced ballads and chapbooks, pamphlets and jestbooks that were cheaply made and sold, and enjoyed until they fell apart.

Q1 of *Arden* sits on a cusp between old and new publishing worlds. One of the primary differences between Q1 and Q2 is a variety of spellings and other features that were old-fashioned by the time of even the former's printing, and were modernized in the latter. For instance, 'head' is spelled 'heede', a spelling that had largely died out in the first half of the sixteenth century (*OED*); 'brake' as a spelling of 'broke' is an early sixteenth-century form, and similarly 'by' for 'buy', 'erre' for 'ear', 'ferse' for 'fierce', 'whill' for 'while', 'hous' for 'house', etc. In terms of verse, the fourteener at the start of the play (1.6) was becoming old-fashioned by the time *Arden* was printed.[2] Given the lack of comparable examples in other texts by Allde and White, these features can be thought of as representative of the age or outlook of the scribe or one of the authors.[3]

---

1   B&T, 9. Wine states that they 'vary only slightly in their states of press correction, minor variants being recorded on the formes of inner A, inner D, outer F, outer H, inner I, and inner K' (xxxii). See Appendix 3.

2   Lucy Munro states that 'The 1590s also saw fast-paced developments in both poetic and theatrical style, developments that rendered certain metrical forms (notably the fourteener and poulter's measure) and dramatic genres (in particular the morality play) archaic, making them available for specific kinds of stylistic experimentation' (6). Other examples of metrical diversity include *Rare Triumphs of Love and Fortune* (printed by Allde in 1589).

3   B&T, 13. The old-fashioned spellings occur across the play.

The end of Q1 is decorated with an ornament printed from a piece of type which had been in use since the 1540s; it was part of a much larger original, which had apparently broken in half in the early 1570s. The sill piece used to end *Arden*, showing off its worm holes, is printed upside down, with its cherubs standing on their heads. It seems a fitting symbol for a quick job, scantily decorated by classical ornament but fully rooted in the materiality of working life.[1]

Arden *as material text*

So, what more can we say about *Arden* from the material qualities of these first quartos? First, *Arden* is printed in black letter type in both Q1 and Q2, and this situates it once again on the cusp, between two different attitudes towards plays.[2] Until 1583, the majority of plays were printed in black letter, a more traditional, even old-fashioned typeface imitating medieval book hands that was, by the 1590s, used mainly in official documents and at the 'cheap print' end of the market, in ballads. The typeface used on the hornbooks with which reading was initially taught (see, for instance, the Folger Library's example, STC 21.6) was associated with lower-status, less sophisticated readers without a great deal of education. After the playwright Lyly's entry into (roman) print in 1584 with *Campaspe* and *Sapho and Phao*, most plays came to be printed in roman text, and thereby associated with higher levels of literacy. According to Bourus and Taylor, 'After 1590, there was never again a year in which black letter plays exceeded roman plays', and crucially, in 1592 *Arden* was 'the only first edition of a dramatic text printed that year in black letter'.[3] That would have made it look

---

1 Sill piece of compartment 53 in McKerrow and Ferguson; McKerrow also notes the worm holes.
2 The title-page, which presumably also functioned as an advertisement, is in roman type.
3 B&T, 9.

old-fashioned or perhaps comfortingly familiar and demotic (also possibly with a nod towards the provincial), in particular in comparison to Lyly's strikingly clean, clear and humanistically inspired texts.

To understand why *Arden* was less than modish visually, despite its generic novelty, we need to see it in the context of its publisher's and printer's output as a whole. They collaborated frequently and, although Allde printed for around eighty-six different booksellers, with Edward White senior and junior he printed more than fifty titles between 1587 and 1621.[1] *Arden* comes at the beginning of a long and fruitful relationship, then, when Allde's printing business was small (Erne estimates, from texts for which evidence survives, that only around 100 sheets 'roughly the equivalent of 800 quarto pages' were printed in 1592), and he had previously printed only four plays.[2] Allde, and his father before him, had printed plays only in black letter (twelve between them) until 1591. White's output of plays had not used roman type before 1592, and after that date he only used black letter in two reprints, *Arden* in 1599 (Q2) and *2 Tamburlaine* in 1606. But that second edition of *Arden*, also in black letter, is curious – it may represent an attempt to tie the second edition to the first, or at least indicate an enduring desire to signal visually the nature of the material by linking it to other types of text still being produced in that typeface. It might be that publisher and printer saw *Arden* as more like sensational crime and less like a play, occupying a ground somewhere between narrative history and drama, as explored above in generic terms (see pp. 12–13): in that year White also published a pamphlet on the *Murder of John Brewen*, an investigation of the *Strange and Wonderful Accidents . . . in the House of M. George Lee* and a prose *History of the*

---

1 McKerrow, 138.
2 Erne, xviii. The other plays were *Cambises* in 1569/70, *Like Will to Like* Q3 in 1587, *The Rare Triumphs of Love and Fortune* in 1589 and Q3 *Gorboduc* in 1590.

Damnable Life and Deserved Death of Dr John Faustus, all in black letter with roman title-pages, like *Arden*. Bourus and Taylor suggest that the choice of black letter for Q2 might also point to something even older, the period in which the events themselves took place: 'White, or Allde, or the two together, decided to use the black letter typeface for *Arden of Faversham* because they wanted to suggest, typographically, the period of the events represented in the play: the 1550s, the reign of Edward VI, the early Reformation'.[1] Old story, new type of drama.

While this feature sets *Arden*'s face backwards to the mid-century, in other ways it is closely linked to the playtexts of the early 1590s. In 1592 (possibly into early 1593), the three plays that White and Allde were working on, *Arden*, *Spanish Tragedy* and *Soliman and Perseda*, made up perhaps a third of White's surviving output that year, and formed the single largest generic category within it, seen in modern terms at least. This is such a suggestive grouping, forming such a significant financial investment for both businesses in that year, that it repays further attention. We have already seen a connection between *Arden* and *Spanish Tragedy* in the court case mentioned above, with the suggestions about mutual saleability, perhaps as a result of success in performance. *Spanish Tragedy* and *Soliman and Perseda* are also closely related to one another. Both were probably written by Kyd, the latter presenting as its full subject-matter the compressed action of the play-within-the-play that brings the former to its bloody climax. These two plays were printed in roman type, rather than *Arden*'s black letter, using printing conventions that are similar, although not identical to one another.[2] This indicates that the three texts were not seen as

---

1 B&T, 10.
2 In *Spanish Tragedy*, 'stage directions are in roman except for names and the words "Exit" and "Exeunt", which are usually in italics. In *Soliman & Perseda*, stage directions are mostly in italics, except for names, which are in roman' (Erne, xx).

a group for marketing purposes, at least not in ways that necessitated visual similarity.

Arden and *Soliman and Perseda*, on the other hand, share a unique distinctive feature in the large number of stage directions they contain beginning with '*Then*'. Given at the start of a stage direction, '*Then*' is very rarely used, and these are the only two contemporary plays to use it so extensively.[1] Its pervasiveness, across the whole of what is apparently a co-authored play, might suggest a common scribe. Conversely, *Arden* lacks stage directions for the use of props, and it has no sound cues. Both kinds of direction feature in *Soliman and Perseda*. This tends to indicate a different provenance for the underlying manuscripts, as such prompts might be expected in a text emanating from the playhouse. One other noteworthy typographical 'tic' of *Arden*'s is not, however, shared with either *Soliman and Perseda* or *Spanish Tragedy*. Each entry begins with '*Here enters*', a feature relatively common in early Tudor plays but one uncommon in later drama.[2] It does creep into printed plays of the 1570s, featuring, for example, in *Common Conditions* (1576; Wiggins 486); EEBO-TCP shows sixty-three hits for *Arden*, but only twenty-nine for the next most frequent usage, in *Damon and Pythias* (1571; Wiggins 389). *Fair Em the Miller's Daughter* (1591; Wiggins 852), the only other play published in the first years of the 1590s to contain the same direction, shows only four instances. This might suggest either a writer or a scribe for *Arden* well versed in older forms. These connections are suggestive about provenance and scribal practice, but they are not conclusive – they offer further complexity to a curious puzzle that sees *Arden* as distinctive typographically, orthographically and in relation to

---

1   B&T, 12. See, e.g., *Soliman and Perseda*, where '*Then he kils* Haleb' is swiftly followed by '*Then* Soliman *kils* Amurath' (ll. 651, 654).
2   Jackson, *Determining*, 107.

the rendering of its dramatic action in print.[1] Overall, however, they do suggest that there is something rather distinctively old-fashioned in *Arden*'s textual materiality.

Q3 and the woodcut

The context for the third quarto of *Arden* – printed nearly forty years after the first – gives us a different view of the play's popularity. Edward White had died, and his widow sold the rights to twenty of his titles, one of which was *Arden*, on 29 June 1624.[2] The purchaser was Edward Allde, printer of Q1. But it was Elizabeth, his wife, who both printed and published Q3 in 1633, after his death, at which point *Arden*'s story becomes one of female publication of the tale of a notorious murder instigated by a woman.[3] Probably shortly before *Arden* Q3 was printed in 1633, someone printed a ballad called 'The complaint and lamentation of Mistresse Arden of Feversham in Kent', for C. Wright. It is not improbable that Elizabeth Allde was the printer of both ballad and quarto, as the striking woodcut in Fig. 14 was clearly made for the former, across whose width it fits perfectly.[4] Reproduced in the smaller quarto

---

1   Taylor and Loughnane state that 'the combination of systematic "*Here enters*" with mid-scene stage directions beginning with "*Then*" distinguishes *Arden of Faversham* from every other extant play of the period' (437). With one exception, scene-end exits in *Arden* are set right, whereas the mid-scene exits are usually centred (Bourus and Taylor count 23 out of 35), also likely to be a feature of the manuscript from which Q1 was set (12–13).

2   Stationers' Register, Liber B, fol. 286[r].

3   A variant to the title-page that identifies the quarto as 'Printed by Eliz. Allde dwelling neere Christs-Church' advertises the book as 'to be sold by *Stephen Pemel*'; see DEEP: deep.sas.upenn.edu/viewrecord.php?deep_id=145; Elizabeth remained the publisher.

4   'Lamentation'. On the practice of co-registration of pamphlets and ballads and occasionally plays and ballads (especially from 1590 to 1616), planned by the publisher to promote sales, see Levin.

14 Woodcut illustration for the ballad 'The complaint and lamentation of Mistresse Arden of Feversham in Kent', *c.* 1633

format of the play, it has to be squeezed in sideways on the verso of the title-page.

The appearance of the woodcut at this stage in the play's history gives further insight into how it related to other contemporary plays. Partly, illustrated plays were in vogue – there were four times as many in the 1630s as in the 1590s,[1] so this was the moment to give visual form to the power of *Arden*'s denouement. John H. Astington, writing about the woodcuts used to advertise Middleton's plays, suggests that booksellers did not specialize in illustrated plays, rather in titles with woodcuts more generally (231–2). That shows how images connected different types of output by the same printer, and suggests that they were perhaps investments that would be especially likely if they could be used across different genres. In the early 1630s, around the time of Q3, Elizabeth Allde also published a reprint of *Friar Bacon and Friar Bungay* (1630; first published by Edward White in 1594), with an impressive woodcut, and a series of illustrated ballads. As plays 'inhabited ambiguous territory in the marketing world of seventeenth-century bookstalls',[2] such links between genres might be more flexibly made, and they connected the plays most firmly to sensational works of the ballad and true crime variety, just as Q1 had done with its black letter type. These woodcuts are likely to have been produced by craftsmen whose main body of work was in wood carving in a domestic context, where their lively skills were appreciated in moralizing and biblical scenes on overmantles and pieces of furniture,[3] and

---

1 Astington, 227. It is, however, hard to calculate this in relation to the rising rate of play publication more generally. Alan B. Farmer and Zachary Lesser, in one method of calculation, identify the two periods relevant here as '1576–1597: an initial period of low production (48 first editions, 11 second-plus editions)', and '1629–1640: a second boom (122 first editions, 84 second-plus editions)' (7).

2 Astington, 229.

3 For more on the skills involved in carved decoration see Hamling, and https://middlingculture.com/tag/carving/.

they epitomize the vernacular, demotic qualities of a variety of domestic tales.

The *Arden* woodcut once more links the play in several different directions at once. Its prominently placed gaming tables relate it, counter-intuitively, to the first *engraved* frontispiece for an early modern play, Thomas Middleton's *A Game at Chess*, a satirical take on Anglo-Spanish politics in the form of a chess match.[1] Games boards had been represented in print since 1499 and in manuscript for much longer, symbolizing conflict between individuals and the workings of fortune.[2] Like the *Game at Chess* illustration, the *Arden* Q3 woodcut is set apart from similar fare by its particularity to one play, when other images tended to be more generic. *Spanish Tragedy* was reprinted in 1615, now featuring for the first time a very strikingly specific woodcut showing the murdered Horatio and Bell-Imperia's and Hieronimo's horrified reactions, with which it has also become inextricably associated in subsequent years, and this image too has a focus on a particular dramatic moment. *Spanish Tragedy*'s woodcut appears to have been made first for the play, as it fits across the quarto page, but it was later added to a *c.* 1620 ballad called 'The Spanish Tragedy, Containing the lamentable Murders of Horatio and Bellimperia: With the pittiful Death of old Hieronimo. To the tune of Queene Dido'. The woodcuts share further features unusual for the genre, in their careful realization of an event in which individuals of the same size interact with one another, and their precise depiction of details of clothing and setting. Unlike the 'exaggerated, non-realistic style' of other cuts[3] with their topsy-turvy folktale world of distorted sizes and unlocated action, these woodcuts situate their action carefully within

1 Astington, 239. The engraving first appeared in some copies of the undated 'Q1' (STC 17882). See *Middleton Companion*, 717–18.
2 Astington, 242.
3 Astington, 229.

spaces that may depict the scenery used, or at least expected, in a stage performance. Interestingly, the carefully delineated clothing of *Arden* and *Spanish Tragedy* in particular belongs to an earlier time, with features that are both Jacobean and Elizabethan, highlighting the fact that these were old plays, and perhaps gesturing towards the type of costumes originally staged.[1]

In the first half of the seventeenth century, then, *Arden* and *Spanish Tragedy*, both originally printed in the early 1590s, again became popular, probably because of theatrical revivals, but perhaps also more broadly as stories of murder and injustice that had entered the public consciousness alongside and beyond their stage history. While Alice's crime remained famous in chronicles, ballads and other writings, *Spanish Tragedy* had a vivid afterlife in oral culture as famous lines from the play entered everyday speech.[2] In the production of fully realized images that accompanied ballads, whose first person narration itself invited amateur, quotidian performances sung in the persona of the protagonist, *Arden* and *Spanish Tragedy* entered a different phase of their imaginative lives, a phase that probably helped to ensure the plays' popularity into the eighteenth century, and therefore beyond to our own times.

This edition: how it differs from the quarto, what it adds and why that matters

Fig. 15 shows two pages of Q1 that equate to 14.46–112 in this edition (pp. 252–4). Looking at the differences between the

---

1 Elly Lowe and Daniel Rosen have dated the costumes in the *Arden* woodcut, on the basis of the male character on the far right and the hair, to 1620 at the earliest, but recognise echoes of earlier dress in, e.g., the hanging sleeves on the woman's gown. The *Spanish Tragedy* woodcut shows an even wider range, with the heels of the shoes *c*. 1615, the hair suggestive of the first decade of the seventeenth century and the pinned flounces on the gown alluding to the 1590s (personal correspondence).

2 *Spanish Tragedy*, 1.

The Tragedy of M. Arden

And this night shal thou and Susan be made sure,
  Mic. Ile go tell him.
  Ales. And as thou goest, tell John cooke of our guests,
And bid him lay it on, spare for no cost.   Exit Michaell.
  Wil. Nay and there be such cheere, we wil bid our selues
Mistres Arden, Dick Greene & I do meane to sup wt you,
  Ales. And welcome shail you be, ah gentlemen,
How mist you of your purpose yesternight?
  Gre. T was long of Shakebag that v̇. luckye villaine.
  Sha. T ou doest me wrong, I did as much as any.
  Wil. Nay then M. Ales, Ile tell you how it was,
When he should haue lockt with both his hilts,
He in a brauery florisht ouer his head
With that comes Francklin at him lustely
And hurts the slaue, with that he slinks away,
Now his way had bene to haue come hand and foote,
  one and two round at his costerd.
He lyke a foole beares his sword point halfe a yarde out
  of danger, I lye here for m lyfe.
If the deui'l come, and he haue no more strength then fence
He shall neuer beat me from this warde,
Ile stand to it, a buckler in a skilfull hand,
Is as good as a castell.
Nay tis better then a sconce, for I haue tryde it.
Mosbie perceiuing this, began to faint,
With that comes Arden with his arming sword,
And thrust him through the shoulder in a tryce.
  Ales. I but I wonder why you both stode still.
  Wil. Faith I was so amazed I could not strike.
  Ales. Ah sirs had he yesternight bene slaine,
For euery drop of his detested blood,
I would cramme in Angels in thy fist.
And kist thee too, and hugd thee in my armes,
  Wil. Patient your selfe, we can not help it now,
Greene and we two, will dogge him through the faire,
And stab him in the croud, and steale away,

                       Here

15   Q1, sig. H2ᵛ–H3ʳ

sixteenth- and twenty-first-century lines makes it possible to
explore the rationale for alterations that this edition has made to
its base text and the extra information it offers for interpretation
of the play. Some additions of information to pre-existing stage
directions have been made throughout, as here, where to Q1's
'Here enters Mosby' has been added '[*with his arm and
shoulder bandaged*]' (in square brackets to show it is a modern

of *Feuershame.*

Here enters Mosbye.

Ales. It is vnpossible, but here comes he,
That will I hope inuent some surer meanes.
Sweete Mosbie hide thy arme, it kils my hart.

Mos. I murdres Arden, this is your fauour,

Ales Ah say not so for when I sawe thee hurt,
I could haue toke the weapon thou letst fall,
And runne at Arden, for I haue sworne,
That these mine eyes offended with his sight,
Shall neuer close, til Ardens be shut vp.
This night I rose and walkt about the chamber,
And twise or thrise, I thought to haue murthred him,

Mos. What in the night, then had we bene vndone.

Ales Why, how long shall he liue?

Mos. Faith Ales no longer then this night.
Black Will and shakbag, will you two
Performe the complot that I haue laid.

Will. I or els think me as a villaine.

Gre. And rather then you shall want,
Ile helpe my selfe.

Mos. You M. Græne shal single Francklin foorth,
And hould him with a long tale of strange newes:
That he may not come home till suppertime.
Ile fetch M. Arden home, & we like frends,
Will play a game or two at tables here,

Ales But what of all this?
How shall he be slaine?

Mosbie Why black Will and shakebag lockt within
the countinghouse,
Shall at a certaine watchword giuen, rush foorth,

Wil. What shall the watch word be?

Mos. (Now I take you) that shall be the word,
But come not foorth before in any case.

Wil. I warrant you, but who shall lock me in?

Ales. That will I do, thou't kepe the key thy selfe.

Mos. Come M. Græne, go you along with me.

H. 3   See

addition) (14.80 SD).[1] The aim is to make it easier for actors to prepare for and readers to imagine more fully the visual impact that Mosby's entrance has at this point. The intention, however, has been to open up possibilities rather than to close them down, and additions have therefore been confined to those that the text seems to ask for, rather than allude to, and with details

1   Stage directions in Q1 are printed in roman type, contrasting with the black letter type used for the spoken text. The textual notes to this edition follow convention in printing Q1's stage directions in italic type, to distinguish them from spoken text, which is printed in roman.

that are suggestive rather than prescriptive. Stage directions have, on the same logic, been added where none exists in Q1, for example at 1.371, to identify the person whom Alice addresses: '[*to Arden*] Here's he that you cast in my teeth so oft', or at 10.46 SD, where a prop is needed: '*Here enters* [CLARKE] *the Painter* [*with a crucifix covered*]'.

Visually, the largest difference in the section illustrated is in ll. 57–68. Q1 sets Black Will's speech as verse (the textual notes on lineation show the original line endings), but the lack of a regular metre and the irregular flow of his speech suggests that it is really prose, as he describes to Alice the scene of the fight in swift, lively language using, we might presume, a considerable amount of gesture.

Emendations to Q1 have been made sparingly, given the irregularity of the text explored above (see pp. 41–2). Metre has in the main been left as originally printed rather than being regularized.[1] Phrases have been altered only where the evidence for their inaccuracy is strong – for instance in this section where Q1 has Will's description as 'Now his way had beene to have come hand and feete' (61–2). To 'come *in* hand and feet' is a technical term in swordsmanship, so we can assume that the missing 'in' is an error. Another possible emendation occurs at 108, where Bourus and Taylor point out that the watchword specified by Mosby here is different from its operative use at 236 ('now I can take you'; Holinshed has 'now may I take you', Southouse MS has 'can take'), and therefore add 'can'. This emendation has not been adopted here, however, as it seems to

---

1 The irregularities of line-setting in Q1 include a number of long verse turnover lines. Where these are of note, the word preceding the turnover in the middle of a probable verse line has been noted in parentheses. For example, at 12.26–9, Q1 prints a final long line, 'You are well enough served, to goe without a guyde, such weather as this.', with a turnover after 'guyde,'; the line is annotated in the textual notes as 26–9] *Delius; Q1 lines* help, / ditch? / *(*guyde, / *)* this. /

demand a level of consistency that the text of a play, as written or printed, or as seen in performance, does not necessitate.

The intention here is to understand the text of *Arden* in the widest possible context. In editorial and linguistic terms, as with its generic and print history, the notes aim to explore its typicality. Quantitative use has therefore been made of the EEBO-TCP database of early modern text transcriptions in cases such as the one mentioned above, in order to assess which word or phrase is most likely to have been intended at a given point. Although EEBO-TCP does not currently contain transcriptions of all extant early modern editions, it still offers extensive and valuable information about typicality. At other points, online resources have been used that it is not possible to search in such a quantitative way because of the way their data is organized. For example, the catalogues of the National Archives and the Kent History and Library Centre have been consulted to give a sense of how manuscript sources spell names, in particular, in the period, and for examples of early modern spoken idiom. In an ideal world, we would understand the valence of particular names, spellings and phrases in both the mouths of audiences and the pens of a wider range of published and unpublished authors, and would therefore be able to give weight to the language as spoken at the time the play was written, and to the vernacular as written in manuscript form, when establishing the veracity and meaning of our texts. Such information as is given here is a small and partial step in that direction, using the imperfect electronic tools currently at our disposal.

The commentary notes' role of explaining the meaning of words and phrases no longer in common usage has also been expanded to consider 'meaning' as holistically as possible, by giving a sense of the social and cultural valence of the phrases, actions and objects of which *Arden* is made. As a play based in the quotidian and obsessed by small distinctions of status in the competitive middle of society, *Arden* demands that we understand the way it deploys such detail if we are to grasp its full significance. So, in the note to l4.103, for instance, readers can learn what 'tables' are; they are pointed not only to the printed evidence for them in *OED* and the 1633 Q3 woodcut, but also to an extant material example in the collections of the Mary Rose museum. A list of repositories with online visual evidence for objects from this period is included in the bibliography, in order to open up our study of early modern theatrical display to the wealth of visual and material evidence beyond the printed sources habitually referenced in editions of plays.

One more piece of information is also given in the note to 'tables' at 103: 'ownership of such "leisure items" was a key indicator of elevated social status, and late-16th-century Faversham inhabitants owned over thirty pairs, present in 13% of households, valued at up to 3s 4d each'. Such information, provided wherever possible for prominent objects within the play, aims to be both quantitatively informative about the likelihood of early modern ownership and precise about details of individual objects. It is based on all probate inventories from the town from the start of the record in the 1560s to 1600, covering the estates of those who remembered Arden and those who may have witnessed the play if toured around the time of Q1 or Q2. It is not intended to suggest that knowing what happened in Faversham per se when *Arden* was written is important to a broader contemporary experience of the play as staged. Instead, Faversham has been chosen as a representative community for which good enough records survive to suggest the percentage of the inventory-making population who might have owned such goods, their relative value, and therefore what kind of impact their inclusion in the playwright's making of character through things is likely to have had. Because inventories for London do not exist in large enough numbers to make such an exercise fruitful or meaningful, Faversham, as a representative of provincial towns in general in the period, is as good as any other – in fact better, as many early modern audiences in London and the south-east at least are likely to have had a sense of its social and material identity. And Faversham's objects do have an added frisson, given that some of the goods listed in its inventories at the end of the sixteenth century can be traced back to the Ardens' ownership. Plays like *Arden*, whose roots are in localized and particularized true crime, and whose mode is mainly one of realism, invite us to extend the traditional types of information in relation to which we understand early modern drama as gripping entertainment and metonymic pieces of a cultural whole. They call on us to continue that movement outwards from the particularity of domestic life in the provinces – from Faversham, to London, and beyond through print culture – that Alice set in motion when she first murdered her husband.

THE
LAMENTA=
BLE AND TRVE TRA-
GEDIE OF M. AR-
DEN OF FEVERSHAM
IN KENT.

Who was most wickedlye murdered, by
the meanes of his disloyall and wanton
wyfe, who for the loue she bare to one
Mosbie, hyred two desperat ruf-
fins Blackwill and Shakbag,
to kill him.

Wherin is shewed the great mal-
lice and discimulation of a wicked woman, the vnsatiable desire of filthie lust
and the shamefull end of all
murderers.

Imprinted at London for Edward
White, dwelling at the lyttle North
dore of Paules Church at
the signe of the
Gun, 1592.

*

THE LAMENTABLE AND TRUE TRAGEDY
OF MASTER ARDEN OF FAVERSHAM
IN KENT.

Who was most wickedly murdered, by
the means of his disloyal and wanton
wife, who for the love she bore to one
Mosby, hired two desperate ruffians,
Black Will and Shakebag,
to kill him.

Wherein is showed the great malice
and dissimulation of a wicked woman,
the insatiable desire of filthy lust
and the shameful end of all
murderers.

Imprinted at London for Edward
White, dwelling at the little north
door of Paul's Church at
the sign of the
Gun. 1592.

*

Title-page Although the elegantly formatted and sensational title-page, which presumably also functioned as an advertisement for the publication, is in roman type, the play itself is in black letter. For its material features see pp. 95–9.

Arden of Faversham was entered into the Stationers' Register to Edward White on 3 April 1592, as 'The tragedie of Arden of Feuersham & blackwill'; the play was printed by Edward Allde (*c.* 1560–1627; printer in London from 1584). The murder on which the play is based took place in 1551.

5–10 *Who ... him* The long-form title foregrounds Arden's wife's role as instigator of the crime.

17–18 *Edward White* (*c.* 1548–*c.* 1612) Apprenticed as a printer in 1565 and admitted to the livery of the Stationers' Company in 1588, from 1577 to 1612 White was a bookseller with a shop in St Paul's Churchyard in London, a centre for the book trade, specializing in crime literature, current affairs and ballads and other cheap print forms. For the other plays with which White and Allde were involved around the time of *Arden*'s printing, see pp. 92–5.

THE TRAGEDY
OF MASTER
ARDEN OF
FAVERSHAM

LIST OF ROLES

Lord Cheyne's men, a London crowd, the Faversham Watch

1 MASTER ARDEN The character is 'by birth a gentleman of blood' (1.35), but the historical Thomas Arden was a 'self-made man from the provinces' (Hyde, 39), born *c.* 1508 and murdered in 1551. Holinshed's *Chronicles* (the play's main source) describe him as 'a man of a tall and comelie personage' (see below, p. 290). For his life see Hyde; Orlin, *Private*; for discussion of his status see above, pp. 33–5.

2 FRANKLIN Franklin is not a historical character and no such person features in Holinshed's version of the story. The character provides Arden with a friend with whom he can share his feelings in front of the audience. A franklin was a member of a class of medieval landowners who were born free but not noble, ranking below the gentry, and by the sixteenth century the term was employed metaphorically to mean a liberal and hospitable host. The role also calls to mind the Franklin in Chaucer's *Canterbury Tales*, who travels the same London–Canterbury road. Franklin was a (relatively uncommon) surname (TNA's Discovery search engine gives 87 sixteenth century hits); for instance, one of Arden's daughters' second husband's friends was a Master Francklinge.

3 ALICE Holinshed describes the historical Alice, stepdaughter of Sir Edward North, as 'a gentlewoman, yoong, tall, and well fauoured of shape and countenance' (see below, p. 290). Her daughter Margaret appears briefly in Holinshed but does not feature in the play.

4 ADAM **Fowle** Innkeepers are uncommon characters in plays (Wiggins lists from 1567–97, with another two as 'other characters' of whom mention is made); their appearance is often associated with vice of one kind or another. The historical Adam was a Common Councillor of the town when Arden was mayor, and the Fowles were an important local family.

5 MICHAEL Michael accompanies Arden on his journeys, acting as a personal servant ('his man' as Holinshed describes him), but also serves drinks and is responsible for locking doors, taking his domestic orders from Alice as well as her husband. While Holinshed mentions many more servants, the play uses Michael and Susan as a representative pair whose actions can be compared to those of their master and mistress. On the pattern of Michael's entrances and exits see p. 50.

6 MOSBY Mosby is identified as a social climber, who has risen from tailor to steward in a noble household. Holinshed describes him as 'a blacke swart man' (see below, p. 290).

7 CLARKE Although frequently employed in the construction of entertainments, painters were infrequently staged as characters in contemporary plays. Clarke's role is comically split between jobbing provincial painter and classical master of the art.

8 GREENE Greene states that he has been reduced to poverty by Arden (1.477–8). In Holinshed, he is 'seruant to sir Anthonie Ager [Aucher]' (see below, p. 291).

9 SUSAN Susan is expected to serve guests at table and wash the floor in the play, taking her orders from Alice. As Mosby's sister, her marriage partner is in his gift, and he promises her to both Michael and Clarke the painter, forming a comic low-status echo of his own love triangle. Historically, Mosby's sister was called Cicely Ponder, suggesting she was a widow, and she 'dwelt in a tenement of maister Ardens néere to his house in Feuersham' (see below, p. 296).

10 BRADSHAW While goldsmithing was a high-status trade in the sixteenth century, Bradshaw's standing as an ex-soldier and his involvement with stolen plate complicate his reputation.

11, 12 BLACK WILL, SHAKEBAG The two ex-soldiers are 'masterless men', a social category that held a specially terrifying place in the early modern imagination; answerable to no one, placeless and apparently roaming the countryside causing disorder, they are hired to murder Arden solely for financial gain. Holinshed describes Will as 'a terrible cruell ruffian' (see below, p. 292).

13 PRENTICE Apprenticeship was the most common way of acquiring craft skills as varied as goldsmithing, printing and acting in early modern England. Young men (and occasionally young women) were bound by legal agreement to a master to learn their trade for a set number of years;

prentices were famed for being unruly both individually and as groups.

14 LORD CHEYNE Lord Cheyne is the play's most socially elevated character and the only onstage representative of the upper gentry. His presence on the road to London and his invitation to his property on the Isle of Sheppey respectively frustrate and set up murder plots. However, he is only onstage in one scene, and his direct influence on the action is limited.

Historically, Sir Thomas Cheyne (c. 1485–1558), administrator and diplomat, of Shurland on the Isle of Sheppey, joined the royal household in the reign of Henry VII and served each succeeding monarch until his death at the start of Elizabeth's reign. Henry VIII made him Knight of the Body (1515) and of the Garter (1539), and named him assistant executor of his will. Cheyne had substantial Kentish influence as constable of four of its castles, Sheriff, JP, MP and Lord Warden of the Cinque Ports; his relationship with Arden helped the latter to advance his career. He expressed his enduring religious conservatism in his will by leaving provision for a priest to say masses for his soul.

15 FERRYMAN In literal terms the Ferryman's role is in operating the passenger and goods ferry from near the head of Faversham creek to Harty Ferry on the Isle of Sheppey; however, the role also alludes to that of Charon, the ferryman of hell. The latter appeared in the contemporary play *The Cobbler's Prophecy* (1594; Wiggins 920).

16 **Dick** REEDE Faversham, on a creek that discharges into the sea near the rivers Medway and Thames, was known as a thriving port and home to many mariners. Holinshed's version of the story states that Arden's body was found in a field which 'he had most cruellie taken from a woman' whose second husband was 'one Richard Read a mariner', as a result of which she had 'exclaimed against him' and 'curssed him most bitterlie euen to his face, wishing manie a vengeance to light vpon him'. As a result, the 2014 RSC production of *Arden* replaced the character with Mrs Reede.

18 MAYOR The key representative of justice in the play, the Mayor appears in its closing phase.

19 **Lord Cheyne's men** originally likely to have been wearing their master's livery (clothing displaying his heraldic badges)
Faversham Watch men who patrolled the town to enforce order before the establishment of a national police force

ARDEN
OF FAVERSHAM

[**Sc. 1**]   *Enter* ARDEN *and* FRANKLIN [*carrying deeds*].

FRANKLIN
    Arden, cheer up thy spirits and droop no more.
    My gracious lord the Duke of Somerset
    Hath freely given to thee and to thy heirs,
    By letters patents from his majesty,

Title Faversham is variously spelled 'Feuershame', 'Feueshame' and 'Feversham' in Q1. The spellings Feversham/Faversham are used interchangeably in the period (see The National Archives search engine for multiple examples).

Sc. 1 Table and chairs are apparently set out from the start, as they are needed at 361. The whole scene, which is loosely located around Arden's Faversham house, may therefore be played out against a backdrop of domestic properties, reminders of the ideals of Arden's authority and Alice's submission under patriarchy (see pp. 22–6).

   Ludwig Tieck first divided the play into acts and scenes in his 1823 German translation, Henry Tyrrell following suit in English in 1851: Tyrrell's Act 1, Sc. 2 begins at 177 below; 1.3 at 359; 2.1 at 536. F. Victor Hugo's 1867 French translation used only scenes, a division followed by all modern editions.

0 SD *deeds* Property deeds were usually large vellum documents from which hung elaborate wax seals. Their physical presence onstage, here as in other contemporary plays, introduces fundamental questions about possession, ownership and action.

1 **droop** be despondent, perhaps with postural suggestion for the actor

2 **Duke of Somerset** Edward Seymour, Duke of Somerset, was beheaded in 1552. He received large grants of land from Henry VIII, and his position as Lord Protector 1547–9 during Edward VI's minority led to rewards that made him England's wealthiest subject. Naming him helps to set the action in Edward's reign (see also 33), as Seymour was the last and most prominent sixteenth century holder of the ducal title, which he awarded himself whilst Protector.

4 **letters patents** document issued by a monarch to confer right or title. The adjectival plural was usual in this expression. See also 300, 458.

   his majesty Edward VI, thirteen years old at the time of Arden's murder

TITLE] THE LAMENTA= / *BLE AND TRVE TRA-* / GEDIE OF M. AR- / *DEN OF FEVERSHAM* / IN KENT. / *(title-page);* The Tragedy of Arden of Faversham and Black Will *Stationer's Register; The Tragedy of M. Arden of Feueshame.* | *head title (uncorrected; 'Feuershame', corrected); The Tragedye of M. Arden of Feuershame.* | *running title (except sig. A4ᵛ, 'Fewersham')*

Sc. I] *Hugo;* ACT I. SCENE I. *Tyrrell   carrying deeds*] *this edn*

All the lands of the Abbey of Faversham.   5
Here are the deeds, sealed and subscribed with his
    name and the King's.
Read them, and leave this melancholy mood.

ARDEN

Franklin, thy love prolongs my weary life;
And, but for thee, how odious were this life,
That shows me nothing but torments my soul,   10
And those foul objects that offend mine eyes;
Which makes me wish that, for this veil of heaven,
The earth hung over my head and covered me.
Love letters passed 'twixt Mosby and my wife,
And they have privy meetings in the town.   15
Nay, on his finger did I spy the ring
Which at our marriage day the priest put on.

5   **Abbey of Faversham** Cluniac monastery founded in 1148 by King Stephen
and Queen Matilda (who were buried
there), initially with monks from
Bermondsey Abbey. Dissolved in 1538,
much of it was demolished to provide
stone to fortify Calais (English territory
at the time); the outer gateway that
became Arden's house was one of the
few buildings to remain intact.

6   Q1 has this as a (by 1592 rather old-
fashioned) fourteener, which is retained
here on the strength of B&T's suggestion
(*CRE*) that the lineation of the underlying manuscript is being followed in the
turn-up of 'kings,'. In performance, in
contrast, the line tends to break at *deeds*,
in order for Franklin to produce, and perhaps unfold and inspect, the prop for
Arden and the audience.

9–11 **how ... eyes** His life presents or offers
nothing (good) to him, rather tormenting his
soul, whereas the offensive things he actually sees with his eyes (evidence of Alice's
adultery) make him wish he was dead.

10 **shows** presents or offers; makes
evident or clear. Thomas Churchyard
similarly describes a ruined castle whose
'walles, which cannot still endure, /
Through sore decay, shewes nothing
fayre to sight' (*Worthiness of Wales*
(1587), sig. B2ᵛ).
    but but that which

11 **foul objects** i.e. evidences of adultery,
including the love-letters and the ring
described in this speech

12–13 **for ... me** He wants *earth*, rather than
(*for*) sky, above his head, i.e. the grave.

15 **privy** carried out in secret; furtive.
Privacy was largely viewed pejoratively
in the period, and concepts of good
neighbourliness determined it a Christian
duty to look out for one's neighbours'
wrongdoings at all times, in order to save
their souls (see p. 27).

16–17 **ring ... on** Early modern wedding
rings had no standard form, so an individual one was likely to be easy to recognize as belonging to a particular person
(see pp. 30–2).

6] *Delius lines* deeds, / King's. / ; *Sturgess lines* subscribed / King's. /   14 passed] *(past); pass SMS*

Can any grief be half so great as this?

FRANKLIN

Comfort thyself, sweet friend; it is not strange
That women will be false and wavering.   20

ARDEN

Ay, but to dote on such a one as he
Is monstrous, Franklin, and intolerable!

FRANKLIN

Why, what is he?

ARDEN

A botcher and no better at the first,
Who, by base brokage getting some small stock,   25
Crept into service of a nobleman;
And by his servile flattery and fawning
Is now become the steward of his house,

---

18   **grief** mental pain or sorrow, the modern
     meaning; also hardship or suffering
     (*OED* 1), and (*OED* 2) injury caused by
     another, which could be the subject of a
     formal complaint

19–20 **it . . . wavering** Women were prover-
     bially said to be wavering, unstable or
     inconstant (Dent, W703.1). Franklin's
     sexist platitudes help to set up the con-
     trast between positive homosocial and
     negative heterosocial relationships for
     Arden; see also 51–2.

24   **botcher** repairer of worn garments rather
     than a maker of new ones. The word also
     carried connotations of poor-quality, low-
     skilled and incompetent work. Holinshed
     identifies Mosby as a tailor (see below,
     p. 290), showing that the playwright
     means Arden to insult here.
     at the first from the start; i.e. at birth, as
     opposed to the 'gentle' birth status the
     play claims for Arden (see 35)

25   **brokage** buying and selling on behalf
     of others. Like botching (24), nothing

new is created in this work, and the
word therefore carried overtones of
deceitful or immoral trade, swindling or
pimping.
     stock either a capital sum to invest, or
     property that produces income, but also
     the social capital to rise into noble service

26   **Crept into** wormed his way into. The
     phrase is frequently used in the period to
     describe the movement of a variety of sin
     and abuses, including the stealthiness of
     religious error.

28   **steward** official in charge of the domestic
     affairs of a household, supervising table
     service, servants and expenditure. Usually
     of relatively high social status themselves,
     stewards enjoyed considerable domestic
     authority: Malvolio's ambitious dreams of
     marriage to Olivia from such a position in
     TN (see, e.g., 2.5), and the Duchess of
     Malfi's tragic version of such a relation-
     ship with Antonio in John Webster's play
     (1.3), suggest the troubling ambiguity of
     stewards' rank.

And bravely jets it in his silken gown.
FRANKLIN
No nobleman will countenance such a peasant.   30
ARDEN
Yes, the Lord Clifford, he that loves not me.
But through his favour let not him grow proud;
For, were he by the Lord Protector backed,
He should not make me to be pointed at.
I am by birth a gentleman of blood,   35
And that injurious ribald that attempts

29 **jets it** struts. Part of a moralized rhetoric of excessive display, the word suggests boasting, but also particular gestures and movements associated with over-fine clothing; see, e.g., Alexander Barclay's translation of Pope Pius II's views on those who 'Jet in theyr sylkes / and bragge in the market / As they were lordes' (1530, sig. B3ʳ).
    silken Under the 1533 Act of Apparel, only knights were permitted to wear silk gowns. This probably refers to Mosby's livery as a high-ranking official in a nobleman's household, the gown representing both that household's status and his own (elevated) servitude as its lower-ranked representative (the referent of *his* in the sentence permits ambiguity around actual ownership). Holinshed has Mosby answering Arden's door in a silk nightgown before the murder (see below, p. 297).

30 **countenance** favour; pronounced as two syllables
    peasant labourer, but with the implication of baseness, rudeness and ignorance as well as lower status and economic dependence (compare the nobility assumed in *nobleman*, with its similar blurring of social and moral status). Arden's and Franklin's contempt sets up the play's edge of social competition.

31 **Lord Clifford** The historical Mosby was servant to Lord North (see p. 290), step-

father to Alice Arden. Edward North, having risen from merchant's son to member of the Privy Council under Protector Somerset (see 2, 33nn.), died in 1564. His son Roger was, when the play was written, 2nd Baron North, a soldier, courtier and diplomat. The scandal caused to the family name by Edward's chief steward's and stepdaughter's crimes is mitigated by the play's substitution of his name with a fictional Lord Clifford (a Henry Clifford, Earl of Cumberland, died in 1570).

33 **the Lord Protector** the Duke of Somerset; see 2n. The pseudo-monarchical power and authority of the role is invoked here.

35 **gentleman of blood** gentleman by birth. The historical Arden was not born a gentleman. His family are likely to have been urban administrators, and his claim to elevated status was built on his ownership of land. His family were midway through the transition from provincial elite to gentry status.

36 **ribald** villain. Term of abuse suggestive of low social status, often with a hint of sexual impropriety. Q1 has 'riball', but *OED* finds only Scottish contemporary examples of this form. Hopkinson[2] suggests that the Q1 spelling might be read 'rebel', which might warrant the violent punishment imagined in 39–42.

30 countenance] *(countnaunce)*   36 ribald] *Q3;* riball *Q1*

To violate my dear wife's chastity
(For dear I hold her love, as dear as heaven)
Shall on the bed which he thinks to defile
See his disseuered joints and sinews torn,   40
Whilst on the planchers pants his weary body,
Smeared in the channels of his lustful blood.

FRANKLIN

Be patient, gentle friend, and learn of me
To ease thy grief and save her chastity:
Entreat her fair – sweet words are fittest engines   45
To raze the flint walls of a woman's breast.
In any case be not too jealous,
Nor make no question of her love to thee;
But, as securely, presently take horse
And lie with me at London all this term.   50
For women, when they may, will not;
But being kept back, straight grow outrageous.

ARDEN

Though this abhors from reason, yet I'll try it,

37 **chastity** abstinence from sex outside of her marriage
39–42 Arden talks bloody talk, reminiscent of Marlowe's Tamburlaine: 'Thy streetes strowed with disseuered iointes of men' (*1 Tamburlaine*, 5.1.323). In doing so, he crosses a line between the need to maintain gentlemanly decorum and his desire for revenge.
41 **planchers** floorboards
42 **channels** rivers
45 **Entreat** deal with, persuade
    engines machines used in warfare
46 **raze** tear or cut; erase; but also demolish and thereby end a siege. Q1 has 'race', a variant spelling which *OED* lists separately (race *v.*[2] 3a, 4). See also 117.
47 **jealous** pronounced 'jealious', as indicated by Q1's spelling 'jelyouse'; see

also 133, 211, 378, 413.
49 **as securely** as though free from anxiety
    presently immediately
50 **lie . . . at** stay . . . in
    term word for each of the four periods in the year during which the business of the law courts is undertaken
52 **straight** immediately
    outrageous excessive, unrestrained
53 **Though . . . reason** As well as seeming contrary to good sense, Franklin's suggestion flies in the face of all advice literature. Husbands' absence from wives was permitted only for warfare, service to Church and commonwealth, or their own essential business affairs, and was then to be kept as short as possible.
    abhors from recoils, diverges or departs from

46 raze] *(race)*   47 jealous] *Q3;* Ielyouse *Q1;* iealious *Q2; similarly 133, 211, 378, 413*

And call her forth, and presently take leave.
Ho, Alice!   55

Here enters ALICE.

ALICE

Husband, what mean you to get up so early?
Summer nights are short, and yet you rise ere day.
Had I been wake, you had not ris so soon.

ARDEN

Sweet love, thou know'st that we two, Ovid-like,
Have often chid the morning when it 'gan to peep,   60
And often wished that dark Night's purblind steeds
Would pull her by the purple mantle back

---

55 **Ho** call to stop or to cease what one is doing. See also 245.

55 SD Alice's clothing would underline her gentry status; a list of the garments belonging to the historical Alice, including a wide range of dresses, skirts and sleeves, in velvets, satins and damasks, as well as 'A chayne of golde for a gentlewomen's neck' and two bracelets, was entered into the borough records as part of a petition by her daughter.

58 **ris** risen. Obsolete form of the past participle, pronounced 'riss', as in Edward Wilkinson, *Thameseidos* (1600), 'Cheekes which with lively Cynab're ore spred, / Seemd like the Morning, new risse from her bed' (sig. B1ʳ).

59 **Ovid-like** There are clear similarities to Ovid's *Elegies*, 1.13, whose first English translation was only published after 1592. The author must therefore have had access to Christopher Marlowe's unpublished MS, or read the *Elegies* in a European edition of the Latin. Marlowe's translation runs as follows: 'Now o'er the sea from her old love comes she / That

draws the day from heaven's cold axle-tree. / Aurora, whither slidest thou? down again / . . . How oft wished I night would not give thee place, / Nor morning stars shun thy uprising face. / How oft that either wind would break thy coach, / Or steeds might fall, forced with thick clouds' approach' (*Elegies*, 1.13.1–3, 11–30).

60 **often** The word repeats in the line below, suggesting eye-skip in the print house. One of a series of repetitions in this part of the play; see p. 41.

61 **dark . . . steeds** The goddess Nyx was the personification of Night in Greek mythology. It was a poetic commonplace, inspired by Ovid, for lovers to want to hold back the light, and much early modern poetry focuses on the moment when night becomes day.
purblind completely blind. Often used in relation to Cupid, see, e.g., *RJ*, 2.1.11–12, 'Speak to my gossip Venus one fair word, / One nickname for her purblind son and heir'.

62 **purple mantle** darkness, personified as the purple mantle, or cloak, of night

54–5] *Delius; one line Q1*   55 Ho] *(How)*

And cast her in the ocean to her love.
But this night, sweet Alice, thou hast killed my heart:
I heard thee call on Mosby in thy sleep.   65

ALICE

'Tis like I was asleep when I named him,
For being awake he comes not in my thoughts.

ARDEN

Ay, but you started up, and suddenly,
Instead of him, caught me about the neck.

ALICE

Instead of him? Why, who was there but you?   70
And where but one is, how can I mistake?

FRANKLIN

Arden, leave to urge her over-far.

ARDEN

Nay, love, there is no credit in a dream.
Let it suffice I know thou lovest me well.

ALICE

Now I remember whereupon it came: 75
Had we no talk of Mosby yesternight?

FRANKLIN

Mistress Alice, I heard you name him once or twice.

ALICE

And thereof came it, and therefore blame not me!

ARDEN

I know it did, and therefore let it pass.
I must to London, sweet Alice, presently.   80

---

63 **her love** Tithonus, a mortal to whom
Aurora asked Jupiter to grant immor-
tality, though she failed to request eternal
youth to accompany it

66 **like** likely

72 **leave ... over-far** 'Don't press her too
far.' The line might be spoken as an aside
to Arden, a warning from Franklin
alluding to his earlier suggestions for
handling Alice.

73 **no credit** nothing to believe. Although
dreams were hard to interpret, their
status as portents was a subject of considerable interest in the period, and they
were scrutinized for potential medical,
political and religious implications.

76–7 The memory of their talk about Mosby
suggests a context of evening socializing
that is picked up later in the mention of
table-talk (343); it indicates the Ardens'
leisured, and therefore elevated, social
and financial status (see p. 108).

ALICE

But tell me, do you mean to stay there long?

ARDEN

No longer than till my affairs be done.

FRANKLIN

He will not stay above a month at most.

ALICE

A month? Ay me, sweet Arden, come again
Within a day or two, or else I die!   85

ARDEN

I cannot long be from thee, gentle Alice.
Whilst Michael fetch our horses from the field,
Franklin and I will down unto the quay,
For I have certain goods there to unload.
Meanwhile, prepare our breakfast, gentle Alice,   90
For yet ere noon, we'll take horse and away.

Exeunt Arden and Franklin.

ALICE

Ere noon he means to take horse and away.
Sweet news is this! Oh that some airy spirit
Would, in the shape and likeness of a horse,
Gallop with Arden 'cross the ocean   95
And throw him from his back into the waves!
Sweet Mosby is the man that hath my heart,

---

82 ***than** Q1 gives 'there', probably an eye-skip from the line above.
88 **quay** A busy and prosperous 'limb' (adjunct port) to Dover, and one of the Cinque Ports responsible for raising a defensive fleet before the establishment of the Royal Navy, Faversham traded with London and the Continent, to which it supplied wheat, gunpowder, wool and oysters. As the King's customer there, collecting customs on imports and exports, Arden's business on the quay, only 100 metres or so from his house, must have been considerable.
90 **prepare . . . Alice** Breakfast was a light, informal meal that could be prepared by the housewife of a middling-status family, so no cook was needed, and broth might be reheated.
91 **yet ere** before (*OED* yet 7d)
95 **ocean** trisyllabic

82 than] *SMS (*then*); there *Q1*

And he usurps it, having nought but this:
That I am tied to him by marriage.
Love is a god, and marriage is but words,   100
And therefore Mosby's title is the best.
Tush, whether it be or no, he shall be mine
In spite of him, of Hymen, and of rites.

Here enters ADAM *of the Fleur-de-Lis.*

And here comes Adam of the Fleur-de-Lis.
I hope he brings me tidings of my love.   105
How now, Adam, what is the news with you?
Be not afraid, my husband is now from home.

ADAM

He whom you wot of, Mosby, Mistress Alice,
Is come to town and sends you word by me:
In any case you may not visit him.   110

---

98 **he** i.e. Arden
100 This daring defiance flies in the face of
     recent changes in the status of marriage.
     Protestant reformers had increased the
     Church's role after the Reformation,
     developing a ceremony that took place in
     front of the altar and involved instruction
     and oath-taking before God, rather than
     simply expressing mutual consent at the
     church door. With the disappearance of
     influential Catholic monastic models of a
     chaste life, the Protestant view of mar-
     riage as an ideal state of human existence
     became increasingly significant.
101 **title** entitlement; a suggestive pairing
     with Arden's title over the Abbey lands
     at the start of the scene, as well as his
     legal rights as husband
102 **Tush** exclamation of impatient contempt
     whether monosyllabic
102–3 **he . . . him** Mosby. . . Arden

103 **Hymen** in Greek and Roman mythology
     the god of marriage, and therefore by
     extension of its ceremony or 'rite'
     rites wordplay on rites/rights
103 SD *Fleur-de-Lis* one of the town's inns,
     near the marketplace; it was leased to the
     historical Adam Fowle, who was a
     common councillor (and therefore a man
     of means) when the historical Arden was
     mayor.
106 **How now** abbreviation of 'How is it now?'
107 **Be not afraid** suggests a hesitancy in
     Adam's behaviour.
     Husband is spoken 'husband's' for metre.
108 **wot of** know of or about
110 **In any case** whatever happens. It is rather
     redundant to send a message to say you
     are here but may not be visited, and the
     line may therefore have comic potential.
     This begins the series of rather petulant
     exchanges between Mosby and Alice.

103 SD] *after 105 Hopkinson*[2] *Fleur-de-Lis] (Flourdeluce)* 104 Fleur-de-Lis] *(flourdeluce)*

ALICE

Not visit him?

ADAM

No, nor take no knowledge of his being here.

ALICE

But tell me, is he angry or displeased?

ADAM

Should seem so, for he is wondrous sad.

ALICE

Were he as mad as raving Hercules,   115
I'll see him, I. And were thy house of force
These hands of mine should raze it to the ground,
Unless that thou wouldst bring me to my love.

ADAM

Nay, an you be so impatient, I'll be gone.

ALICE

Stay, Adam, stay – thou wert wont to be my friend –   120
Ask Mosby how I have incurred his wrath.
Bear him from me these pair of silver dice
With which we played for kisses many a time,
And when I lost, I won, and so did he –
Such winning and such losing, Jove send me! –   125

---

112 **take no knowledge** take no notice; admit no knowledge
115 **raving Hercules** Hercules raved in madness, having been induced by the gods to kill his wife and children in a story that formed the subject of plays by Seneca the Younger and Euripides. On the point of committing suicide in remorse, he was persuaded by Theseus to go to Athens instead.
116 **I'll ... I** B&T (*CRE*) argues convincingly for this formulation (employing the pleonastic, emphatic pronoun), rather than 'I'll see him. Ay', favoured by pre-

vious editors, citing Tarlinskaja, *Versification* (108) and other uses in the scene at 168, 243, 374.
of force strongly fortified (*OED* force *n.*[1] 3b)
119 **an** if
120 **wert wont** used
friend The type of friendship that might be possible between a gentlewoman and an innkeeper is not at all clear. Whilst the dominant meaning is ally or helper (in her relationship with Mosby), a past physical relationship could be indicated in performance.

116 him, I. And] *(*him, I and*)*; him, I, and *Q2;* him. Ay and *Delius*   117 raze] *(*race*)*

And bid him, if his love do not decline,
Come this morning but along my door
And as a stranger but salute me there.
This may he do without suspect or fear.
    [*Then Adam takes the dice.*]

ADAM

I'll tell him what you say, and so farewell.   *Exit.*

ALICE

Do, and one day I'll make amends for all.   131
I know he loves me well, but dares not come
Because my husband is so jealous,
And these, my marrow-prying neighbours, blab –
Hinder our meetings when we would confer.   135

---

127 **but ... door** only alongside my door;
  just passing by
128 **salute** greet
129 SD B&T (*CRE*) points out that the play's
  'stage directions are systematic and unusual: almost all entrance directions use
  the formula "Here enters", and directions
  for onstage action (other than entrances
  or exits) all begin with "Then" '. The editorial stage directions added to this edition follow this formula.
130 SD Q1 often gives exits rather earlier than
  modern readers or actors might expect
  them, indicating the point at which characters begin to leave, rather than go offstage.
  Editors have traditionally moved them to a
  later position, but this edition keeps their
  original placings, as they encourage 'long'
  exits in which characters speak to one
  another from some distance, animating
  this lengthy and complex scene.
133 **jealous** trisyllabic. See 47n.
134 **these** suggests a gesture indicating other
  houses nearby. See p. 83 for discussion
  of this scene in production.
  marrow-prying Q1's reading is dismissed
  in B&T (*CRE*) as a 'minim misreading', but

contemporary publications talk of a meta-
phorical search of 'the marrow and sinewes'
(Aelian, *A Register of Histories Containing
Martial Exploits of Worthy Warriors* (1576),
sig. Lliii'), or of 'searching into the marow,
depth, and substance of matters' (Marin
Barleti, *The History of George Castriot*
(1596), 196). See also *OED* marrow $n.^2$ 2 for
the now chiefly regional meaning of husband, wife or lover. Both 'narrow' and
'marrow' fit with the claustrophobia of the
play's Faversham, but the latter is the more
striking reading.
neighbours, blab Editors have considered
whether *blab* functions here as a verb,
meaning to talk indiscreetly (*OED v.* 4), or
as a noun meaning loose talk (*OED n.* 2).
See, e.g., B&T (*CRE*)'s 'neighbour blabs',
which assumes *neighbour* as adjective and
blab as noun (*OED n.* 1 meaning a tell-tale).
Since the majority of EEBO-TCP instances
of the word 1580–1600 are for the verb or
refer to 'playing the blab', which also
underscores the agency of the person blab-
bing, this edition retains the Q1 reading.
134–5 **blab ... Hinder** The *neighbours* both
  blab and *Hinder*.

---

127 Come] To come *Q2*   129 SD] *B&T (Wiggins subst.)*   130 SD] *(Exit Adam.); after 131 Hugo*   134
marrow-prying] narrow prying *Q2;* narrow, prying *SMS*   neighbours, blab] *(*neighbours blab*); neighbours'
blab *Delius;* neighbour blabs *B&T;* neighbours' blabs *(conj. Jowett in B&T (CRE))*

But, if I live, that block shall be removed,
And, Mosby, thou that comes to me by stealth
Shalt neither fear the biting speech of men
Nor Arden's looks. As surely shall he die
As I abhor him and love only thee.   140

Here enters MICHAEL.

How now, Michael, whither are you going?

MICHAEL

To fetch my master's nag. I hope you'll think on me?

ALICE

Ay, but Michael, see you keep your oath,
And be as secret as you are resolute.

MICHAEL

I'll see he shall not live above a week.   145

ALICE

On that condition, Michael, here is my hand:
    [*Then they shake hands.*]
None shall have Mosby's sister but thyself.

MICHAEL

I understand the painter here hard by
Hath made report that he and Sue is sure?

136 **block** obstacle, obstruction
138 **biting speech** The phrase, denoting slander, is prominent in publications relating to the Martin Marprelate controversy (satirical attacks and counter-attacks on the Church's government by bishops); see, e.g., John Lyly's *Pap with an Hatchet* (1589), 'Now comes a biting speach, let mee stroake my beard thrice like a Germain, before I speak a wise word' (sig. D1r).
140 SD Michael is the first character to enter in working dress. Visibly of lower status, his clothing would provide a socially instructive contrast to Mosby's liveried

finery, as described by Arden (29).
142 **nag** small horse for riding
    think on me think about me; remember my suit
146 **here ... hand** The bargain is sealed with a handshake, a pattern that is shortly repeated with Clarke (260).
148 **hard by** in very close proximity, i.e. a near neighbour
149 **sure** contracted to be married, in this period in a 'handfasting ceremony' where the couple held hands in front of witnesses while stating their commitment to one another, in advance of the church ceremony (*OED* 8a)

142] *Hopkinson²; Q1 lines* nagge, / mee. /   144 you] *Q2;* yon *Q1*   146 SD] *this edn*

ALICE

There's no such matter, Michael; believe it not. 150

MICHAEL

But he hath sent a dagger sticking in a heart,
With a verse or two stolen from a painted cloth,
The which I hear the wench keeps in her chest.
Well, let her keep it. I shall find a fellow
That can both write and read, and make rhyme too. 155
And if I do – well, I say no more.
I'll send from London such a taunting letter
As she shall eat the heart he sent with salt,

151 **dagger ... heart** now a classic tattoo, then an emblem. Love was usually represented as a heart pierced by an arrow (e.g. on the V&A's 'Shepherd Buss' embroidery, T.219-1953), but the use of a dagger suggests rather lust (dagger as a phallic symbol) and/or death. Clarke has painted the image for Susan with an accompanying text as a kind of love-letter. Eumenides, in John Lyly's *Endymion* (*c.* 1588), states that 'such is my unspotted faith to Endymion that whatsoever seemeth a needle to prick his finger is a dagger to wound my heart' (3.1.21–3).

152 **stolen** pinched, as an idea (for someone who has none of their own) see the clichéd nature of moralizing on painted cloths discussed in the next note.
painted cloth linen cloth onto which bold images, often imitating the patterns of Italian silks, and aphorisms were painted. Forming cheaper alternatives to tapestries, they were extremely common until the end of the sixteenth century, when their moralizing began to be mocked. See *Luc*, 'Who fears a sentence or an old man's saw / Shall by a painted cloth be kept in awe' (244–5). They were painted by itinerant house-painters, so both the workmanship and originality indicated mock Clarke's pretensions of professional aesthetic skill.

153 **chest** As individuals living in the houses

of others, servants kept their possessions in locked chests. For women, such chests often housed dowry items, the contents representing their value on the marriage market and therefore their future prospects. See Joan the servant's dream in the anonymous *A Warning for Fair Women*, from which she wakes when falling, 'as I ran to my chest to fetch ye a handkercher' (1599; Sc. 6); servant Jane Page of Sandwich, dying in 1593, kept her possessions (all clothing) in a little chest priced at 12d (KHLC 10.21.439).

157 **taunting** provoking, answering back, but also insulting

158 ***As she shall** Delius's addition of *she* clarifies and regularizes the line, assuming an eye-skip from *sh[e]* to *sh[all]*. The emendation is necessary in order to make sense of the speech, but it does not entirely resolve Michael's confused emotions: while his letter must be intended for Susan, as it is she who must *fling the dagger* in the next line, the 'taunting' is clearly directed at Clarke. This petulant response to a rival mimics the tiff between Alice and Mosby.
eat ... salt 'consume' the heart seasoned and spiced, either by her tears at his rebuke, or by the letter's verbal 'salt' and hence hot and likely to induce enough anger to lead to dagger-flinging

158 As she shall] *Delius;* As shall *Q1*

And fling the dagger at the painter's head.

ALICE

What needs all this? I say that Susan's thine!　　　160

MICHAEL

Why, then I say that I will kill my master,
Or anything that you will have me do.

ALICE

But, Michael, see you do it cunningly.

MICHAEL

Why, say I should be took, I'll ne'er confess
That you know anything. And Susan, being a maid,　　165
May beg me from the gallows of the shrieve.

ALICE

Trust not to that, Michael.

MICHAEL

You cannot tell me: I have seen it, I.
But mistress, tell her, whether I live or die
I'll make her more worth than twenty painters can;　　170
For I will rid mine elder brother away,
And then the farm of Boughton is mine own.

164 **took** arrested

165–6 **Susan ... shrieve** Michael shows his naivety and lack of learning (also evident in his illiteracy) by believing this 'urban myth' about being saved from hanging by a virgin. B&T (*CRE*) argues, in not updating *shrieve*, that a monosyllabic ending was probably intended, as the author of this scene used few feminine endings.

166 **shrieve** sheriff

170 **make ... worth** offer her more as a jointure, money she would receive in the event of his death

171 **rid ... away** murder. As a younger son Michael has little wealth of his own; farms were usually passed on to the eldest son intact so that they remained economically functional units.

172 **Boughton** a village on the main London–Canterbury road, four miles from Faversham. In 1545 Thomas Arden took a 21-year lease on 1,100 acres of woodland there. Jacob emends Q1's 'Bolton' to 'Bocton', an early modern spelling of Boughton that B&T (*CRE*) points out is more likely to have been misread as 'Bolton'.

172 Boughton] *(Bolton)*

Who would not venture upon house and land
When he may have it for a right-down blow?

Here enters MOSBY.

ALICE

Yonder comes Mosby. Michael, get thee gone,   175
And let not him nor any know thy drifts.   *Exit Michael.*
Mosby, my love.

MOSBY

Away I say, and talk not to me now.

ALICE

A word or two, sweetheart, and then I will.
'Tis yet but early days, thou needest not fear.   180

MOSBY

Where is your husband?

ALICE

'Tis now high water, and he is at the quay.

MOSBY

There let him be. Henceforward know me not.

ALICE

Is this the end of all thy solemn oaths?
Is this the fruit thy reconcilement buds?   185
Have I, for this, given thee so many favours,

---

173 **venture** dare; risk
174 **right-down** without reserve; outright, knock-out
174 SD Despite his intention not to see Alice, announced by Adam at 110 and 112, Mosby nevertheless arrives within 44 lines of Adam's departure with her message. He may therefore enter indirectly or furtively, as per her instruction, or convey barely suppressed eagerness.
176 **drifts** intentions, schemes. The visual pull of Mosby's entry on the audience's attention, paired with Michael's exit, sets up the busy, episodic nature of this scene, stressing the complexity of Alice's plotting.
180 **early days** early in the day; too early for something to happen
182 **high water ... quay** These mentions of the quay and the timing of the (here high) tide (cf. 88, 406) give a rhythm and timescale of work against which the murder attempts are set.
185 **buds** begins to grow
186 **favours** love tokens (*OED* 7); actions that further or aid an individual (*OED* 5)

Incurred my husband's hate and – out alas! –
Made shipwreck of mine honour for thy sake?
And dost thou say, 'Henceforward know me not'?
Remember when I locked thee in my closet?   190
What were thy words and mine? Did we not both
Decree to murder Arden in the night?
The heavens can witness, and the world can tell,
Before I saw that falsehood look of thine,
'Fore I was tangled with thy 'ticing speech,   195
Arden to me was dearer than my soul,
And shall be still. Base peasant, get thee gone,
And boast not of thy conquest over me,
Gotten by witchcraft and mere sorcery.
For what hast thou to countenance my love,   200
Being descended of a noble house
And matched already with a gentleman
Whose servant thou mayst be? And so, farewell.

MOSBY

Ungentle and unkind Alice, now I see
That which I ever feared and find too true: 205
A woman's love is as the lightning flame,
Which even in bursting forth consumes itself.

---

187 **out alas** exclamation of reproach
188 **shipwreck ... honour** The metaphor
picks up on the mention of the *quay* in
182. The phrase was a common one, with
shipwreck said to have been made of
many intangible assets in the period,
including hopes, fortunes, judgement,
fame, faith, piety, chastity, credit, affec-
tion and souls.
190 **closet** Closets in most urban properties
were small spaces, generally set in
alongside chimney-breasts or staircases
and used chiefly for storage. Alice imagines a rather grander version in an elite
house: a chamber off the main room.

197 **Base** low-born; worthless; despicable
and ignoble
199 **mere** pure; nothing short of
200 **countenance** set off, grace by making
look good
201–3 **Being ... be** referring to Alice
203 **mayst** might fittingly
204 **Ungentle** not gentle; unkind or discour-
teous. The word mixes questions of
status and behaviour in interesting ways.
206–7 See also the instability Juliet notes in
her contract with Romeo, which she
describes as 'Too like the lightning which doth cease to be / Ere one can
say "it lightens"' (*RJ*, 2.1.119–20).

To try thy constancy have I been strange.
Would I had never tried, but lived in hope.

ALICE

What needs thou try me, whom thou never found false?   210

MOSBY

Yet pardon me, for love is jealous.

ALICE

So lists the sailor to the mermaid's song;
So looks the traveller to the basilisk.
I am content for to be reconciled,
And that I know will be mine overthrow.   215

MOSBY

Thine overthrow? First let the world dissolve!

ALICE

Nay, Mosby, let me still enjoy thy love,
And, happen what will, I am resolute.
My saving husband hoards up bags of gold
To make our children rich, and now is he   220
Gone to unload the goods that shall be thine,
And he and Franklin will to London straight.

MOSBY

To London, Alice? If thou'lt be ruled by me,
We'll make him sure enough 'fore coming there.

208 In order to test your determination, or faithfulness, I've been distant (strange).
210 **never** monosyllabic for metre
211 **jealous** See 47n.
212 *lists** emended to Q3's 'lists' from Q1's 'list' for rhetorical balance with following line (see B&T (*CRE*)'s argument) **mermaid's song** Sirens, with whom mermaids were confused, tried to lure sailors, including Odysseus, to their deaths with beguiling songs.
213 **basilisk** familiar to some early modern audience members from medieval bestiaries, a legendary reptile that can kill with a single glance

216 **world dissolve** apocalyptic imagery, the earliest example of the phrase of only four identified by EEBO-TCP to 1642, the other three 1631–40, on high political subjects in Rome and Turkey
219 **hoards ... gold** Arden is described in language reminiscent of descriptions of the figure of Avarice, familiar from morality plays, and staged by Christopher Marlowe in *Doctor Faustus* as Covetousness, one of the seven deadly sins.
224 We'll make him securely dead before he gets to London; we'll make sure he gets there safely (ironic).

212 lists] *Q3;* list *Q1*   224 'fore] *Sturgess;* for *Q1*

ALICE

    Ah, would we could.   225

MOSBY

    I happened on a painter yesternight,

    The only cunning man of Christendom;

    For he can temper poison with his oil

    That whoso looks upon the work he draws

    Shall, with the beams that issue from his sight,   230

    Suck venom to his breast and slay himself.

    Sweet Alice, he shall draw thy counterfeit,

    That Arden may, by gazing on it, perish.

ALICE

    Ay, but Mosby, that is dangerous,

    For thou, or I, or any other else,   235

    Coming into the chamber where it hangs, may die.

MOSBY

    Ay, but we'll have it covered with a cloth,

    And hung up in the study for himself.

ALICE

    It may not be, for when the picture's drawn

    Arden, I know, will come and show it me.   240

---

227 **only** pre-eminent, best
cunning man learned or skilled person; crafty man; conjurer or wizard; person 'possessing magical knowledge or skill' (*OED* cunning 3)

228 **temper** prepare by mingling or mixing

229 **draws** makes as representation, depicts (here in paint)

230 **beams ... sight** Sight was considered a much more material and active process in early modern England: Galenic theory suggested that vital spirits (here *beams*) came out of the eyes as one looked, causing the air to connect the viewer directly to the object of their interest.

Part of what was viewed might then be absorbed into the viewer's body.

237 **covered ... cloth** Paintings owned by the upper-middling and their social superiors were often covered with curtains to protect them and permit their revelation to honoured guests: Robert Fagg of Faversham left a 'hanging picture with a curtain' in the chamber over his hall when he died in 1574, valued at 20s (KHLC 10.7.173).

238 **study** a small room, usually windowless, often used for accounting and paperwork and therefore most likely to be occupied by the master of the house

236] *Brooke lines* hangs, / die. /

MOSBY

Fear not, we'll have that shall serve the turn.
This is the painter's house, I'll call him forth.

ALICE

But Mosby, I'll have no such picture, I.

MOSBY

I pray thee, leave it to my discretion.
Ho, Clarke!   245

Here enters CLARKE
[*with a vial of poison concealed*].

Oh, you are an honest man of your word; you served
    me well.

CLARKE

Why, sir, I'll do it for you at any time,
Provided, as you have given your word,
I may have Susan Mosby to my wife.
For, as sharp-witted poets, whose sweet verse   250

241 **that** that which
244–5 B&T (*CRE*) conjectures that the initial pronoun in 244 was a repetition from the previous line. Unable to hear regular verse in these lines, the editors give 244–5 as one line and 246 as prose. It is possible, however, to speak 'leave't' as one syllable, and such elisions are common in this text.
244 **discretion** four syllables
245 **Ho** See 55n.
245 SD Clarke may well enter holding a symbol of his craft such as brushes or palette. Although frequently employed in the construction of entertainments, painters were infrequently staged as characters in contemporary plays. Warwick's Men staged the lost play *The*

Painter's Daughter at court in 1576 (Wiggins 600); Apelles appears in Lyly's *Campaspe* (printed 1584; Wiggins 746); *Spanish Tragedy* B-text (1602, Wiggins 783) features Bazardo, a painter.
246 The line suggests the dialogue in which the two men have been engaged in the past, leading to Clarke's assertion in 247 and to Mosby's statement to Alice in 264 that he has *talked sufficient*. The absence of the specifics invites speculation about Mosby's character, Clarke's service to him perhaps having required poison (suggesting previous immorality) or a portrait (suggesting a social climber).
248–9 **given . . . wife** referring to the agreement between the two men for Susan's hand in marriage

244–5] *Delius; one line Q1*   244 I pray] Pray *(conj. B&T (CRE))*   245 Ho] *(How)*   245.2] *this edn*
246] *Tyrrell lines* word, / well. /

Make heavenly gods break off their nectar draughts
And lay their ears down to the lowly earth,
Use humble promise to their sacred Muse,
So we, that are the poets' favourites,
Must have a love. Ay, love is the painter's Muse,   255
That makes him frame a speaking countenance;
A weeping eye that witnesses heart's grief.
Then tell me, Master Mosby, shall I have her?

ALICE
'Tis pity but he should; he'll use her well.

MOSBY
Clarke, here's my hand: my sister shall be thine.   260
[*Then they shake hands.*]

CLARKE
Then, brother, to requite this courtesy,
You shall command my life, my skill, and all.

ALICE
Ah, that thou couldst be secret.

---

251 **nectar draughts** drinks of nectar (the drink of the gods in classical mythology)

252 **lay ... to** turn their ears towards, i.e. listen to

253 **sacred Muse** The Muses were classical goddesses who presided over the arts and inspired their practitioners, here especially poets.

254–5 **we ... love** Painters, like poets, must have a divine inspiration. Clarke aims to elevate his art to equal that of the poet by alluding to Horace's '*Ut pictura poesis*' ('as is painting, so is poetry'), a quotation often used in the wider rivalry between art forms, the paragone. These Italian Renaissance debates sit rather comically as motivation for the love of a servant.

256 **frame** shape; compose or produce
speaking countenance expressive face;

striking likeness of the subject of a portrait. Although not a common phrase in EEBO-TCP (appearing in only three other texts to 1642), it does appear in Marlowe's translation of Ovid's *Elegies*, 'View me, my becks and speaking countenance' (1.4.17). See 59n.

257 **witnesses** bears witness to, i.e. demonstrates the inner emotion externally (with wordplay on the meaning 'sees')

259 Alice appears swayed by Clarke's elevated language, perhaps ironically.
'Tis ... should 'It would be a pity if he didn't.'
use treat

260 **here's my hand** The pair to Alice's promise to Michael (146); the repetition underlines both Susan's lack of agency and Mosby and Alice's lack of respect for their own credit.

260 SD] *this edn*

MOSBY
> Fear him not. Leave; I have talked sufficient.

CLARKE [*to Alice*]
> You know not me, that ask such questions. 265
> Let it suffice I know you love him well,
> And fain would have your husband made away,
> Wherein, trust me, you show a noble mind,
> That, rather than you'll live with him you hate,
> You'll venture life, and die with him you love. 270
> The like will I do for my Susan's sake.

ALICE
> Yet nothing could enforce me to the deed
> But Mosby's love. [*to Mosby*] Might I without control
> Enjoy thee still, then Arden should not die.
> But, seeing I cannot, therefore let him die. 275

MOSBY
> Enough sweet Alice, thy kind words makes me melt.
> [*to Clarke*] Your trick of poisoned pictures we dislike;
> Some other poison would do better far.

ALICE
> Ay, such as might be put into his broth,
> And yet in taste not to be found at all. 280

CLARKE
> I know your mind, and here I have it for you.
> Put but a dram of this into his drink,
> Or any kind of broth that he shall eat,
> And he shall die within an hour after.

---

264 **Leave** Leave off; stop speaking, let it go, rather than leave us. Tyrrell emends to 'Fear him not, love', which suggests less tension between Alice and Mosby in their desire to control the situation, but as a result implies that Alice's interventions have less force.

265 **questions** trisyllabic
267 **made away** killed
270 **venture** risk, gamble on
273 **control** restraint, check
282 **dram** ⅛ fluid ounce (*c.* 3.6ml)

264 not. Leave; I] *(*not, leaue, I*);* not, love, I *Tyrrell* 265 SD] *B&T* 273 SD] *B&T* 277 SD] *Sturgess* 284 SD] *Wiggins*

[*Then he gives Alice the poison.*]

ALICE

    As I am a gentlewoman, Clarke, next day   285
    Thou and Susan shall be married.

MOSBY

    And I'll make her dowry more than I'll talk of, Clarke.

CLARKE

    Yonder's your husband. Mosby, I'll be gone.

Here enters ARDEN *and* FRANKLIN.

ALICE

    In good time, see where my husband comes.
    Master Mosby, ask him the question yourself.   290
                                  Exit Clarke.

MOSBY

    Master Arden, being at London yesternight,
    The Abbey lands whereof you are now possessed
    Were offered me, on some occasion,
    By Greene, one of Sir Antony Aucher's men.
    I pray you, sir, tell me, are not the lands yours?   295
    Hath any other interest herein?

---

285 **As ... gentlewoman** on my honour as a
gentlewoman; as surely as I am of gentle
birth
286 **married** trisyllabic
289 **In good time** at the right moment
293 **occasion** casual occurrence; event or
incident; four syllables
294 **Sir Antony Aucher** (d. 1558), gentleman,
administrator and landowner from
Otterden, eight miles from Faversham. He
worked for Thomas Cromwell, who procured for him the paymastership of the

royal haven works at Dover. A major purchaser of crown lands after the dissolution, he did business with Arden over
property. Charging extortionate rates for
victualling the fortifications of Boulogne
and handling large amounts of church
plate at the Reformation, his honesty was
often in question. In Holinshed, the
Greene of the plot is servant to Aucher
(see below, p. 291), whose name is there
spelled Ager, as in Q1.
296 **any other** anyone else

288 SD FRANKLIN] FRANKLIN *and* MICHAEL *Sturgess*   294 Aucher's] *(Agers)*

ARDEN

Mosby, that question we'll decide anon. –
Alice, make ready my breakfast; I must hence.   *Exit Alice.*
As for the lands, Mosby, they are mine
By letters patents from his majesty.   300
But I must have a mandate for my wife:
They say you seek to rob me of her love.
Villain, what makes thou in her company?
She's no companion for so base a groom.

MOSBY

Arden, I thought not on her; I came to thee.   305
But rather than I pocket up this wrong –

FRANKLIN

What will you do, sir?

MOSBY

Revenge it on the proudest of you both.
Then Arden draws forth Mosby's sword.

ARDEN

So, sirrah, you may not wear a sword:
The statute makes against artificers.   310

---

301 **mandate** authorization, specifically the King's command relating to a private suit, and therefore equivalent to the *letters patents* in the previous line

302–3 Arden shifts from addressing Mosby using the more flatteringly deferential *you*, suggesting a formal conversation between social equals, to *thou*, an indication of contempt and his sense of his rival's social inferiority.

303 **what makes thou** what are you up to

304 **companion** friend and company-keeper, but also wife (*OED n.* 3a)

306 **pocket up** suppress without responding

310 **statute** Arden apparently assumes a law, and editors cite the statute of 37 Edward III, c. 9, which reserved the wearing of swords for the gentry and above. Swords were not mentioned specifically in the contemporary sumptuary legislation, and research into their ownership suggests that they were considerably more widespread, owned by merchants and craftsmen as well as the elite (Hayward). Six per cent of householders in sixteenth-century Faversham owned swords (in a total of 215 inventories from the start of the record in 1565 to 1600), none named as gentlemen (occupations included maltman, yeoman and grocer); the swords had the low average value of 2s (KHLC).

makes against artificers does not pertain to, or is unfavourable to, craftsmen

artificers stressed on the second syllable

I warrant that I do. Now use your bodkin,
Your Spanish needle and your pressing iron,
For this shall go with me. And mark my words –
You, goodman botcher, 'tis to you I speak –
The next time that I take thee near my house,   315
Instead of legs I'll make thee crawl on stumps!

MOSBY

Ah, Master Arden, you have injured me;
I do appeal to God, and to the world.

FRANKLIN

Why, canst thou deny thou wert a botcher once?

MOSBY

Measure me what I am, not what I was.   320

ARDEN

Why, what art thou now? But a velvet drudge,
A cheating steward and base-minded peasant.

311 **warrant** express strong belief; guarantee as true (the fact that artificers are not to wear swords)
bodkin pointed instrument used by tailors for piercing holes in cloth, here used in ironic contrast to its other meaning, dagger
312 **Spanish needle** very fine needle, enabling detailed stitching. Made by techniques apparently inherited from Islamic refugees from Spain, such a needle cost around three times as much as a tailors' needle (Arnold, 9).
pressing iron another of the tailor's (or botcher's) tools. Holinshed records Mosby as wearing it at his girdle and striking Arden with it when the latter was murdered (see below, p. 298).
313 **this** i.e. Mosby's sword
314 **goodman** courtesy title for men below the gentry, used ironically here with the insulting *botcher* (see 24)

315 **take** apprehend, arrest; lay hold of; come upon
317 **injured me** insulted me; injured my reputation
318 Mosby's appeal to a wider public indicates his perception of the need for witnesses to a slanderous utterance. Slander, or defamation, was tried in the ecclesiastical courts as a form of moral and civil disobedience; calling into question gentry honour, in 'scandalous words provocative of a duel', could at certain times in early modern England be tried in the Court of Chivalry.
321 **velvet drudge** Mosby still undertakes menial and demeaning work (as a drudge), while wearing velvet, which as a soft, luxurious and expensive fabric is inappropriate for hard manual work. It is worn here as livery, rather than as the clothing of the gentry.

321 thou now? But] *this edn;* thou now, but *Q1;* now, but *SMS;* thou but *(conj. Jackson, 'Material');* thou now but *Wine*

MOSBY

> Arden, now thou hast belched and vomited
> The rancorous venom of thy mis-swoll'n heart,
> Hear me but speak: as I intend to live   325
> With God and his elected saints in heaven,
> I never meant more to solicit her;
> And that she knows, and all the world shall see.
> I loved her once, sweet Arden, pardon me.
> I could not choose; her beauty fired my heart.   330
> But time hath quenched these over-raging coals,
> And, Arden, though I now frequent thy house,
> 'Tis for my sister's sake, her waiting-maid,
> And not for hers. Mayst thou enjoy her long.
> Hellfire and wrathful vengeance light on me   335
> If I dishonour her or injure thee.

ARDEN

> Mosby, with these thy protestations
> The deadly hatred of my heart is appeased,
> And thou and I'll be friends if this prove true.
> As for the base terms I gave thee late,   340

---

324 **mis-swoll'n** inappropriately or unnecessarily distended with emotion. This is the only example listed in EEBO-TCP, and the word does not appear in *OED*. For 'swollen' in this context see Thomas Kyd's *Soliman and Perseda* (1588; Wiggins 799), 'And here my tongue dooth stay, with swolne harts greefe' (1.1400).

326 **elected saints** those predestined to salvation in the Protestant understanding of the afterlife. The phrase was familiar from Protestant wills after the Reformation: see, for instance, Shakespeare's fellow-actor Henry Condell's assertion that he would 'enioy everlasting life in the Kingdome of Heaven amongest the elect Children of God' (Honigmann and Brock, 156). Mosby outrageously stakes the veracity of his statement of his feelings towards Alice on his future entry to heaven, a state of affairs rendered less than likely by his committing adultery and intending murder.

337–43 Somewhere during this speech it seems likely that Arden returns Mosby's sword. The qualification he provides, *if this prove true*, and the identification of the *table-talk* after his injunction to *Forget* might suggest a grudging, conditional and perhaps threatening return.

337 **protestations** five syllables

334 Mayst] *(maiest);* maist *Q3;* May'st *Delius*

141

Forget them, Mosby. I had cause to speak
When all the knights and gentlemen of Kent
Make common table-talk of her and thee.

MOSBY

Who lives that is not touched with slanderous
. tongues?

FRANKLIN

Then, Mosby, to eschew the speech of men,   345
Upon whose general bruit all honour hangs,
Forbear his house.

ARDEN

Forbear it? Nay, rather frequent it more!
The world shall see that I distrust her not.
To warn him on the sudden from my house   350
Were to confirm the rumour that is grown.

MOSBY

By my faith, sir, you say true.
And therefore will I sojourn here a while
Until our enemies have talked their fill.
And then, I hope, they'll cease, and at last confess   355
How causeless they have injured her and me.

342 **When** considering that
343 **table-talk** talk on hospitable dinner occa-
    sions that indicates the elevated social
    circles in which Arden moves whilst
    undercutting his credit within them
344 **slanderous** sland'rous
346 **general bruit** common talk, rumour
347 **Forbear** keep away from, shun
350 **warn ... from** notify him without

warning to go from. *OED* (*v.*[1] 6c) gives
this as the earliest instance of this
meaning of 'warn'.
352 ***By ... sir** Q1 reads 'By faith my sir';
B&T (*CRE*) argues that both '"by faith"
and "my sir" are anomalous', suggesting
scribal or compositorial transposition, or
a misplaced proof correction.
353 **sojourn** lodge

352 my faith] *SMS;* faith, my *Q1*

ARDEN

> And I will lie at London all this term,
> To let them see how light I weigh their words.

Here enters ALICE [*and* MICHAEL, *with a bowl of broth*].

ALICE

> Husband, sit down; your breakfast will be cold.

ARDEN

> Come, Master Mosby, will you sit with us?   360

MOSBY

> I cannot eat, but I'll sit for company.
> [*Then Arden, Franklin and Mosby sit at the table.*]

ARDEN

> Sirrah Michael, see our horse be ready.   [*Exit Michael.*]
> [*Then Arden begins to eat the broth, but pauses.*]

ALICE

> Husband, why pause ye? Why eat you not?

ARDEN

> I am not well. There's something in this broth
> That is not wholesome. Didst thou make it, Alice?   365

ALICE

> I did, and that's the cause it likes not you.
> *Then she throws down the broth on the ground.*

358 SD Michael needs to enter at some stage in the scene so that Arden can address him at 362, and entry at this point offers the opportunity for him to set up breakfast (see p. 50 for discussion of his entrances and exits). He may bring stools for Arden and Mosby to sit on. If he brings the broth, his service makes the meal more formal; if Alice serves her husband, her personal attention sets the murder attempt in the context of domestic intimacy.

361 Mosby's refusal to eat shows his knowl-edge of the poison but also offers the audience the emblematic disruption of a meal intended as a symbol of amity.

362 SD1 Q1 gives an exit for Michael at 415. Whilst he does not have to exit here and re-enter later (394), it would be a very insubordinate servant who ignored his master's command.

366 **cause . . . you** reason you don't like it

366 SD Franklin might go to taste the broth here, and Alice throw it down to avoid discovery.

358 SD *and Michael*] *White   with . . . broth*] *Wiggins*   361 SD] *B&T (Wiggins subst.)*   362 SD1] *Wiggins; Exit Michael and re-enter | Sturgess*   SD2] *Wiggins subst.*

There's nothing that I do can please your taste;
You were best to say I would have poisoned you.
I cannot speak or cast aside my eye
But he imagines I have stepped awry.   370
[*to Arden*] Here's he that you cast in my teeth so oft;
Now will I be convinced, or purge myself.
[*to Mosby*] I charge thee speak to this mistrustful
    man –
Thou that wouldst see me hang, thou, Mosby, thou –
What favour hast thou had more than a kiss   375
At coming or departing from the town?

MOSBY

You wrong yourself and me to cast these doubts;
Your loving husband is not jealous.

ARDEN

Why, gentle mistress Alice, cannot I be ill
But you'll accuse yourself?   380
Franklin, thou hast a box of mithridate;
I'll take a little to prevent the worst.

FRANKLIN

Do so, and let us presently take horse.
My life for yours, ye shall do well enough.

369–70 spoken openly and publicly, to the
    audience on- or offstage, or both
371 **cast ... teeth** reproach me for; prover-
    bial, see Dent, T429.
    so oft suggests that Arden's knowledge
    of the affair has considerable history,
    thereby casting him in an unfavourable
    light as an ineffective patriarchal house-
    hold head. Holinshed says that Arden
    'was contented to winke at hir [Alice's]
    filthie disorder' in order not to lose the
    'benefit' he hoped to gain from her

friends (see below, p. 290).
372 **convinced** proven guilty (*OED v.* II 4)
    purge myself clear myself (of the suspi-
    cion), establish innocence
378 **jealous** See 47n.
381 **mithridate** compound medicinal prepa-
    ration, believed to be a universal antidote
    to poison. It was for sale at the start of the
    seventeenth century in Canterbury, near
    Faversham, for fourpence ('The diary of
    Thomas Cocks', Canterbury Cathedral
    Archives and Library, DCc-LitMs/E/31).

371 SD] *this edn*   373 SD] *Wiggins*   379–80] *Brooke lines* I / selfe? / ; *Delius lines* Alice, / yourself? /

ALICE

    Give me a spoon, I'll eat of it myself.   385

    Would it were full of poison to the brim;

    Then should my cares and troubles have an end!

    Was ever silly woman so tormented?

ARDEN

    Be patient, sweet love: I mistrust not thee.

ALICE

    God will revenge it, Arden, if thou dost;   390

    For never woman loved her husband better

    Than I do thee.

ARDEN

    I know it, sweet Alice. Cease to complain,

    Lest that in tears I answer thee again.

                 [Here enters MICHAEL.*]*

FRANKLIN

    Come, leave this dallying, and let us away.   395

ALICE

    Forbear to wound me with that bitter word.

    Arden shall go to London in my arms.

        [Then she embraces Arden.]

ARDEN

    Loath am I to depart, yet I must go.

ALICE

    Wilt thou to London then, and leave me here?

---

385 Alice may try to grab Arden's spoon.

388 **silly** defenceless, powerless (with suggestion of innocence or undeserved suffering)

393 **complain** lament

394 **answer** respond or reply to the (pretend) tears which this line suggests Alice is now weeping

394 SD Michael's re-entry at this point, apparently having readied the horses, would then prompt Franklin's attempt in the following line to break in on Arden and Alice's passionate conversation.

395 **dallying** flirting, idle chat; deferring or putting off

396 **Forbear to** abstain, refrain from

391–2] *W&P; one line Q1*   394 SD] *B&T (Wiggins subst.)*   397 SD] *Wiggins*

Ah, if thou love me, gentle Arden, stay.   400
    [*Then Arden hesitates.*]
Yet, if thy business be of great import,
Go if thou wilt – I'll bear it as I may –
But write from London to me every week,
Nay, every day. And stay no longer there
Than thou must needs, lest that I die for sorrow.   405

ARDEN

I'll write unto thee every other tide,
And so farewell, sweet Alice, till we meet next.

ALICE

Farewell, husband, seeing you'll have it so.
And, Master Franklin, seeing you take him hence,
In hope you'll hasten him home I'll give you this.   410
    And then she kisseth him.

FRANKLIN

And if he stay, the fault shall not be mine.
Mosby, farewell, and see you keep your oath.

MOSBY

I hope he is not jealous of me now.

ARDEN

No, Mosby, no; hereafter think of me
As of your dearest friend. And so, farewell.   415
    Exeunt Arden, Franklin and Michael.

---

405 **thou must needs** you absolutely have to
406 **every other tide** i.e. once a day (there
are two high tides every 24 hours 50
mins). Boats carrying goods and passen-
gers made regular journeys from London
to Kent. John Taylor states that a hoy
(small passenger and goods vessel) went
directly from Faversham to St
Katherine's Dock, and that 'Tydeboats'
and barges went from the Lion Key to
Greenhithe or from Billingsgate to

Gravesend and Milton at the mouth of
the Thames (at which they were met on
foot or horseback) (*The Carriers'
Cosmography* (1637), sig. C4ʳ⁻ᵛ).
410 SD In performance, the kiss is often
unwelcome. It enacts the reception Alice
claims to offer Mosby (375–6), and demonstrates that the jest she and Mosby perform at 13.80 may not have been as fundamentally inappropriate as it now seems.
413 **jealous** See 47n.

400 SD] *B&T*

ALICE

    I am glad he is gone. He was about to stay,
    But did you mark me then, how I broke off?

MOSBY

    Ay, Alice, and it was cunningly performed.
    But what a villain is this painter Clarke!

ALICE

    Was it not a goodly poison that he gave?   420
    Why, he's as well now as he was before!
    It should have been some fine confection,
    That might have given the broth some dainty taste;
    This powder was too gross and palpable.

MOSBY

    But, had he eaten but three spoonfuls more,   425
    Then had he died and our love continued.

ALICE

    Why, so it shall, Mosby, albeit he live.

MOSBY

    It is unpossible, for I have sworn
    Never hereafter to solicit thee
    Or, whilst he lives, once more importune thee.   430

ALICE

    Thou shalt not need; I will importune thee.
    What, shall an oath make thee forsake my love?
    As if I have not sworn as much myself,
    And given my hand unto him in the church!

---

422 **confection** compound. The word was used to refer to both a medicine and a poison. Four syllables.

424 ***gross and palpable** Gross (*OED adj.* 3) means 'palpable, conspicuous, striking'. The pairing 'gross and palpable' (as opposed to Q1's 'populo[u]s') was widely current in the period,

appearing as a phrase 154 times in 85 texts to 1600 on EEBO-TCP, especially as a description of sin and ignorance, a context which may set up suggestive echoes for the audience.

428–30 ironic morality of course, as, both socially and theologically, murder is the greater breach

417 broke] *(*brake*)*   424 palpable] *Delius;* populos *Q1;* popular *SMS*   430, 439 whilst] *Q2;* whylest *Q1*

Tush, Mosby, oaths are words, and words is wind,   435
And wind is mutable. Then, I conclude,
'Tis childishness to stand upon an oath.

MOSBY

Well proved, Mistress Alice. Yet, by your leave,
I'll keep mine unbroken whilst he lives.

ALICE

Ay, do, and spare not. His time is but short;   440
For, if thou beest as resolute as I,
We'll have him murdered as he walks the streets.
In London many alehouse ruffians keep,
Which, as I hear, will murder men for gold.
They shall be soundly fee'd to pay him home.   445

Here enters GREENE.

MOSBY

Alice, what's he that comes yonder? Knowest thou him?

ALICE

Mosby, be gone! I hope 'tis one that comes
To put in practice our intended drifts.   *Exit Mosby.*

---

435 **oaths ... wind** Much of this speech is based on common proverbial sayings: 'Words are but wind' (Dent, W833), 'As wavering as the wind' (Dent, W412); the shock comes in their extension to the marriage vows. The phrase is near-quoted by Samuel Butler in *Hudibras* ('*Oaths* are but *words*, and *words* but *wind*', 281), but similar sentiment is also found in Edmond Bicknoll's 1579 *A Sword Against Swearing* ('Hubidras, bynde euery mans bargayne sure by writing', sig. Biiiᵛ), part of the religious debate on oaths in the period (Spurr), and

quoted as the words of deponents in early modern court cases (TNA STAC 8/288/16, fol. 35; Hindle, Peace).

444 **Which** who

445 **pay him home** punish him as much as he deserves (i.e. to death), playing on the financial sense ('recompense him fully') that the murderers will be paid to *pay* Arden what he has got coming to him.

446 **he that comes** Jowett (B&T (*CRE*)) suggests 'he comes', pointing to *that comes* in the following line as the source of an error of repetition.

448 **drifts** schemes, plots

445 fee'd] *SMS;* fed *Q1*

GREENE

    Mistress Arden, you are well met.

    I am sorry that your husband is from home   450

    Whenas my purposed journey was to him.

    Yet all my labour is not spent in vain,

    For I suppose that you can full discourse

    And flat resolve me of the thing I seek.

ALICE

    What is it, Master Greene? If that I may,   455

    Or can with safety, I will answer you.

GREENE

    I heard your husband hath the grant of late,

    Confirmed by letters patents from the King,

    Of all the lands of the Abbey of Faversham,

    Generally entitled so that all former grants   460

    Are cut off, whereof I myself had one;

    But now my interest by that is void.

    This is all, Mistress Arden; is it true nor no?

ALICE

    True, Master Greene: the lands are his in state,

    And whatsoever leases were before   465

    Are void for term of Master Arden's life.

    He hath the grant under the Chancery seal.

GREENE

    Pardon me, Mistress Arden, I must speak,

    For I am touched. Your husband doth me wrong

    To wring me from the little land I have.   470

---

451 **Whenas** at the time at which

454 **flat** downright, absolutely (as in 'that's flat', *OED* II 6b)

460 **Generally entitled** Arden's right to the estate is without qualification.

462 **interest by** right or title to, claim upon

464 **in state** in possession

467 **under . . . seal** in a document attested by

the seal of the Court of Chancery (the highest court next to the House of Lords)

469 **touched** moved emotionally

471 **My . . . life** The income from my land (living) is all I have to live on.

471–2 **only . . . portion** that is all that remains of my inheritance

My living is my life: only that
Resteth remainder of my portion.
Desire of wealth is endless in his mind,
And he is greedy-gaping still for gain;
Nor cares he though young gentlemen do beg,   475
So he may scrape and hoard up in his pouch.
But, seeing he hath taken my lands, I'll value life
As careless as he is careful for to get.
And tell him this from me: I'll be revenged,
And so as he shall wish the Abbey lands   480
Had rested still within their former state.

ALICE

Alas, poor gentleman, I pity you;
And woe is me that any man should want.
God knows, 'tis not my fault. But wonder not
Though he be hard to others, when to me –   485
Ah, Master Greene, God knows how I am used!

GREENE

Why, Mistress Arden, can the crabbed churl
Use you unkindly? Respects he not your birth,
Your honourable friends, nor what you brought?
Why, all Kent knows your parentage and what you
   are.   490

ALICE

Ah, Master Greene – be it spoken in secret here –
I never live good day with him alone.
When he is at home, then have I froward looks,
Hard words, and blows to mend the match withal.

---

476 **pouch** small bag or pocket (latter in this
   period not fixed to clothing)
477 **taken** pronounced ta'en
478 **careless** carelessly, casually
   get gain profit
485 **Though** if
487 **crabbed** irritable, bad-tempered; **crabbèd**
   churl low-born and rude man. See also
   508. Like Arden's taunting of Mosby,

this exchange calls into question the relationship between Arden's status and his
behaviour.
489 **what you brought** i.e. the dowry
   (money) which you brought to your husband when you married
493 **froward** perverse and hard to please
494 **mend ... withal** correct or restore our
   marriage with (ironic)

And though I might content as good a man,   495
Yet doth he keep in every corner trulls;
And, weary with his trugs at home,
Then rides he straight to London. There, forsooth,
He revels it among such filthy ones
As counsels him to make away his wife.   500
Thus live I daily in continual fear,
In sorrow, so despairing of redress
As every day I wish with hearty prayer
That he or I were taken forth the world.

GREENE

Now trust me, Mistress Alice, it grieveth me   505
So fair a creature should be so abused.
Why, who would have thought the civil sir so sullen?
He looks so smoothly. Now fie upon him, churl,
And if he live a day, he lives too long!
But frolic, woman, I shall be the man   510
Shall set you free from all this discontent.
And if the churl deny my interest,
And will not yield my lease into my hand,
I'll pay him home, whatever hap to me.

ALICE

But speak you as you think?   515

GREENE

Ay, God's my witness. I mean plain dealing,
For I had rather die than lose my land.

ALICE

Then, Master Greene, be counselled by me:
Endanger not yourself for such a churl,

---

496 **trulls** whores
497 **trugs** whores
500 **make away** kill
504 **forth** away from
507 **sullen** obstinate, ill-humoured (*OED* 1a); 'moodily silent' (*OED* 1b)
508 **smoothly** mild

fie exclamation of disgust or reproach
510 **frolic** make merry
511 **Shall** who will
514 **hap** happens (as verb), or the chance or fortune that falls (as noun)
518 **counselled** counsellèd

But hire some cutters for to cut him short.   520
And here's ten pound to wager them withal;
  [*Then she gives Greene money in a purse.*]
When he is dead you shall have twenty more,
And the lands whereof my husband is possessed
Shall be entitled as they were before.

GREENE

Will you keep promise with me?   525

ALICE

Or count me false and perjured whilst I live.

GREENE

Then here's my hand: I'll have him so dispatched.
  [*Then they shake hands.*]
I'll up to London straight; I'll thither post,
And never rest till I have compassed it.
Till then, farewell.   530

ALICE

Good fortune follow all your forward thoughts.
                          Exit Greene.
And whosoever doth attempt the deed,
A happy hand I wish; and so farewell.
All this goes well. Mosby, I long for thee,
To let thee know all that I have contrived.   535

Here enters MOSBY *and* CLARKE.

---

520 **cutters** persons over-ready to resort to weapons; cutthroats or highway robbers. May also suggest 'gelders', those who castrate animals (*OED* 2d).

521 **ten pound** Ten pounds could be made up of ten gold sovereigns or twenty angels. A sovereign weighed approximately 11g and an angel 8g. As the combined weight is relatively small (110g), Alice is likely to have carried it in a purse at her waist.

524 i.e. the right, or title, to the lands will be restored to Greene

528 **post** travel with speed

529 **compassed** accomplished

531 **forward** eager, spirited

533 **happy** fortunate

---

520 cutters] *Oliphant;* cutter *Q1*   521 them] then *Wiggins*   SD] *this edn (Wiggins subst.)*   527 SD]
Wiggins subst.   531 SD] *after 534 Hugo*   535 SD] ACT II. SCENE I. *Tyrrell*

MOSBY

How now, Alice, what's the news?

ALICE

Such as will content thee well, sweetheart.

MOSBY

Well, let them pass a while, and tell me, Alice,
How have you dealt and tempered with my sister –
What, will she have my neighbour Clarke, or no?   540

ALICE

What, Master Mosby? Let him woo himself!
Think you that maids look not for fair words?
Go to her, Clarke – she's all alone within.
Michael, my man, is clean out of her books.

CLARKE

I thank you, Mistress Arden; I will in.   545
And, if fair Susan and I can make a gree,
You shall command me to the uttermost:
As far as either goods or life may stretch.   *Exit.*

MOSBY

Now, Alice, let's hear thy news.

ALICE

They be so good that I must laugh for joy   550
Before I can begin to tell my tale.

MOSBY

Let's hear them, that I may laugh for company.

ALICE

This morning, Master Greene – Dick Greene I mean,
From whom my husband had the Abbey land –
Came hither railing, for to know the truth   555

---

538 **let . . . while** i.e. tell me your news later
  (*news* is plural in this period)
539 **tempered with** persuaded
544 **out . . . books** out of her favour (proverbial, Dent, B534)

546 **Susan** monosyllabic for metre
  make a gree come to terms; make an
  agreement
555 **railing** complaining, ranting

548 SD] *(Exit Clarke)*

Whether my husband had the lands by grant.
I told him all, whereat he stormed amain,
And swore he would cry quittance with the churl
And, if he did deny his interest,
Stab him, whatsoever did befall himself.   560
Whenas I saw his choler thus to rise,
I whetted on the gentleman with words;
And, to conclude, Mosby, at last we grew
To composition for my husband's death:
I gave him ten pound to hire knaves,   565
By some device to make away the churl;
When he is dead, he should have twenty more,
And repossess his former lands again.
On this we 'greed, and he is ridden straight
To London, to bring his death about.   570

MOSBY
But call you this good news?

ALICE   Ay, sweetheart, be they not?

MOSBY
'Twere cheerful news to hear the churl were dead!
But trust me, Alice, I take it passing ill
You would be so forgetful of our state
To make recount of it to every groom.   575
What, to acquaint each stranger with our drifts,
Chiefly in case of murder? Why, 'tis the way
To make it open unto Arden's self,
And bring thyself and me to ruin both.

---

557 **stormed amain** raged violently
558 **cry quittance** get even
562 **whetted on** urged on
564 **composition** agreement
565 **to hire** B&T (*CRE*) proposes 'for to hire',
    pointing out that Q1 uses the formulation
    'for to' three times in this scene (at 214,
    478, 520) 'always in verse, always in
    mid-line and for metrical reasons'.

566 **device** plot, stratagem
567 **he ... he** Arden ... Greene
573 **passing** beyond, surpassing; exceed-
    ingly
574 **forgetful ... state** unmindful of our sit-
    uation
577 **in case of** as regards
578 **open ... self** known to Arden himself

Forewarned, forearmed; who threats his enemy   580
Lends him a sword to guard himself withal.

ALICE

I did it for the best.

MOSBY

Well, seeing 'tis done, cheerly let it pass.
You know this Greene; is he not religious?
A man, I guess, of great devotion?

ALICE   He is.   585

MOSBY

Then, sweet Alice, let it pass. I have a drift
Will quiet all, whatever is amiss.

Here enters CLARKE *and* SUSAN.

ALICE

How now, Clarke, have you found me false?
Did I not plead the matter hard for you?

CLARKE

You did.

MOSBY   And what; wilt be a match?   590

CLARKE

A match, i'faith, sir; ay, the day is minc!
The painter lays his colours to the life;
His pencil draws no shadows in his love:
Susan is mine!

---

580 **Forewarned, forearmed** proverbial
(*OED* forearmed)

583 **cheerly ... pass** 'let's be cheerful and
not dwell on it'
cheerly Tyrrell's reading, 'clearly',
meaning completely (*OED adv.* 8, which
also means 'cleanly'), and without
entanglement (*OED adv.* 10), is worth
noting as it gets to the heart of the need to
move on and find a solution to a potentially dangerous situation.

585 **devotion** four syllables

591 **the day is mine** I've won the battle.

592 **lays ... life** applies his paint (in layers)
to make a lifelike picture

593 **pencil** small paintbrush for delicate work
such as faces
shadows suggestions of emotional darkness, foreboding or doubt
his love i.e. both his painting of his
beloved and their relationship

155

ALICE. You make her blush.

MOSBY
What, sister, is it Clarke must be the man? 595

SUSAN
It resteth in your grant. Some words are passed,
And haply we be grown unto a match
If you be willing that it shall be so.

MOSBY
Ah, Master Clarke, it resteth at my grant –
You see my sister's yet at my dispose – 600
But, so you'll grant me one thing I shall ask,
I am content my sister shall be yours.

CLARKE
What is it, Master Mosby?

MOSBY
I do remember once, in secret talk,
You told me how you could compound by art 605
A crucifix empoisoned,
That whoso look upon it should wax blind,
And with the scent be stifled that, ere long,
He should die poisoned that did view it well.
I would have you make me such a crucifix, 610
And then I'll grant my sister shall be yours.

---

596 **It ... grant** It remains for you to give
your consent to the marriage.
Some words See 149n. for the handfasting ceremony.

597 **haply** The dominant meaning is 'perhaps', as the match is conditional on
Mosby's agreement, but the quartos all
have the trisyllabic spelling 'happely',
and the word also carries, secondarily,
the more modern sense 'fortunately'.
The shift between these spellings and
meanings comes up repeatedly across the
play.

600 **yet** still, a reference to her unmarried
state, and possibly a suggestion that she
has not yet come of age

601 **so** in order that you will; if you will

605 **compound** combine elements together
(here including pigments) to make; a
word suggesting technical and professional skill

606, 618, 622 **empoisoned** trisyllabic at 606,
622, four syllables at 618

607 **That** such that
whoso anyone who
wax grow, become

597 haply] *Delius;* happely *Q1;* happily *Q2–3*

CLARKE

> Though I am loath, because it toucheth life,
> Yet, rather or I'll leave sweet Susan's love,
> I'll do it, and with all the haste I may.
> But for whom is it? 615

ALICE

> Leave that to us. Why, Clarke, is it possible
> That you should paint and draw it out yourself,
> The colours being baleful and empoisoned,
> And no ways prejudice yourself withal?

MOSBY

> Well questioned, Alice. Clarke, how answer you that? 620

CLARKE

> Very easily. I'll tell you straight
> How I do work of these empoisoned drugs:
> I fasten on my spectacles so close
> As nothing can any way offend my sight.
> Then, as I put a leaf within my nose, 625
> So put I rhubarb to avoid the smell,
> And softly, as another work, I paint.

MOSBY

> 'Tis very well. But against when shall I have it?

CLARKE

> Within this ten days.

---

612 **toucheth** involves, relates to, has a harmful effect on, but with a pun on 'touch' as paint 'by touching the surface lightly or delicately . . . to make small additions or modifications to an artwork' (*OED* 7a)

613 **rather or** rather than (*OED* rather III 8a), 'preference for one outcome over another' (*OED* IV 10). B&T has 'rather ere', but the Q1 reading retains the sense of Clarke weighing up the options.

624 **nothing** Emending to 'nought' would regularize the metre.

626 **rhubarb** exotic plant, eventually domestically grown, valued for its medicinal rootstock which was considered good for the liver and used as a purgative

627 **softly** gently, carefully
as another work as with any other painting

628 **against** by

620] *Tyrrell; Q1 lines* Ales, / that? /

MOSBY   'Twill serve the turn.
    Now, Alice, let's in, and see what cheer you keep.   630
    I hope, now Master Arden is from home,
    You'll give me leave to play your husband's part?
ALICE
    Mosby, you know who's master of my heart,
    He well may be the master of the house.   *Exeunt.*

[Sc. 2]   *Here enters* GREENE *and* BRADSHAW.

BRADSHAW
    See you them that comes yonder, Master
        Greene?
GREENE
    Ay, very well. Do you know them?

        Here enters BLACK WILL *and* SHAKEBAG.

629 **serve the turn** do the trick
632 **play ... part** metatheatrical way of
    expressing not only his easier and more
    regular sexual access to Alice, but also
    the opportunity to act like a propertied
    member of the gentry
633–4 As he rules her heart and enjoys her
    body, Mosby may fittingly take over con-
    trol of the household. Involving taking
    Arden's rightful place as patriarchal head
    and usurping his rule over servants and
    property as well as Alice herself, this is a
    truly shocking suggestion.
Sc. 2 The scene makes few demands on staging
    as all the characters are in transit. Its
    implied location, established when Black
    Will questions Bradshaw about his desti-
    nation, is on the road between Faversham
    and Rochester (where Will suggests they
    rest, 116), on the way to London.

2 SD Holinshed describes Black Will as 'a
    terrible cruell ruffian with a sword and a
    buckler', and also mentions 'an other
    [i.e. Shakebag, not named by him until
    the murder attempt at Harty Ferry], and
    an other with a great staffe on his necke'
    (see below, p. 292). The play was written
    in a period when continental rapiers were
    replacing swords and bucklers as fitting
    arms for gentlemen (William Bas's
    *Sword and Buckler, or, Servingman's
    Defence* (1609) calls the latter 'ancient'
    (sig. B4ʳ)), so carrying a sword and
    buckler would mark Will out as old-
    fashioned (or from the 1550s), and a pro-
    fessional soldier rather than a member of
    the elite. The two may enter from the
    opposite door to Bradshaw and Greene,
    allowing the latter pair to comment
    unheard.

634 SD] *Q2; Eeunt, Q1* **Sc. 2**] *Hugo;* ACT II. SCENE II. *Tyrrell;* ACT II. SCENE I. *Delius* 1 comes]
come *Q3* 2 SD] *after 13 Tyrrell*

BRADSHAW

The one I know not, but he seems a knave,
Chiefly for bearing the other company;
For such a slave, so vile a rogue as he,   5
Lives not again upon the earth.
Black Will is his name. I tell you, Master Greene,
At Boulogne he and I were fellow soldiers,
Where he played such pranks
As all the camp feared him for his villainy.   10
I warrant you, he bears so bad a mind
That for a crown he'll murder any man.

GREENE [*aside*]

The fitter is he for my purpose, marry.

[*Then Bradshaw makes to leave.*]

BLACK WILL   How now, fellow Bradshaw, whither away
so early?   15

---

3   **knave** man of low status; dishonest villain.
The word extends the terms of mixed
social and moral abuse from the first scene.

5   The vehemence of Bradshaw's language
mirrors Arden's description of Mosby in
1.25–7, 36, and the disdain inherent in it
similarly indicates his wish to draw a
social and moral distinction between
himself and others.

8   **Boulogne** French port in the English
Channel. Captured by Henry VIII in
1544, it was surrendered in 1550 by
Edward VI, a year before Arden's
murder. Soldiers returning from France
were a common sight in Kent in the first
half of the sixteenth century, as were the
trained bands of militia mustering
against the threat of invasion in the
1580s and early 1590s, including 7,000
Kentish men.

12   **crown** silver or gold coin (*c.* 30g or *c.*
2.8g in weight respectively) worth 5s (a
quarter of a pound). They are mentioned
again at 33 and 80. Average wages for
servants 1560–99 were under 50s a year
(Jane Whittle, 'Servants in rural England
1560–1650: Kussmaul revisited',https://
www.campop.geog.cam.ac.uk/events/
richardsmithconference/papers.html).

13   **marry** originally an oath (referring to
Mary, mother of God); by this period used
to emphasize a point (*OED* marry *int.*)

14   **fellow** colleague. Will insists on his and
Bradshaw's previous comradeship in the
army. The tense exchange 14–33 tests
out the relationship between their sta-
tuses in war and peacetime, and the relative hierarchies of army and town.

---

7 name.] *Jacob (name:);* name *Q1;* name, *Q2–3*   13 SD1] *Tyrrell*   SD2] *Wiggins*   14–15] *W&P; Q1*
lines Bradshaw, / *earely?* /

BRADSHAW

    O Will, times are changed – no fellows now,
    Though we were once together in the field –
    Yet thy friend, to do thee any good I can.

BLACK WILL   Why, Bradshaw, was not thou and I fellow
    soldiers at Boulogne, where I was a corporal and thou   20
    but a base, mercenary groom? 'No fellows now'
    because you are a goldsmith, and have a little plate in
    your shop? You were glad to call me 'fellow Will' and,
    with a curtsy to the earth, 'One snatch, good corporal'
    when I stole the half ox from John the victualler and   25
    domineered with it amongst good fellows in one night.

BRADSHAW

    Ay, Will, those days are past with me.

BLACK WILL

    Ay, but they be not past with me,
    For I keep that same honourable mind still. Good

---

17 **field** (of war)

20 **corporal** non-commissioned military officer ranking under a sergeant but above a private. Ranks emerged in English armies in the 1570s, so use of this term belongs to the world of the play rather than the historical period it depicts. *OED* gives a first date of 1579, so the word may have struck the audience as part of a wider recent explosion of new military language.

21 **mercenary** hired, or serving for wages
    groom inferior; servingman. See *TS*, 4.1.111–12, 'You logger-headed and unpolished grooms. / What, no attendance?'.

22 **plate** high-status gold or silver vessels, usually for dining

24 **curtsy** bow, expressing Will's superior

and Bradshaw's inferior military status. Contraction of 'courtesy' (*OED n.* 8).
    snatch possibly a brief song, but more likely hasty meal or snack (*OED n.* 6a). The story then casts Will as a kind of anti-victualler (see 25), dispensing stolen army rations.

25 **victualler** person responsible for supplying an army with provisions. Sir Anthony Aucher, mentioned in 1.294 as the employer of a man who offered Arden's lands for sale, was chief victualler of Boulogne and Le Havre 1545–50.

26 **domineered** tyrannized (*OED v.* 1a), or 'lorded it'; but also feasted riotously (*OED v.* 2)

29 **honourable** (ironic)

19–26] *W&P; Q1 lines* 1 / *Bulloine*: / groome? / gouldsmith, / shoppe, / Will, / earth, / corporall. / vitler. / fellowes, / night. /   28–34] *prose W&P; Q1 lines* me. /still, / fellow, / down / more, / you to. / goe. / ; *31–3* (But were . . . more) *prose Q2; 28–33* (Ay? . . . too.) *prose Delius*   28 Ay, but] *(*I but*)*; Ay? But *Delius*

neighbour Bradshaw, you are too proud to be my 30
fellow; but, were it not that I see more company
coming down the hill, I would be fellows with you
once more, and share crowns with you too. But let
that pass, and tell me whither you go.

BRADSHAW

To London, Will, about a piece of service 35
Wherein haply thou mayst pleasure me.

BLACK WILL

What is it?

BRADSHAW   Of late Lord Cheyne lost some plate,
Which one did bring and sold it at my shop,
Saying he served Sir Anthony Cooke.
A search was made, the plate was found with me, 40

31–3 **were … too** again, suggestion of a possible threat from Will: either that the company he sees would be fitter targets for robbery than Bradshaw, or that their presence frustrates his plans. His professed desire to *share crowns* (*OED* share *v.* 1d gives this as first usage for the meaning 'To divide (what one has or receives) into portions, and give shares to others as well as one's self' – another new word at the end of the sixteenth century) could refer to his ill-gotten gains.

33–4 **let that pass** forget about that

35 **service** work done for a master or superior. The word is also part of the developing military lexicon (see, e.g., *MA*, 'He hath done good service, lady, in these wars', 1.1.45–6), and so may call here upon shared martial experience.

36 **haply** See 1.597n.
   pleasure gratify or help

37–41 The question of the lost plate blurs the previously clear line between

Bradshaw's respectable lifestyle and Will's dishonest one, as the basis of the former's new status turns out to be stolen property. Theft of plate was a constant problem, ways of recovering it shifting in the early modern period from sovereigns' searches of London shops for stolen Court plate to the Goldsmiths' Company's creation of the office of Warning Carrier who distributed notices of lost and stolen property. The episode may, therefore, be based on a particular crime (as Cust suggested), or a more generally plausible occurrence.

37 **Lord Cheyne** See List of roles, 14n.

39 **Sir Anthony Cooke** (1505/6–76) Essex knight, educator and humanist, Protestant companion and guide to Edward VI. Men of his standing would be expected to have impressive plate collections, and the historical Cooke bequeathed all his surviving sons and his exceptionally well-educated daughters a share in his will.

---

36 haply] *Delius;* happely *Q1;* happily *Q2*   39–41] *Oliphant lines* search / I / 'size /

And I am bound to answer at the 'size.
Now Lord Cheyne solemnly vows,
If law will serve him, he'll hang me for his plate.
Now I am going to London upon hope
To find the fellow. Now, Will, I know   45
Thou art acquainted with such companions.

BLACK WILL   What manner of man was he?

BRADSHAW

A lean-faced, writhen knave,
Hawk-nosed and very hollow-eyed,
With mighty furrows in his stormy brows.   50
Long hair down his shoulders curled;
His chin was bare, but on his upper lip
A mutchado, which he wound about his ear.

BLACK WILL   What apparel had he?

---

41 **answer** defend himself, counter the charge
   'size assize; regular county sessions at which civil and criminal justice was administered
48 **writhen** twisted or contorted; often used of snakes and other curled and writhing things
50 **furrows** deep wrinkles, like the lines a plough makes in a field
51 **Long hair** as symbolizing lawlessness and criminality. B&T (*CRE*) finds late sixteenth-century examples of 'long hair down to his shoulders' and argues for the addition of Q3's 'to' here, partly to aid the metre.
53 **mutchado** moustache; a new and obviously foreign word. *OED* gives a first date for 'mustachio', from the Spanish and Italian, as 1551 (W. Thomas's MS translation of Barbaro's *Travels to Tana and Persia*, 'They [the Persians] suffer their mostacchi to growe a quarter of a yarde longer than their beardes' (publ. 1873)), and for 'moustache' as 1585 (Thomas Washington's translation of

Nicolas de Nicolay's *Navigations, Peregrinations and Voyages made into Turkey*). Its initial exoticism as a foreign word used primarily in travel narratives is clear. The scene in the barber's shop in Guillaume de la Mothe's *French Alphabet* (1592) translates 'Ne couppez pas ceste moustache' as '*Doe not cut that locke*' (148–9), suggesting that the term was still unfamiliar in English. Its moral implications are hinted at by Philip Stubbes: 'it is a world to consider, how their mow-chatowes must be preserued and laid out, from one cheke to another, yea, almost from one eare to another.' (*2 Anatomy*, sig. G8ᵛ). In both foreign and domestic contexts, the length of such hair was noteworthy: cf. *Jew of Malta*, 'a fellow met me with a mustachio like a raven's wing' (4.2.31–2), where length indicates villainy.
54 Identifying people by describing their clothing was the usual way of recognizing individuals when most only had one suit of clothes, and garments were not purchased ready-made.

42–3] *prose Oliphant; W&P lines* law / plate. /   44–6] *prose Oliphant*   51 down] downe *to* Q3

BRADSHAW

A watchet satin doublet all to-torn – 55
The inner side did bear the greater show –
A pair of threadbare velvet hose, seam-rent,
A worsted stocking rent above the shoe,
A livery cloak, but all the lace was off –
'Twas bad, but yet it served to hide the plate. 60

BLACK WILL Sirrah Shakebag, canst thou remember since
we trolled the bowl at Sittingbourne, where I broke the
tapster's head of the Lion with a cudgel-stick?

SHAKEBAG Ay, very well, Will.

BLACK WILL Why, it was with the money that the plate 65
was sold for. Sirrah Bradshaw, what wilt thou give
him that can tell thee who sold thy plate?

55 **watchet** light blue
doublet close-fitting upper-body garment for men; with hose, the usual masculine attire
56 i.e. the lining was more presentable than
the outside.
57 **velvet** an expensive fabric, here much
decayed (see also 1.321n.)
seam-rent falling apart at the seams
58 **worsted stocking** close-fitting garment
covering foot and leg, here made of a
woollen fabric of well-twisted yarn from
combed, long-staple wool
rent pulled apart
59 **livery cloak** cloak given to a servant of
an elite household as part of their wages,
marked in such a way that it identified
their master and therefore gave legiti-
macy to his servants, ensuring they were
not seen as 'masterless men'. It may,
then, have borne Cooke's armorial badge.
See also the *velvet hose* at 57, likely to
have been part of the outfit, and 1.29.
60 **bad** poorly made; perhaps also 'rotten'
61–6 **Sirrah . . . for** Wiggins has these lines as
an aside between Will and Shakebag, but

the villains' general brazen openness suggests that they are spoken in the hearing of
the other characters, and the circumstan-
tial detail gives (an ostensible) plausibility
to the (in other ways dubious, see 69n.)
identification Will offers Bradshaw.
62 **trolled the bowl** passed a drinking bowl
around the company, pledging one
another. For the social cohesion it induced,
see, e.g., Thomas Dekker's *Shoemaker's
Holiday*'s 'Second Three-Man's Song':
'Troll the bowl, the jolly nut-brown bowl,
/ And here, kind mate, to thee!' (p. 7).
Sittingbourne town around seven
miles outside Faversham, on the London
road
63 **tapster's** innkeeper's. The word originally applied to women (*OED* 1; see next
note).
Lion the Red Lion in Sittingbourne (just
outside Faversham) on the road to
London), an upmarket inn. In November
1531 Henry VIII's Privy Purse expenses
record his journey from Calais to
Greenwich, including '19th. To the wife
of the Lyon in Sittingbourne, 4*s.* 8*d.*'.

59 off] *(of)* 61–3 *Delius; Q1 lines* remember / Sittingburgh, / Lyon / sticke? / 62 Sittingbourne] *Q3*
*(*Sittingburne*)*; Sittingburgh *Q1*; Sittenbourn *SMS* 65–7] *Delius; Q1 lines* for: / him / plate? /

163

BRADSHAW   Who, I pray thee, good Will?

BLACK WILL   Why, 'twas one Jack Fitten. He's now in
Newgate for stealing a horse, and shall be arraigned   70
the next 'size.

BRADSHAW   Why then, let Lord Cheyne seek Jack Fitten
forth, for I'll back and tell him who robbed him of
his plate. This cheers my heart! Master Greene, I'll
leave you, for I must to the Isle of Sheppey with speed.   75
[*Then he hands over a letter.*]

GREENE   Before you go, let me entreat you to carry this
letter to Mistress Arden of Faversham, and humbly
recommend me to herself.

BRADSHAW
That will I, Master Greene, and so farewell.

---

69   **Jack Fitten** A fitten is a lie or an invention (*OED n.*), suggesting that this man
is a figment of Will's imagination.
Spelled 'Fitton' it was also a surname,
although not a very common one (TNA
Discovery gives 129 sixteenth-century
instances). Either Will is playing a trick
on Bradshaw, or they are both sharing
the joke on Cheyne. Wiggins's casting
of the exchange between Will and
Shakebag (60–4) as asides would
underscore the former reading, by suggesting that they profited from the sale
of the plate because they themselves
stole it.

70   **Newgate** a London prison, just inside the
city wall
arraigned called to answer, indicted.
The punishment for stealing a horse was
death.

72–3 **seek . . . forth** seek . . . out (*OED* forth
adv. 3b)

75   **Isle of Sheppey** i.e. Cheyne's house at

Shurland, to which Arden and Franklin
travel in Sc. 12; Henry VIII and Anne
Boleyn stayed at the house for two days
in 1532. Sheppey is in the Thames
estuary, just off the Kent coast north of
Faversham.

75 SD This letter presents a problem in the
plot and, more locally, for performance.
It appears here that Greene is letting
Alice know that he has found the right
men for the job (Holinshed has, 'We
haue got a man for our purpose, we maie
thanke my brother Bradshaw'; see
below, p. 293). If so, he might write it
quickly, while Bradshaw discusses the
plate, perhaps leaning on another character's back. When it is read by Alice in Sc.
8, however, the letter gives information
that could not have been known at this
point in the action.

78   **recommend . . . herself** commend me to
her remembrance or regard; convey my
regards to her. A very formal phrase.

69–71] *Delius; Q1 lines* Fitten, / horse, / sise. /   72–5] *Wiggins; Q1 lines* forth / plate, / you, / speede, /   75
SD] *Wine (Oliphant subst.)*   76–8] *Oliphant; Q1 lines* you / Feuershame, / selfe. /

Here, Will, there's a crown for thy good news.   80
[*Then he gives him the coin.*]   *Exit.*

BLACK WILL   Farewell Bradshaw. I'll drink no water, for
thy sake, whilst this lasts. Now, gentleman, shall we
have your company to London?

GREENE

Nay, stay, sirs:
A little more I needs must use your help,   85
And in a matter of great consequence
Wherein, if you'll be secret and profound,
I'll give you twenty angels for your pains.

BLACK WILL   How? Twenty angels? Give my fellow George
Shakebag and me twenty angels? And if thou'lt have   90
thy own father slain that thou mayst inherit his land,
we'll kill him.

SHAKEBAG   Ay, thy mother, thy sister, thy brother, or all
thy kin.

GREENE

Well, this it is: Arden of Faversham   95

---

80   **there's a crown** a further suggestion of
the ambiguity of Bradshaw and Will's
relationship, as this type of tip expresses
Will's lower standing; see Cesario's
response to Olivia's offer of coins to take
her message to Orsino, 'I am no fee'd
post, lady; keep your purse' (*TN*, 1.5.276).
80   SD2 See 1.130 SDn. for the timing of
exits in the play.
81   **drink no water** as he can now afford
alcohol
83   **company to London** Travellers over
Rainham Down often went in groups,
partly for companionship and partly as it

was known to be dangerously open
ground. Holinshed gives a sense of its
busy traffic when he states that Bradshaw
accompanied Greene because he had
money to transport, and that they met
both servingmen coming down from
Leeds (in Kent) and Will, 'comming vp
the hill from Rochester' (see below,
p. 292).
87   **profound** able to conceal things deeply
88   **angels** English gold coins worth 10s
(half a pound), featuring the archangel
Michael slaying the dragon. See 1.521n.
91   **that** in order that

80 SD1] *this edn* (*Wiggins subst.*)   SD2] (*Exit Bradshaw*); *after* lasts *82 Hugo*   81–3] *Delius; Q1 lines*
Bradshaw, / lasts: / London. /   84–5] *W&P; one line Q1*   89–92] *Delius; Q1 lines* fellow / Angels, /
slaine, / him. /   93–4] *Delius; one line Q1*

Hath highly wronged me about the Abbey land,
That no revenge but death will serve the turn.
Will you two kill him, here's the angels down,
And I will lay the platform of his death.

BLACK WILL　　Plat me no platforms! Give me the money, 100
and I'll stab him as he stands pissing against a wall,
but I'll kill him.

SHAKEBAG　　Where is he?

GREENE　　He is now at London, in Aldersgate Street.

SHAKEBAG　　He's dead, as if he had been condemned by 105
an Act of Parliament, if once Black Will and I swear
his death.

GREENE　　Here is ten pound [*giving them Alice's purse
of money*]; and when he is dead ye shall have twenty
more.　　　　　　　　　　　　　　　　　　　　110

96　**wronged** Two syllables makes the line a
regular hexameter; alternatively elision
of 'me' and ''bout' allows a pentameter.

97　**serve the turn** be appropriate, do

98　**down** on the spot, up front (*OED adv.*
7a)

99　**lay ... of** devise the plan for; *platform*
could mean 'foundation', 'diagram' or
'strategy' (*OED n.* 3a; *n.* 12; *n.* 14a).
Several contemporary meanings of the
word relate to military activity.

100　**Plat** partly said for the point made by
repetition with *platform* (compare the
jokingly formulaic 'Grace me no grace,
nor uncle me no uncle', *R2*, 2.3.87), but
plat means 'plan, sketch out'. It therefore
represents the abstract, schematic version of an action.

101–2　**I'll ... him** i.e. even if I have to stab
him in that way, I will do it (conditional
use of *but* introducing a threat (*OED*
8b(c)))

101　**pissing ... wall** a dishonourable, unsol-
dierly way to kill a man as he has no
means of defence; a spontaneous, unpre-
meditated action as opposed to the plat-
ting of platforms

104　**Aldersgate Street** upmarket residential
area running from Aldersgate in the city
wall to Cheapside, the main shopping
district; home to many gentry and members of the aristocracy at the time this
play was put on including – as suggestive of the social and cultural context the
playwright's inclusion of the street name
sets up for Arden and Franklin – the first
recorded purchaser of Shakespeare's
Venus and Adonis, Richard Stonley.
Holinshed has Arden lodging in 'a
certeine parsonage which he held in
London' (see below, p. 294).

106　**Act of Parliament** law or statute, and so
executive order. This is one of several
instances of the 'ruffians' elevating their
schemes by speaking about them as legitimate legal business; see also 112–15.

100–2] *Delius;* Plat ... money *verse,* And ... him. *prose Q1*　105–7] *Delius; Q1 lines* condemned / I /
death, /　108–10] *BH&N; Q1 lines* dead, / more. /　108 SD] *this edn (B&T subst.)*

BLACK WILL   My fingers itch to be at the peasant. Ah, that I might be set awork thus through the year, and that murder would grow to an occupation! That a man might, without danger of law – Zounds, I warrant I should be Warden of the Company! Come, let us 115 be going, and we'll bait at Rochester, where I'll give thee a gallon of sack to handsel the match withal.   *Exeunt.*

---

111 ***fingers itch** denotes a craving to (usually violent) action. Q1 has 'fingers itches' but EEBO-TCP, in 89 hits for 'finger itch' including variant forms 1570–1642, gives 84 instances of the plural 'fingers' and only four 'itches' (of which only one other is 'fingers itches' (a 1624 ballad)). The Q3 verb is therefore adopted here.

113 **grow to** become

114 **might, without** B&T (*CRE*) has 'might [worke] without', arguing that there is 'little dramatic point' reading Will's *Zounds* as 'self-interruption' (the editors posit a faulty copyist who skips over one *w* to the next). The point seems, however, to be Will's visionary movement into a fantasy about his own status, where his mind travels faster than his words and arrives at an elevated position for him before the first thought about what might be done 'without danger of law' is ended.

Zounds a strong oath: contraction of 'God's wounds'

115 **Warden ... Company** Will imagines a Company of Murderers, with 'murderer' as a legitimate occupation. Wardens were members of the governing bodies of the guilds or companies that organized labour and controlled the quality of products in early modern towns, most prominently the livery companies of London; they were often extremely wealthy and influential men.

116 **bait** stop at an inn for refreshment whilst travelling

Rochester cathedral town *c.* 23 miles from Faversham, on the banks of the Medway, where travellers could cross the river on an important bridge whose management was established by royal patent in 1399

117 **sack** Spanish wine

handsel seal a bargain or contract

111–18] *Delius; Q1 lines* pesant, / yeere, / occupation: / law, / company, / Rochester, / Sack, / all. /   111 itch] *Q3;* itches *Q1*   114 might, without] might [follow it] without *Hopkinson²;* might [worke] without *B&T (CRE)*

[Sc. 3]   *Here enters* MICHAEL *[with a letter]*.

MICHAEL   I have gotten such a letter as will touch the
painter, and thus it is:

Here enters ARDEN *and* FRANKLIN, *and hears*
Michael read this letter.

My duty remembered, Mistress Susan, hoping in God
you be in good health as I, Michael, was at the making
hereof. This is to certify you that, as the turtle true,   5
when she hath lost her mate, sitteth alone, so I,
mourning for your absence, do walk up and down

Sc. 3 The implied location of the scene is Paul's Yard, the area around St Paul's Cathedral. One of the busiest parts of London, it was filled with booksellers and other vendors, their customers, and those passing through this central space on their way south to the river Thames, north to Aldersgate Street, east to Cheapside and west along Fleet Street to Westminster. See Map of Early Modern London (https://mapoflondon.uvic.ca/). It is represented by the passage of actors across the stage and the apprentice's stall (51).

0 SD *with a letter* The prop letter may have been folded to suggest its amorous contents: often repeatedly folded, with the ends tied with coloured ribbon, love-letters were small enough to hide in the palm of the hand or up a sleeve, thereby intimately engaging an audience by sharing their unwrapping when they were displayed and producing potential humour in the folding and unfolding.

1   gotten . . . letter As he promised in Sc. 1

(154–7), Michael has found someone to write his letter for him.

touch produce an effect on (*OED v.* 16b) or strong emotion in (*OED v.* 28b); move. Although it is addressed to Susan, Michael sees the letter's effect as being on Clarke.

3–17 Editors have seen links between the letter and Euphuism, the elaborate prose style of John Lyly, with its balanced syntax and analogies with classical mythology and natural history. Contemporary letter-writing manuals, however, contain examples of all these features; see e.g. Angel Day, who gives over the last *c.* 20 pages of his 1586 *English Secretary* to love-letter outlines.

5   *turtle* dove whose legendary faithfulness to its mate appeared in contemporary poetry; see, e.g., Robert Chester and William Shakespeare, *Love's Martyr*, 'Let the bird of loudest lay' (*Poems*). The phrase is proverbial: 'As true as a turtle to her mate', Dent, T624.

Sc. 3] Hugo; ACT II. SCENE III. *Tyrrell;* ACT II. SCENE II *Delius*   **0 SD** *with a letter B&T (Wiggins subst.)*   1–2] *Delius; Q1 lines* letter, / is. / ; *W&P lines* Painter: / is: /

Paul's, till one day I fell asleep and lost my master's
pantofles. Ah, Mistress Susan, abolish that paltry
painter, cut him off by the shins with a frowning look   10
of your crabbed countenance, and think upon Michael
who, drunk with the dregs of your favour, will cleave
as fast to your love as a plaster of pitch to a galled
horseback. Thus hoping you will let my passions
penetrate, or rather impetrate, mercy of your meek   15
hands, I end.

               Yours, Michael, or else not Michael

ARDEN [*coming forward*]
  Why, you paltry knave!
  Stand you here loitering, knowing my affairs –
  What haste my business craves to send to Kent?   20

8   *Paul's* The central aisle of St Paul's Cathedral, known as Paul's Walk, was frequented by merchants and the professions for business, by the gentry, gallants and courtiers to show off new fashions, and by the news hunters and pickpockets who followed them. It is staged in Ben Jonson's *Every Man Out of His Humour* (1599) and written about by Dekker in his *Gull's Horn-book* (1609).

9   *pantofles* high shoes that elevated walkers above the dirt of the street. Increasingly richly decorated, they drew the wrath of Stubbes: 'handsome how should they be, when as with their flipping & flapping vp and down in yᵉ dirte they exaggerate a mountain of mire' (*Anatomy*, sig. E4ᵛ). The detail shows Arden's status, and its inclusion indicates Michael's inability to judge what is pertinent to a love-letter.
   paltry worthless, contemptible or base

10 *cut ... shins* don't leave him a leg to stand on, undermine him (*OED* shins 2b)

11 *crabbed* bad-tempered, irritable and churlish; another example of Michael's misjudged letter-writing

12 *cleave* stick

13–14 *plaster ... horseback* cure for a galled, or chafed, sore back. Recommended by Leonard Mascall for gored cattle amongst other ailments (47), the very painful separation that would be necessitated therefore proves Michael's steadfastness.

15 *impetrate* obtain by request or entreaty (*OED*). Through malapropism the letter slips from sex ('*penetrate*') to this semi-spiritual request for mercy.

17 i.e. unless I am yours I am not myself.

20 **haste ... Kent** (knowing) the speed my affairs demand in order to send word to Kent. The word or message is implied, as in Kyd's *Spanish Tragedy* (1588), 'I'll send to him to meet / The Prince and me' (3.2.88–9) (*OED* send *v.* 6c).

18 SD] *Tyrrell*

FRANKLIN

Faith, friend Michael, this is very ill,
Knowing your master hath no more but you;
And do ye slack his business for your own?

ARDEN

Where is the letter, sirrah? Let me see it.
Then [Michael] gives him the letter.
See, Master Franklin, here's proper stuff: 25
Susan my maid, the painter and my man,
A crew of harlots, all in love, forsooth.
[*to Michael*] Sirrah, let me hear no more of this!
Now, for thy life, once write to her a word –

Here enters GREENE, [BLACK] WILL *and* SHAKEBAG.

Wilt thou be married to so base a trull?   30
'Tis Mosby's sister! Come I once at home,
I'll rouse her from remaining in my house.
Now, Master Franklin, let us go walk in Paul's.
Come, but a turn or two, and then away.
                    Exeunt [Arden, Franklin and Michael].

22 **your ... you** i.e. you're his only servant.
23 **slack** neglect, delay
27 **harlots** rogues or vagabonds of either
     gender, with suggestion of immorality,
     sexual and otherwise
29 The Q1 reading gives Arden a sentence
     which he must break off in frustration
     with his next thought of being married to
     a trull; B&T (*CRE*) emends to SMS's
     'Nor', arguing for a minim misreading,
     which makes the two lines a coherent
     thought but loses the passion of Arden's
     thoughts about another potentially adul-
     terous marriage. The erratic nature of his
     thought-pattern here is picked up again
     at the start of Sc. 6.
     for thy life on pain of death

29 SD B&T points out the threatening environ-
     ment produced by the multiple overhearing
     in this scene, as Greene, Will and Shakebag
     enter behind Arden and Franklin, who had
     previously been overhearing Michael.
30 **trull** prostitute
31–2 **Come ... house** 'As soon as I get
     home I'll throw her out.'
32 **rouse her from** startle her from her state
     of comfort (*OED* rouse $v.^1$ 4c). *OED*
     gives the first use in this sense as 1583,
     although Holinshed uses it in a related
     way in his 1577 *Chronicles*: 'from the
     conquest to this day, the Irish enemy
     could never rouse them from thence'
     (*Description of Ireland*, sig. A2^v).
34 **turn** short walk in a confined space

24 SD Michael] *Sturgess (Hugo subst.)*   28 SD] *Wiggins*   29 Now] Nor *SMS*   34 SD *Arden ... Michael*]
Oliphant

GREENE

  The first is Arden, and that's his man; 35
  The other is Franklin, Arden's dearest friend.

BLACK WILL Zounds, I'll kill them all three.

GREENE

  Nay, sirs, touch not his man in any case;
  But stand close, and take you fittest standing,
  And at his coming forth speed him. 40
  To the Nag's Head – [*aside*] there is this coward's
    haunt –
  But now I'll leave you till the deed be done. *Exit.*

SHAKEBAG If he be not paid his own, ne'er trust
  Shakebag.

BLACK WILL Sirrah Shakebag, at his coming forth I'll 45

37–8 Holinshed reports that 'Gréene shewed blacke Will maister Arden walking in Poules. Then said blacke Will, What is he that goeth after him? Marie said Gréen, one of his men. By his bloud (said blacke Will) I will kill them both. Naie (said Greene) doo not so, for he is of counsell with vs in this matter' (see below, p. 293). The playwright has added Franklin to this scenario.

38 **in any case** on any account

39 **fittest standing** the best position. The term *standing* suggests both the place where a hunter stands to shoot at game and a stall from which to serve customers, such as the one staged in this scene (*OED* standing 4c, 5).

40 **speed** i.e. kill

41–2 B&T (*CRE*)'s argument for the transposition of these lines makes the sense more obvious in modern terms, as Greene first says he will leave and then

states his destination – to wait for them at the tavern rather than stay to see Arden killed in Paul's Yard. However, 'but now' carried the sense of 'just now, only this moment' (*OED* but *P4*), which makes the import clearer and allows the lines dynamically to signal Greene's nervous speed.

41 **Nag's Head** tavern on the corner where Friday Street met Cheapside at the Cross, two roads east of St Paul's Cathedral

this coward's meaning (and perhaps gesturing towards) himself

43 **paid his own** given his dues or just deserts

45 **coming forth** from St Paul's. See 8n. Francis Osborne, writing in the seventeenth century, describes men walking 'after dinner from three to six, during which times some discoursed on business, others of news' (209).

41–2] *B&T transposes these lines* 41 SD] *this edn* 42 SD] *(Exit Greene); after 44 Oliphant* 45–7] *Delius; Q1 lines* foorth / blackfreers, / way. /

run him through; and then to the Blackfriars, and there take water and away.

SHAKEBAG
Why that's the best; but see thou miss him not.

BLACK WILL   How can I miss him when I think on the forty angels I must have more?   50

Here enters a PRENTICE.

PRENTICE   'Tis very late; I were best shut up my stall, for here will be old filching when the press comes forth of Paul's.

Then lets he down his window, and it breaks
Black Will's head.

---

46   **Blackfriars** district south-west of St Paul's, on the north bank of the Thames. It provided both a place of sanctuary, due to its status as a previously monastic liberty, and a convenient exit to the river. For later audiences it also had theatrical associations: in addition to housing the Royal Wardrobe from which costumes were borrowed, drama was staged there, first in a smaller space where plays by boy actors were put on (1576–84), and from 1599 in a new space, which became the indoor home of the King's Men from 1609.

47   **take water** take a boat across the Thames

51   **stall** standing (see 39n.); table in front of a shop on which goods are offered for sale (*OED* 6a). Pairs of shutters, hinged at the top and bottom of a window, opened outwards, the lower of them supported on two legs to form a counter, and met in the middle horizontally when closed, thereby sealing the merchandise inside. The killers are waiting in Paul's

Yard (see Sc. 3n.). Edward White, on the play's Q1 title-page, describes his shop as 'at the lyttle North dore of Paules Church at the signe of the Gun', in other words fronting onto Paul's Alley, a public thoroughfare which ran right through Old St Paul's from south to north (Raven).

52   **old filching** recurrent stealing. The apprentice is protecting his master's property.
press crowd. Suggests that a service is ending, although see also 45n.

53.1 *window* i.e. upper shutter (see 51n.). B&T proposes a stall on wheels (necessitating a considerable investment in a fairly particular type of property). Wine points out 'i wooden canepie' in Henslowe's inventory (Foakes, 319), although this is more likely to represent a royal 'state' covering a throne. A board set up over the discovery space, perhaps with a less specific table with merchandise underneath, may have been used.

49–50] *Delius; Q1 lines* fortye / more. /   51–3] *Delius; Q1 lines* stall, / foorth / Paules. / ; *BH&N lines* stall, / press / Paul's. /

BLACK WILL   Zounds, draw, Shakebag, draw, I am almost
killed!   55

> [*Then Black Will and Shakebag draw
> their swords, and the press comes forth
> and passes over the stage.*]

PRENTICE   We'll tame you, I warrant.

BLACK WILL   Zounds, I am tame enough already.

Here enters ARDEN, FRANKLIN *and* MICHAEL.

ARDEN
What troublesome fray or mutiny is this?

FRANKLIN
'Tis nothing but some brabbling, paltry fray,
Devised to pick men's pockets in the throng.   60

ARDEN
Is't nothing else? Come, Franklin, let us away.
                    Exeunt [Arden, Franklin and Michael].

BLACK WILL
What 'mends shall I have for my broken head?

55.3 'Pass over the stage' commonly signifies
entry at one door and exit through the
other. See Dessen and Thomson, 158–9.

56   **We'll** As Wiggins points out, the word
indicates additional actors (B&T suggests they enter through central doors,
although this would mean the stall could
not be sited in the discovery space), and
Franklin describes a *throng* at 60. Such
an entry would signal disorder to an
urban audience particularly sensitive to
crowds (hence Arden's *mutiny*, 58). The
threatening presence of apprentices, who
traditionally rioted on Shrove Tuesday,
was increasing at the end of the sixteenth
century, and they were said to muster
thousand-strong bands in the city.

tame This, with Will's use of the word in
his reply in the following line, plays on
the meanings 'subdue' (*OED v.* 1) and
'pierce or cut into' (*OED v.* 2).

58   **fray** brawl, disturbance

60   **throng** Holinshed says that 'blacke
Will thought to haue killed maister
Arden in Poules churchyard, but
there were so manie gentlemen that
accompanied him to dinner, that he
missed of his purpose' (see below,
p. 293). The play isolates Arden and
Franklin against the crowd, rather than
offering gentlemen-diners, but retains
the sense that he is protected by his
habits of sociability.

62   **'mends** amends

55 SD] *this edn (B&T subst.)*   61 SD *Arden . . . Michael*] *Oliphant*

PRENTICE   Marry, this 'mends: that if you get you not
away all the sooner, you shall be well beaten and sent
to the Counter.   *Exit.*

BLACK WILL   Well, I'll be gone; but look to your signs,   66
for I'll pull them down all. Shakebag, my broken head
grieves me not so much as by this means Arden hath
escaped.

Here enters GREENE.

I had a glimpse of him and his companion.   70

GREENE   Why, sirs, Arden's as well as I. I met him and
Franklin going merrily to the ordinary. What, dare
you not do it?

BLACK WILL   Yes, sir, we dare do it; but, were my consent
to give again, we would not do it under ten pound   75
more. I value every drop of my blood at a French
crown. I have had ten pound to steal a dog, and we
have no more here to kill a man. But that a bargain is
a bargain, and so forth, you should do it yourself.

GREENE   I pray thee, how came thy head broke?   80

---

65   **Counter** small prison attached to a may-
or's court. There was one in Wood Street
from 1556, opposite Friday Street at
Cheapside Cross, and one in the Poultry
at the eastern end of Cheapside.

65 SD   Retaining the earlier Q1 position for
the exit, rather than its common editorial
position, means that Will's next sentence
(*Well . . . all*) is spoken to the back of the
departing Prentice, on a stage left empty
except for Will and Shakebag, conveying
a sense of the emptiness of Will's threats
and the deflation of his usual aggressive
confidence, either through pain or

because he realizes that the job will not
be straightforward.

66   **signs** shop signs. Pulling them down
would create social confusion, akin to
changing the direction of road signs, as
they were used as aids to navigation in
the city.

68   **as** as that

72   **ordinary** inn where meals were provided at a fixed price

76–7   **French crown** English name for *écu*,
worth 4s

79   **and so forth** 'you know how the saying
goes . . .'

63–5] *Q2; Q1 lines* away / counter. /   65 SD] *(Exit Prentice); after 69 Hugo*   66–70] *Delius; Q1 lines*
signes, / all. / much, / escaped. / *[SD]* / companion. /   69 SD] *after 70 Oliphant*   69–70 I had . . . GREENE
Why] GREENE I had . . . Why *Jacob*   71–3] *Delius; Q1 lines* as I, / ordinary, / it? / ; / *W&P lines* met /
ordinary. / it? /   74–9] *Delius; Q1 lines* againe, / more. / Crowne. / dogge, / man, / foorth, / selfe. /

BLACK WILL   Why, thou seest it is broke, dost thou not?

SHAKEBAG   Standing against a stall, watching Arden's
coming, a boy let down his shop window and broke
his head; whereupon arose a brawl, and in the tumult
Arden escaped us, and passed by unthought on. But   85
forbearance is no acquittance; another time we'll do
it, I warrant thee.

GREENE

I pray thee, Will, make clean thy bloody brow,
And let us bethink us on some other place
Where Arden may be met with handsomely.   90
Remember how devoutly thou hast sworn
To kill the villain; think upon thine oath.

BLACK WILL

Tush, I have broken five hundred oaths!
But, wouldst thou charm me to effect this deed,
Tell me of gold, my resolution's fee;   95
Say thou seest Mosby kneeling at my knees,

---

85   **unthought on** not thought of, and therefore unnoticed

86   **forbearance ... acquittance** 'putting
up with it doesn't make amends'; proverbial, Dent, F584

90   **handsomely** skilfully or cleverly (*OED*
2); but also 'readily' (*OED* 4)

91   **devoutly** ironically referring to a religious oath, as Will's mind has mainly
been on the money; it suggests a later
meaning, 'earnestly', the first instance of
which is given in *OED* as Hamlet's ' 'tis
a consummation / Devoutly to be
wished' (1604, 3.1.62–3).

94   **charm** bewitch, enchant

95   **resolution's fee** payment for my determination

96   **kneeling ... knees** another of Will's fan-

tasies of power and deference; see also
2.23–6, 105–6. The phrase is unusual, and
B&T (*CRE*) emends to 'kneeling at my
feet' following SMS, arguing contamina-
tion and a lack of contemporary parallels.
In support of the Q1 reading, however,
also common was the idea of falling on
one's knees before royalty (temporal and
divine) as a display of subjection (see,
e.g., the 1581 translation of Seneca, 'Why
liest thou prostrate at my knees?' (*Seneca*,
sig. G7^r), 'layde humbly at thy Knees'
(sig. K2^v), 'at thy knees I fal' (sig. Q1^r)),
so it is possible that *kneeling* is in error,
rather than *knees*. The phrase as it stands
is sensitive to the mental image of the
relative proximity of the kneeler, whose
head would be level with Will's knees.

82–7] *W&P; Q1 lines* coming, / head. / tumult / on. / acquittance, / thee. /   96 knees] feet *SMS*

Offering me service for my high attempt;
And sweet Alice Arden, with a lap of crowns,
Comes with a lowly curtsy to the earth,
Saying, 'Take this but for thy quarterage;   100
Such yearly tribute will I answer thee.'
Why, this would steel soft-metalled cowardice,
With which Black Will was never tainted with.
I tell thee, Greene, the forlorn traveller,
Whose lips are glued with summer's parching heat,   105
Ne'er longed so much to see a running brook
As I to finish Arden's tragedy.
Seest thou this gore that cleaveth to my face?
From hence ne'er will I wash this bloody stain
Till Arden's heart be panting in my hand.   110

GREENE

Why, that's well said; but what sayeth Shakebag?

97 **high** superior, honourable; contrasted with the lowness of Mosby's kneeling
98 **lap of crowns** skirt full of money; with sexual overtones
99 **curtsy** The word signifies his desire for authority; see also 2.24.
100 **quarterage** money paid every quarter of the year, often as wages or allowance. The full *lap* of 98 is therefore only a quarter of the *yearly tribute* of the next line.
101 **answer** satisfy, fulfil a wish (with a sexual suggestion)
102 **steel** point or edge a soft metal with steel, as in an arrowhead, and therefore harden it (*OED* 1), and, figuratively, strengthen or fortify like steel (*OED* 2a). See *VA*, 374–5, '"Give me my heart . . . O, give it me, lest thy hard heart do steel it"'.

soft-metalled Two readings of Q1's 'metled' are possible: either 'mettled', meaning having a particular (in this case gentle) temperament, or 'metalled', meaning made of or containing metal (*OED adj*. 1a). *OED* metal *v*. 1 suggests slippage between the two spellings in the period, and a word-play is in any case clearly intended. In the context of *steel*, this spelling more obviously connects the phrase (unique in EEBO-TCP) to the military language developing at the time (see e.g. William Bourne, *The Art of Shooting in Great Ordnance* (1587), 'For to knowe whether that any peece of Ordnaunce bee sufficiently metalled to beare her charge with Pouder' (62).
110 **panting** violent throbbing of the heart (*OED* 2)

102 soft-metalled] *(*soft metled*);* soft melted *Q2;* soft-mettled *Tyrrell*

SHAKEBAG

    I cannot paint my valour out with words;
    But, give me place and opportunity,
    Such mercy as the starven lioness,
    When she is dry-sucked of her eager young,   115
    Shows to the prey that next encounters her,
    On Arden so much pity would I take.

GREENE

    So should it fare with men of firm resolve.
    And now, sirs, seeing this accident
    Of meeting him in Paul's hath no success,   120
    Let us bethink us on some other place
    Whose earth may swallow up this Arden's blood.

Here enters MICHAEL.

    See, yonder comes his man. And wot you what,
    The foolish knave is in love with Mosby's sister;
    And for her sake, whose love he cannot get   125
    Unless Mosby solicit his suit,
    The villain hath sworn the slaughter of his master.
    We'll question him, for he may stead us much.
    How now, Michael, whither are you going?

MICHAEL

    My master hath new supped,   130
    And I am going to prepare his chamber.

GREENE   Where supped Master Arden?

---

112 **paint ... words** express or display my courage in words. For figurative use see, e.g., George Puttenham, *Art of English Poesie* (1589), 1.15.27, 'their miserable ends painted out in playes and pageants, to shew the mutability of fortune'.

115 **dry-sucked** sucked until she has no milk left to give her young (and so is desperate)
119 **accident** incident, event
123 **wot** know
126 **solicit his suit** urge or plead his petition
128 **stead** help, profit

122 SD] *after 129 Tyrrell*

MICHAEL   At the Nag's Head, at the eighteenpence
ordinary. How now, Master Shakebag; what, Black
Will! God's dear Lady, how chance your face is so   135
bloody?

BLACK WILL   Go to, sirrah! There is a chance in it. This
sauciness in you will make you be knocked.

MICHAEL
Nay, an you be offended I'll be gone.

GREENE
Stay, Michael, you may not scape us so.   140
Michael, I know you love your master well.

MICHAEL
Why, so I do, but wherefore urge you that?

GREENE
Because I think you love your mistress better.

[MICHAEL]
So think not I. But say, i'faith, what if I should?

SHAKEBAG [*to Greene*]
Come to the purpose! Michael, we hear   145

133–4 **eighteenpence ordinary** room with
an 18d set menu in the Nag's Head. The
prices went as low as 6d, so the detail
shows Arden's status.
135 **God's dear Lady** by the Virgin Mary (an
oath)
   chance come
137 **There . . . it** It was chance, i.e. bad luck.
138 **sauciness** insolent presumption. Will
feels Michael's directness is inappropriate, coming from a servant.
   knocked Perhaps more than simply
'beaten', as being knocked on the head
meant being put to death, in the way
cattle were killed (*OED v.* 3a); a third of
EEBO-TCP uses of the word to 1600
carry this meaning.
142 **wherefore . . . that** 'why do you bring
that up'
'143–4 Greene's statement causes resent-

ment, because Michael takes him to
mean that he (Michael) has romantic or
sexual feelings for Alice.
145 **Come . . . purpose** The first of two
attempts by Will and Shakebag to alter the
course of the interrogation of Michael.
Here, Shakebag indicates that Greene is
proceeding too circuitously and making
no headway; see also 147 and 158. Q1
gives no punctuation for the line, and
other editors have attached the vocative to
the following sentence (e.g. Wine, 'Come
to the purpose, Michael. We hear . . . ').
B&T (*CRE*) offers structural support to
the present reading, arguing that 'the line
is metrically more regular, and more characteristic of the blank verse of the 1580s
and early 1590s, if the caesura comes after
"purpose": the caesura is the preferred
location for mid-line syllabic variation'.

133–6] *Bayne; Q1 lines* ordinarye, / Wil, / bloody? /   137–8] *Bayne; Q1 lines* it. / knockt. /   144 SP] *Q2;*
not in Q1   145 SD] *this edn*

You have a pretty love in Faversham.

MICHAEL

Why, have I two or three; what's that to thee?

BLACK WILL [*to Shakebag*]

You deal too mildly with the peasant!

[*to Michael*]   Thus it is:

'Tis known to us you love Mosby's sister;

We know besides that you have ta'en your oath   150

To further Mosby to your mistress' bed,

And kill your master for his sister's sake.

Now, sir, a poorer coward than yourself

Was never fostered in the coast of Kent.

How comes it, then, that such a knave as you   155

Dare swear a matter of such consequence?

GREENE   Ah, Will.

BLACK WILL

Tush, give me leave, there's no more but this:

Sith thou hast sworn, we dare discover all.

And hadst thou or shouldst thou utter it,   160

We have devised a complot under hand,

Whatever shall betide to any of us,

To send thee roundly to the devil of hell.

And therefore thus: I am the very man,

Marked in my birth-hour by the Destinies,   165

To give an end to Arden's life on earth;

---

151 **further** assist or promote
154 **fostered** nourished, brought up
157 In contrast to Greene's own subtle approach, Will's direct questioning, giving away all their confidential information, provokes this resigned or exasperated interjection.
159 **Sith** since

161 **complot under hand** scheme or conspiracy which is both stealthy (as in 'underhand') and in hand, or under way
162 **betide** happen
165 **Destinies** classical beings who presided over life and determined its direction and duration, ensuring that fate took its course

148 SD1] *this edn (Oliphant subst.)*   SD2] *Wiggins*   161 complot] *(complat)*

Thou but a member, but to whet the knife
Whose edge must search the closet of his breast.
Thy office is but to appoint the place
And train thy master to his tragedy;   170
Mine to perform it when occasion serves.
Then be not nice, but here devise with us
How and what way we may conclude his death.

SHAKEBAG

So shalt thou purchase Mosby for thy friend,
And by his friendship gain his sister's love.   175

GREENE

So shall thy mistress be thy favourer,
And thou disburdened of the oath thou made.

MICHAEL

Well, gentlemen, I cannot but confess,
Sith you have urged me so apparently,
That I have vowed my master Arden's death;   180
And he whose kindly love and liberal hand
Doth challenge naught but good deserts of me
I will deliver over to your hands.
This night, come to his house at Aldersgate;
The doors I'll leave unlocked against you come.   185
No sooner shall ye enter through the latch,

---

167 **member** limb; lesser part of the plan
167–8 **whet . . . breast** This intimate language
may indicate that Will performs threatening stage business with his weapon.
168 **closet . . . breast** Breasts were often
compared to closets, as intimate places
for the storage of secrets and knowledge
(see, e.g., John Foxe, *Christ Jesus
Triumphant* (1579), 'what is done
inwardly in his owne secret closet of his
brest, & hart' (sig. E1)); here viscerally
imagined as searched by the knife-blade
for Arden's heart.

170 **train** lure or entice
172 **nice** cowardly and unmanly (*OED* 4a);
scrupulous, punctilious (*OED* 3a)
179 **apparently** clearly, openly
182 **challenge** lay claim to, demand
184 **Aldersgate** See 2.104 and n.
185 A servant's most important task at night
was to ensure that the house was secure,
so this is a shocking offer.
against in anticipation of when, in time
for when
186 **latch** fastening for door or gate, here
standing for the gate itself

Over the threshold to the inner court,
But on your left hand shall you see the stairs
That leads directly to my master's chamber.
There take him, and dispose him as ye please.   190
Now it were good we parted company.
What I have promised, I will perform.

BLACK WILL

Should you deceive us, 'twould go wrong with you.

MICHAEL

I will accomplish all I have revealed.

BLACK WILL   Come, let's go drink – choler makes me as   195
dry as a dog.   *Exeunt [Black] Will, Greene and*
Shakebag. Michael remains.

MICHAEL

Thus feeds the lamb securely on the down,
Whilst through the thicket of an arbour brake
The hunger-bitten wolf o'erpries his haunt,
And takes advantage to eat him up.   200
Ah, harmless Arden, how, how hast thou misdone,
That thus thy gentle life is levelled at?

---

187 **inner court** Large urban houses were built around a courtyard that sat behind the main street gate and from which the various ranges of rooms could be accessed, making the street doors the main point of protection after dark. Arden's own house in Faversham was such a property, although the entrance range no longer survives, as was Shakespeare's New Place in Stratford.

188–9 **stairs ... chamber** Ralph Treswell's *London Surveys* provides examples of stairs leading directly off inner courts, which would suggest that the sense of threat an audience felt would come partly from the realism of the description.

190 **dispose** do with, dispose of
194 **revealed** declared publicly
195 **choler** anger
197 **securely** with (false) freedom from care
    down elevated, open land
198 **thicket ... arbour brake** All three words mean dense vegetation, behind which the *wolf* (199) could watch unseen.
199 **o'erpries his haunt** surveys (literally 'overlooks') his usual feeding place
201 **misdone** done wrong or harmed (anyone)
202 **levelled at** aimed at

The many good turns that thou hast done to me,
Now must I quittance with betraying thee.
I, that should take the weapon in my hand   205
And buckler thee from ill-intending foes,
Do lead thee with a wicked, fraudful smile,
As unsuspected, to the slaughterhouse.
So have I sworn to Mosby and my mistress;
So have I promised to the slaughtermen.   210
And should I not deal currently with them,
Their lawless rage would take revenge on me.
Tush, I will spurn at mercy for this once.
Let pity lodge where feeble women lie.
I am resolved, and Arden needs must die.   *Exit.*   215

[Sc. 4]   *Here enters* ARDEN *and* FRANKLIN.

ARDEN

No, Franklin, no – if fear or stormy threats,
If love of me or care of womanhood,
If fear of God, or common speech of men
(Who mangle credit with their wounding words

---

204 **quittance** repay
206 **buckler** protect, like the shield so
named; defend, ironically like the shield
Holinshed states that Black Will carries
(see below, p. 292).
208 **As unsuspected** not regarded with suspicion
211 **deal currently** do business obligingly and
honestly. 'Currently' means 'smoothly' or
'readily', like a flowing stream's current
(*OED adv.* 1), but 'current' also means
'genuine' coinage, as opposed to counterfeit money (*OED current adv.* 5).
213 **spurn at** kick against
Sc. 4 The scene is set at Franklin's London
home, the stage doors being used by all

three characters to represent entry into its
farther reaches. The unspecified space
that the stage represents could be imagined as either indoors (the characters
leaving to go to bedchambers) or outside
in its courtyard (the characters leaving to
go inside).
0 SD Arden and Franklin enter mid-way
through a conversation apparently
arising from one of Franklin's attempts
to convince Arden that all will be well.
See 43–7 for Franklin's suggestions for
Arden's grief-afflicted gestures.
2 **care of womanhood** consideration of
the reputation of womankind
4 **credit** reputation; good name

215 SD] *(Exit Michaell)*   **Sc. 4**] *Hugo;* ACT III. SCENE I. *Tyrrell*

And couch dishonour as dishonour buds)   5
Might 'join repentance in her wanton thoughts,
No question then but she would turn the leaf
And sorrow for her dissolution.
But she is rooted in her wickedness,
Perverse and stubborn, not to be reclaimed.   10
Good counsel is to her as rain to weeds,
And reprehension makes her vice to grow
As Hydra's head that plenished by decay.
Her faults, methink, are painted in my face
For every searching eye to over-read;   15
And Mosby's name, a scandal unto mine,

5   **couch** To *couch* is lay in the earth to grow (*OED v.*[1] 3c). The word was also used more specifically in the malting process, where it described the spreading of grain on the floor to sprout (*OED v.*[1] 5), hence, in both the specific and the general case, *buds*. The line as a whole therefore suggests that gossip nurtures the first shoots of dishonour and makes it grow. *OED* gives the Q1 spelling 'cooch' only for the noun (*n.* 2).

6   **'join** enjoin; impose
    wanton undisciplined, rebellious as well as lustful

7   **turn the leaf** turn over a new leaf, or page of a book (proverbial; *OED* leaf *n.* 1 *P2*b)

8   **dissolution** dissolute or unrestrained, morally lax living; five syllables

12 **reprehension** reproof, censure

13 **Hydra's head** Hydra was the many-headed snake of classical myth. Its heads re-grew as fast as they were cut off, and it was only eventually slain by Hercules using a special golden sword.

*plenished stocked, supplied or furnished. Q1's 'perished' is clearly an error; Delius emends to 'flourished', which B&T follows, stating (in *CRE*) that *OED* gives only Scottish examples of 'plenish' in the sixteenth century. However, 'plenished' was in use in England: George North's translation of Philibert's *The Philosopher of the Court* (1575) has a 'poore purse ruthfully plenished', and John Norden's only slightly later *Vicissitudo* (1600) describes countries yielding 'precious things . . . / Wherewith all *other parts* are plenished' (118, sig. E2ᵛ). Although 'flourish' pairs well with *decay*, *plenished* seems considerably more likely to be misread as 'perished'.

14 His face expresses his reaction to her deeds; his moral standing is damaged by her faults. Suggests the superimposition of Alice's faults on Arden's face as a kind of portrait that signals the impact of her immorality on his credit, but also perhaps alludes to her 'painting' of her own face: the make-up which makes her sexually alluring to other men.

5 couch] *Q3*; cooch *Q1*   13 plenished] *W&P*; perisht *Q1*; nourished *conj. Tyrrell*; flourish'd *Delius*

Is deeply trenched in my blushing brow.
Ah Franklin, Franklin! When I think on this,
My heart's grief rends my other powers
Worse than the conflict at the hour of death.   20

FRANKLIN

Gentle Arden, leave this sad lament.
She will amend, and so your griefs will cease;
Or else she'll die, and so your sorrows end.
If neither of these two do haply fall,
Yet let your comfort be that others bear   25
Your woes, twice-doubled, all with patience.

ARDEN

My house is irksome; there I cannot rest.

FRANKLIN

Then stay with me in London; go not home.

ARDEN

Then that base Mosby doth usurp my room,
And makes his triumph of my being thence.   30
At home or not at home, where'er I be,

---

17 **trenched** cut or carved into a surface;
    trenchèd. See *Mac*, 3.4.24–5, 'safe in a
    ditch he bides, / With twenty trenched
    gashes on his head'. Arden is marked with
    Mosby's name in a metaphor that recalls the
    practice of branding the faces of criminals.
19 **rends** tears, lacerates; removes from
    their place
20 **conflict** spiritual struggle
21–6 Franklin's less-than-comforting speech
    gives a further suggestion (see 1.19–20,
    51–2) that he is not good with relation-
    ships, and opens up the possibility of

performances that bring out a vested
(homosocial/homosexual) interest in
keeping Arden in London.
24 **haply** fortunately
    fall befall; come to pass
26 **patience** three syllables
29 **usurp my room** take my place (a patriar-
    chally dangerous situation where another
    man has control of one's household
    including goods, servants and wife)
30 **triumph** glory in his victory, in gaining
    the mastery
    thence absent, away

21 SP] *Q2 (Franc.); Farn. Q1*

Here, here it lies, ah, Franklin, here it lies
That will not out till wretched Arden dies.

Here enters MICHAEL.

FRANKLIN
Forget your griefs awhile – here comes your man.

ARDEN
What o'clock is't, sirrah?

MICHAEL   Almost ten.   35

ARDEN
See, see how runs away the weary time!
Come, Master Franklin, shall we go to bed?
                Exeunt Arden and Michael. Franklin remains.

FRANKLIN
I pray you go before; I'll follow you.
Ah, what a hell is fretful jealousy!
What pity-moving words, what deep-fetched sighs,   40
What grievous groans and overlading woes

---

32 **here** The passions, and especially grief, were associated first and foremost with the heart, so it is most likely that Arden points there as he speaks. However, grief was exacerbated by thought, so it is possible that he points to his head to express his inability to stop thinking about his problems or to indicate the cuckold's horns that were imagined to grow from the forehead. In performance, as Wiggins argues, this has implications for our sense of the type of pain (shame or emotional hurt) Arden is suffering.
    it his pain

33 SD Entering with a portable lantern, here or at 54, would suggest darkness and the night-time duties of a servant; it was a common way of signalling night, Dessen and Thompson listing over sixty instances (1580–1642); see also the start of Sc. 5.

37 **go to bed** Most people in early modern England shared a bed, either with a spouse or with an individual of the same sex. It was seen as an antidote to both loneliness and cold, and being made to sleep alone was considered privation or punishment.

37 SD See 1.130n. for the timing of exits in the play.

39 **fretful** corrosive, irritating. For the phrase *fretful jealousy* see Kyd's translation of Robert Garnier's *Cornelia*, 2.4.1–2.

40 **deep-fetched** drawn from deep inside, and therefore amplified in their impact

41 **overlading** overloading; woes enough to sink one emotionally

---

37 SD] *after 38 Hopkinson[2]   Franklin remains] (Manet Franklin.)*   40 pity-moving] *Q2 (*Pitty mouing*);* pitty moning *Q1*

Accompanies this gentle gentleman!
Now will he shake his care-oppressed head,
Then fix his sad eyes on the sullen earth,
Ashamed to gaze upon the open world;   45
Now will he cast his eyes up towards the heavens,
Looking that ways for redress of wrong.
Sometimes he seeketh to beguile his grief
And tells a story with his careful tongue;
Then comes his wife's dishonour in his thoughts,   50
And in the middle cutteth off his tale,
Pouring fresh sorrow on his weary limbs.
So woe-begone, so inly charged with woe,
Was never any lived and bare it so.

Here enters MICHAEL.

MICHAEL

My master would desire you come to bed.   55

FRANKLIN

Is he himself already in his bed?   *Exit. Michael remains.*

MICHAEL

He is, and fain would have the light away.
Conflicting thoughts encamped in my breast
Awake me with the echo of their strokes;

43–7 Franklin gives suggestions here for
gestures for the actor playing Arden,
based on contemporary humoral theories. A melancholic temperament, caused
by an excess of black bile, affected both
physical and mental processes, mani-
festing itself both inside and out.

43   **oppressed** oppressèd
45   **open** public
48   **beguile** divert attention from
49   **careful** full of care
53   **woe-begone** overwhelmed with mis-
     fortune

charged loaded; burdened
54 SD See 33 SDn.
57   **have … away** have the evening candle
     taken out of the room. Michael's line of
     farewell, followed by a thoughtful
     speech, forms a pair with Franklin's
     soliloquy at 38–54.
58–61 Michael imagines his thoughts as rival
     armies.
58   **encamped** encampèd
59   **strokes** blows

56 SD] *(Exit Fran. Manet Mic.); after 57 Hugo*

And I, a judge to censure either side,   60
Can give to neither wished victory.
My master's kindness pleads to me for life
With just demand, and I must grant it him.
My mistress, she hath forced me with an oath
For Susan's sake, the which I may not break,   65
For that is nearer than a master's love.
That grim-faced fellow, pitiless Black Will,
And Shakebag, stern in bloody stratagem –
Two rougher ruffians never lived in Kent –
Have sworn my death if I infringe my vow,   70
A dreadful thing to be considered of:
Methinks I see them with their bolstered hair,

60 **censure** form an opinion of; criticize
61 **wished victory** i.e. the victory Michael desires for one of his thoughts, so that he knows what to do; wishèd
66 **nearer** closer, more intimate
71 **considered** thought carefully
72 **bolstered** stuffed or padded; puffed up or increased. While neither this reading nor the alternative 'boltered' is entirely secure, as both words are so rare in other contemporary texts, enlargement is clearly the key idea. Although not otherwise applied to hair, 'bolstered' was used of various aspects of the appearance and clothing, and was moralized in ways that indicated threat: it appears in John Studley's translations of Seneca (1566), e.g., from *Medea*, 'Theyr kyngly corage bolstred out / with maiestie of might' (11, sig. C3ʳ). It is also linked to the bolster, or pillow, on which the head was laid at night, pertinent as Michael has just returned from Arden's chamber. The association of fear with hair standing on end (and therefore increased in size) is prominent in the period: see, e.g., Hercules Furens' 'staring bush of hayre'

(*Seneca*, sig. B1ᵛ), and Thomas Fenne's 'Hecubae's Mishaps' (1590), '*With quaking corps and haire vpright full still I stoode at gaze*' (Fenne, sig. Bb4ʳ). Here, of course, it is the hair that is causing, rather than expressing, fear. B&T has 'boltred', which the editors link to 'balter' (in *CRE*), whose meanings of matted or clogged with lumps date from 1601 (see Philemon Holland's 1601 translation of Pliny for balls of excrement sticking to a sheep's rear end or the knotting of a goat's beard). The reading is linked to Macbeth's description of the 'blood-boltered' apparition of Banquo (4.1.122), although this does not directly describe hair either, and could just refer to lumps of gore. Versions of 'bolt' meaning to spring or start (*OED v.*[2] 1b) appear most frequently in relation to hair in EEBO-TCP to 1642, but begin in 1620 (e.g. 'stiffe-bolting haire' of a distracted man 'With staring eyes' (Quarles, sig. D1ᵛ), also suggesting enlargement of the hair. They suggest a connection between 'boltered' and 'bolstered'.

72 bolstered] *(bolstred); boltered Sturgess*

Staring and grinning in thy gentle face,
And in their ruthless hands their daggers drawn,
Insulting o'er thee with a peck of oaths   75
Whilst thou, submissive, pleading for relief,
Art mangled by their ireful instruments.
Methinks I hear them ask where Michael is,
And pitiless Black Will cries, 'Stab the slave!
The peasant will detect the tragedy.'   80
The wrinkles in his foul, death-threatening face
Gapes open wide like graves to swallow men.
My death to him is but a merriment,
And he will murder me to make him sport.
He comes, he comes. Ah, Master Franklin, help!   85
Call up the neighbours or we are but dead!

Here enters FRANKLIN *and* ARDEN.

FRANKLIN
What dismal outcry calls me from my rest?
ARDEN
What hath occasioned such a fearful cry?
Speak, Michael! Hath any injured thee?
MICHAEL
Nothing, sir, but as I fell asleep   90

---

73 **thy** Arden's
75 **Insulting o'er** exulting or triumphing
    over. As in William Lambarde's
    Perambulation of Kent (1576), 'what
    was it els for this proude *Prelate* thus
    to insult ouer simple men' (140).
    peck lot; technically a quarter of a bushel
    of dry goods (*OED* 2a)
77 **ireful instruments** angry weapons;
    weapons of anger
80 **detect** expose; reveal, discover
84 **make him sport** entertain him. The idea

of murder as a parody of entertainment is
picked up again later when Michael is
accused of *pranks*, 104.
86 The threat of night-time disorder and
    housebreaking is evoked here.
87 The line is reminiscent of two of
    Hieronimo's in *Spanish Tragedy*: 'What
    outcries pluck me from my naked bed'
    (2.5.1) and 'I hear, / His dismal outcry
    echo in the air' (4.4.107–8).
90 **Nothing** nobody, if *any* in 89 is taken to
    mean 'anybody' (*OED* B *pron.* and *n.* 1)

75 thee] *Q3;* there *Q1*   81 death-threatening] *(death threatning)*   87 SP] *Q2 (Fran.); Eran Q1*

Upon the threshold leaning to the stairs
I had a fearful dream that troubled me,
And in my slumber thought I was beset
With murderer-thieves that came to rifle me.
My trembling joints witness my inward fear.   95
I crave your pardons for disturbing you.

ARDEN

So great a cry for nothing I ne'er heard.
What, are the doors fast locked, and all things safe?

MICHAEL

I cannot tell; I think I locked the doors.

ARDEN

I like not this, but I'll go see myself.   100
[*Then he checks the doors.*]
Ne'er trust me but the doors were all unlocked.
This negligence not half contenteth me.
Get you to bed and, if you love my favour,
Let me have no more such pranks as these.
Come, Master Franklin, let us go to bed.   105

---

91 **threshold leaning to** doorway leaning
against, or towards (like a lean-to, which
OED dates to 1461), or at the bottom of
94 **rifle** rob (with the sense of physical
searching)
95 **witness ... fear** picks up on the theme of
inner emotion and outer evidence, which
Arden began above (17, 32). Michael's
uncontrolled body offers the suggestion that
lower-status emotion is more visible, or at
least that it is more fitting that it should be so.
100 SD Editors have imagined that Arden tries
the doors at the back of the stage (BH&N,
Wine), or that he '*Goes out, and returns a
moment or two later*' (Oliphant), or 'may
exit through one door and return through
another' (B&T). Wine points out the connection between this action and the tense
of the verb in the following line: Q1's

'were' suggests that the others do not see
him try them, whereas Q2's 'are' indicates
a shared discovery. In either case, Michael
and Franklin are left watching after Arden
with no particular action stated, which
offers the audience a similarly static and
anticipatory type of staging to the passages
during which the characters are playing at
tables and cleaning up blood in Sc. 14.
101 In Holinshed it is Michael who re-locks
the doors, 'fearing least blacke Will
would kill him as well as his maister,
after he was in bed himselfe, he rose
againe and shut the doores, bolting them
fast', although he later tells the murderers
that it was Franklin (see below, p. 294).
102 **not half contenteth** is a long way from
pleasing
104 **pranks** malicious tricks or deceptions

91 leaning] leading *Tyrrell*   100 SD] *Wiggins subst.; Goes out, and returns a moment or two later.* |
Oliphant   101 were] are *Q2*

FRANKLIN

Ay, by my faith, the air is very cold.
Michael, farewell. I pray thee, dream no more.   *Exeunt.*

[Sc. 5]   *Here enters* [BLACK] WILL, GREENE *and* SHAKEBAG.

SHAKEBAG

Black night hath hid the pleasures of the day,
And sheeting darkness overhangs the earth
And with the black fold of her cloudy robe
Obscure us from the eyesight of the world,
In which sweet silence such as we triumph.   5
The lazy minutes linger on their time,
Loath to give due audit to the hour,
Till in the watch our purpose be complete

---

107 SD B&T suggests that servant and masters might go their separate ways, which would underline the distance of rank by indicating different sleeping quarters, and show Michael's isolation.

Sc. 5 The implied location of the scene is in the street near Franklin's house, where the characters make use of a stage door to represent the property's outermost entrance.

0 SD Q1 has the entry after Shakebag has spoken his first line, which Wiggins therefore supposes to be from within, 'adding to the suspense'. Coupled with the positioning of '*Exeunt*' on the penultimate line of Sc. 4, it appears that the transition between scenes at the top of sig. E1ᵛ was subject to disruption.

2 **sheeting** covering; enfolding. This is the only early modern adjectival use in EEBO-TCP or *OED*, and the latter gives the verb's earliest instance as *AC* ('when snow the pasture sheets', 1.4.66), therefore *c.* 1606.

4 **Obscure** Modern readers would expect 'obscures' here; a disagreement between singular and plural has been introduced, perhaps through omitted type, here or at another place in the sentence.

5 **such as we** i.e. robbers, criminals. The aim here is apparently to conjure up the atmosphere of dangerous night, rather than to choose language that characterizes Shakebag. The initial image is fairly conventional as a scene opener (Wine lists *1* and *2 Tamburlaine*, *Faustus*, *Spanish Tragedy*, *1H4*, *R3* and *Woodstock*).

triumph gain mastery, prevail; stress on second syllable

6–7 i.e. time runs slowly.

7 **due audit** proper reckoning

8 **the watch** either one of the periods into which the night was divided in the classical and biblical eras, or, perhaps more likely here as its duration is determined by Arden's death, the more general action of watching for him, as in 'keeping watch'

---

106 SP] *Fran. Q2; Farn. Q1*   by] *Q2; be Q1*   107 SD] *Q2; opp. 106 Q1*   **Sc. 5**] *Hugo;* ACT III. SCENE II. *Tyrrell*   0 SD] *Q2; after 1 Q1*   2 sheeting] *(sheting)*

And Arden sent to everlasting night.
Greene, get you gone and linger here about,   10
And at some hour hence, come to us again,
Where we will give you instance of his death.

GREENE

Speed to my wish whose will soe'er says no;
And so I'll leave you for an hour or two.   *Exit.*

BLACK WILL

I tell thee, Shakebag, would this thing were done.   15
I am so heavy that I can scarce go.
This drowsiness in me bodes little good.

SHAKEBAG

How now, Will, become a precisian?
Nay, then let's go sleep, when bugs and fears
Shall kill our courages with their fancy's work.   20

BLACK WILL

Why, Shakebag, thou mistakes me much,
And wrongs me too in telling me of fear.
Were't not a serious thing we go about,
It should be slipped till I had fought with thee
To let thee know I am no coward, I.   25
I tell thee, Shakebag, thou abusest me.

SHAKEBAG

Why, thy speech bewrayed an inly kind of fear
And savoured of a weak, relenting spirit.
Go forward now in that we have begun,

---

9   **everlasting night** death
12   **instance** evidence; proof
13   'May my desire be successful, despite
     the wishes of others.'
16   **heavy** sluggish (*OED* 19); weighed
     down with grief (*OED* 27)
     go walk
18   **precisian** strict observer of religious
     rules; Puritan, in the sense of someone
     incapacitated by their conscience
19–20 i.e. we might as well go home to sleep,

if our courage can so easily be killed.
19   **bugs** imaginary terrors
20   **fancy's work** hallucinatory power
24   **slipped** made to wait; overlooked tem-
     porarily, as in 'slipped the mind'
27   **bewrayed** exposed, revealed
     inly inwardly felt. It raises again the
     question of inner feelings and outer
     show, see 4.14–17.
28   **savoured** was suggestive or redolent
29   **Go forward** continue

And afterwards attempt me when thou darest.   30

BLACK WILL

And if I do not, heaven cut me off!
But let that pass, and show me to this house
Where, thou shalt see, I'll do as much as Shakebag.

SHAKEBAG

This is the door. [*Then he tries it.*] But soft, methinks
'tis shut.
The villain Michael hath deceived us!   35

BLACK WILL

Soft, let me see. [*Then he tries it.*] Shakebag, 'tis shut
indeed.
Knock with thy sword; perhaps the slave will hear?
[*Then Shakebag knocks.*]

SHAKEBAG

It will not be: the white-livered peasant
Is gone to bed, and laughs us both to scorn.

BLACK WILL

And he shall buy his merriment as dear   40
As ever custrel bought so little sport.
Ne'er let this sword assist me when I need,
But rust and canker after I have sworn,

---

30 **attempt** try your luck with; attack
31 **cut me off** sever me (from life)
33 **do as much** be as involved, brave, active
34 SD The sense of threat to the household built up in Scs 4 and 5 is partly achieved through the use of the stage doors, which the audience see tried from either side as the stage represents first their interior and then their street faces.
34 **soft** imperative to silence or slackened pace, in this case close to 'hang on a moment'
35 **deceived** deceivèd
37 **thy sword** For sword-wearing, see 1.310n. on *statute*; Shakebag's possession of one is a threat to social order as it is clearly meant for violence rather than to mark status.
37 SD Wiggins argues that Shakebag may not knock, as the noise might draw attention to their activities, but the action's boldness and untempered aggression, as opposed to careful planning, seems to fit the villain's character.
38 **white-livered** cowardly
41 **custrel** rogue
     sport See 4.84, 14.343 for the theme of entertainment and leisure in the murder attempts.
43 **canker** corrode, decay

34 SD] *this edn (Wine subst.)*   36 SD] *this edn (Wiggins subst.)*   37 SD] *this edn (B&T subst.)*   38–9] *Delius; Q1 lines* bed / scorne. /   41 custrel] *(coistrell)*

If I, the next time that I meet the hind,
Lop not away his leg, his arm, or both.   45
SHAKEBAG
And let me never draw a sword again,
Nor prosper in the twilight, cockshut light,
When I would fleece the wealthy passenger,
But lie and languish in a loathsome den,
Hated and spit at by the goers-by,   50
And in that death may die unpitied,
If I, the next time that I meet the slave,
Cut not the nose from off the coward's face
And trample on it for this villainy.
BLACK WILL
Come, let's go seek out Greene; I know he'll swear.   55
SHAKEBAG
He were a villain an he would not swear;
'Twould make a peasant swear amongst his boys,
That ne'er durst say before but 'yea' and 'no',
To be thus flouted of a custrel.

---

44 **hind** domestic servant, but also female
    deer and hence quarry, prey
47 **cockshut light** twilight, 'edge of the
    evening' (Cotgrave). The phrase refers
    either to putting chickens to roost or to
    catching woodcocks who, because they
    were so easy to snare, lent their names to
    dupes or fools.
51 **unpitied** unpitièd
56 **an** if
57 If we see this as referring to a solemn oath,
    a parody of which they themselves have
    just sworn, then the meaning is that peas-
    ants had no need to swear because they had
    nothing important to vow to do (Black Will
    mocks Michael at 3.155–6 for being too

knavish and cowardly to swear). If we see it
as a profane oath, then peasants may be
thought of as less foul-mouthed, wishing to
appear respectable and devout. Sturgess's
suggested emendation, 'pedant', meaning
schoolmaster, is adopted by B&T, but
Stubbes's *Motive to Good Works* (1593)
describes inveterate swearers who account
'him a peasant and no man, that cannot
sweare it out lustely' (176), suggesting the
currency of Q1's idea that swearing is for
higher-status irreligious types.
58 **durst** dared
59 **flouted of** mocked by
    custrel The Q1 spelling, 'coisterel', sug-
    gests trisyllabic pronunciation.

---

57 peasant] pedant *(conj. Sturgess)*   59 custrell] *(coisterel)*

BLACK WILL

Shakebag, let's seek out Greene, and in the morning,   60
At the alehouse 'butting Arden's house,
Watch the outcoming of that prick-eared cur,
And then let me alone to handle him.   *Exeunt.*

[Sc. 6]   *Here enters* ARDEN, FRANKLIN *and* MICHAEL.

ARDEN [*to Michael*]

Sirrah, get you back to Billingsgate
And learn what time the tide will serve our turn.
Come to us in Paul's. First go make the bed,
And afterwards go hearken for the flood.   *Exit Michael.*
Come, Master Franklin, you shall go with me.   5
This night I dreamed that, being in a park,
A toil was pitched to overthrow the deer,
And I, upon a little rising hill,
Stood whistly watching for the herd's approach.

---

61 **'butting** abutting
62 **prick-eared cur** pointy-eared dog
63 **handle** deal with
Sc. 6 The energetic bustle with which the scene begins makes it plain that it is now morning. The characters are clearly still in the vicinity of Franklin's house, as Michael leaves to make the beds.
1   **Billingsgate** London's principal dock once the new London Bridge stopped boats travelling further west, on the north bank of the Thames between London Bridge and the Tower of London. A daily barge ran from there to Gravesend in Kent.
2   **serve our turn** satisfy our need
3–4 Arden's disordered volley of commands indicates his preoccupied state of mind. Billingsgate is around five miles from St Paul's.
3   **Paul's** Arden's identification of a return to Paul's and the ordinary in this scene

suggests a London routine for the men, centred around business and sociability.
4   **hearken . . . flood** listen for information about the incoming tide
6   The dream interrupts their exit, delaying it until 46 and creating an intimate moment of disclosure amongst friends and equals, in the absence of the lower-status Michael.
    park deer park, for hunting
7   **toil** net forming an enclosed area into which the object of the hunt is driven
    pitched set up and made fast with stakes (*OED* 9), referring to a snare
9   **whistly** softly, without noise. Relatively common as an adjective ('whist'), though EEBO-TCP gives only one other adverbial use in the century before 1642 ('as whistly he withdrew thence', Pedro Mexia, *The Treasury of Ancient and Modern Times* (1613)).

Sc. 6] *Hugo;* ACT III. SCENE III. *Tyrrell*   1 SD] *Wine (Hugo subst.)*

Even there methoughts a gentle slumber took me   10
And summoned all my parts to sweet repose.
But in the pleasure of this golden rest
An ill-thewed foster had removed the toil,
And rounded me with that beguiling home
Which late, methought, was pitched to cast the deer.   15
With that he blew an evil-sounding horn,
And at the noise another herdman came
With falchion drawn, and bent it at my breast,
Crying aloud, 'Thou art the game we seek.'
With this I waked, and trembled every joint,   20
Like one obscured in a little bush
That sees a lion foraging about,
And, when the dreadful forest king is gone,
He pries about with timorous suspect
Throughout the thorny casements of the brake,   25
And will not think his person dangerless,
But quakes and shivers though the cause be gone.

---

13 **ill-thewed foster** bad-mannered or ill-natured forester. 'Foster' was a contracted form of forester up to 1607 (*OED n.* 3), see, e.g., *FQ*, 'A grisly foster forth did rush' (3.1, sig. Bb7ʳ).
removed the toil moved the deer-catching net
14 **rounded** surrounded
home the snare as a place of deceptive and appealing (*beguiling*) safety, linked to other meanings of the word: resting place (*OED* 6) and the grave (*OED* 3; see also *long home* at 10.46). Some editors have found the semi-metaphorical use of the word problematic: B&T adopts Craik's 'snare', arguing (in *CRE*) for a complex misreading; Jowett conjectures a misreading of 'yarne', citing its meaning 'net' (*OED* 1b), but Arden's description of

his dreaming self, sleeping in the spot as the snare is moved, and Franklin's explicit linking of this dream to Michael's one (32–5), which disrupts the household in Sc. 4, renders emendation unnecessary in the context of the play's repeated questioning of the protective qualities of domestic space.
15 **late** previously
cast bring down; throw on its side
18 **falchion** broad curved sword with the edge on the convex side. Q1's 'fauchon' is disyllabic, as is required here.
21 **obscured** obscurèd
24 **suspect** suspicion; suspèct
25 **thorny casements** 'windows' made by gaps in the thorn bushes
brake thicket
26 **dangerless** free from danger

13 foster] forester *SMS;* fors'ter *B&T*   14 home] snare *Craik*   18 falchion] *(*fauchon*)*   21 obscured] *Q2;* oscured *Q1*   27 shivers] Q3 *(*shiuers*);* shewers *Q1*

So, trust me, Franklin, when I did awake,
I stood in doubt whether I waked or no,
Such great impression took this fond surprise. 30
God grant this vision bedeem me any good!
FRANKLIN
This fantasy doth rise from Michael's fear
Who, being awaked with the noise he made,
His troubled senses yet could take no rest;
And this, I warrant you, procured your dream. 35
ARDEN
It may be so – God frame it to the best –
But oftentimes my dreams presage too true.
FRANKLIN
To such as note their nightly fantasies
Some one in twenty may incur belief.
But use it not: 'tis but a mockery. 40
ARDEN
Come, Master Franklin, we'll now walk in Paul's,
And dine together at the ordinary,
And by my man's direction draw to the quay
And with the tide go down to Faversham.
Say, Master Franklin, shall it not be so? 45
FRANKLIN
At your good pleasure sir; I'll bear you company. *Exeunt.*

---

30 **great impression** Cf. *R3*, 1.4.63, 'Such terrible impression made my dream'. The more common phrase in EEBO-TCP texts to 1600 is 'deep impression'.
fond surprise foolish emotion; sudden attack
31 **bedeem** presage
33 **awaked** awakèd
35 **procured** brought about
36 **frame** direct (*OED v.* 5a)

37 **presage** predict, foretell; presàge
39 **incur** meet with
40 **use it not** don't do it (don't pay attention to your dreams); see the discussion of Alice's dream, 1.73n.
43–4 i.e. go to the quay at the right time of the tide to sail to Faversham, as advised by Michael.
46 **At ... pleasure** as it pleases you

46] *W&P; Q1 lines* sir, / companye. /

[Sc. 7]   *Here enters* MICHAEL *at one door.*
              Here enters GREENE, BLACK WILL *and*
                  SHAKEBAG *at another door.*

BLACK WILL

Draw, Shakebag, for here's that villain Michael!

GREENE

First, Will, let's hear what he can say.

BLACK WILL

Speak, milksop slave, and never after speak!

MICHAEL

For God's sake, sirs, let me excuse myself;

For here I swear, by heaven and earth and all,   5

I did perform the utmost of my task

And left the doors unbolted and unlocked.

But see the chance: Franklin and my master

Were very late conferring in the porch,

And Franklin left his napkin where he sat,   10

With certain gold knit in it, as he said.

Sc. 7 The scene is loosely set between Franklin's house, which Michael is presumed just to have left (for which reason Tyrrell located it in Aldersgate), and the quay to which he is bound. Also in play is the Salutation Inn, towards which the characters are presumed to depart at the end. None of these locations makes any particular material demands on staging.

3   **milksop** feeble; timid
    never after speak don't speak again (indicating that he will be dead after this excuse)

6   **utmost of** 'the most or greatest possible or attainable' (*OED* 2a)

8   **see the chance** look at (or imagine) the mischance (bad luck)

9   **porch** Often fairly substantial in size, early modern porches demonstrated the status of the house behind. They offered a

liminal space in which individuals could have relatively private conversations.

10 **napkin** table napkin or handkerchief. Ownership of such linens defined middling status and above, and they could be very expensive and highly embellished.

11 **gold . . . it** Either gold (coin) is tied up in the cloth (as candied fruits are in Middleton's *Chaste Maid*, where the Nurse enters with comfits and Allwit comments, 'Now out comes all the tasselled handkerchers, / They are spread abroad between their knees already; / Now in goes the long fingers . . . Now we shall have such pocketing' (3.2.51–5)), or the cloth has gold knitted or woven into it (most usually as a border lace of metal thread) and is hence intrinsically valuable (like the work in Desdemona's handkerchief in *Oth*).

Sc. 7] *Hugo;* ACT III. SCENE IV. *Tyrrell*   6 utmost] *(outmost)*

Being in bed, he did bethink himself
And, coming down, he found the doors unshut.
He locked the gates and brought away the keys,
For which offence my master rated me.   15
But now I am going to see what flood it is,
For with the tide my master will away,
Where you may front him well on Rainham Down,
A place well fitting such a stratagem.

BLACK WILL

Your excuse hath somewhat mollified my choler.   20
Why now, Greene, 'tis better now nor e'er it was.

GREENE

But, Michael, is this true?

MICHAEL

As true as I report it to be true.

SHAKEBAG   Then, Michael, this shall be your penance: to
feast us all at the Salutation, where we will plot our   25
purpose thoroughly.

GREENE   And, Michael, you shall bear no news of this
tide because they two may be in Rainham Down
before your master.

---

12   **bethink himself** remember
15   **rated** berated, severely told off
16   **what flood it is** the timing of the tides
18   **front** confront face-to-face
     Rainham Down open land near Rainham,
     approximately half-way between
     Gravesend (where the boat stopped) and
     Faversham, on the London road. It had a
     reputation for robberies, hence its descrip-
     tion as *well fitting* (19) the stratagem. In
     Holinshed it is Arden's maid who tells
     Greene that 'This night will my maister go
     downe' (see below, p. 294).
21   **'tis** it (the plot/chance of killing Arden)
     is

nor than
23   'as true as I tell you it is'. Disingenuous
     phrase, intended to befuddle. Wiggins
     has, 'As true as the fact that I'm telling it
     to you'.
25   **Salutation** a Billingsgate tavern, prob-
     ably (ironically, given the context) with a
     sign showing the Angel Gabriel
     announcing Jesus's impending birth to
     the Virgin Mary
28   **tide** the *flood* (16). If Arden misses this
     high tide then the murderers will be able
     to overtake him.
     because . . . be so that they may be
     they two Black Will and Shakebag

24–6 *Wiggins; Q1 lines* penance, / Salutation, / throughly. /   25 plot] *(plat)*   26 thoroughly] *(throughly)*
27–9 *Wiggins; Q1 lines* tide / M. / ; *Delius lines* tide, / Down / master. /

MICHAEL   Why, I'll agree to anything you'll have me, so   30
you will accept of my company!   *Exeunt.*

[**Sc. 8**]   *Here enters* MOSBY.

MOSBY
Disturbed thoughts drives me from company
And dries my marrow with their watchfulness.
Continual trouble of my moody brain
Feebles my body by excess of drink
And nips me, as the bitter north-east wind   5

---

30   **so** provided that
31   ***accept ... company** The difference
between Q1's 'except' and Q3's 'accept'
changes our sense of Michael's character.
Of his choice of 'except', which suggests
that Michael wants above everything to
avoid Black Will and Shakebag's company, Wine states that it is 'one of the
most ambiguous readings in the text'. In
a period when eating together was a sign
of confraternity and drinking together
could mean pledging allegiance, it is psy-
chologically plausible that Michael is
prepared to pay to save his skin, but
wants to avoid the implications of joining
them around the table for reasons of cowardice and also perhaps moral queasi-
ness. However, as a contemporary authorial word choice, 'accept' seems the more
likely. B&T 'modernizes' to 'accept' in
MCE, and points (in *CRE*) to Barnabe
Rich's 1574 address 'To the Gentle
Reader' in his *A Right Excellent and
Pleasant Dialogue Between Mercury and
an English Soldier*, where he asks them
to 'beare with my inabylitie, and except
of my good wyll' (sig. A3ᵛ) and to *OED*
except *v.* 6, which also indicates confusion of the two words. EEBO-TCP produces only two hits for 'except of my'

1560–1600, of which this is one, but
forty-six for 'accept of my', the majority
of which are deferential phrases that set
up hierarchical relationships around the
labour, service or goodwill that the writer
proffers.

Sc. 8 Tyrrell imagined the scene set within
Arden's Faversham house, perhaps
because its passion and intimacy give an
interior feel, but it is loosely located on
the outskirts of the property chiefly by
Alice's insistence that first Bradshaw and
then she and Mosby go inside.

1   **Disturbed** disturbèd
2   **marrow** various 'central substances',
including that within the cavity of bones,
therefore used to signify the innermost
part of a person's being (*OED n.*¹ 1d).
See also *marrow-prying*, 1.134, and n.
their watchfulness the wakefulness or
insomnia that the thoughts induce in him
3   **trouble** vexation, distress
moody subject to moods of depres-
sion, melancholy. The word was also
linked to anger as another intemperate
emotion.
4   **Feebles ... by** enfeebles ... by provoking
5   **nips** pinches painfully, as with cold
(*OED v.*¹ IV 11)

30–1 *Wiggins; Q1 lines* me. / company. /   31 accept] *Q3;* except *Q1*   **Sc. 8**] *Hugo;* ACT IV. SCENE I.
Tyrrell; Act III. Scene V. *Delius*

Doth check the tender blossoms in the spring.
Well fares the man, howe'er his cates do taste,
That tables not with foul suspicion;
And he but pines amongst his delicates
Whose troubled mind is stuffed with discontent.   10
My golden time was when I had no gold:
Though then I wanted, yet I slept secure.
My daily toil begat me night's repose;
My night's repose made daylight fresh to me.
But, since I climbed the top bough of the tree   15
And sought to build my nest among the clouds,
Each gentle starry gale doth shake my bed
And makes me dread my downfall to the earth.

6 **check** stop, hold back the growth of (*OED* 13); perhaps also rebuke (*OED* 11)

7 **cates** dainty, choice foods (often bought in rather than home-produced)

8 **tables** dines; shares a table (here with a personified *foul suspicion*)
suspicion four syllables

9 **pines** endures pain (*OED* 2); wastes away with hunger (*OED* 3a)
delicates similar to *cates* (7): tasty and refined foods

10 **stuffed** as with food

11 **golden** very favourable, propitious

12 **wanted** lacked the necessities; did without

13 **begat** produced, gave

17 **gentle starry gale** Neither of the two main editorial options for this phrase, the one given here (following Q1) or 'gentlest airy', is unproblematic; both are apparently unique phrases in the period. Q1 has 'stary', an alternative spelling of 'starry', and this reading makes poetic sense of a movement coming from the night sky, or 'Relating to, or caused by, the influence of the stars' (*OED* 2b). B&T, following Sturgess, adopts 'gentlest airy gale', suggesting (in *CRE*) the movement of *st* from the end of the first word to the start of the next. Both 'starry' and 'airy' refer primarily to a region and/or its nature. The former, generally denoting the heavens, is most commonly encountered in the period in *The Whole Book of Psalms* (1578), which gives both 'starry heavens' and 'starry skye' (*Psalms*, sigs 43ʳ, B3ʳ). 'Airy' refers to elemental properties opposed to fire and water, but also to lofty, open and breezy places. While either 'airy' or 'starry' would then describe the gale's location around a treetop, and both may be used poetically, the latter offers the most striking extension of the imagery to include notions of astrological influence and elevation of the sightline. There are analogous uses of 'starry': for instance, in Marlowe's *Dido, Queen of Carthage* (1594), a throne is described as being built 'amidst those starrie towers, / That earth-borne *Atlas* groning vnderprops' (A3ᵛ).

12 Though] *Q2;* Thought *Q1*   17 gentle starry] *Jacob;* gentle stary *Q1;* Gentle Steary *SMS;* gentle stirring *Hopkinson²* (conj. Collier); gentle stirry *Delius;* gentlest airy *Sturgess (conj. McElwaine)*

But whither doth contemplation carry me?
The way I seek to find where pleasure dwells   20
Is hedgcd behind me, that I cannot back
But needs must on, although to danger's gate.
Then, Arden, perish thou by that decree.
For Greene doth ear the land and weed thee up
To make my harvest nothing but pure corn.   25
And for his pains I'll hive him up a while,
And after smother him to have his wax;
Such bees as Greene must never live to sting.
Then is there Michael and the painter too,
Chief actors to Arden's overthrow,   30

Readings must also make sense of *gale* which, contrary to B&T's assertion, is not used poetically to mean a breeze until 1728 (*OED n.*³ 1b). Its use here connects to the pillar of inconstant love that 'shakes with every blast of wind' at 10.96–9, echoing the image of a gust that threatens security up high. Given the way 'gentle' was usually connected to wind: e.g. *VA*, 'I'll sigh celestial breath, whose gentle wind / Shall cool the heat of this descending sun' (189–90), *gentle* is best read ironically, linked to the social meaning of the word that runs throughout *Arden* (the wind is rough and ill-behaved like a base-born man, rather than measured in its behaviour like a gentleman). This ironic play on the meaning, so pertinent to the following exchange between Alice and Mosby, is made clearer by *gentle* than by 'gentlest'.

bed figuratively the nest and literally the bed in which he lies at night

19 Mosby catches his mind wandering and brings himself back to earth.

20 **way** pathway, road
   where to the place at which (*OED* 5b)

21 **hedged** blocked

back retreat

23 **that decree** cither Mosby's decision that the only way is forwards or, conversely, an event or circumstance foreordained as part of God's purpose (*OED* 3)

24–5 Greene plots to kill Arden (the weed) so that Mosby's *harvest* (what comes to him after the murder) will contain only the *corn* (Alice and Arden's wealth and her love/body).

24 **ear** plough

26 ***hive him up** shelter him. Q1 has 'heaue', and the phrase could mean elevate him socially (*OED v.* 2b), which would not be inappropriate, but makes little sense with the following line. To 'hive' which, as B&T (*CRE*) points out could be spelled 'heue' and is therefore perhaps the source of the error, meant to afford shelter (*OED v.* 2) as a beehive does to bees (see 27 for extension of the image).

27 **smother ... wax** Smothering, or suffocating with smoke, is used to calm bees by (it is now known) masking their alarm pheromones so that they are less likely to sting the beekeeper. In Greene's case figurative, as Mosby wishes not to calm him but to kill him.

26 hive] *Delius;* heaue *Q1*

Who, when they shall see me sit in Arden's seat,
They will insult upon me for my meed,
Or fright me by detecting of his end.
I'll none of that, for I can cast a bone
To make these curs pluck out each other's throat,   35
And then am I sole ruler of mine own.
Yet Mistress Arden lives; but she's myself,
And holy Church rites makes us two but one.
But what for that? – I may not trust you, Alice;
You have supplanted Arden for my sake,   40
And will extirpen me to plant another.
'Tis fearful sleeping in a serpent's bed,
And I will cleanly rid my hands of her!

31   **sit ... seat** literally occupy the best
     position at the table (see 14.291);
     metaphorically play the part of husband
     and householder (see 1.633–4)
32   **insult upon me** be elated at, or glory in
     my defeat
     meed reward, deserts, but especially
     here corrupt gain (*OED n.* 2a)
33   **his** Arden's
34–5 **cast ... throat** proverbial way of
     causing a diverting contention (Dent,
     H88). Mosby is implicitly referring to
     his sister here, as the bone cast before
     Clarke and Michael.
37–8 **myself ... one** Husband and wife were
     joined as one flesh and therefore consid-
     ered inseparable and of common pur-
     pose; common law held that wives, so
     conjoined, could not give evidence
     against their husbands (the defendant's
     protection against self-incrimination
     being extended to them). On the other
     hand, Alice should also therefore have
     been inseparable from Arden.

38   **And** B&T emends to 'An', meaning
     'if' (i.e. we would be one *if* we were
     married), a meaning that also stands with
     And, assuming that Mosby continues
     using the present tense for his projected
     future (*makes* = will make). But there
     may also be a submerged reference to
     the source material here: Holinshed
     says the couple made a solemn promise
     to each other 'to be in all points as man
     and wife togither, and therevpon they
     both receiued the sacrament on a
     sundaie at London' (see below, p. 296),
     in which case they would already be
     married.
39   **what for that?** so what?
     may not cannot and must not (Abbott,
     310)
40   **supplanted** ousted, dispossessed
41   **extirpen** extirpate, pull out by the roots.
     The word is not in *OED* and this is the
     unique example in EEBO-TCP.
43   **cleanly** completely, wholly (*OED adv.* b)

Here enters ALICE [*with a prayer-book*].

But here she comes, and I must flatter her.
How now, Alice? What, sad and passionate?   45
Make me partaker of thy pensiveness;
Fire divided burns with lesser force.

ALICE

But I will dam that fire in my breast
Till, by the force thereof, my heart consume.
Ah, Mosby!   50

MOSBY

Such deep pathaires, like to a cannon's burst
Discharged against a ruinated wall,
Breaks my relenting heart in thousand pieces.
Ungentle Alice, thy sorrow is my sore.
Thou know'st it well, and 'tis thy policy   55
To forge distressful looks to wound a breast
Where lies a heart that dies when thou art sad.

43 SD Here, as well perhaps as in previous scenes, Alice is likely to enter with a prayer-book (as she uses it at 116), perhaps hung from her waist on a chain from her girdle (see, as an example, V&A LOAN:MET ANON.2:4-1998).

45 **sad** distressed or downcast
passionate intensely emotional (*OED* 3); sorrowful (*OED* 5b); angry (*OED* 2a). Alice's strong emotions are given a spiritual colour if they are linked to her reading of her prayer-book.

47 **Fire** the fire of her *sad and passionate* emotions (45); two syllables

48 **dam ... breast** i.e. keep it within myself, as opposed to dividing it as Mosby suggests

49 i.e. until it burns itself out
*heart** Q1 reads 'part', but Craik's conjecture of a straightforward misreading of 'heart' spelled 'hart' (and by analogy love)

then allows a sympathetic parallel with Mosby's broken organ (which is indeed spelled 'hart' in Q1), in 53.

51 **pathaires** passionate outbursts. EEBO-TCP gives only one other example of the word, dated 1615, and suggests a link to petard, meaning a small bomb used to blow a hole in a wall (hence *Ham*, 3.4.204–5, 'to have the enginer / Hoist with his own petard').
cannon's burst explosion of a cannon or impact of its ball

54 **sore** pain, suffering; grief

56 **forge** fashion, make, as with metal: hence the *looks*' ability to wound. The phrase continues the martial metaphors.

57 *when** Q1's 'where' is an easy misreading/repetition of the line's previous *Where*.

43 SD *with a prayer-book*] *Sturgess* 49–50] *Delius; one line Q1* 49 heart] *Craik* (hart); part *Q1*
57 when] *Q2;* where *Q1*

It is not love that loves to anger love.

ALICE

It is not love that loves to murder love.

MOSBY

How mean you that?   60

ALICE

Thou know'st how dearly Arden loved me.

MOSBY

And then?

ALICE

And then conceal the rest, for 'tis too bad,
Lest that my words be carried with the wind
And published in the world to both our shames.   65
I pray thee, Mosby, let our springtime wither;
Our harvest else will yield but loathsome weeds.
Forget, I pray thee, what hath passed betwixt us,
For now I blush and tremble at the thoughts.

MOSBY

What, are you changed?   70

ALICE

Ay, to my former happy life again:
From title of an odious strumpet's name,
To honest Arden's wife. Not Arden's honest wife –
Ha, Mosby, 'tis thou hast rifled me of that,

58–9 On the distinctive pattern of 'repetition of a reflexive pronoun' in these lines and its links to early Shakespearean style, see Jackson, 'Quarrel', 266–7, 282–3.

58   The thing that calls itself love is not love when it desires to make the beloved angry. For a similar construction, see *Son*, 116.2–3, 'Love is not love / Which alters when it alteration finds'.

61   **loved** lovèd

62   **And then?** so what?

66–7 **let ... weeds** Reversing Mosby's earlier image of harvest (24–5), Alice suggests that they should let their initial love (*springtime*) die, as it can only turn to something undesirable (*loathsome weeds*) in the end.

67   **else** otherwise

71   **happy** fortunate (*OED* 1); content (*OED* 5)

74   **rifled** robbed; see 4.94.

And made me slanderous to all my kin. 75
Even in my forehead is thy name engraven,
A mean artificer, that low-born name.
I was bewitched – woe worth the hapless hour
And all the causes that enchanted me!

MOSBY

Nay, if thou ban, let me breathe curses forth, 80
And, if you stand so nicely at your fame,
Let me repent the credit I have lost:
I have neglected matters of import
That would have stated me above thy state,
Forslowed advantages and spurned at time – 85
Ay, Fortune's right hand Mosby hath forsook,
To take a wanton giglot by the left.
I left the marriage of an honest maid,
Whose dowry would have weighed down all thy
wealth,
Whose beauty and demeanour far exceeded thee. 90

---

75 **slanderous** a source of shame or disgrace
76 **engraven** engraved, carved. See 4.14–17, cf. Revelation, 17.4–5, 'And the woman was arayed in purple & scarlet colour, and decked with golde, precious stone, and pearles, and had a cup of golde in her hande, full of abhominations and fylthynesse of her fornication. / And in her forehead was a name written, a misterie, great Babylon, the mother of whoredome, and abhominations of the earth.' (Bible, sig. T8ᵛ)
77 **mean artificer** low-born craftsman; *artificer* is stressed on the second syllable.
78 **woe worth** a curse on; literally, 'woe equal to'
80 **ban** curse

81 **stand ... fame** are so scrupulous about your reputation
84 **stated** ranked, or placed in the social hierarchy (in this case above Alice)
85 **Forslowed** delayed, neglected
spurned at kicked against, rejected with contempt. A combination of the proverbial follies of striving against the stream of time (Dent, S927) and spurning (kicking) against a prick (spur) (*OED* spurn *v.*¹ 2b).
86 **Fortune's right hand** Fortune's friendship, alliance or favour; metonymically (*OED* right hand A 1b) the right hand seen as the stronger and more useful
87 **wanton giglot** uncontrolled and lustful girl
89 **weighed down** weighted more heavily in the scales than, i.e. been worth more than

75 slanderous] *(slaundrous)*

205

This certain good I lost for changing bad,
And wrapped my credit in thy company.
I was bewitched – that is no theme of thine –
And thou, unhallowed, hast enchanted me.
But I will break thy spells and exorcisms,   95
And put another sight upon these eyes
That showed my heart a raven for a dove.
Thou art not fair – I viewed thee not till now;
Thou art not kind – till now I knew thee not.
And now the rain hath beaten off thy gilt,   100
Thy worthless copper shows thee counterfeit.
It grieves me not to see how foul thou art,
But mads me that I ever thought thee fair.
Go, get thee gone, a copesmate for thy hinds!
I am too good to be thy favourite.   105

ALICE

Ay, now I see, and too soon find it true,
Which often hath been told me by my friends:
That Mosby loves me not, but for my wealth,

91 **for changing bad** by exchanging for something bad; but also 'for a bad that is varying and inconstant'
92 **wrapped** concealed, muffled up
credit reputation; good name
93 **that ... thine** 'you're not the only one who can say that'; 'you can't say that about yourself'
94 **unhallowed** unholy, wicked
96 **put ... eyes** assume another way of looking
97 **for** as being, as if it were
100 **beaten ... gilt** taken off the thin layer of gold
101 i.e. she is like a fake coin whose base metal is revealed when the gold plating comes off. The image picks up on the giving of gold coins in earlier scenes.
103 ***I ever** B&T, following SMS, reverses

Q1's syntax here, and posits (in *CRE*) a transposition of the common word order (on Shakespeare's characteristic use of which they cite Tarlinskaja, *Versification*). Q1's 'ever I' is particularly jarring, coming as it does in the centre of the second of a pair of otherwise metrically well-balanced lines, so the emendation is adopted here.
104 **copesmate** partner, lover, accomplice in crime. One copy of Q1 has 'copsemate', and B&T emends to this, suggesting (in *CRE*) a pun on copse as an appropriate place for hinds and citing two 1591 works by Abraham Fraunce. As hinds are female deer, however, and Mosby is suggesting Alice's liaison with male servants, the primary spelling is given here.
108 **but** only

103 I ever] *SMS*; ever I *Q1*   thought] *Q2–3*; chought *Q1*   104 copesmate] *Q1a*; copsemate *Q1b*

Which too incredulous I ne'er believed.
Nay, hear me speak, Mosby, a word or two –   110
I'll bite my tongue if it speak bitterly –
Look on me, Mosby, or I'll kill myself!
Nothing shall hide me from thy stormy look:
If thou cry war there is no peace for me.
I will do penance for offending thee   115
And burn this prayer-book, where I here use
The holy word that had converted me.
See, Mosby, I will tear away the leaves,
And all the leaves, and in this golden cover
Shall thy sweet phrases and thy letters dwell;   120
And thereon will I chiefly meditate,

110 **Nay ... speak** suggests that Mosby tries to leave, turns away, or blocks his ears or possibly her mouth

114–22 Several editors speculate about possible censorship in this passage, given the shocking nature of the actions it suggests. B&T (*CRE*) argues suggestively that it is remarkable 'that the passage contains no explicit reference to God', pointing to *2 Tamburlaine*, 5.1, where the Koran is burned, during which 'God' is named six times and 'Mahomet' five. They suggest that *The holy word* might have read 'God's holy word', and that there may be omissions of lines, perhaps after *dwell*. The repetition in 'leaves, / And all the leaves' may also suggest disruption.

115 **penance** performance of a penalty of some kind to express sorrow and make amends for a sin. In Catholic practice the equivalence between sin and recompense is worked out by the priest.

116 **prayer-book** probably, and if so especially shockingly, the *Book of Common Prayer* (*BCP*): the post-Reformation prayer-book in English, first published in 1549 and reissued in a more strongly Protestant form in 1552. Although banned under Mary, it was reissued on Elizabeth I's accession. Rather than prayers for personal devotion, it contained forms of service for worship at all times of the day and year, daily readings, collects and psalms; in other words, the complete liturgy of the Church.

116–17 **use ... me** i.e. read the words that have turned me from a Catholic to a Protestant, kept me from error and wrongdoing more generally, or taught me specifically to turn away from an immoral relationship with Mosby (cf. John Northbrooke, *Spiritus Est Vicarius Christi* (1557), 'Least the custome of pleasure shoulde ... converte us ... from God and good workes' (62)).
use practise or observe (*OED* 1a)

119 **golden** precious, but probably also literally made with gold (the V&A object cited in 43 SDn. is an example). The book is therefore a sign of Alice's status and the wealth she brings with her.

117 had] hath *Q3*

And hold no other sect but such devotion.
Wilt thou not look? Is all thy love overwhelmed?
Wilt thou not hear? What malice stops thine ears?
Why speaks thou not? What silence ties thy tongue?　　125
Thou hast been sighted as the eagle is,
And heard as quickly as the fearful hare,
And spoke as smoothly as an orator,
When I have bid thee hear, or see, or speak;
And art thou sensible in none of these?　　　　　　　130
Weigh all thy good turns with this little fault
And I deserve not Mosby's muddy looks.

122 **hold ... sect** adhere to no other cult. B&T's substitution of 'faith' for *sect* aims to reconstitute the pre-censorship line. The editors state (in *CRE*) that the awkward construction of 'hold no other sect' has no EEBO-TCP parallels, unlike the more regular 'hold faith'. Although this is a plausible and interesting suggestion, the potent and divisive meanings of *sect* have considerable force here: the word is most often pejoratively used in post-Reformation discourse by one group to describe another, in an attempt to define orthodoxy in opposition to others' heresy. In the year *Arden* was printed at least two sermons were preached at Paul's Cross decrying various sects, including '*Paules Jesuits,* a Murrain Sect of Heretics That Infect the Pureness of the Gospel' (Robert Temple, *A Sermon Teaching Discretion in Matters of Religion*, sig. B7ʳ). The word's presence in moral literature around women's behaviour is also interesting: Henry Smith's *A Preparative to Marriage* (1591) states that '*Salomon* mounteth the envie of women above all other envies, stubborne, sullen, taunting, gainsaying, outfacing ... We say not, all are alike, but this sect hath manie Disciples' (82–3). The period also saw the inception of compound words such as sect-maker, sect-master and sect-follower, which indicates its divisiveness and the way this might characterize Mosby and Alice's love.

123 **overwhelmed** overpowered

126 **been ... is** had the eyesight of an eagle. For the proverbially sharp-eyed eagle see Dent, E6.

127 **heard as quickly** had hearing as alert

128 **as smoothly ... orator** i.e. using attractive or convincing language, with a show of sincerity

130 **sensible** capable of perceiving
these his senses

131 **Weigh ... with** balance against, as on scales
thy good turns the good things I have done for you

122 sect] faith *B&T*

A fount once troubled is not thickened still;
Be clear again, I'll ne'er more trouble thee.

MOSBY

Oh no, I am a 'base artificer';   135
My wings are feathered for a lowly flight,
Mosby, fie no, not for a thousand pound;
Make love to you, why, 'tis unpardonable.
We beggars must not breathe where gentles are!

ALICE

Sweet Mosby is as gentle as a king,   140
And I too blind to judge him otherwise.
Flowers do sometimes spring in fallow lands,
Weeds in gardens; roses grow on thorns.
So whatsoe'er my Mosby's father was,
Himself is valued gentle by his worth.   145

---

133 ***fount once troubled** spring or fountain
when it has been disturbed, stirred up and
so made cloudy (compare the modern
sense of *trouble* in 134). In a period when
natural springs provided the only reliable
sources of clean water, this would be a
significant problem. Q1 has 'fence of
trouble', an obvious error; Headlam conjectured eye-skip from an intermediate
mistake, from 'on' in one word to 'on' in
the other, 'fon[t on]ce troubled', of which
an attempt was then made to make sense.
B&T (*CRE*) conjectures 'fonte once'
(which spelling they point out is more
likely to be confused, given the similarity
of *t* and *c* in secretary hand).

thickened still made permanently more
murky or opaque (with mud caused by
the 'troubling' of the water)

135 **artificer** stressed on the second syllable

136 **feathered for** have feathers appropriate
to: i.e. like a low-flying garden bird,

rather than an eagle

139 **gentles** gentlemen and gentlewomen

142–3 Plants grow in the wrong places, just
as people's natures might be inappropriate for their social standing.

143 **Weeds** B&T emends to 'Weed breeds' in
order to provide the extra syllable to
regularize the verse, suggesting (in *CRE*)
eye-skip from 'one "eede" to the next'
and pointing out that the word 'is' has
been missed from 145. But the full
phrase appears to be asking the hearer to
carry *spring* over from flowers to weeds.
'Weeds spring' appears thirteen times to
1642 in an EEBO-TCP search, whereas
'weeds breed' does not appear.

145 *His worth to her gives him equivalent
value to a gentleman. See pp. 15–36 for
contemporary debates about the under-
pinnings of social status. The verb (*is*) is
added here, as per the SMS addition, as
the line does not make sense without it.

---

133 fount once troubled] *Schelling (conj. Headlam)* (font . . .); fence of trouble *Q1*; sense of trouble
Tyrrell   139 gentles] *Tyrrell*; gentiles *Q1*   143 Weeds] Weed breeds *B&T*   145 is] *SMS; not in Q1*

MOSBY

Ah, how you women can insinuate,
And clear a trespass with your sweet-set tongue!
I will forget this quarrel, gentle Alice,
Provided I'll be tempted so no more.

Here enters BRADSHAW.

ALICE

Then with thy lips seal up this new-made match.   150

MOSBY

Soft, Alice, for here comes somebody.

ALICE

How now Bradshaw, what's the news with you?

BRADSHAW

I have little news, but here's a letter
That Master Greene importuned me to give you.

ALICE

Go in, Bradshaw, call for a cup of beer.   155
'Tis almost supper time, thou shalt stay with us.

Exit [Bradshaw].

Then she reads the letter.

*We have missed of our purpose at London, but shall
perform it by the way. We thank our neighbour
Bradshaw.*

Yours, Richard Greene   160

How likes my love the tenor of this letter?

---

146 **insinuate** worm oneself artfully into another's favours (*OED* 2a)
147 **clear a trespass** wipe away a fault
sweet-set positioned or fixed in such a way that it is pleasing to the senses
149 **so** in this manner

150 **seal up** ratify, as one would a document; kiss
153 **letter** See 2.77.
155–6 Alice demonstrates her domestic authority and the hospitality that her house can offer.
161 **tenor** sense, import

149 SD] *after 151 Tyrrell; after 150 Hugo*   156 SD] *Q2; opp. 155 Q1 (Exit)   Bradshaw] Tyrrell*

MOSBY

Well were his date complete and expired!

ALICE

Ah, would it were! Then comes my happy hour.
Till then my bliss is mixed with bitter gall.
Come, let us in to shun suspicion.   165

MOSBY

Ay, to the gates of death to follow thee!   *Exeunt.*

[**Sc. 9**]   *Here enters* GREENE, [BLACK] WILL *and*
                    SHAKEBAG [*with pistols*].

SHAKEBAG

Come, Will, see thy tools be in a readiness:
Is not thy powder dank, or will thy flint strike fire?

BLACK WILL

Then ask me if my nose be on my face,
Or whether my tongue be frozen in my mouth.
Zounds, here's a coil!   5
You were best swear me on the intergatories

---

162 **Well** to a great extent (*OED adv.*, *n.*[4] III)
were . . . expired i.e. were he dead
expired expirèd. legal term for the end of
a contract that relates to the letter's date; it
recalls the image of sealing up in 150.

164 **gall** bile

165 **suspicion** four syllables

Sc. 9 Set on the open road which Will defines
as a *down* (12). Michael and Arden pin-
point it geographically later in the scene
(51, 55–6; see also 127).

0.2 *with pistols* See Dessen and Thomson,
164, for the frequency of entries with
pistols, e.g. *Spanish Tragedy*, 3.3.

1 **tools** weapons

2 **powder . . . fire** Struck with iron or steel,
the flint produces sparks that ignite the

gunpowder. Elizabethan trained bands
often carried touch-boxes and flasks filled
with priming (or touch-) powder for their
weapons, and this was, therefore, familiar
equipment for many in the audience who
were required to keep them at home. In
1591 Nicholas Ady, Faversham innkeeper,
kept touch-box and flask in the garret over
his buttery, and a 30lb barrel of gunpowder in his study (KHLC 10.19.359).

3 **nose . . . face** perhaps related to the proverbial 'As plain as the nose on a man's
face' (Dent, N215)

5 **coil** fuss or ado

6 **intergatories** interrogatories, legal questions addressed to the accused or witnesses in court

---

163] *Delius; Q1 lines* were, / howre. /   166] Ay] *(I);* Ile *SMS;* I *Wiggins*   **Sc. 9**] *Hugo;* ACT IV. SCENE
II. *Tyrrell;* Act III. Scene VI. *Delius*   0.2 *with pistols*] *this edn*   2] *Delius; Q1 lines* dancke, / fyre /   5–7]
Delius; Q1 lines (the /) hand. /

How many pistols I have took in hand,
Or whether I love the smell of gunpowder,
Or dare abide the noise the dag will make,
Or will not wink at flashing of the fire.   10
I pray thee, Shakebag, let this answer thee:
That I have took more purses in this down
Than e'er thou handledst pistols in thy life.

SHAKEBAG

Ay, haply thou hast picked more in a throng;
But, should I brag what booties I have took,   15
I think the overplus that's more than thine
Would mount to a greater sum of money
Than either thou or all thy kin are worth.
Zounds, I hate them as I hate a toad
That carry a muscado in their tongue   20
And scarce a hurting weapon in their hand.

BLACK WILL

O Greene, intolerable!
It is not for mine honour to bear this!
Why, Shakebag, I did serve the King at Boulogne,
And thou canst brag of nothing that thou hast done.   25

---

9   **dag** heavy pistol or handgun. The tanner Robert Wroting kept one in his hall in Faversham in 1590 (KHLC 10.19.152).
10 **wink** shut my eyes
12 **down** elevated, open land
14 **haply** perhaps. Q1, here and at 54, reads 'happely'.
    throng crowd
16–18 'The amount by which my ill-gotten gains exceed yours is more than your whole family's fortune.'
16 **overplus** addition, that which is in excess
18 **kin** either Will's relations, or the wider

family of thieves with which his actions associate him
19 **them** those who carry *a muscado* (20) in their tongue
20 **muscado** probably a confusion of 'moschetto', the Italian for 'musket' (B&T). Other suggestions have included 'mosquito' (Hopkinson) or the Spanish for gadfly (Bullen), but these meanings do not deal well with Shakebag's slur on Will's family, whom he clearly sees as 'all mouth and no weapons'.
23 **for** in accordance with
24 See 2.8.

14, 54 haply] *SMS;* happely *Q1;* happily *Q2*   17 mount to . . . money] mount up to . . . money *(conj. Jowett);* to . . . money mount *(conj. Taylor)*   20 muscado] *moschetto B&T*

212

SHAKEBAG

Why, so can Jack of Faversham,
That swooned for a fillip on the nose
When he that gave it him holloed in his ear,
And he supposed a cannon-bullet hit him.
Then they fight.

GREENE

I pray you, sirs, list to Aesop's talk: 30
Whilst two stout dogs were striving for a bone,
There comes a cur and stole it from them both.
So, while you stand striving on these terms of
    manhood,
Arden escapes us and deceives us all.

SHAKEBAG

Why, he begun.

BLACK WILL   And thou shalt find I'll end.   35
I do but slip it until better time.
But if I do forget –

Then he kneels down and holds up
his hands to heaven.

GREENE

Well, take your fittest standings, and once more
Lime your twigs to catch this weary bird.

---

26 **so can** i.e. brag that he served the
    King
    Jack generic name, 'everyman', as in
    'Jack of all trades'
27 **swooned** fainted; swoonèd
    fillip blow
28 **holloed** shouted loudly, hollered
30 **Aesop's talk** sayings of the legendary
    Greek story-teller, credited with the
    authorship of many animal fables
31–3 In the original story, a lion and a bear
    fight over a kid, but while they lie

exhausted and wounded a fox takes their
prey. Cf. Mosby's plan, 8.34–5.
32 **cur** low-bred dog
33 **striving ... manhood** arguing about
    who is the most manly
36 **slip it** let it go
38 **take ... standings** See 3.39, where
    Greene gives the same instruction.
39 **Lime your twigs** Bird lime, a sticky sub-
    stance made from holly tree bark, was
    spread on twigs to catch small birds who
    landed there.

27 swooned] *(sounded)*   34 deceives] *Q2;* deceaue *Q1*

I'll leave you, and at your dags' discharge   40
Make towards, like the longing water-dog
That coucheth till the fowling-piece be off,
Then seizeth on the prey with eager mood.
Ah, might I see him stretching forth his limbs
As I have seen them beat their wings ere now!   45

SHAKEBAG

Why, that thou shalt see if he come this way.

GREENE

Yes, that he doth, Shakebag, I warrant thee.
But brawl not when I am gone in any case,
But, sirs, be sure to speed him when he comes;
And in that hope I'll leave you for an hour.   50
Exit. [Black Will and Shakebag conceal themselves.]

Here enters ARDEN, FRANKLIN *and* MICHAEL.

MICHAEL

'Twere best that I went back to Rochester.
The horse halts downright; it were not good
He travailed in such pain to Faversham.
Removing of a shoe may haply help it.

ARDEN   Well, get you back to Rochester; but, sirrah, see   55
ye overtake us ere we come to Rainham Down,
For it will be very late ere we get home.

41 **Make towards** come towards you
    water-dog dog trained to retrieve water-fowl
42 **coucheth** lies down
    fowling-piece light gun used for shooting wild fowl
48 **in any case** on any account
49 **speed** kill
50 SD Greene's exit picks up on his similar avoidance of violence in 3.41–2.

51 **back to Rochester** The party are apparently to be imagined by the audience part-way between Rochester and Rainham; see also 127 and n.
52 **halts** limps
    downright thoroughly, completely
53 **travailed** laboured; but also, as heard onstage, 'travelled'
54 **haply** perhaps
56 **overtake** catch up with

50 SD *Exit*] *(Exit Gre.) Black ... themselves*] *Wiggins*   54 shoe may] *Q2;* shoemay *Q1*   55–7] *Hopkinson² lines* sirrah, / Down. / home. / ; *Delius lines* see, / Down, / home. /   56 Rainham] *(Raynum)*

MICHAEL *[aside]*

> Ay, God he knows, and so doth Will and Shakebag,
> That thou shalt never go further than that Down;
> And therefore have I pricked the horse on purpose,   60
> Because I would not view the massacre.   *Exit.*

ARDEN

> Come, Master Franklin, onwards with your tale.

FRANKLIN

> I assure you, sir, you task me much.
> A heavy blood is gathered at my heart,
> And on the sudden is my wind so short   65
> As hindereth the passage of my speech.
> So fierce a qualm yet ne'er assailed me.

58 **God ... and** formulaic phrase, but fairly rare with only five instances to 1600. See, e.g., George Gascoigne, *The Poesies of George Gascoigne Esquire* (1575), 'As God he knowes and men can witnesse beare' (cxxxv); *R3*, 'For God he knowes, and you may partly see' (Q1 (1597), sig. H3ʳ).

60 **pricked** wounded by piercing. The word was familiar from farriery, where it referred to the piercing of a horse's foot to the quick whilst shoeing, resulting in lameness.

62 **Franklin ... tale** There is a literary joke here about a man called Franklin telling a tale on the old Pilgrim Road from London to Canterbury (Wiggins). Chaucer's 'Franklin's Tale' (based on Boccaccio) concerns a married couple committed to equality, parted by the husband's quest for fame. Their relationship faces a test when the wife's unwelcome suitor unexpectedly fulfils his side of her wild bargain offering her sexual favours in return for the removal of all the coastal rocks of Brittany. The story eventually told in this scene, in contrast, has its roots in the gossip that surrounded local court cases for adultery. Its basis in social life and the portentous context of Franklin's shortness of breath give it a power greater than its length.

    onwards carry on

63 **task** to set to a task, with suggestions of the slightly later meaning (*OED v.* 3a, citing *MW*, 1616, as the first example) to put a strain upon

64 **heavy blood** originally a humoral term, it also had portentous overtones. EEBO-TCP gives only three other pre-1600 uses, including the 1526 *Great Herbal*'s description of the melancholic individual who 'hath in hym heuy blode of the nature of erthe and is comynly pale of colour' (sig. Cc4ᵛ), and Churchyard, *Churchyard's Challenge* (1593), telling of bugbears that, 'are fancies of thy head: / Or on thy hart some heauy blood, / that haunts thee in thy bed' (183).

65 **on the sudden** suddenly
    wind breath

67 **qualm** sudden pang of fear or misgiving (*OED n.³* 1a); attack of faintness or sickness (*OED n.³* 2)
    assailed assailèd

58 SD] *Tyrrell*   61 SD] *(Exit Micahell.)*

ARDEN

Come, Master Franklin, let us go on softly.
The annoyance of the dust, or else some meat
You ate at dinner, cannot you brook.   70
I have been often so, and soon amended.

FRANKLIN

Do you remember where my tale did leave?

ARDEN

Ay, where the gentleman did check his wife.

FRANKLIN

She being reprehended for the fact,
Witness produced that took her with the deed,   75
Her glove brought in, which there she left behind,
And many other assured arguments,
Her husband asked her whether it were not so.

ARDEN

Her answer then? I wonder how she looked,
Having forsworn it with such vehement oaths,   80
And at the instant so approved upon her?

FRANKLIN

First, did she cast her eyes down to the earth,
Watching the drops that fell amain from thence;

---

70   *brook digest, retain in the stomach (*OED* 2a); tolerate or endure (*OED* 3a). Q1 has 'brooke you', but it is Franklin who should brook the meat, rather than the other way round. EEBO-TCP records no instances of 'brook with you' (the Q2 reading) to 1642, so this edition adopts B&T (*CRE*)'s conjectured reversed syntax, despite the metre.

72   **where ... leave** where I stopped my story

73   **check** stop; rebuke; also perhaps 'challenge' (*OED* 4a). As the audience have not heard the first part of the tale, this

word sets it up strikingly as a marital dispute.

74   **fact** crime

75   **took ... deed** came upon her doing it; caught her at it (*OED* take 6a)

76   See 7.8–11 for the story of Franklin's own mislaid napkin, which establishes the significance of personal objects as evidence (in Sc. 7 certainly fabricated) of behaviour.

77   **assured** verified; assurèd
     arguments proofs, evidence

81   **approved** proved

83   **amain** with full force; quickly

70 ate] *(eat)*   you brook] *conj. B&T (CRE);* brooke you *Q1;* brooke with you *Q2*   78 Her] *Q1b;* He *Q1a*

Then softly draws she forth her handkerchief,
And modestly she wipes her tear-stained face;   85
Then hemmed she out, to clear her voice, should
    seem,
And with a majesty addressed herself
To encounter all their accusations.
Pardon me, Master Arden, I can no more:
This fighting at my heart makes short my wind.   90

ARDEN
Come, we are almost now at Rainham Down.
Your pretty tale beguiles the weary way;
I would you were in state to tell it out.

SHAKEBAG [*aside to Black Will*]
Stand close, Will, I hear them coming.

Here enters LORD CHEYNE *with his men.*

BLACK WILL [*aside to Shakebag*]
Stand to it, Shakebag, and be resolute.   95

LORD CHEYNE [*to his men*]
Is it so near night as it seems,
Or will this black-faced evening have a shower? –
What, Master Arden, you are well met!

---

86   **hemmed she out** she cleared her throat
     to make her voice more distinct (perhaps
     in a way that suggested her hesitancy)
     should seem it would seem
88   **encounter** contest, dispute
92   Cf. *R2*, 2.3.8–12, 'But I bethink me what a
     weary way / From Ravenspurgh to
     Cotshall will be found / In Ross and
     Willoughby, wanting your company, /
     Which I protest hath very much beguiled /
     The tediousness and process of my travel'.

pretty skilful; well-wrought
beguiles diverts attention from, wiles
     away
93   **in state** fit, ready to do it (*OED* state *n.*
     P2b); see also *OED* 7a, healthy
     tell it out finish it
94   SD2 In Holinshed, Arden is protected by
     'diuerse gentlemen of his acquaintance,
     who kept him companie' (see below,
     p. 295), and the incident is separate to his
     visit to Cheyne's house.

84 handkerchief] *(handkercher)*   94 SD1] *Wiggins (aside to Will), (Hugo subst.)*   95 SD] *Wiggins (Hugo
subst.)*   96 SD] *this edn*

I have longed this fortnight's day to speak with you.
You are a stranger, man, in the Isle of Sheppey.   100

ARDEN

Your honour's always, bound to do you service.

LORD CHEYNE

Come you from London, and ne'er a man with you?

ARDEN

My man's coming after.
But here's my honest friend, that came along with me.

LORD CHEYNE [*to Franklin*]

My Lord Protector's man I take you to be.   105

FRANKLIN

Ay, my good lord, and highly bound to you.

LORD CHEYNE [*to Arden*]

You and your friend come home and sup with me.

ARDEN

I beseech your honour, pardon me.
I have made a promise to a gentleman,
My honest friend, to meet him at my house.   110
The occasion is great, or else would I wait on you.

---

99 **this fortnight's day** for a fortnight
100 i.e. you don't visit me often enough; a public demonstration of favour and patronage from Cheyne to Arden.
101 The line would be accompanied by a show of deference, the actor probably bowing and removing his hat as he speaks.
102 **man** servant
105 The audience are told very little of Franklin's affairs; at the start of the play he speaks with authority about the Lord Protector's land grant to Arden (1.2–5), and Cheyne's assertion here indicates that Franklin is in Somerset's service. It is possible that Franklin's display of Somerset's arms, on his costume or riding gear, alerts Cheyne to the connection.

106 **highly bound** strongly obliged; having a duty of respect and service, with a suggestion of the technical sense of pertaining to the nature of the role of retainer (dependant who gives service in return for patronage) that is linked to the status of Franklin's relationship with the Lord Protector.
107 **sup** take supper; eat the last meal of the day
109–10 **promise . . . house** The audience are not told about such a promise in advance, which suggests that Arden is inventing an excuse to allow him to see Alice.
111 **wait on** attend, with a suggestion of service due to one of higher rank, though not to wait at table; see also *wait upon*, 115.

---

100 Sheppey] *Q1b* (Sheppy); *Q1a*   103–4] *W&P lines* here's /me. / ; *prose Wiggins (conj. Wine)*   105 SD] *Wine*   107 SD] *this edn*

LORD CHEYNE

Will you come tomorrow and dine with me,
And bring your honest friend along with you?
I have diverse matters to talk with you about.

ARDEN

Tomorrow we'll wait upon your honour.   115

LORD CHEYNE [*to his men*]

One of you stay my horse at the top of the hill.
What, Black Will, for whose purse wait you?
Thou wilt be hanged in Kent when all is done.

BLACK WILL

Not hanged, God save your honour.
I am your beadsman, bound to pray for you.   120

LORD CHEYNE

I think thou ne'er saidst prayer in all thy life.
[*to his men*] One of you give him a crown,
[*to Black Will*] And, sirrah, leave this kind of life.
If thou beest 'tainted for a penny matter
And come in question, surely thou wilt truss.   125
Come, Master Arden, let us be going;
Your way and mine lies four mile together.

Exeunt all but Black Will and Shakebag.

112 **dine** take the main meal of the day
116 One of Cheyne's retinue could leave here, but they may gesture offstage to a supposed other, depending on the number of actors available.
stay stop, bring to a halt. The command indicates both the size of retinue the audience are to imagine for Cheyne and the landscape in which the action takes place.
117 Cheyne perhaps notices Will as he turns round to address his servants.
120 **beadsman** servant; originally one charged with or taking on the duty of praying regularly for another's soul
124 **'tainted** attaindered, condemned

penny matter trifling, unimportant crime
125 **come in question** become an issue; here, specifically, are examined in court under suspicion
truss hang
127 This suggests that they are at Sittingbourne, travelling together towards Faversham until Cheyne's party take the lower road (nearer the coast) to Harty Ferry. As Arden previously told Michael to overtake them before they got to Rainham Down (55–6), the audience are to imagine that the time spent listening to Franklin's tale has advanced them on their journey by some five miles.

116 SD] *Wiggins* 121 saidst] *(saidest)* 122 SD] *Wiggins* 123 SD] *Wiggins (To Will)* 127 SD] *(Exeunt. Manet Black Wil & Shakbag)*

Arden of Faversham

BLACK WILL

The devil break all your necks at four miles' end!
Zounds, I could kill myself for very anger!
His lordship chops me in,   130
Even when my dag was levelled at his heart.
I would his crown were molten down his throat!

SHAKEBAG

Arden, thou hast wondrous holy luck.
Did ever man escape as thou hast done?
Well, I'll discharge my pistol at the sky,   135
For by this bullet Arden might not die.
    [*Then he fires his gun.*]

Here enters GREENE.

GREENE

What, is he down, is he dispatched?!

SHAKEBAG

Ay, in health towards Faversham, to shame us all.

GREENE

The devil he is! Why, sirs, how escaped he?

SHAKEBAG

When we were ready to shoot,   140
Comes my Lord Cheyne to prevent his death.

GREENE

The Lord of heaven hath preserved him.

130 **chops me in** interrupts me, butts in
131 **his** Arden's
136 **by … die** The bullet is now deemed unlucky as it has not been used to kill Arden, or is superfluous as the chance to kill him has passed.
137 **dispatched** killed, in Greene's meaning, but sent on his journey *towards Faversham*, as Shakebag puns on the term in the following line
138 A pun on 'Fevershame', the Q1 spelling, seems likely here, in the context of *health* and *shame*; see B&T, 15–16.
142 **preserved** preservèd

130–1] *Delius; Q1 lines* when / hart. /   136 SD1] *this edn (Wiggins subst.)*   140–1] *one line Wiggins*

BLACK WILL   'The Lord of heaven', a fig! The Lord
    Cheyne hath preserved him, and bids him to a feast to
    his house at Shurland.   145
    But, by the way, once more I'll meet with him,
    And, if all the Cheynes in the world say no,
    I'll have a bullet in his breast tomorrow.
    Therefore come, Greene, and let us to Faversham.

GREENE
    Ay, and excuse ourselves to Mistress Arden.   150
    Oh, how she'll chafe when she hears of this!

SHAKEBAG
    Why, I'll warrant you she'll think we dare not do it.

BLACK WILL
    Why then, let us go and tell her all the matter,
    And plot the news to cut him off tomorrow.   *Exeunt.*

143 *'**The Lord ... fig** Q1 has 'Preserued, a
figge', and the curious nature of Will's
echo of Greene, repeating the verb rather
than its subject, indicates that this passage was censored. Jackson's proposed
emendation, followed here, extends
Cheyne's characterization of Will as
impious, and harks back to Alice's abuse
of the *BCP* in the previous scene in its
shock value (Jackson, 'Material').
Whilst this cannot be proved to be the
speech that was originally intended,
it is in keeping with the outrageous
nature of Will's language at other points
and his lack of respect for any kind
of authority. Jackson also points out the
balance between the agency ascribed

to the heavenly and then the earthly
Lord.
   fig insulting gesture involving thrusting
the thumb rudely between two closed
fingers. Its performance in this context
adds considerably to Will's heavenly
insult. See, e.g., Marlowe's *Edward II*,
where Prince Edward says to Queen
Isabella, 'please my father well, and then
a Fig / For all my vnckles friendship here
in France' (sig. G4ᵛ).
151 **chafe** rage; scold
154 **plot the news** make a new plot involving
this news; plot tomorrow's news that he
is killed
   cut him off both head him off on his
journey and kill him

143–5] *B&T; Q1 lines* him / shorlow: /   143 'The Lord ... fig!] *Sturgess (conj. Jackson, 'Material');*
Preserued, a figge, *Q1*   145 Shurland] *Jacob;* Shorlow *Q1;* Shorland *Hopkinson²;* Shorlan *B&T*
(CRE)   152 do it] *Q2;* doit *Q1*   154 plot] *(plat)*

[Sc. 10]   *Here enters* ARDEN *and his wife* [ALICE],
             FRANKLIN *and* MICHAEL.

ARDEN

See how the Hours, the guardant of heaven's gate,
Have by their toil removed the darksome clouds,
That Sol may well discern the trampled pace
Wherein he wont to guide his golden car.
The season fits. Come, Franklin, let's away.   5

ALICE

I thought you did pretend some special hunt
That made you thus cut short the time of rest.

ARDEN

It was no chase that made me rise so early
But, as I told thee yesternight, to go
To the Isle of Sheppey, there to dine with my Lord
     Cheyne;   10
For so his honour late commanded me.

Sc. 10 Franklin and Arden are just about to leave the Faversham house as the scene opens, and Clarke enters shortly after their departure. The scene is therefore linked to the house, but not specifically set within it; Alice may be taken to exit 'within' at 34, but it is not clear from where she returns with Mosby and Greene at 77.

1   **the Hours** the Horae, daughters of Aphrodite and Zeus in Greek mythology, responsible for the changing of the seasons
   guardant guardian, keeper or protector. The Horae were the guardians of the gates of Mount Olympus. Cf. the Poet's welcoming speech in *Elvetham*: 'And light-foot *Howrs, the* guardians *of heaven's gate*' (B3ᵛ).

3   **Sol** personification of the sun. See 1.61 for a corresponding passage of classical allusion.
   pace passage, route

4   **wont** is accustomed
   golden car i.e. the sun, as a golden carriage drawn by horses

5   **The season fits** It is the right moment (to leave).

6   **pretend** both 'plan' (*OED* 10) and 'use as a pretext' (*OED* 2b). The word adds to the atmosphere of dissembling and mistrust between the couple.
   hunt a common reason for rising early amongst the elite, and often used in a literary context. See *Tit*, 'The hunt is up, the morn is bright and grey' (2.1.1).

11   **late** recently

Sc. 10] *Hugo;* ACT IV. SCENE III. *Tyrrell;* Act IV. Scene I. *Delius*   3 discern] *(deserne) Q2;* deserue *Q1*   9–10] *W&P; Q1 lines* Sheppy: / Cheiny. / ; *Delius lines* yesternight, / dine / Cheiny; /

ALICE

Ay, such kind husbands seldom want excuses;
Home is a wild cat to a wandering wit.
The time hath been – would God it were not past –
That honour's title nor a lord's command　　　　　　　15
Could once have drawn you from these arms of mine.
But my deserts or your desires decay,
Or both. Yet if true love may seem desert,
I merit still to have thy company.

FRANKLIN

Why, I pray you, sir, let her go along with us.　　　　20
I am sure his honour will welcome her,
And us the more for bringing her along.

12　**kind** affectionate and loving (used sarcastically); with a suggestion of high social rank (associated with Cheyne), picking up on Arden's previous speech (*OED* II 6b, akin to 'gentle' in its double meaning of behaviour and status)
　　want lack

13　Although it sounds proverbial, Dent gives no entry. EEBO-TCP to 1642 offers Thomas Cooper's 1617 *Mystery of Witchcraft*, in which the idle and vagrant generation are described as 'alwaies gadding: their own house is a wild-cat, they must needs be stirring whom the Diuel driues' (309), and the anonymous *Women's Sharp Revenge* (1640): 'in your Lecture of the wife to her husband, Is the house a wild-cat to you? and why a wild-cat you tame foole? unlesse you study to set odds betwixt man and wife, and to make them agree in a house like dogs and cats together' (104). Wildcats were famously vicious and the name was often given to shrewish women (see *TS*, 1.2.113–14; Tusser's *Hundred Good*

Points of Husbandry (1570), 'Where windows stand open ye cattes make a fray yet wilde cats with two legs are worser then they' (fol. 30)). There may have been a slippage of the idea of inhospitable wildness from the wife to the house itself (see 25–6 for an analogous idea).
　　wandering wit both an 'unhinged brain' and a 'person who thinks only of getting out of the house'

15　**That ... nor** that neither ... nor
　　honour's title Jacob's suggestion, 'honours, title', is also plausible.

17　**deserts** merits
　　***desires** Q1 reads 'deserues', and Q2 appears to try to emend to 'desernes', perhaps meaning 'perceptions' (*OED* discern *n.*), although the first example given is 1599. The move is interestingly similar to the textual confusions between quarto readings in 1.3 ('deserue'/'deserne'), and may indicate an isolated feature of the MS.
　　decay decrease

18　**desert** deserving

13 wandering] *(wandring)*　15 honour's title] *(honors tytle);* honours, title *Jacob*　17 desires] *W&P;* deserues *Q1;* desernes *Q2*

ARDEN

Content! [*to Michael*] Sirrah, saddle your mistress' nag.

ALICE

No, begged favour merits little thanks.
If I should go, our house would run away   25
Or else be stolen; therefore I'll stay behind.

ARDEN

Nay, see how mistaking you are. I pray thee, go.

ALICE

No, no, not now.

ARDEN

Then let me leave thee satisfied in this:
That time, nor place, nor persons alter me,   30
But that I hold thee dearer than my life.

ALICE

That will be seen by your quick return.

ARDEN

And that shall be ere night an if I live.
Farewell, sweet Alice; we mind to sup with thee.

Exit Alice.

24 **No** Alice's swift refusal can be played as coming soon enough to keep Michael from exiting.
begged beggèd
25–6 **If ... stolen** The association of women with household security is strong in this period, linked to their husbanding of domestic resources and the impact of their chastity on household credit; see also proverbs with curiously mobile houses, e.g. to keep one's house on one's back like a snail (Dent, S580). The lines can be delivered to suggest Alice's sarcastic humour towards Arden, indicating a 'shrewish' nature.
27 **mistaking** misunderstanding, misconceiving

29 **satisfied** contented, answered
32 **seen** shown
quick speedy, but with a pun on 'alive' that Arden picks up on in the following line. Used with the second meaning in its most widely heard contemporary context in the Apostles' Creed from the *BCP*, where Christ is imagined at the Last Judgement: 'he shal come againe with glory, to judge both the quicke and the deade'.
33 ***an if** if, provided that (*OED* if 8b); 'and if' and 'an if' were used interchangeably.
34 **mind** intend
sup take supper; eat the last meal of the day

23 SD] *Sturgess (Hugo subst.)*   27] *W&P; Q1 lines* are, / goe. /   33 an] *Delius; and Q1*

FRANKLIN

Come, Michael, are our horses ready? 35

MICHAEL Ay, your horse are ready, but I am not ready,
for I have lost my purse with six and thirty shillings in
it, with taking up of my master's nag.

FRANKLIN [*to Arden*]

Why, I pray you, let us go before,
Whilst he stays behind to seek his purse. 40

ARDEN [*to Michael*]

Go to, sirrah!
See you follow us to the Isle of Sheppey,
To my Lord Cheyne's, where we mean to dine.

Exeunt Arden and Franklin. Michael remains.

MICHAEL So, fair weather after you, for before you lies
Black Will and Shakebag, in the broom close, too close 45
for you. They'll be your ferrymen to your long home.

---

37 **six and thirty shillings** a large sum of money for a servant (for average wages see 2.12n.). The clothing of John Lie, a Faversham bachelor, was thus valued in 1599, and was his most valuable possession (KHLC 10.28.205).

38 **taking up** bringing from pasture (*OED* take up 2b)
master's Q1 has 'M.', which could refer either to Arden's or to Alice's horse as Michael is addressing Franklin. Although there is more comic potential in the latter given the pointlessness of the task, it would necessitate taking Michael offstage and back on again in quick succession for one joke.

41 **Go to** expression of mock disbelief or (usually) playful impatience; 'get away' (*OED v.* go to 1b *imper.*)

44 **fair ... you** 'May fair weather follow you.' A common farewell (see Dent,

W217), here contrasted with *before you*.

45 **broom close** enclosed field of the yellow-flowered heathland shrub. Broom had a wide variety of uses, from medicine to bedding, but was best known as a material to make besoms (brooms). One of the few commercially viable plants that grew on sandy heathland, it was found all around the creeks on this part of the coast, lending its name to several areas and a farm called Broomfield, situated just above the road to Harty Ferry.

46 ***your long home** the afterlife, as the place where the longest period of existence is spent. In Greek mythology, Charon carried the souls of the deceased across the rivers Styx and Acheron and into the realm of the dead. This edition follows B&T's adoption of SMS's 'your', due to the overwhelming use of a possessive pronoun with the phrase in the period.

36–8] *Delius; Q1 lines* ready, / purse, / in it, / Nagge. / 38 master's] *W&P;* M. *Q1;* mistris *Q3* 41–2] *Wiggins; one line Q1* 43 SD *Michael remains*] *(Manet Michaell)* 44–8] *W&P; Q1 lines* you, / shakebag, / you, / home, / [SD] / corriual, / Susan. / ; *44–6 prose, 47–8 verse Delius* 46 to your long home] *(y'*long-home) *SMS;* to long home *Q1*

225

Here enters [CLARKE] *the Painter* [*with a crucifix covered*].

But who is this? The painter, my co-rival, that would
needs win Mistress Susan.

CLARKE   How now, Michael, how doth my mistress and
all at home?   50

MICHAEL   Who, Susan Mosby? She's your mistress too?

CLARKE   Ay, how doth she, and all the rest?

MICHAEL   All's well but Susan; she is sick.

CLARKE   Sick? Of what disease?

MICHAEL   Of a great fear.   55

CLARKE   A fear? Of what?

MICHAEL   A great fever.

CLARKE   A fever? God forbid!

MICHAEL   Yes, faith, and of a lurdan too, as big as
yourself.   60

CLARKE   O Michael, the spleen prickles you. Go to; you
carry an eye over Mistress Susan.

MICHAEL   Ay, faith, to keep her from the painter.

CLARKE   Why more from a painter than from a serving-
creature like yourself?   65

47 **co-rival** one of several competitors with
equal claims (*OED n.* 1a)
51 **She's** Q1's unspaced 'Sheis' suggests a
contraction.
55 **fear** dread, but with pun on 'fere'
meaning 'spouse' (*OED* fere *n.*[1] 2a): i.e.
fear of ending up with Clarke as her husband (59–60). Clarke hears only the primary meaning.
59 **lurdan** general term of abuse, usually of
men, suggesting dim-wittedness and/or

laziness. It is linked to a semi-facetious
medical condition, 'fever-lurden': see
Andrew Boorde, *Breviary of Helthe*
(1547), 'I had almost forgotten the fever
lurden with the which many ... yonge
persons be sore infected nowe a dayes'
(55).
61 **spleen prickles** violent ill-temper goads
you
62 **carry ... over** have an eye on; have eyes
for

46 SD CLARKE] *Tyrrell   with ... covered*] *this edn*   47 co-rival] *(corriual)*   49–50] *W&P; Q1 lines*
Mistresse, / home? /   51 She's] *(Sheis); She is Q2*   55 fear] fever *Delius;* fe'er *McIlwraith*   59–60]
Delius; Q1 lines too, / selfe. /   61–2] *Delius; Q1 lines* you. / susan. /   64–5] *Tyrrell; Q1 lines (*seruing /*)*
selfe. / *; Q3 lines* Serving / selfe. /

MICHAEL   Because you painters make but a painting-
table of a pretty wench, and spoil her beauty with
blotting.

CLARKE   What mean you by that?

MICHAEL   Why, that you painters paint lambs in the   70
lining of wenches' petticoats, and we servingmen put
horns to them, to make them become sheep.

CLARKE   Such another word will cost you a cuff or a
knock.

MICHAEL   What, with a dagger made of a pencil? Faith, 'tis   75
too weak, and therefore thou too weak to win Susan.

CLARKE   Would Susan's love lay upon this stroke!
Then he breaks Michael's head.

Here enters MOSBY, GREENE *and* ALICE.

66–7 **painting-table** painted table, i.e.
painting. Paintings were owned by the
upper middling sort and above in provincial towns, keeping provincial artists in
business, and here the term gives a sense
of the cultural circles in which the
Ardens move. Robert Fagg of Faversham
had two 'hanging painted tables' in his
hall, valued at 2s, and two in his parlour
at 12d, when he died in 1574 (KHLC
10.7.173), indicating the kind of numbers in which they were owned; 11 per
cent of households owned them.

68   **blotting** spoiling with ink or paint; but
also stigmatizing (morally), and
throwing dirt at, therefore obliterating or
effacing

70–2 The joke is obscure, but clearly linked
to two later jest-book stories of a young
painter who, forced to go overseas,
paints a lamb on his wife's belly. A merchant, sleeping with her in her husband's

absence, adds two horns with a pencil
(fine paintbrush), telling her he has just
refreshed the old painting. When her
husband returns she tells him, 'yea sir,
remember that it is a yeir past and mair
sen [since] ye went, and thocht it war bot
a lambe quhen ye went, now perdie, it
must neids be a sheip and haue hornes by
the course of nature' (John Rolland,
Thrie Tailes of the Thrie Priests of Peblis
(1603), sig. A2^{r–v}; see also William
Fennor, *Cornucopiae* (1612), 91).

72   **horns** the sign of the cuckold, whose
wife has had sex with another man. A
powerful shaming image.

75   **dagger … pencil** perhaps alluding to
painting as a less manly trade, but primarily suggesting Clarke's short, thin and
ineffective manhood
pencil small paintbrush suitable for delicate work (*OED* 1a)

77   **Would** if only; I wish that

70–2] *Delius; Q1 lines* (the /) peticots / (be- /) sheepe. /   75–6] *Delius; Q1 lines* pensell? / weake, / susan. /

227

ALICE

I'll lay my life, this is for Susan's love.
[*to Michael*] Stayed you behind your master to this
    end?
Have you no other time to brabble in   80
But now, when serious matters are in hand?
Say, Clarke, hast thou done the thing thou promised?

CLARKE

Ay, here it is; the very touch is death.
    [*Then he shows the poisoned crucifix.*]

ALICE

Then this, I hope, if all the rest do fail,
Will catch Master Arden,   85
And make him wise in death that lived a fool.
Why should he thrust his sickle in our corn,

---

80 **brabble** noisily brawl or squabble; but also 'quibble' (*OED* 1), suggesting perhaps that Alice doesn't find their fighting very manly or physical

81 Oliphant has Michael exit here, and B&T suggests he may leave '*nursing his head*'. It would be strikingly disobedient for a servant to leave without express instruction, especially when chastised (unless one takes 79–81 as an implicit instruction to 'stay behind' no longer); Michael's perhaps marginal presence onstage throughout the rest of the scene would echo the way he silently witnesses other aspects of his superiors' plotting.

83 The crucifix has to be brought onstage wrapped up, given its deadly power. The 1982/3 RSC rehearsal notes list a 'Crucifix bound with string and cloth so its shape is obvious'. When it was ordered in 1.610, it followed Mosby's question to Alice 'You know this Greene; is he not religious?' (1.584), suggesting that the object was intended to silence

him after Alice has told him too much. Nine scenes later, the crucifix's appearance as another scheme for Arden's death may suggest to the audience that either Alice and Mosby, or two playwrights writing different scenes, have misunderstood one another's intentions. John Nicholls, in *John Niccols Pilgrimage* (1581), describes a tyrant whose 'Chamberlaines had besméered his Crucifix with poyson' (sig. C1[r]).

86 i.e. make him see the truth, as he dies, of her feelings towards him (as opposed to the usual kind of spiritual wisdom that might come with gazing on a crucifix)

87–94 The speech is ostensibly spoken to Mosby but, as Greene's intervention at 104 shows, the exchange, which is rhetorically passionate in nature, has a wider audience.

87 **thrust ... corn** impede, interfere. Proverbial and sexual: 'Put not thy sickle in another man's corn', where 'sickle' is read as penis (Williams, 1248).

79 SD] *Wine (Hugo subst.)*   83 SD] *Wiggins*

Or what hath he to do with thee, my love?
Or govern me that am to rule myself?
Forsooth, for credit sake I must leave thee? 90
Nay, he must leave to live, that we may love!
May live, may love, for what is life but love?
And love shall last as long as life remains,
And life shall end before my love depart.

MOSBY

Why, what's love without true constancy? 95
Like to a pillar built of many stones,
Yet neither with good mortar, well compact,
Nor cement, to fasten it in the joints,
But that it shakes with every blast of wind
And, being touched, straight falls unto the earth, 100
And buries all his haughty pride in dust.
No, let our love be rocks of adamant
Which time, nor place, nor tempest can asunder.

GREENE

Mosby, leave protestations now,
And let us bethink us what we have to do: 105
Black Will and Shakebag I have placed
In the broom close, watching Arden's coming.
Let's to them, and see what they have done. *Exeunt.*

89 A particularly wild and seditious line, as the rule of wives by their husbands indirectly underpinned the political stability of the realm, which was conceived of as a series of supervised component parts of which the household was the smallest. See pp. 14–15.

96–101 A loosely proverbial image, based on various biblical ideas about good and bad builders (Christ as cornerstone from Ephesians, 2.19–22; the wise man who builds a stone house on the rock, Matthew, 7.24–7); see also 'Hard with hard (i.e. stones and hard mortar) never made a good wall', a slightly later proverb (No. 96, 'Choice and Wittie Proverbs', in *The Book Of Merry Riddles*, 1617).

98 ***cement** Q1 reads 'semell', and B&T (*CRE*) plausibly suggests 'semētt' as the form that led to the error.

102 **adamant** proverbially hard rock symbolizing unchangeableness

103 **asunder** divide

92 may love] my love *B&T*   98 cement] *Q3;* semell *Q1*   106–8] *Delius lines* broom, / them, / done. /

[Sc. 11]   *Here enters* ARDEN *and* FRANKLIN.

ARDEN   O ferryman, where art thou?

Here enters the FERRYMAN.

FERRYMAN   Here, here! Go before to the boat and I will
follow you.

ARDEN
We have great haste; I pray thee, come away.

FERRYMAN   Fie, what a mist is here!   5

ARDEN
This mist, my friend, is mystical,
Like to a good companion's smoky brain,
That was half-drowned with new ale overnight.

FERRYMAN   'Twere pity but his skull were opened to
make more chimney-room.   10

Sc. 11 This scene and the following one, neither of which features in the historical
accounts, extend the theme of the
journey of death facilitated by a ferryman. They therefore implicitly allude
to Charon, the ferryman of Hades, who
carried the souls of the dead over the
rivers Styx and Acheron from the world
of the living to that of the dead. Charon
appears in Virgil's *Aeneid*, Bk 6, as
Aeneas descends to the underworld, and
Jasper Heywood's translation of
Seneca's *Hercules Furens* describes 'His
Bearde unkempt, his bosome foule
deform'de in filthy wyse' (*Seneca*, sig.
C4ʳ). He is mentioned in *Spanish
Tragedy* by the Ghost of Andrea, who
recounts in the opening speech of the
play how he is prevented from entering
the underworld by 'churlish *Charon*',
who 'Said that, my rites of burial not performed, / I might not sit amongst his pas-
sengers' (1.1.20–2). Unlike these literary

and dramatic depictions, however, in
Arden the theme is in comic mode, and
exploits the humorous potential of the
physical difficulties of ferry travel.

1   See 10.46n. The line, accompanied by
appropriate stage business of searching,
sets the foggy scene.

2–3 The Ferryman is apparently otherwise
engaged; perhaps, for comic potential,
saying goodbye to his wife.

6   **mystical** mysterious and enigmatic; used
here comically to allude to the obfusca-
tory power of the mist

9   **'Twere ... opened** it would be a shame
if his skull wasn't opened

10 **chimney-room** vent for smoke to clear,
here from the brain. Chimneys as semi-
enclosed flues over fires were a new
fashion in the sixteenth century, slowly
(and unevenly across the country)
replacing open central hearths whose
smoke escaped between the rafters of
full-height central halls.

Sc. 11] *Hugo;* ACT IV. SCENE IV. *Tyrrell;* ACT IV. SCENE II. *Delius*   2–3] *W&P; Q1 lines* boat. /
you. /   9–10] *W&P; Q1 lines* opened, / roome. /

FRANKLIN   Friend, what's thy opinion of this mist?

FERRÝMAN   I think 'tis like to a curst wife in a little house,
that never leaves her husband till she have driven him
out at doors with a wet pair of eyes. Then looks he as
if his house were afire, or some of his friends dead.   15

ARDEN   Speaks thou this of thine own experience?

FERRYMAN   Perhaps ay, perhaps no; for my wife is as
other women are, that is to say, governed by the moon.

FRANKLIN   By the moon? How, I pray thee?

FERRYMAN   Nay, thereby lies a bargain, and you shall   20
not have it fresh and fasting.

ARDEN   Yes, I pray thee, good ferryman.

FERRYMAN   Then, for this once, let it be midsummer
moon; but yet my wife has another moon.

FRANKLIN   Another moon?   25

---

11   Given their stated hurry in 4, Franklin's question seems oddly nonsequitous. Like his story in Sc. 9, we might see the stand-alone, bawdy comic routine to which this gives rise as moving the travellers some way along the route.

12–14   **a curst . . . eyes** extension of a proverbial phrase into simile, see, e.g., 'wyves and smoke cause men there hous to for go' (Copland, sig. C2ʳ); 'A smoking house and a chiding wife make a man run out of doors' (Dent, H781).

12   **curst** cantankerous, shrewish (*OED* 4a, which gives this spelling as usual for the meaning, in contrast to the more typical 'cursed')

18   **governed . . . moon** The inconstancy of the moon was proverbial ('As changeful as the moon', Dent, M1111), so the Ferryman's point is partly that his wife is

ungovernable (or self-governed as Alice wants to be, 10.89); also with reference to her menstrual cycle, which was often thought to be influenced by the moon, and which he might perceive as making her emotionally unpredictable.

20   **bargain** negotiation over a service to be provided (*OED n.* 1a)

21   **fresh and fasting** eager and hungry (*fresh*, meaning ready to eat or drink, having an appetite (*OED* 2b), is the opposite of *fasting*). The speech means something like 'just because you're keen to have it'.

22   **Yes . . . thee** yes please

23–4   **midsummer moon** on Midsummer Day, or the phase of the moon in which Midsummer Day falls, often said to be a time of particular lunacy

24   **another moon** not the midsummer moon, but her vagina

12–15] *Delius; Q1 lines* house, / (him /) eyes, / fire, / dead. /   17–18] *Q3 lines* other / Moone. /   20–1] *Delius; Q1 lines* bargane. / fasting. /   20 Nay] *Q3;* Na *Q1*   23–4] *Delius; Q1 lines* Moone, / moone. / 24 has] *Q3;* as *Q1*

FERRYMAN   Ay, and it hath influences and eclipses.

ARDEN   Why then, by this reckoning you sometimes
play the man in the moon?

FERRYMAN   Ay, but you had not best to meddle with that
moon, lest I scratch you by the face with my bramble   30
bush.

ARDEN   I am almost stifled with this fog. Come, let's away.

FRANKLIN   And, sirrah, as we go, let us have some more
of your bold yeomanry.

FERRYMAN   Nay, by my troth, sir, but flat knavery.   35

Exeunt.

[**Sc. 12**]   *Here enters* [BLACK] WILL *at one door, and*
SHAKEBAG *at another.*

SHAKEBAG   O Will, where art thou?

---

26 **influences** supposed ethereal fluid
streaming from the heavens and shaping
destiny on earth (*OED n.* 2a); the flowing
in of any fluid, perhaps here semen
eclipses obscurations of the light of the
moon as it passes into the earth's
shadow; when his wife closes her legs in
refusal of his sexual advances

28 **man ... moon** mythical person who
dwells in the moon, suggested by the
semblance of a face in the lunar seas
when full; the man (or penis) in her
vagina

30–1 **bramble bush** traditional attribute of
the man in the moon; see *MND*,
5.1.252–3, 'I, the man i'th' moon; this
thorn-bush my thorn-bush'.

34 **bold yeomanry** upfront, 'homely' talk
of the 'common man', often bawdy and
bordering on insolent

35 **but** no more than, only (*OED* 2a);
making the distinction with the more
honest yeomanry Franklin suggests
flat knavery dishonest or crafty, unscru-
pulous talk

Sc. 12 The imagined setting is the same
marshy area as the previous scene,
around the Harty Ferry that ran from the
head of Faversham Creek to the Isle of
Sheppey. The drainage ditches on the
marsh may be represented by a trap door.

1   Shakebag's line echoes Arden's opening
line in Sc. 11, highlighting the sense that
the two scenes function as a pair.

27–8] *Delius; Q1 lines* sometimes / Moone. /   29–31] *Delius; Q lines* moone / bush, /   33–4] *Tyrell; Q1
lines (*your /) yeomandrie. / ; Q3 lines* your / yeomandrie. /   34 yeomanry] *(*yeomandry)   **Sc. 12**] *Hugo;*
Act IV. Scene III. *Delius*

232

BLACK WILL   Here, Shakebag, almost in hell's mouth,
    where I cannot see my way for smoke.
SHAKEBAG   I pray thee, speak still, that we may meet by
    the sound, for I shall fall into some ditch or other   5
    unless my feet see better than my eyes.
BLACK WILL   Didst thou ever see better weather to run
    away with another man's wife, or play with a wench
    at pot-finger?
SHAKEBAG   No, this were a fine world for chandlers, if   10
    this weather would last, for then a man should never
    dine nor sup without candle-light. But sirrah Will,
    what horses are those that passed?

---

2   **hell's mouth** The entrance to hell (envis-
aged as the mouth of a great beast) was
associated with smoky confusion partly
through its staging in medieval mystery
plays. Often related to the whale which
swallowed Jonah (as in Thomas Lodge
and Robert Greene's *A Looking Glass for
London and England*, a play whose
depiction of Jonah being '*cast out of the
Whales belly vpon the Stage*' shows the
currency of the image in the early
modern theatre (1594, probably written
1589–91, 4.2.1460–1); sig. F3ᵛ). Its mention here brings water, fog and moral
judgement into the scene. It is likely that
Jonah entered via the trap door in
Looking Glass, and B&T suggests that
the trap door may have been open during
Black Will and Shakebag's entrances
here.

3   **smoke** fog (in line with the allusion to
hell's mouth). No fog is mentioned in
Holinshed, who says Will 'mist the waie,
& taried in a wrong place' (see below,
p. 295); Dessen and Thomson suggest
that fog was generally '*fictional* rather
than linked to a special onstage effect'

(143).
4–5   **speak ... sound** carry on speaking so
that I can move towards your voice
5   **ditch** drainage ditches on the marsh
(making it possible to graze sheep there)
8–9   **play ... pot-finger** referring to the children's game of making popping sounds
by putting a finger in the mouth and popping it out against the corner of the lips.
OED (pot *n.* 3) cites John Withals's
Shorte Dictionarie (1553): 'A potte made
in the mouth, with one fynger, as children use to doo', the only other instance
given. Here it has a sexual innuendo; see
Williams, 'finger' (485–6) for context.
12   **dine ... candle-light** i.e. in such
weather, both midday and evening meals
would need artificial light. Eating by
candle-light, in the evening, was a new
activity for the middling sorts in this
period as the main meal was traditionally
taken at lunchtime, as Cheyne's is.
13   **horses** Dessen and Thomson list as
common the sound of horses offstage
(117), although here Arden and Franklin
may be taken to have passed by before
the scene begins.

2–3] *Delius; Q1 lines* mouth, / smoake. /   10–13] *Delius; Q1 lines* chandlers, / man / candle light, / past? /

BLACK WILL   Why, didst thou hear any?

SHAKEBAG   Ay, that I did.   15

BLACK WILL   My life for thine, 'twas Arden and his
companion, and then all our labour's lost.

SHAKEBAG   Nay, say not so, for if it be they, they may
haply lose their way as we have done, and then we
may chance meet with them.   20

BLACK WILL   Come, let us go on like a couple of blind
pilgrims. (*Then Shakebag falls into a ditch*).

SHAKEBAG   Help, Will, help, I am almost drowned.

Here enters the FERRYMAN.

FERRYMAN   Who's that that calls for help?

BLACK WILL   'Twas none here, 'twas thou thyself.   25

FERRYMAN   I came to help him that called for help. Why,
how now, who is this that's in the ditch? [*to Shakebag*]

---

16   **My ... thine** i.e. I assure you

17   **all ... lost** proverbial (Dent, L9)

19   **haply** perhaps, possibly; but also with
modern sense of 'luckily for us'

21–2   **blind pilgrims** a common trope in
medieval art; linked to placeless jour-
neying, beggary and deceit, so increasing
the atmosphere of moral judgement here.
The idea of pilgrimage (and its Catholic
implications) is picked up again in
14.220; such pilgrims would have been a
common sight on the road between
London and Canterbury before the
Reformation. Although EEBO-TCP
shows this as the earliest instance of the
phrase, Richard Mulcaster offers a related
idea: 'This were better then brauerie, and
more triumphant then trauelling, to
remaine at home with their prince, not to
rome abroad with the pilgrime, to see
farre in other countries, and be starke

blinde in their owne' (*Positions*, 209),
suggesting the connection between journeys and knowledge or ignorance. The
speech and ensuing action also references
the related proverb (Dent, B452), given
by Canterbury resident John Bale as,
'Into the dytche, the blynde the blynde
maye lede' (*Three Laws*, sig. D4ʳ).

22 SD   Shakebag probably falls through a trap
door in the stage (see 2n.). Here the play's
topographical realism most obviously
runs into theatrical challenges: Holinshed
says only that 'blacke Will lost his way'
(see below, p. 296), so the expansion of
the business to falling into the ditch was
apparently intended both to offer comedy
and to use the stage space effectively.

25   Either below-stage or behind Will,
Shakebag is apparently unseen at this
moment and only becomes visible during
the Ferryman's next speech.

16–17] *Q2; Q1 lines* companion / lost, /   19 haply] *(happely)*   18–20] *Delius; Q1 lines (*happely / *)* done
/ them. /   26–9] *Delius; Q1 lines* help, / ditch? / *(*guyde, / *)* this. /   27 SD] *B&T*

You are well enough served, to go without a guide such weather as this.

BLACK WILL   Sirrah, what companies hath passed your   30
ferry this morning?

FERRYMAN   None but a couple of gentlemen that went to
dine at my Lord Cheyne's.

BLACK WILL   Shakebag, did not I tell thee as much?

FERRYMAN   Why sir, will you have any letters carried to   35
them?

BLACK WILL   No, sir; get you gone.

FERRYMAN   Did you ever see such a mist as this?

BLACK WILL   No, nor such a fool as will rather be hocked
than get his way.   40

FERRYMAN   Why, sir, this is no Hock Monday; you are
deceived. [*Then Shakebag comes out of the ditch.*]
[*to Shakebag*] What's his name, I pray you, sir?

---

28 **You ... served** 'serves you right'
30 **companies** collective noun: people gathered or travelling together; people associated in a group or as companions (*OED* company *coll.n.* 6a)
passed been conveyed, especially across a river (*OED* pass 7a); harking back to the connection the play sets up between Charon and this Ferryman, an ironic reference to the word's secondary meaning, to die (*OED* II 6b)
35 **letters carried** The ferry was the quickest way of getting letters to Harty, and in the absence of a regular postage service (before Charles I opened up the royal post to private letters) this would have been one of the ferryman's jobs.
39 **hocked** disabled by cutting the tendons of the ham or hock; hamstrung
40 **get his way** get going, leave
41 **Hock Monday** Hocktide, the second Monday and Tuesday after Easter Day, a holiday period during which money was collected for the parish through festive customs including, before the

Reformation, the tying up of men and women on alternate days for a ransom. Oxford and London parishes continued the custom after the Reformation, and *The Old Coventry Play of Hock Tuesday* was revived as part of the entertainment at Elizabeth I's 1575 visit to Kenilworth. The move from violent incapacitation to harmless game epitomizes the often-comic brutality of the play's lower-status characters.
42 SD The following line is the first direct address to Shakebag that receives an answer since he fell into the ditch, and hence the latest moment at which he is likely to escape it. It appears in any case that the Ferryman switches interlocutors at this point. The Ferryman's refusal to leave the stage (35–42) and his non-sequitur (38) suggest a space for comic business which could be filled by Will pulling Shakebag out. Editors have had Shakebag emerging at 29, but Will's conversation with the Ferryman could equally ignore his plight. This would make his address at 34 comic and explain the lack of a reply.

---

39 hocked] (hought)   41–3] *Delius; Q1 lines* deceiud / sir? /   42 SD] *this edn*   43 SD] *this edn*

SHAKEBAG His name is Black Will.

FERRYMAN

I hope to see him one day hanged upon a hill. *Exit.*

SHAKEBAG

See how the sun hath cleared the foggy mist. 46

Now we have missed the mark of our intent.

Here enters GREENE, MOSBY *and* ALICE.

MOSBY

Black Will and Shakebag, what make you here?

What, is the deed done? Is Arden dead?

BLACK WILL

What could a blinded man perform in arms? 50

Saw you not how till now the sky was dark,

That neither horse nor man could be discerned?

Yet did we hear their horses as they passed.

GREENE

Have they escaped you then, and passed the ferry?

SHAKEBAG

Ay, for a while; but here we two will stay, 55

And at their coming back meet with them once more.

---

45 The Ferryman's line of verse, rhyming with Shakebag's prose, seems to effect a broader transition to verse. The resulting doggerel gives the lines a portentous edge that returns the scene to earlier forms of drama, here the morality tradition where the name Black Will can be read as a vice figure, equivalent of Evil Wilfulness, and he therefore deserves hanging on account of his name. It is also possible that he recognizes the name as that of a notorious villain, see pp. 17–18.
hanged echoes Lord Cheyne's prophecy at 9.118.
upon a hill may reflect actual punish-

ments, but also has a moral resonance in the implication 'for all to see' (as Holinshed puts it in his *Chronicles*, 'the dauntyng of the vicious, by soure penall examples' (1577, 'Preface to the Reader', sig. 4ʳ)

47 **missed** Modern spelling loses the repetition of *mist*, with its comic/portentous effect.

48 **make you** are you doing

50 **blinded** blind, but also made blind or blindfolded (with fog)
perform in arms accomplish with weapons

54 **passed** See 30n.

45 SD] *(Exit Ferryman.)*

Zounds, I was ne'er so toiled in all my life
In following so slight a task as this.

MOSBY [*to Shakebag*]
How cam'st thou so berayed?

BLACK WILL
With making false footing in the dark.   60
He needs would follow them without a guide.

ALICE [*giving money*]
Here's to pay for a fire and good cheer.
Get you to Faversham to the Fleur-de-Lis,
And rest yourselves until some other time.

GREENE
Let me alone, it most concerns my state.   65

BLACK WILL
Ay, Mistress Arden, this will serve the turn
In case we fall into a second fog.

> *Exeunt Greene, [Black] Will and Shakebag.*

57   **toiled** worn-out, weary, but also 'pulled about violently' (in the ditch) (*OED v.*[1] 1) and 'trapped in a toil', like a hunted quarry, as Arden imagines in 6.13 (*OED v.*[2] 1)

59   **berayed** dirtied, defiled, befouled

61   No guide was mentioned; perhaps a suggestion that Will covers up for their incompetence here.

62   **pay . . . cheer** Payment would be needed for both the drink (good cheer) and the fire in the inn.

65   **Let me alone** Wiggins glosses, 'let me deal with this', but it could also mean 'leave me alone (here)', rather than including me in the group drinking at the Fleur-de-Lis. B&T emends to 'along', glossing 'let me go along', i.e. the opposite. The meaning of the line hangs on *it*, which would mean either the murder, or organizing fire and cheer in the inn, the latter a comic line and the former deadly serious. Will's *this* in the next line indicates that he takes the money, so if the line is played as comic there might be a tussle between them for the coins.

concerns my state relates to, or is more appropriate to, my social status as a gentleman; or concerns my situation (see 1.475)

66   **serve the turn** satisfy our need

67   **second fog** more bad weather, but also with suggestion that the drink might lead them into a *second fog* of inebriation

59 SD] *Wine (Hugo subst.)*   62 SD] *Oliphant*   63 Fleur-de-Lis] *(flowre deluce)*

MOSBY

These knaves will never do it; let us give it over.

ALICE

First tell me how you like my new device:
Soon, when my husband is returning back,   70
You and I, both marching arm in arm
Like loving friends, we'll meet him on the way
And boldly beard and brave him to his teeth.
When words grow hot, and blows begin to rise,
I'll call those cutters forth your tenement,   75
Who, in a manner to take up the fray,
Shall wound my husband Hornsby to the death.

MOSBY

Ah, fine device! Why this deserves a kiss.
    [*Then he kisses her.*]   *Exeunt.*

---

68 **give it over** leave off or abandon it
72 **loving friends** good friends, both to
     Arden and to one another, but with
     obvious ironies
73 **beard** oppose openly and resolutely,
     with daring or with effrontery; thwart
     brave treat with bravado; challenge,
     defy; threaten, menace
75 **cutters** cutthroats or highway robbers
     forth out of
     tenement dwelling-place; specifically
     rented property, 'held of another by any
     tenure' (*OED* 2a), suggesting Mosby's
     status within the town as less secure than
     Arden's
76 **in ... to** in a way likely to; with the
     intention of

take up join in with something started
by others (*OED* 4a)
77 **Hornsby** offensive, shaming name for a
     cuckold, part of a wide vernacular
     vocabulary of popular shaming language
     and actions focused on the cuckold's
     supposed horns that makes its way into
     contemporary court records, but rarely
     into print. EEBO-TCP gives only two
     examples, one of which is Matteo
     Bandello's *Certain Tragical Discourses*,
     trans. Geoffrey Fenton (1567), which
     features a wife who is careful to 'brydel
     goodman hornsbye (her husband) with
     obedience' so that her lover can enter her
     chamber (sig. H8^r).

78 SD1] *this edn (Wine subst.)*

[Sc. 13]   *Here enters* Dick REEDE *and a* SAILOR.

SAILOR

Faith, Dick Reede, it is to little end.

His conscience is too liberal and he too niggardly

To part from anything may do thee good.

REEDE

He is coming from Shurland as I understand.

Here I'll intercept him, for at his house   5

He never will vouchsafe to speak with me.

If prayers and fair entreaties will not serve,

Or make no battery in his flinty breast,

Here enters FRANKLIN *and* ARDEN.

I'll curse the churl and see what that will do!

See where he comes to further my intent.   10

Sc. 13 The scene is implicitly set on the way back from Shurland, in Faversham (Reede says Arden refuses to entertain him in his house). The fact that Alice is expected to meet Arden on the way walking suggests that it is to be imagined taking place roughly on the outskirts of the town.

0 SD Both men are likely to have been dressed in mariners' costumes to make clear their profession. Inventories suggest sea gowns or cassocks were worn over jerkins. See the Museum of London sailors' slops, 53.101/1b; Mary Rose leather jerkin 81A2592.

1 **to little end** pointless

2 **liberal** unrestrained by moral considerations, and therefore uncaring. In its other meaning of 'generous' the word con-

trasts ironically with *niggardly*.

3 **part from** give up

6 **vouchsafe** agree, condescend

8 **battery** bombardment of fortifications, hence *flinty breast*

8 SD Although Q1 gives Michael as entering here with his master, he plays no role in the scene, and his entrance is therefore often omitted in performance (see p. 50). As he does not speak, and was not with Arden and Franklin when they left the ferry in the previous scene, his entry has been omitted in this edition as superfluous in both performance and narrative terms.

9 **churl** low-status, rudely behaved man, with suggestion of financial meanness that picks up on the earlier use of *niggardly*

Sc. 13] *Hugo;* ACT IV. SCENE V. *Tyrrell;* ACT IV. SCENE IV. *Delius*   4 Shurland] *Jacob;* Shorlow *Q1*   6 vouchsafe] *Q2;* vouchafe *Q1*   8 SD] *after 10 Tyrrell; after 9 Delius*   FRANKLIN *and* ARDEN] *this edn;* Here enters Fra. Ard. and Michaell *Q1*   9 churl] *(carl)*

Master Arden, I am now bound to the sea.
My coming to you was about the plot of ground
Which wrongfully you detain from me.
Although the rent of it be very small,
Yet will it help my wife and children   15
Which here I leave in Faversham, God knows,
Needy and bare. For Christ's sake let them have it!

ARDEN

Franklin, hearest thou this fellow speak?
That which he craves I dearly bought of him,
Although the rent of it was ever mine.   20
[*to Reede*] Sirrah, you that ask these questions,
If with thy clamorous impeaching tongue

11 **bound ... sea** about to embark on a voyage
15 **children** trisyllabic
17 **For Christ's sake** compelling and powerful form of supplication that counts strongly against Arden's character for his lack of charity in response. Holinshed only mentions Arden's dealings with Reede in relation to the land where the body is found, saying he 'most cruellie' took it from a woman who was at that stage a widow and later married the mariner (see below, p. 303), so the playwright's inserted scene is pointed in casting doubt on our response to Arden.
20 **rent of it** i.e. rent from it, payable to Arden as landlord; Arden suggests that he has bought out Reede's lease when taking possession of the Abbey properties. The terms of Arden's ownership of Faversham property are very complex and apparently indicate some sharp practices (see Hyde, 50–8). Contemporary accounts make his fault clear: Holinshed states that the Reeds 'had long inioied it [the land] by a lease, which they had of it for manie yeares, not then expired: neuerthelesse, he [Arden] got it from them' (see below, p. 303). John

Stowe's MS account of the murder gives a clear moral steer by stating that Arden acquired the field 'by like title as Ahab got Naboths vyneyard for he had taken it frome one Reade and his wyfe by vyolence' (fol. 36ʳ). In 1 Kings, 21, Naboth refuses to sell King Ahab his vineyard, so false witness is borne against him at the instigation of Ahab's wife, Jezebel, and he is stoned to death; God sends Elijah to Ahab to tell him, 'In the place where dogs licked the blood of Naboth, shall dogs lick even thy blood also' (Geneva Bible (1599), v. 19). The story was very popular in sermons, texts and wall-paintings, as evidence of poor leadership, over-powerful women, God's just judgements, property rights and the power of the cries of the righteous; see, e.g., a sermon given at Paul's Cross in London in 1591 by William Fisher, printed by Edward Allde in 1592 (sig. B3ʳ).
22 **impeaching** accusing, often in a legal sense. The formal language and delay in Arden's direct address to Reede while he talks to Franklin underline the social distance between the two men in a way that suggests Arden's disdain and perhaps arrogance.

12–13] *W&P lines* plat / me: /   12 plot] *(*plat*)*

Thou rail on me, as I have heard thou dost,
I'll lay thee up so close a twelvemonth's day
As thou shalt neither see the sun nor moon!   25
Look to it, for, as surely as I live,
I'll banish pity if thou use me thus.

REEDE

What, wilt thou do me wrong and threat me too?
Nay, then I'll tempt thee: Arden, do thy worst!
God, I beseech thee, show some miracle   30
On thee or thine in plaguing thee for this.
That plot of ground which thou detains from me –
I speak it in an agony of spirit –
Be ruinous and fatal unto thee!
Either there be butchered by thy dearest friends,   35
Or else be brought for men to wonder at,
Or thou or thine miscarry in that place,
Or there run mad, and end thy cursed days.

FRANKLIN

Fie, bitter knave, bridle thine envious tongue!
For curses are like arrows shot upright   40
Which, falling down, light on the shooter's head.

---

23 **rail** complain, rant
24 **lay thee . . . close** have you imprisoned
    a twelvemonth's day for a year
25 **As** that
29 **tempt** put to the test; incite; call out
30 Reede must make a gesture of prayer or
    supplication to indicate the change of
    addressee from Arden to God; see his
    description at 46–7 of the sailors praying
    and his falling down.
31 **thee** Arden
    in by
32 **thou detains** you withhold, with a fur-
    ther meaning for 'detain' of 'keeping
    prisoner' that links it to Arden's threat at
    24–5

36 **brought . . . at** as is the case with
    Arden's body (Epil.9–13), making these
    lines prophetic
37 **miscarry** come to harm, perish
38 **cursed** cursèd
39 **bridle** restrain, as one would a horse. The
    image was a common one for control of
    the emotions, something considered
    harder for lower status men and all
    women.
    envious malicious (*OED adj.* 2)
40–1 **curses . . . head** proverbial: 'Curses
    return upon the heads of those that curse'
    (Dent, C924)

31 plaguing] *(plauging)*   41 shooter's] *Q3;* sutors *Q1*

REEDE

Light where they will! Were I upon the sea,
As oft I have in many a bitter storm,
And saw a dreadful southern flaw at hand,
The pilot quaking at the doubtful storm   45
And all the sailors praying on their knees,
Even in that fearful time would I fall down
And ask of God, whate'er betide of me,
Vengeance on Arden, or some misevent,
To show the world what wrong the carl hath done.   50
This charge I'll leave with my distressful wife:
My children shall be taught such prayers as these.
And thus I go, but leave my curse with thee.

                          Exeunt Reede and Sailor.

ARDEN

It is the railingest knave in Christendom,
And oftentimes the villain will be mad.   55
It greatly matters not what he says,
But I assure you, I ne'er did him wrong.

FRANKLIN

I think so, Master Arden.

---

43 **have** have been
44 **flaw** sudden gust or squall of wind
45 **pilot** helmsman or navigator of the ship
    doubtful to be dreaded; of uncertain outcome
48 **betide of** happens to
49 **misevent** bad happening; only early modern use of the word listed in EEBO-TCP and *OED*
51 **charge** responsibility
    distressful full of distress
54 **railingest knave** most abusive ranter; describing the result of the unbridled tongue mentioned in 39

58 **I think so** The phrasing is ambiguous nowadays, meaning either that Franklin agrees Arden did Reede no wrong, or that he thinks he did do him wrong, and in performance the enthusiasm or reservation with which the line is spoken has considerable impact on the audience's attitude to Arden as a character (see p. 36). It is very hard to gauge its early modern weight, but the most straightforward reading is Franklin's (brief) agreement: 'I think [that it is] so.'

51 my] *Q2; wy Q1*

ARDEN

Now that our horses are gone home before,
My wife may haply meet me on the way;   60
For, God knows, she is grown passing kind of late,
And greatly changed from the old humour
Of her wonted frowardness,
And seeks by fair means to redeem old faults.

FRANKLIN

Happy the change that alters for the best!   65
But see, in any case, you make no speech
Of the cheer we had at my Lord Cheyne's,
Although most bounteous and liberal,
For that will make her think herself more wronged
In that we did not carry her along;   70
For sure she grieved that she was left behind.

ARDEN

Come, Franklin, let us strain to mend our pace,
And take her unawares playing the cook;

Here enters ALICE *and* MOSBY [*arm in arm*].

For I believe she'll strive to mend our cheer.

FRANKLIN

Why, there's no better creatures in the world   75

---

59 **before** before us
61 **passing** exceedingly
62 **changed** changèd
    humour temperament
63 **wonted frowardness** usual perverseness,
    hardness to please or ungovernableness
65 proverbial (Dent, B26, 'To change (the
    bad) for the better')
66 **in any case** whatever happens
67 **cheer** both the food and drink offered as

hospitality and the merriment it produces. See also 74.
70 **carry her along** take her with us
72 **strain . . . pace** try hard to hurry up
73 SD As B&T points out, the entry here (as
    located in Q1) draws out the rich irony of
    the next three lines, during which Alice
    and Mosby remain unseen by Arden and
    Franklin.
74 **mend** increase, like the men's *pace* (72)

62–3] *Delius lines* from / frowardness. /   73 SD] *after*

243

Than women are, when they are in good humours.

ARDEN

Who is that? Mosby! What, so familiar?
Injurious strumpet, and thou, ribald knave,
Untwine those arms!

ALICE

Ay with a sugared kiss let them untwine.   80
[*Then she kisses Mosby.*]

ARDEN

Ah Mosby, perjured beast! Bear this and all!

MOSBY

And yet no horned beast: the horns are thine.

FRANKLIN

Oh, monstrous! Nay, then 'tis time to draw.
[*Then Arden, Franklin and Mosby draw.*]

ALICE

Help, help, they murder my husband!

Here enters [BLACK] WILL *and* SHAKEBAG.

SHAKEBAG

Zounds, who injures Master Mosby?

[*Then they fight. Shakebag and
Mosby are wounded.*]

Help, Will, I am hurt.   85

78 **Injurious** insulting, harmful
    ribald knave villainous rogue
80 **sugared** sweet and alluring
81 **perjured** forsworn, having deliberately
    broken an oath
    Bear . . . all 'If I accept this I'll accept

anything'; proverbial (Dent, A172)
82 **horned beast** cuckold, see 10.72n.;
    hornèd
85 **Zounds . . . Mosby** comic intervention
    as a reply to Alice's cry about her hus-
    band

76 Hugo   arm in arm] Sturgess (Hugo subst.)   80 SD] *this edn (Wine subst.)*   82] *Q2; Q1 lines* beast, /
thine. /   83 SD] *BH&N (Hugo subst.)*   85 SD] *this edn (Wiggins subst.)*

MOSBY

    I may thank you, Mistress Arden, for this wound.

                 Exeunt Mosby, [Black] Will and Shakebag.

ALICE

    Ah, Arden, what folly blinded thee?

    Ah, jealous, harebrain man, what hast thou done?

    When we, to welcome thee, intended sport,

    Came lovingly to meet thee on thy way,   90

    Thou drew'st thy sword, enraged with jealousy,

    And hurt thy friend whose thoughts were free from

        harm,

    All for a worthless kiss and joining arms,

    Both done but merrily to try thy patience;

    And me unhappy, that devised the jest,   95

    Which, though begun in sport, yet ends in blood.

---

85 SD This complex and impressive fight scene takes its structure from the contrast between the two gentlemen (perhaps fighting with rapiers) and Mosby (with the weapon Arden removed from him at 1.309), and two lower-status fighters (perhaps with swords and bucklers). Both their weapons and their styles of swordsmanship are likely to have been very different, and what the audience sees here as evidence of their skills feeds into their sense of Will and Shakebag's professional competence and Arden, Franklin and Mosby's bravery and martial masculine identity. If this action is played very differently to the narrative that Will recounts at 14.57–71 then the effect will be comic, suggesting the emptiness of his boasts throughout the play as a soldiering professional; if the two match, the villains' dark threat is increased.

88 **harebrain** reckless

89 **sport** entertainment, but also 'love-making' or 'amorous play' (*OED* 1c). See also 96.

90 **lovingly** in a loving manner which, like *sport*, is capable of multiple interpretations

94 **merrily** Q1 reads 'mirrely'; Sturgess adopts W&P's conjectured 'merely', which has the effect of playing down the *jest*, but loses the balance with *unhappy* in 95. B&T (*CRE*) points out the rarity of Q1's spelling, further examples with this meaning only being found in Churchyard's *Charge* (1580; his 1575 use means 'merely') and the work of two Scottish writers.

95 **And me** Whilst this does make sense as an opening to Alice's next thought, editorial conjectures such as 'Aye me' and 'Ah me' are also credible.

jest trivial sport; prank or practical joke

---

88 jealous] *Q3;* Ielious *Q1;* iealious *Q2*   89 thee,] *BH&N;* thy *Q1*   92] *Delius; Q1 lines* freende, / harme. /   94 merrily] *(*mirrely*);* merely *Sturgess (conj. W&P)*   95 And] Aye *Delius;* Ah *(conj. Sturgess)*

FRANKLIN

Marry, God defend me from such a jest!

ALICE

Couldst thou not see us friendly smile on thee
When we joined arms, when I kissed his cheek?
Hast thou not lately found me overkind?   100
Didst thou not hear me cry they murder thee?
Called I not help to set my husband free?
No, ears and all were 'witched. Ah me accurst,
To link in liking with a frantic man!
Henceforth I'll be thy slave, no more thy wife,   105
For with that name I never shall content thee.
If I be merry, thou straightways thinks me light;
If sad, thou sayest the sullens trouble me;
If well-attired, thou thinks I will be gadding;
If homely, I seem sluttish in thine eye.   110
Thus am I still, and shall be while I die,
Poor wench abused by thy misgovernment.

ARDEN

But is it for truth that neither thou nor he
Intendedst malice in your misdemeanour?

ALICE

The heavens can witness of our harmless thoughts.   115

---

103 **'witched** bewitched
104 **link in liking** fall for; see also *Soliman and Perseda*, 1.1855, 'And is she linkt in liking with my foe?'.
   frantic insane, frenzied
106 **with . . . thee** I'll never content you as a wife
107 **light** lacking gravity; unchaste
108 **sullens** gloomy ill-humour, sulks
109 **gadding** wandering purposelessly in a way likely to suggest or lead to sin, here to show oneself off

110 **homely** plainly dressed, in a way suitable for being at home
   sluttish unclean, untidy and immoral
112 **misgovernment** misconduct and anarchy (Arden's lack of control over himself), but also and more damningly, maladministration (his lack of appropriate government of his wife)
113 **for truth** true
114 **misdemeanour** originally an offence less serious than a felony (*OED* 1), so a stronger misconduct than its current meaning suggests

116] *Tyrrell; Q1 lines* Ales, / faulte: /

ARDEN

Then pardon me, sweet Alice, and forgive this fault.
Forget but this, and never see the like.
Impose me penance, and I will perform it;
For in thy discontent I find a death,
A death tormenting more than death itself. 120

ALICE

Nay, hadst thou loved me as thou dost pretend,
Thou wouldst have marked the speeches of thy friend
Who, going wounded from the place, he said
His skin was pierced only through my device.
And if sad sorrow taint thee for this fault, 125
Thou wouldst have followed him, and seen him
dressed,
And cried him mercy whom thou hast misdone.
Ne'er shall my heart be eased till this be done.

ARDEN

Content thee, sweet Alice, thou shalt have thy will,
Whate'er it be. For that I injured thee 130
And wronged my friend, shame scourgeth my
offence.
Come thou thyself and go along with me,
And be a mediator 'twixt us two.

FRANKLIN

Why, Master Arden, know you what you do?
Will you follow him that hath dishonoured you? 135

---

124 **device** plan
125 **taint** convict, prove guilty (of crime)
(*OED v. 1*)
126 **him dressed** his wounds tended
127 **cried him** asked him for
misdone wronged; injured physically
130 **For that** because
131 **scourgeth** punishes, and therefore corrects
134–46 B&T suggests that this exchange might

be staged with Arden flanked by Alice and
Franklin on either side, reminding early
modern audiences of the visual structure of
morality play action, in which good and
bad angels or councillors speak in a
character's ears in succession (see,
e.g., Marlowe, *Doctor Faustus*, Scs. 5
and 13). Although they are abusing one
another more than advising him, his pas-
sivity in the passage is.

ALICE

Why, canst thou prove I have been disloyal?

FRANKLIN

Why, Mosby taunts your husband with the horn!

ALICE

Ay, after he had reviled him
By the injurious name of perjured beast!
He knew no wrong could spite a jealous man   140
More than the hateful naming of the horn.

FRANKLIN

Suppose 'tis true, yet is it dangerous
To follow him whom he hath lately hurt.

ALICE

A fault confessed is more than half amends,
But men of such ill spirit as yourself   145
Work crosses and debates 'twixt man and wife.

ARDEN

I pray thee, gentle Franklin, hold thy peace;
I know my wife counsels me for the best.
I'll seek out Mosby where his wound is dressed,
And salve his hapless quarrel if I may.   150

Exeunt Arden and Alice.

FRANKLIN

He whom the devil drives must go, perforce.

137 *taunts your Q1's 'traunt you' is a peculiar misreading, in which an *r* from 'your'
is missing and an extra one inserted in the
previous word. Jowett (private communication) conjectures a mis-correction in
proof or press correction.
139 injurious hurtful
144 proverbial: 'Confession of a fault is half
amends' (Dent, C589)
146 Work crosses cause trouble, vexation or
annoyance
149 is is being

150 salve heal
hapless unfortunate
150 SD The narrative logic of the exit
through different doors that B&T proposes is suggested in the next scene,
when Alice has no knowledge of Mosby
and Arden's reconcilement; its symbolic
impact here would be considerable.
151 He . . . go proverbial: 'He must needs go
that the devil drives' (Dent, D278), here
referring to Alice as the devil
perforce of necessity

137 taunts your] *Q3;* traunt you *Q1;* taunt you *Q2*   140 a] *Q3;* an *Q1*   jealous] *Q3;* Ielious *Q1;* iealious *Q2*

Poor gentleman, how soon he is bewitched!
And yet, because his wife is the instrument,
His friends must not be lavish in their speech. *Exit.*

[**Sc. 14**] *Here enters* [BLACK] WILL,
SHAKEBAG *and* GREENE.

BLACK WILL Sirrah Greene, when was I so long in killing
a man?
GREENE I think we shall never do it; let us give it over.
SHAKEBAG Nay, zounds, we'll kill him, though we be
hanged at his door for our labour! 5
BLACK WILL Thou knowest, Greene, that I have lived in
London this twelve years, where I have made some
go upon wooden legs for taking the wall on me, divers
with silver noses for saying 'There goes Black Will'.
I have cracked as many blades as thou hast done nuts. 10
GREENE O monstrous lie!

---

154 **lavish** unrestrained; i.e. they cannot
mention it.
Sc. 14 Textually, the scene becomes localized only when Will asks 'Which is the
counting-house?' (137), although the
preceding action must be played in front
of the door leading to it (probably the
door to the discovery space), and further
doors to other areas within the house and
the outside. A chair, stools, a table and
set of tables (backgammon board) are
also needed, as is drinking equipment.
5 **at his door** i.e. at the scene of the crime
8 **taking the wall** walking on the cleaner
edge of the road by the wall and thereby
leaving the other to walk near the
drain. In a period before pavements

(Faversham's were installed in 1753),
this discourtesy was the source of often
violent tensions.
on Q1's preposition 'on' is rare in this
phrase (although 'on' for 'of' is otherwise
common, Abbott, 181), with only three
other instances in EEBO-TCP to 1642,
two from texts by Thomas Nashe printed
in 1592; compare Q2's 'of' (68 instances).
9 **silver noses** provided as prosthetics for
noses lost through illness (often syphilis)
or in battle, such as that worn by the
astronomer Tycho Brahe after a duel.
They were kept in place with paste or
glue. For an example see A641037 in the
Science Museum Collection (London).
10 **cracked ... blades** broken ... weapons

---

154 SD] *(Exit Fran.)* **Sc. 14**] *Hugo;* ACT V. SCENE I. *Tyrrell* 3] *Delius; Q1 lines* it. / ouer. / 4–5]
Delius; Q1 lines him. / labour. / 6–10] *Delius; Q1 lines* in / yeers. / legges, / me, / saying, / blackwill. /
blades, / Nutes. / 8 on] of *Q2*

BLACK WILL   Faith, in a manner I have. The bawdy houses
    have paid me tribute: there durst not a whore set up,
    unless she have agreed with me first for opening her
    shop windows. For a cross word of a tapster I have   15
    pierced one barrel after another with my dagger, and
    held him by the ears till all his beer hath run out. In
    Thames Street a brewer's cart was like to have run
    over me; I made no more ado but went to the clerk and
    cut all the notches of his tallies, and beat them about   20
    his head. I and my company have taken the constable
    from his watch and carried him about the fields on a
    cowl-staff. I have broken a sergeant's head with his
    own mace, and bailed whom I list with my sword and

12   **in a manner** in some way
      bawdy houses brothels
14   **agreed ... for** bargained or negotiated
      for (*OED* agree *v.* 8c)
14–15 **opening ... windows** starting up her
      business; with a possible sexual pun
15   **tapster** tavern-keeper
18   **Thames Street** following an old Roman
      road beside the river, the longest street in
      early modern London, running east–west
      from the ditch around the Tower in the
      east to Puddle Wharf in the west, almost
      the complete breadth of the city within
      the walls. See Map of Early Modern
      London (https://mapoflondon.uvic.ca/).
      was ... run came close to, narrowly
      missed, running
20   **tallies** sticks marked on one side with
      notches to show the debts due to the
      tradesperson, cut across the notches so
      that creditor and debtor had half each.
      Cutting off the notches effectively can-
      celled all debts and thereby caused com-
      mercial mayhem. Q1's spelling, 'tales',
      reflects the Old French derivation of the

word ('*tailles*') and its sixteenth-century
legal meanings (in tail, etc.).
21   **constable** officer of the peace appointed
      by a parish in the period before a national
      police force was established
23   **cowl-staff** stout stick originally used to
      carry a 'cowl', or water tub, being thrust
      through the two handles of it, but more
      generally a pole or staff used to carry
      heavy burdens, supported on the shoul-
      ders of two bearers. Carrying a person on
      one was a form of popular shaming, often
      aimed at revealing the weakness of men
      abused by their wives; see *MW*, 3.3.136,
      and the plasterwork frieze at Montacute
      House, Somerset (Skimmington Ride).
      sergeant's A sergeant was an officer who
      summoned people to appear before a
      court.
24   **mace** sceptre or staff of office, resem-
      bling an ornamental version of a weapon
      of war; borne before or carried by some
      civic officials in formal procession (*OED*
      *n.*² 2a)
      list liked

12–31] *Delius; Q1 lines* haue. / tribute, / aggreed / windowes. / Tapster, / dager, / out, / In . . . tales *(3 lines
prose)* / and . . . head. *(short indented line)* / watch, / coltstaffe. / mace, / buckler. / morning, / hand, / drinke:
/ his / night / this, / Miracle. /   14 opening] *(*opning*)*   17 by] *Q2;* be *Q1*   20 notches] *(*natches*)*   tallies]
*(*tales*)*   23 cowl-staff] *(*coltstaffe*)*

buckler. All the tenpenny alehouses would stand every   25
morning with a quart pot in their hand, saying, 'Will it
please your worship drink?' He that had not done so
had been sure to have had his sign pulled down and his
lattice borne away the next night. To conclude, what
have I not done, yet cannot do this?   30
Doubtless he is preserved by miracle.

Here enters ALICE *and* MICHAEL.

GREENE

Hence, Will; here comes Mistress Arden.

ALICE

Ah, gentle Michael, art thou sure they're friends?

MICHAEL

Why, I saw them when they both shook hands;
When Mosby bled he even wept for sorrow,   35
And railed on Franklin, that was cause of all.

25 **alehouses** lowest in the hierarchy of early modern drinking establishments. Alehouses and the immoral behaviour they bred were a source of public concern, strictly regulated by public bodies, railed against by moralists and prosecuted for infringements through Quarter Sessions courts (hence the high number of contemporary references to alehouse keepers discovered by B&T (*CRE*)). B&T (*CRE*) emends to 'alehous keepers', but the line makes sense as the house personified. Compare the 'eighteenpence ordinary' at which Arden dines in 3.133–4; a *tenpenny* alehouse was still a rather superior one.

26 **quart pot** vessel for beer, holding a

quarter of a gallon, or around two pints, often made of pewter; see, e.g., National Trust Collections 494979.1.

27 **your worship** respectful form of address to social superior, mayor or magistrate

28 **sign pulled down** See 3.66n.

29 **lattice** lattice-work window, usually painted red or green, which signified that the property sold drink

32 **Hence** suggests that Greene wants Will (and presumably Shakebag, who does not speak again until 56) to make himself scarce, and these actors may move away from the others.

36 **railed on** complained bitterly about; see 13.54.

25 alehouses] alehouse men *Jacob;* alehouses-men *W&P;* alehouse-keepers *B&T*   26 their] *Q2;* his *Q1*
28 sign] *(Signe) Q2;* Singne *Q1*   31 SD] *after 32 Hopkinson²*

No sooner came the surgeon in at doors
But my master took to his purse and gave him money;
And, to conclude, sent me to bring you word
That Mosby, Franklin, Bradshaw, Adam Fowle,   40
With diverse of his neighbours and his friends,
Will come and sup with you at our house this night.

ALICE

Ah, gentle Michael, run thou back again,
And when my husband walks into the fair
Bid Mosby steal from him and come to me;   45
And this night shall thou and Susan be made sure.

MICHAEL

I'll go tell him.

ALICE

And as thou goest, tell John cook of our guests,
And bid him lay it on, spare for no cost.   *Exit Michael.*

BLACK WILL

Nay, an there be such cheer, we will bid ourselves. 50

---

37 **surgeon** qualified individual who performed surgery, more common than the university-educated physician. There were only a few such individuals in sixteenth-century towns; local records identify Thomas Annott in Faversham from the 1580s and John Swayton from the 1590s (Mortimer).

44 **fair** St Valentine's Fair; one of two granted in Faversham's 1546 incorporation charter, it brought vendors, shoppers and their money into the town. Holinshed says it was 'woont to be kept partlie in the towne, and partlie in the abbeie', but that Arden, 'for his owne priuat lucre & couetous gaine', had it kept only on his own property that year, 'bereauing the towne' (see below, p. 300); this action is part of the historical figure's question-

able morality that appears at several points in the play (see pp. 33–7).

45 **steal** slip away

46 **made sure** contracted to marry, in a legally binding ceremony (see also 1.149 and n.)

48 **John cook** Households of this size are unlikely to have had their own cook, but they may have employed one for special occasions.

49 **lay it on** be lavish in expense. *OED* gives the earliest use as 1593, *Edward II*, 'Thou shalt have crowns of us, t'outbid the barons; / And, Spencer, spare them not, but lay it on' (3.1.55–6).

50 **bid** invite. It is possible that Will and Shakebag move forward at this point to address Alice at 50, having retreated at 31.

41 diverse] *(diuers)*

Mistress Arden, Dick Greene and I do mean to sup with you.

ALICE

And welcome shall you be. Ah, gentlemen,
How missed you of your purpose yesternight?

GREENE

'Twas long of Shakebag, that unlucky villain.   55

SHAKEBAG

Thou doest me wrong; I did as much as any.

BLACK WILL   Nay then, Mistress Alice, I'll tell you how
it was: when he should have locked with both his
hilts, he in a bravery flourished over his head. With
that comes Franklin at him lustily and hurts the   60
slave – with that he slinks away. Now his way had
been to have come in hand and feet, one and two
round at his costard. He, like a fool, bears his sword-
point half a yard out of danger. I lie here for my life.
If the devil come, and he have no more strength than   65

51–2 Will's assertion would, under normal circumstances, be considered rude and socially inappropriate; Alice's encouraging response shows a world turned upside down.

55 **long of** because of, on account of

58–9 **locked . . . flourished** Hilts are the handles of swords that protect the hand of the wielder, so locking would parry the opponent's blow, whereas flourishing *in a bravery* (waving a weapon over one's head in triumph or swagger) leaves one open to attack. Use of technical sword-fighting language here is again notable.

59–60 **With that** at that instant

60 **lustily** vigorously

62 ***come . . . feet** technical swordsmanship or fencing term, meaning lunge or thrust with a sword in order to make a decisive hit (*OED* come I 7). See, e.g., *1H4*, 2.4.209–10, 'I followed me close, came in foot and hand'. Wine's addition of 'in' to Q1's 'come' is therefore followed here.

63 **costard** head (literally a kind of large apple)

64 **here** suggests Will demonstrates the defensive posture

65–6 **If . . . ward** If the devil had come with no power other than defensive swordsmanship, he still wouldn't have broken down my defences.

57–68] *Sturgess; Q1 lines* was, / hilts, / head / lustely / away, / (feete, /) costerd. / (out /) lyfe. / fence / warde, / hand, / castell. / it. / ; *W&P lines as Q1, except* foole / danger. / come, / fence, / it; /   61 Now] *new paragraph B&T*   62 come in] *Wine;* come *Q1*

fence, he shall never beat me from this ward. I'll stand
to it: a buckler in a skilful hand is as good as a castle –
nay, 'tis better than a sconce, for I have tried it.
Mosby, perceiving this, began to faint.
With that comes Arden with his arming-sword,   70
And thrust him through the shoulder in a trice.

ALICE

Ay, but I wonder why you both stood still?

BLACK WILL

Faith, I was so amazed I could not strike.

ALICE

Ah, sirs, had he yesternight been slain,
For every drop of his detested blood   75
I would have crammed in angels in thy fist,
And kissed thee too, and hugged thee in my arms.

BLACK WILL

Patient yourself, we cannot help it now.
Greene and we two will dog him through the fair,
And stab him in the crowd, and steal away.   80

66 **fence** skills in the art of fencing, or
swordsmanship more broadly; action of
defending
ward defensive posture, mode of par-
rying: 'positions or placings which with-
stand the enemies blowes, and are as a
shield or safegarde against them'
(Giacomo di Grassi, *True Art of Defence*
(1594), sig. C4ʳ)
66–7 **stand to it** maintain it to be true; stick
to my guns, i.e. maintain my position
68 **sconce** small castle, often fortifying a
particular route such as a ford or a bridge
70 **arming-sword** forming part of his
armour, but also with possible heraldic
associations
73 **amazed** stunned, as by a blow to the

head (*OED* 1), or filled with panic or fear
(*OED* 3), as well as astonished (*OED* 4)
76 ***crammed in angels** Q1 reads 'cramme
in Angels', Q3 gives the reading adopted
here, apparently intended in Q2's
botched correction to 'camd in angels'.
'Cramming in' suggests excess, surplus
and physical effort, and expresses Alice's
profligacy and desperation, fitting
well with the excessive and ungentle-
womanly physicality of her offer to kiss
and hug the murderers in the following
line.
angels English gold coins worth 10s
(half a pound), featuring the archangel
Michael slaying the dragon
78 **Patient** calm

76 have . . . angels] *(*have cram'd in angels) Q3; cramme in Angels Q1; haue camd in angels Q2*

Here enters MOSBY [*with his arm and shoulder bandaged*].

ALICE

It is unpossible. But here comes he
That will, I hope, invent some surer means.
Sweet Mosby, hide thy arm; it kills my heart.

MOSBY

Ay, Mistress Arden, this is your favour.

ALICE

Ah, say not so, for when I saw thee hurt   85
I could have took the weapon thou lett'st fall
And run at Arden! For I have sworn
That these mine eyes, offended with his sight,
Shall never close till Arden's be shut up.
This night I rose and walked about the chamber,   90
And twice or thrice I thought to have murdered him.

MOSBY

What, in the night? – then had we been undone.

ALICE

Why, how long shall he live?

MOSBY

Faith, Alice, no longer than this night.
Black Will and Shakebag, will you two   95
Perform the complot that I have laid?

BLACK WILL

Ay, or else think me as a villain.

---

81 **unpossible** impossible; also at 271
84 **favour** lover's gift to be worn in public,
    or by a knight on the battlefield (here the
    bandage worn as such); the result of
    Alice's affection
89 **Arden's ... shut up** i.e. in death

96 **complot** conspiracy
97 **think me** think of me
    villain insulting term of address
    suggesting a low-status or depraved
    person, and therefore generating
    multiple ironies

80 SD] *after 82 Oliphant*   80.2 *with ... bandaged*] *B&T (Oliphant subst.)*   86 lett'st] *(letst)*   95–6]
W&P lines performe / laid? /

GREENE

    And rather than you shall want, I'll help myself.

MOSBY

    You, Master Greene, shall single Franklin forth,

    And hold him with a long tale of strange news   100

    That he may not come home till supper time.

    I'll fetch Master Arden home, and we like friends

    Will play a game or two at tables here.

ALICE

    But what of all this? How shall he be slain?

MOSBY

    Why, Black Will and Shakebag, locked within the

        counting-house,   105

    Shall, at a certain watchword given, rush forth.

BLACK WILL

    What shall the watchword be?

---

98 B&T points out that, up until this point, Greene has studiously avoided all direct involvement in the murder attempts; these lines may therefore be self-consciously spoken, and other characters may register the change in his attitude.

100 **hold** detain

102 **like friends** as friends do

103 **tables** the two halves of the board on which chess, backgammon, etc. were played. Ownership of such 'leisure items' was a key indicator of elevated social status, and late-sixteenth-century Faversham inhabitants owned over thirty pairs, present in 13 per cent of households, valued at up to 3s 4d each (KHLC). A pair is depicted in the woodcut to the

1633 quarto, showing the game's interest for a contemporary audience (Bloom), and one survives from the carpenter's cabin of the Mary Rose.

105 **counting-house** chamber or closet for business or accounts, likely to have been staged in the discovery space. In Holinshed the room is called 'a closet at the end of [Arden's] parlour' (see below, p. 297) and, although they did signify elite urban status (the only Kentish examples in the sixteenth century belonged to town officers known as jurats), these historical spaces were used much like general closets, for keeping random goods as well as for mercantile business. The term is used here to suggest Arden's greed.

98] *Delius; Q1 lines* want, / selfe. /   104] *Tyrrell; Q1 lines* this? / slaine? /   105–6] *Delius lines* Why- / counting-house, / forth. /

MOSBY

'Now I take you', that shall be the word.

But come not forth before in any case.

BLACK WILL

I warrant you; but who shall lock me in?   110

ALICE

That will I do; thou'lt keep the key thyself.

MOSBY

Come, Master Greene, go you along with me.

See all things ready, Alice, against we come.

ALICE

Take no care for that; send you him home,

Exeunt Mosby and Greene.

And if he e'er go forth again, blame me.   115

Come, Black Will, that in mine eyes art fair;

Next unto Mosby do I honour thee.

Instead of fair words and large promises

My hands shall play you golden harmony.

How like you this? Say, will you do it, sirs?   120

BLACK WILL

Ay, and that bravely too! Mark my device:

---

108 The watchword as specified by Mosby here is different to its operative use at 236 ('now I can take you'; Holinshed has 'Now maie I take you' (see below, p. 298); SMS, 'I can take you'), so B&T adds 'can'. The point is really, however, that they should strike when Mosby defeats Arden, rather than the exact words spoken in doing so; audiences are unlikely to note the loss of one word of the phrase Mosby identifies here, in the context of the tension around the game itself.

114 **Take . . . for** don't worry about
116 **Black . . . fair** Alice plays on *Black* as a name signifying a dark complexion, contrasted with the contemporary connection of beauty with a facial whiteness achieved through lack of exposure to the sun (and therefore manual labour).
119 **play . . . harmony** dispense gold. The image, from lute playing, draws attention to and sexualizes the skills expected of a gentlewoman.
121 **bravely** both valiantly and showily **device** plan; invention

108 'Now . . . you'] Now Mr^(ΛArden) I Can take you *SMS;* 'Now I can take you' *B&T*   111 thou'lt] *Q3;* thou'st *Q1*

Place Mosby, being a stranger, in a chair,
And let your husband sit upon a stool,
That I may come behind him cunningly
And with a towel pull him to the ground,   125
Then stab him till his flesh be as a sieve.
That done, bear him behind the Abbey,
That those that find him murdered may suppose
Some slave or other killed him for his gold.

ALICE

A fine device. You shall have twenty pound;   130
And when he is dead, you shall have forty more.
And, lest you might be suspected staying here,
Michael shall saddle you two lusty geldings.
Ride whither you will – to Scotland or to Wales –
I'll see you shall not lack, where'er you be.   135

BLACK WILL

Such words would make one kill a thousand men!
Give me the key. Which is the counting-house?

122–3 Seating was intended to distinguish sitters from one another socially in mixed gatherings, and chairs were owned in smaller numbers not because furnishings were 'sparse', as Wine suggests, but to demonstrate hierarchy. The chair, in which Will suggests Mosby sits, was traditionally reserved for the head of the household, and may have been marked with his initials; stools, such as the one on which Arden is to be placed, were for women, children and those of lower status, although chairs were provided in larger numbers across the 16th and 17th centuries as the middling sort dined more often with their neighbours (see pp. 22–3). In late-sixteenth-century Kentish urban parlours, stools outnumbered chairs by approximately three to one.

124 **cunningly** skilfully; *OED* gives 1603 as the first instance of the modern meaning 'craftily'.

125 **towel** linen cloth used at meals. Their ownership, often in multiples for special dining occasions, denoted elevated social status.

133 **lusty geldings** energetic castrated horses (better behaved because without hormones, unlike stallions)

137 Alice probably keeps the key with others on her belt. Control of the keys to all rooms and chests in the house defined a wife's executive power over its spaces during the daytime, making her acquiescence to Will's demand for them an especially shocking reversal of her responsibilities.

126 sieve] *Q2 (*siue*); sine *Q1*   136 a thousand] *(*1000*)*

[Then Alice gives him the key and points
to the counting-house door.]

ALICE

Here would I stay and still encourage you,
But that I know how resolute you are.

SHAKEBAG

Tush, you are too faint-hearted; we must do it.   140

ALICE

But Mosby will be there, whose very looks
Will add unwonted courage to my thought
And make me the first that shall adventure on him.

BLACK WILL

Tush, get you gone, 'tis we must do the deed.
When this door opens next, look for his death!   145

[Exeunt Black Will and Shakebag.]

ALICE

Ah, would he now were here, that it might open.
I shall no more be closed in Arden's arms
That, like the snakes of black Tisiphone,
Sting me with their embracings. Mosby's arms
Shall compass me and, were I made a star,   150

---

138 **Here** As Alice does not leave the stage,
her assertion that she would stay *Here*
appears to refer to the counting-house,
indicating her movements. Wiggins
points out that the scene requires three
doors, leading respectively to counting-
house, street, and out of the parlour into
the rest of Arden's property.

140 In other words Alice, as a woman, is too
faint-hearted to commit murder, so has
to hire Black Will and Shakebag.

142 **unwonted** unusual, exceptional

143 **adventure** try, run the risk; unusual with

on, but see, e.g., Costanzo Felice, *The
conspiracie of Catiline* (1557), 'than
thought he not to lose his time: but
to aventure on gretter thynges wherin
was more harde besinesse and laboure
and honoure' (sig. Bb2ᵛ).

145 **look for** expect

148 **snakes ... Tisiphone** One of the three
Furies, Tisiphone is described by Ovid as
clothed in a dress dripping with blood
and with a snake coiled around her waist
and more in her hair. Ironically, she pun-
ished the crime of homicide.

137 SD] *B&T (Wiggins subst.)*   145 SD] *W&P subst.*

I would have none other spheres but those.
There is no nectar but in Mosby's lips.
Had chaste Diana kissed him, she, like me,
Would grow lovesick, and from her watery bower
Fling down Endymion and snatch him up.   155
Then blame not me, that slay a silly man
Not half so lovely as Endymion.

Here enters MICHAEL.

MICHAEL   Mistress, my master is coming hard by.
ALICE   Who comes with him?
MICHAEL   Nobody but Mosby.   160
ALICE   That's well, Michael. Fetch in the tables, and when
    thou hast done, stand before the counting-house door.
MICHAEL   Why so?
ALICE
    Black Will is locked within to do the deed.
MICHAEL   What, shall he die tonight?   165
ALICE   Ay, Michael.
MICHAEL   But shall not Susan know it?

151 **spheres** concentric, hollow circles (like the layers of an onion), imagined to revolve around the earth, carrying the heavenly bodies (*OED* 2a). Figuratively, environments appropriate to one's nature, as each star occupied its own sphere (*OED* 4b), a meaning which is reflected in Alice's 'relocation' from elite to lower-status husband.

153 **Diana** goddess of the moon

154 **watery bower** Diana was often depicted bathing in a secluded spot (e.g. in the story of Actaeon).

155 **Endymion** a shepherd youth of such beauty that the moon had him put to sleep so that she could embrace him perpetually; or a boy incurably in love with the moon. Lyly's play *Endymion, the Man in the Moon* was published in 1591 (Wiggins 794). Its performance before this date may have influenced the reference.

156 **silly** defenceless, powerless

158 **hard by** very close, primarily physically but also in time

153 chaste] *(chast)*   154 watery] *(watrie)*   155 snatch] *Q2;* snath *Q1*   157 SD] ACT V. SCENE II. – *A Room in* Arden's *House. Enter* Michael *and* Alice. *Tyrrell*   161–2] *Delius; Q1 lines* tables, / *(*the / *)* doore. /   165 shall] *(shull)*

ALICE

  Yes, for she'll be as secret as ourselves.

MICHAEL   That's brave! I'll go fetch the tables.

ALICE

  But Michael, hark to me a word or two: 170
  When my husband is come in, lock the street door.
  He shall be murdered ere the guests come in.   *Exit Michael.*

          Here enters ARDEN *and* MOSBY.

  Husband, what mean you to bring Mosby home?
  Although I wished you to be reconciled,
  'Twas more for fear of you than love of him: 175
  Black Will and Greene are his companions,
  And they are cutters, and may cut you short;
  Therefore I thought it good to make you friends.
  But wherefore do you bring him hither now?
  You have given me my supper with his sight.   180

MOSBY

  Master Arden, methinks your wife would have me
      gone.

---

169 **brave** courageous; excellent

172 **ere** before

172 SD1 Michael will need to re-enter at some stage with the playing tables, and he might also bring in the table on which to place them, a chair and stools, and the wine that will be used later for the pledging. This could, as B&T suggests, be accomplished by multiple quick exits and entrances, which would be in keeping with the general physical business that often characterizes servants in early modern plays, or he may be aided by other servants. In any case, the following dialogue is likely to be set against a backdrop of preparative activity that ironically enacts hospitality.

176 Sturgess points out that we might expect Shakebag here, not Greene, but that the latter's name suits the rhythm of the line better; it also fits with B&T's suggestion that Greene's valour and determination steps up a gear (see 98n.).

177 **cutters** bullies, cutthroats and robbers; castrators of animals
    cut you short trim or stop your progress; kill you

179 **wherefore** why

180 **given ... supper** taken away my appetite

172 ere] *Q3;* or *Q1*

ARDEN

No, good Master Mosby, women will be prating.
Alice, bid him welcome; he and I are friends.

ALICE

You may enforce me to it if you will,
But I had rather die than bid him welcome!   185
His company hath purchased me ill friends,
And therefore will I ne'er frequent it more.

MOSBY [*aside*]

Oh, how cunningly she can dissemble!

ARDEN

Now he is here you will not serve me so?

ALICE

I pray you be not angry or displeased.   190
I'll bid him welcome, seeing you'll have it so:
You are welcome, Master Mosby; will you sit down?

MOSBY

I know I am welcome to your loving husband,
But for yourself, you speak not from your heart.

ALICE

And if I do not, sir, think I have cause.   195

MOSBY

Pardon me, Master Arden; I'll away.

ARDEN

No, good Master Mosby.

---

182 **prating** chattering foolishly, at great
length and to little purpose (commonly
seen as a female trait); prattling like a
chicken (*OED* 1a); see also 200
183 **bid him welcome** formally greet him
and offer hospitality; the duty of a housewife to her husband's guests
186 **purchased** acquired in exchange for
something else, not necessarily money

189 **serve** render obedience and service,
fulfil one's duty to a superior
(*OED v.* 8a)
192 Although several modern editors have
Mosby sit here, he is still questioning the
terms of his hosts' hospitality, and it is
more likely that he sits once the pledging
has taken place.
196 **away** leave

188 SD] *Tyrrell*   196 Master] *Jacob;* M. *Q1;* mistris *Q3;* Mʳ *SMS*

ALICE

   We shall have guests enough, though you go hence.

MOSBY

   I pray you, Master Arden, let me go.

ARDEN

   I pray thee, Mosby, let her prate her fill.   200

Enter MICHAEL.

ALICE [*to Mosby*]

   The doors are open, sir, you may be gone.

MICHAEL [*aside*]

   Nay that's a lie, for I have locked the doors.

ARDEN [*to Michael*]

   Sirrah, fetch me a cup of wine. I'll make them friends.

   And, gentle Mistress Alice, seeing you are so stout,

   You shall begin. Frown not; I'll have it so.   205

ALICE

   I pray you, meddle with that you have to do.

ARDEN

   Why, Alice, how can I do too much for him

   Whose life I have endangered without cause?

ALICE

   'Tis true, and seeing 'twas partly through my means,

   I am content to drink to him for this once.   210

---

200 **prate** chatter foolishly

203 SD Michael may leave here to fetch the wine, or he may bring it from the table on which he has already placed it. Editors have had him re-enter at 208. But rather than being fetched by the glass, wine might be served from a 'wine pot', owned as part of a set of drinking and serving vessels in pewter or silver by the urban middling sort, in order to be displayed and used on hospitable occasions such as

this (see p. 87). In other words, the ritual of serving was an important part of the ritual of drinking, and may well have been staged. Silver-topped wine pots were owned by 6 per cent of Faversham households (KHLC; see also 1.310n.).

204 **stout** proud, arrogant

205 **begin** i.e. toast with the wine

206 **meddle ... do** perhaps 'attend to your proper business'; or 'get on with it (the toast)'

---

200 SD] *this edn*   201 SD] *this edn*   202 SD] *Tyrrell*   203] *Delius; Q1 lines* Wine. / friends. /   203 SD] *B&T*

Here, Master Mosby! [*Then she drinks to him.*] And,
  I pray you, henceforth
Be you as strange to me as I to you.
Your company hath purchased me ill friends,
And I for you, God knows, have, undeserved,
Been ill-spoken of in every place;   215
Therefore henceforth frequent my house no more.

MOSBY

I'll see your husband in despite of you!
Yet, Arden, I protest to thee by heaven,
Thou ne'er shalt see me more after this night.
I'll go to Rome rather than be forsworn!   220

ARDEN

Tush, I'll have no such vows made in my house.

ALICE

Yes, I pray you, husband, let him swear,
And on that condition, Mosby, pledge me here.

MOSBY

Ay, as willingly as I mean to live.
    [*Then Alice hands him the cup, and he drinks to her.*]

ARDEN

Come, Alice, is our supper ready yet?   225

ALICE

It will by then you have played a game at tables.
    [*Then Arden sits on a stool and Mosby in the chair.*]

ARDEN

Come, Master Mosby, what shall we play for?

---

212 neatly equivocal phrase
214 **for you** on your account; for your sake
220 **go to Rome** undertake an arduous pilgrimage; metaphorically to convert to Catholicism, thereby showing the strength of his feelings

forsworn perjured by breaking his oath
223 **pledge** drink to someone to show goodwill or allegiance; toast
226 **will ... have** will be by the time you have

211 SD] *B&T* 224 SD] *B&T (Wiggins subst.)* 226 SD] *this edn*

MOSBY

Three games for a French crown, sir, an't please you?

ARDEN

Content.

[Then they play at the tables. Here enter BLACK WILL
and SHAKEBAG *from the counting-house.]*

BLACK WILL *[aside to Alice and Michael]*

Can he not take him yet? What a spite is that!   230

ALICE *[aside to Black Will]*

Not yet, Will. Take heed he see thee not.

BLACK WILL *[aside to Alice and Michael]*

I fear he will spy me as I am coming.

MICHAEL *[aside to Black Will]*

To prevent that, creep betwixt my legs.

MOSBY

One ace, or else I lose the game.

[Then he throws the dice.]

ARDEN

Mary, sir, there's two for failing.   235

---

228 **French crown** French gold coin worth
4s. See 3.76–7n.
229 SD The staging here would work well
with Holinshed's visceral and chilling
assertion that Michael 'stood at his masters backe, holding a candle in his hand,
to shadow blacke Will, that Arden might
by no meanes perceiue him comming
foorth' (see below, p. 298); in any case,
Black Will and Shakebag enter surrepti-
tiously and remain unseen.
230 **Can ... yet** Can he not beat him at the
game? 'Take' is to capture an opponent's
piece (*OED* 1f). See also 238. Whereas
Holinshed suggests that Mosby utters the

'watchword' even though he is unable to
beat Arden, eliciting the response 'Take
me (quoth Master Arden) which waie?'
(see below, p. 298), the play builds tension
by tying Mosby's genuine victory in the
game to Arden's murder (see Bloom, 17).
234 **ace** side of the dice marked with a single
spot, a 'one'
235 **two for failing** two aces (one more than
is needed to win), to prevent failing.
Bloom gives a detailed exposition of the
possible relationship of this throw to
actual gameplay, but admits that the rules
of the game have changed considerably
over time (16–20).

228] *Delius; Q1 lines* sir, / you. / an't] *Wiggins; and Q1*   229.1–2 *Here ... counting-house*] *B&T
(Wiggins subst.)*   230 SD] *this edn (Hugo subst.)*   231 SD] *B&T (Hugo, subst.)*   232 SD] *this edn (Hugo
subst.)*   233 SD] *B&T (Hugo subst.)*   234 SD] *B&T (Sturgess subst.)*

MOSBY

    Ah, Master Arden, 'now I can take you'!

    Then [Black] Will pulls him down with a towel.

ARDEN

    Mosby, Michael, Alice, what will you do?

BLACK WILL

    Nothing but take you up, sir, nothing else.

    [Then Mosby stabs Arden.]

MOSBY

    There's for the pressing iron you told me of.

    [Then Shakebag stabs Arden.]

SHAKEBAG

    And there's for the ten pound in my sleeve.   240

    [Then Arden groans.]

ALICE *[to Arden]*

    What, groans thou? *[to Mosby]* Nay then, give me

    the weapon –

    Take this for hindering Mosby's love and mine!

    [Then Alice stabs Arden, and he dies.]

MICHAEL   O mistress!

BLACK WILL

    Ah, that villain will betray us all.

MOSBY

    Tush, fear him not, he will be secret.   245

---

236 SD *pulls ... towel* as is depicted in the woodcut (see Fig. 14)

237 **what ... do** what are you doing

238 **take you up** wonderfully resonant phrase with many meanings, most prominently here: check you, bring you up short (*OED* take up 11a), arrest or apprehend you (*OED* 9a) or convey you to heaven (*OED* 2a); but also, literally, to capture a piece in chess or backgammon (*OED* 10b)

239 **pressing iron** See 1.312, and Holinshed, who says that Mosby, 'hauing at his girdle a pressing iron of fourtéene pounds weight, stroke him on the hed with the same' (see below, p. 298); the playwright chose to reference rather than stage this action.

240 **in my sleeve** referring to the money he's been paid to do the job

238, 239 SD] *B&T*   240 SD] *this edn (Wiggins subst.)*   241 SD1] *B&T*   SD2] *Wiggins*   242 SD] *B&T (Wiggins subst.)*

MICHAEL

Why, dost thou think I will betray myself?

SHAKEBAG

In Southwark dwells a bonny northern lass,
The widow Chambley. I'll to her house now,
And if she will not give me harborough
I'll make booty of the quean even to her smock.   250

BLACK WILL

Shift for yourselves; we two will leave you now.

ALICE

First lay the body in the counting-house.
Then they lay the body in the counting-house.

BLACK WILL

We have our gold; Mistress Alice, adieu.
Mosby, farewell; and, Michael, farewell too.
                    Exeunt [Black Will and Shakebag. Knocking].

[*Here enters*] SUSAN.

SUSAN

Mistress, the guests are at the doors.   255
Hearken, they knock! What, shall I let them in?

---

247 **Southwark** area on the south bank of the Thames around London Bridge, and therefore outside the liberties of the city, home to various kinds of entertainment in inns, theatres (the Rose and Globe) and bear-baiting arenas, as well as, probably most relevant to Shakebag here, brothels

248 **Chambley** The sixteenth-century spelling of Q1's 'Chambly', which has no sixteenth- or seventeenth-century hits on TNA Discovery.

249 **harborough** harbour, refuge

250 **booty** plunder, spoil, gain; he threatens to rape her
quean prostitute
smock woman's undergarment, worn closest to the skin and therefore her last line of defence

251 **Shift for yourselves** Provide for yourselves; depend on your own efforts. May pick up on the previous line, as the noun 'shift' is a synonym for smock.

254 SD2 *Here enters* B&T (*CRE*) points out that '*Here enters*' is the play's usual form.

249 And] *Q2;* Ind *Q1*   254 SD1 *Black . . . Shakebag*] *Hugo (Will and Shakebag) Hugo   Knocking*] *this edn (B&T subst.)*   SD2 *Here enters*] *this edn (B&T subst.); Enter Q1*

ALICE

> Mosby, go thou and bear them company.   *Exit Mosby.*
> And Susan, fetch water and wash away this blood.
>> [*Exit Susan, returns with a pail of water and*
>>> *begins washing the floor.*]

SUSAN

> The blood cleaveth to the ground and will not out.

ALICE

> But with my nails I'll scrape away the blood.   260
> [*Then she scratches at the floor.*]
> The more I strive, the more the blood appears!

SUSAN

> What's the reason, mistress, can you tell?

ALICE

> Because I blush not at my husband's death.

Here enters MOSBY.

MOSBY

> How now, what's the matter? Is all well?

ALICE

> Ay, well, if Arden were alive again!   265
> In vain we strive, for here his blood remains.

---

257 **bear them company** go with them

258 SD The direction, suggested by Alice's instruction and Susan's complaint at 259, includes within it a period of time onstage without lines for Alice, one which continues as Susan begins to wash. Clearing up after the murder or preparing for the food would involve Alice taking on the role of a servant, continuing the uncertainty the scene raises about the boundaries between service and authority (and see note on Michael's actions at 292); more contemplative activities would develop some tragic gravitas for the character.

259 **cleaveth** sticks fast; also, ironically, remains devoted or steadfast (see 358)

260 **with . . . scrape** (animalistic image more usually associated with dogs)

263 **Because . . . not** The floor 'blushes' on Alice's behalf. She sees the blood whose flow from a murdered corpse was thought to identify a murderer (by cruentation, in which suspects were brought before the body to see if it bled to accuse them) as finding a different route to accuse her. See also 16.4–5.

258 SD] *Wine (Sturgess subst.)*   260 SD] *this edn (Wiggins subst.)*

MOSBY

Why, strew rushes on it, can you not?
This wench doth nothing! [*to Susan*] Fall unto the
      work.

ALICE

'Twas thou that made me murder him.

MOSBY   What of that?

ALICE

Nay, nothing, Mosby, so it be not known.   270

MOSBY

Keep thou it close, and 'tis unpossible.

ALICE

Ah, but I cannot; was he not slain by me?
My husband's death torments me at the heart.

MOSBY

It shall not long torment thee, gentle Alice.
I am thy husband; think no more of him.   275

Here enters ADAM Fowle *and* BRADSHAW.

BRADSHAW

How now, Mistress Arden? What ail you weep?

MOSBY

Because her husband is abroad so late.
A couple of ruffians threatened him yesternight,
And she, poor soul, is afraid he should be hurt.

---

267 **strew rushes** Rushes were strewn on the
floor as a sweet-smelling, renewable
covering, warm and quiet to walk on,
with new green ones laid to welcome
guests. Holinshed says the murderers
'strewed againe the rushes that were
shuffled with struling' (see below,
p. 298). For evidence of their use on the
stage, e.g. in *2H4*, 5.5, see Dessen and
Thomson, 185–6.

268 **Fall unto** begin

271 **close** secret

274–5 A gesture of marital possession from
Mosby, such as a kiss or sexual advance,
seems to be called for here, to take
Alice's mind away from the murder.

276 **What ... weep** What afflicts you to the
extent that it is making you weep? See
Franklin's similar question at 305. 'Ail
you' is twice as common as 'ails you' in
EEBO-TCP searches to 1600.

277 **abroad** away from home

268 SD] *Wine*   276, 281, 357 Mistress] *(M.); Q3 (Mrs)*

269

ADAM

Is't nothing else? Tush, he'll be here anon.   280

Here enters GREENE.

GREENE

Now, Mistress Arden, lack you any guests?

ALICE

Ah, Master Greene, did you see my husband lately?

GREENE

I saw him walking behind the Abbey even now.

Here enters FRANKLIN.

ALICE

I do not like this being out so late.

Master Franklin, where did you leave my husband?   285

FRANKLIN

Believe me, I saw him not since morning.

Fear you not; he'll come anon. Meantime

You may do well to bid his guests sit down.

ALICE

Ay, so they shall. Master Bradshaw, sit you there.

I pray you be content; I'll have my will.   290

Master Mosby, sit you in my husband's seat.

[*Then the guests sit down, and Susan and
Michael speak quietly to one another.*]

---

283 **even now** only a short time ago

290 The line suggests that Bradshaw resists her instructions, perhaps because they require him to move awkwardly around the furniture in order to avoid the spot on the floor where the blood was spilled.

291 This has the effect of elevating Mosby above the other guests on a chair at the head of the table, as they sit on stools below him.

291 SD] *this edn (B&T subst.)*

MICHAEL   Susan, shall thou and I wait on them? Or, an
thou sayest the word, let us sit down too.

SUSAN
Peace, we have other matters now in hand.
I fear me, Michael, all will be bewrayed.   295

MICHAEL   Tush, so it be known that I shall marry thee in
the morning, I care not though I be hanged ere night.
But to prevent the worst I'll buy some ratsbane.

SUSAN
Why, Michael, wilt thou poison thyself?

MICHAEL
No, but my mistress, for I fear she'll tell.   300

SUSAN
Tush, Michael, fear not her; she's wise enough.

MOSBY
Sirrah Michael, give's a cup of beer.
[*Then Michael gives him a cup.*]
Mistress Arden, here's to your husband.
[*Then Mosby drinks.*]

ALICE
My husband!

FRANKLIN
What ails you, woman, to cry so suddenly?   305

ALICE
Ah, neighbours, a sudden qualm came over my heart!
My husband's being forth torments my mind.

---

292 Michael has not spoken since 243; Will
says farewell to him at 254, and he may
exit with Mosby or Susan after this, and
re-enter with one or the other of them.
B&T points out that he must remove the
knife and towel, and may set the table for
food before this point.

293 **let ... too** Michael indicates the wider
implications of Alice's violation of

domestic hierarchy: if Mosby is to sit in
her husband's seat, then the servants
might equally well join them at the table
instead of standing as they are currently
doing, waiting on them.

295 **bewrayed** revealed

298 **ratsbane** rat poison: arsenic compound

302 **Sirrah ... beer** See parallels with
203.

292–3] *B&T; Q1 lines* them? / too. /   292 an] *(and)*   296–8] *Delius; Q1 lines* the / night. / rats bane.
/   302 SD] *B&T (Wiggins subst.)*   303 SD] *Wiggins subst.*   307 being] *Q2;* deing *Q1*

I know something's amiss; he is not well,
Or else I should have heard of him ere now.

MOSBY [*aside*]

She will undo us through her foolishness.   310

GREENE

Fear not, Mistress Arden, he's well enough.

ALICE

Tell not me; I know he is not well.
He was not wont for to stay thus late.
Good Master Franklin, go and seek him forth,
And if you find him send him home to me,   315
And tell him what a fear he hath put me in.

FRANKLIN

I like not this; I pray God all be well.
I'll seek him out, and find him if I can.
                            Exeunt Franklin, Mosby and Greene.

ALICE [*aside to Michael*]

Michael, how shall I do to rid the rest away?

MICHAEL [*aside to Alice*]

Leave that to my charge; let me alone.   320
'Tis very late, Master Bradshaw,
And there are many false knaves abroad,
And you have many narrow lanes to pass.

BRADSHAW

Faith, friend Michael, and thou sayest true;
Therefore I pray thee, light's forth, and lend's a link.   325

---

313 **wont for to** used to
317 W&P and others have this first line as an aside, but Franklin apparently makes no particular secret of his suspicions, as they are plainly read by and Mosby and Alice, 341–2.
319 **how ... do** what shall I do. A mistress asking a servant for advice suggests her loss of control (see also 330–1).

320 **charge** duty, responsibility
325 **light's forth** light us to the door (by going before with the candle); just possibly an injunction: 'lights forth'
link torch (to see our way home). Communal street lighting was installed in most provincial towns only in the eighteenth century, in Faversham in 1751.

310 SD] *SMS*   318 SD] *Tyrrell; after 317 Q1*   319 SD] *B&T*   320 SD] *B&T*   321–2] *one line B&T*

ALICE

> Michael, bring them to the doors, but do not stay,
> You know I do not love to be alone.
>
> > *Exeunt Bradshaw, Adam and Michael.*
>
> Go, Susan, and bid thy brother come.
> But wherefore should he come? Here is nought but
>   fear.
> Stay, Susan, stay, and help to counsel me.   330

SUSAN

> Alas, I, counsel? Fear frights away my wits.

> > *Then they open the counting-house door,*
> > *and look upon Arden.*

ALICE

> See, Susan, where thy quondam master lies!
> Sweet Arden, smeared in blood and filthy gore.

SUSAN

> My brother, you and I shall rue this deed.

ALICE

> Come, Susan, help to lift his body forth,   335
> And let our salt tears be his obsequies.

> > [*Then they bring his body from the counting-house.*]
> > *Here enters* MOSBY *and* GREENE.

MOSBY

> How now, Alice, whither will you bear him?

ALICE

> Sweet Mosby, art thou come? Then weep that will;
> I have my wish in that I joy thy sight.

---

326 **bring . . . doors** show them off the premises
329 The line needs Q3's elision ('here's') for the metre.
332 **quondam** former

336 **obsequies** funeral rites
338 **weep that will** those that want to weep can do so
339 **joy thy sight** joy in the sight of you

327 SD] *Hugo; after 325 Q1*   336.1] *B&T*   338] *Delius; Q1 lines* come? / will. /

GREENE

Well it 'hoves us to be circumspect.   340

MOSBY

Ay, for Franklin thinks that we have murdered him.

ALICE

Ay, but he cannot prove it, for his life.

We'll spend this night in dalliance and in sport.

Here enters MICHAEL.

MICHAEL

O mistress, the Mayor and all the watch

Are coming towards our house with glaives and bills. 345

ALICE

Make the door fast; let them not come in.

[*Then Michael locks the street door.*]

MOSBY

Tell me, sweet Alice, how shall I escape?

ALICE

Out at the back door, over the pile of wood.

And for one night lie at the Fleur-de-Lis.

MOSBY

That is the next way to betray myself.   350

---

340 **'hoves** behoves

343 **dalliance** flirtation, caressing; idle and frivolous play
sport See 13.89.

344 **watch** body of watchmen who patrolled the streets of a town in the days before a national police force was established

345 **glaives** blades fastened to a long handle; halberds
bills concave blades with long handles, or concave axes with spikes at the back and spear-heads topping the shaft; used by constables of the watch, and signi-

fying local justice as opposed to martial endeavour on the stage (Dessen and Thomson, 30)

346 **Make . . . fast** Fasten/secure the door.

346 SD A door or other exit from the stage may be locked to represent the street door, or Michael must exit and return, indicating that the stage represents a room deeper within the house (further from the outer entrance).

348 **pile of wood** The playwright imagines the yard of a house where the wood is kept ready for use in fires.

350 **next** shortest or most direct

346 SD] *B&T (Wiggins subst.)*   349 Fleur-de-Lis] *(floure deluce)*

GREENE

> Alas, Mistress Arden, the watch will take me here,
> And cause suspicion where else would be none.

ALICE

> Why, take that way that Master Mosby doth;
> But first convey the body to the fields.

> > *Then they bear the body into the fields*
> > [*and then all but Susan return*].

MOSBY

> Until tomorrow, sweet Alice, now farewell,   355
> And see you confess nothing in any case.

GREENE

> Be resolute, Mistress Alice; betray us not,
> But cleave to us as we will stick to you.
> >   *Exeunt Mosby and Greene.*

ALICE

> Now let the judge and juries do their worst;
> My house is clear, and now I fear them not.   360

> [*Here enter* SUSAN *and* MICHAEL.]

SUSAN

> As we went it snowed all the way,
> Which makes me fear our footsteps will be spied.

---

354 SD The timing of the exits and entrances needed to clarify the logistics of the murder is complicated in Q1. This solution is succinct, leaving another edgy silence on the stage as Alice waits for their return (see also 254). B&T surmises that Michael and Susan begin to move Arden's body, and are followed by Mosby and Greene when their farewells are said; this helps to shorten an other-wise awkward pause. Other editors have seen Mosby as being involved from the start.

358 **cleave** The word echoes 259.

360 **clear** wide range of meanings around transparency and pellucidity, the main ones here being unsullied; free from fault, offence or guilt, and therefore innocent. See also 1.583n.

361 **snowed** snowèd

354.2] *this edn*   360 SD] *B&T*

ALICE

Peace, fool, the snow will cover them again!

SUSAN

But it had done before we came back again.   [*Knocking*]

ALICE

Hark, hark, they knock! Go, Michael, let them in.   365
[*Then Michael opens the door.*]

Here enters the MAYOR *and the Watch.*

How now, Master Mayor, have you brought my
husband home?

MAYOR

I saw him come into your house an hour ago.

ALICE

You are deceived; it was a Londoner.

MAYOR

Mistress Arden, know you not one that is called
Black Will?

ALICE

I know none such. What mean these questions?   370

MAYOR

I have the Council's warrant to apprehend him.

ALICE [*aside*]

I am glad it is no worse.

Why, Master Mayor, think you I harbour any such?

---

364 **done** finished
365 SD If Michael leaves the stage here (see
     346), he must return immediately with
     the Mayor and Watch.
368 **Londoner** See Holinshed, where Alice

'sent for two Londoners to supper,
the one named Prune, and the other Cole,
that were grosers' (see below, p. 299).
370 **questions** three syllables; as also at 396
371 **Council's** Privy Council's

364 SD] *Wine (Hugo subst.)*   365] *Delius; Q1 lines* knocke, / in. /   SD1] *this edn (Wine subst.)*   369]
*Delius; Q1 lines (*one /) Will. /   372 SD] *Tyrrell*

MAYOR

We are informed that here he is,

And therefore pardon us, for we must search.   375

ALICE

Ay, search and spare you not, through every room.

Were my husband at home, you would not offer this.

Here enters FRANKLIN.

Master Franklin, what mean you come so sad?

FRANKLIN

Arden, thy husband and my friend, is slain.

ALICE

Ah, by whom, Master Franklin, can you tell?   380

FRANKLIN

I know not, but behind the Abbey

There he lies murdered in most piteous case.

MAYOR

But Master Franklin, are you sure 'tis he?

FRANKLIN

I am too sure. Would God I were deceived!

ALICE

Find out the murderers, let them be known.   385

FRANKLIN

Ay, so they shall. Come you along with us.

ALICE

Wherefore?

---

377 **offer** attempt or intend. Often linked
to particular types of injury or harm
(*OED* 5a).
377 SD Franklin must have the hand-towel
and knife concealed about his person.
378 **what ... sad** 'What is the meaning of
your arriving in such a sad mood?'

379 In the play, Franklin takes over the job of
revealing the crime from the Mayor, who
is the sole representative of justice in
Holinshed.
382 **piteous** deserving pity
case physical state; position or circumstance

FRANKLIN

    Know you this hand-towel and this knife?

SUSAN [*aside to Michael*]

    Ah, Michael, through this thy negligence

    Thou hast betrayed and undone us all.   390

MICHAEL [*aside to Susan*]

    I was so afraid I knew not what I did;

    I thought I had thrown them both into the well.

ALICE

    It is the pig's blood we had to supper.

    But wherefore stay you? Find out the murderers.

MAYOR

    I fear me you'll prove one of them yourself.   395

ALICE

    I, one of them? What mean such questions?

FRANKLIN

    I fear me he was murdered in this house

    And carried to the fields for, from that place,

    Backwards and forwards, may you see

    The print of many feet within the snow.   400

    And look about this chamber where we are

    And you shall find part of his guiltless blood;

    For in his slip-shoe did I find some rushes,

---

390 **betrayed** betrayèd

393 SP This, Franklin's next speech (397) and the Mayor's following one (405) have specific addressees in B&T (to Franklin, the Mayor and the Watch respectively), but it is in the nature of the revelation of wrongdoing that such statements have a wider, general audience, underlining their quasi-judicial nature, as part of which the Mayor is judging them as evidence.

    pig's blood Probably intended to allude to blood used in cookery, as part of a dish (perhaps something like black pudding), its spilling as liquid by the table renders Alice's excuse both unconvincing and symbolic of sacrifice. See also 407.

403 **slip-shoe** light shoe or slipper. Holinshed states that Arden is left in the field 'in his night gowne, with his slippers on' (see below, p. 299). It is therefore clear that he was not killed while out walking, and the detail suggests that this is the only room in which rushes were newly strewed (Wiggins).

389 SD] *this edn (Tyrrell subst.)*   391 SD] *this edn (Tyrrell subst.)*

Which argueth he was murdered in this room.

MAYOR

Look in the place where he was wont to sit.   405

See, see, his blood – it is too manifest!

ALICE

It is a cup of wine that Michael shed.

MICHAEL   Ay, truly.

FRANKLIN

It is his blood which, strumpet, thou hast shed!

But if I live, thou and thy complices,   410

Which have conspired and wrought his death, shall

    rue it.

ALICE

Ah, Master Franklin, God and heaven can tell

I loved him more than all the world beside.

But bring me to him; let me see his body.

FRANKLIN [*to the Watch, pointing to Michael and Susan*]

Bring that villain, and Mosby's sister too;   415

And one of you go to the Fleur-de-Lis

And seek for Mosby and apprehend him too.   *Exeunt.*

---

404 **argueth** indicates, offers good grounds to suspect that, proves. The metrical awkwardness would be removed by emending to 'argues'.

405 **wont** accustomed

407 **shed** spilled. The word would be familiar to a contemporary audience in relation to Christ's shedding of his blood as represented in the wine taken at communion, as in *BCP*, '*And the minister that delivereth the cuppe shall saye.* THE bloude of our lorde Jesu Christ, which was shedd for the, preserve thy body and soule into everlasting life: and drinke this in remembraunce that Christes bloude was shedde for thee, and be thankeful.' It harks back to 393's *pig's blood* had *to supper.*

410 **complices** accomplices

411] *Delius; Q1 lines* death, / it. /   415 SD] *this edn (Wine, B&T subst.)*   416 Fleur-de-Lis] *(*flowre deluce*)*

[Sc. 15]   *Here enters* SHAKEBAG *alone.*

SHAKEBAG

    The widow Chambley in her husband's days I kept,
    And now he's dead she is grown so stout
    She will not know her old companions.
    I came thither thinking to have had
    Harbour, as I was wont,   5
    And she was ready to thrust me out at doors.
    But, whether she would or no, I got me up,
    And as she followed me I spurned her down the stairs,
    And broke her neck, and cut her tapster's throat;
    And now I am going to fling them in the Thames.   10
    I have the gold; what care I though it be known?
    I'll cross the water and take sanctuary.   *Exit.*

Sc. 15.1 in ... days i.e. when her husband
was alive
    kept maintained as a mistress
2   **stout** proud, haughty; obstinate or
defiant
5   **Harbour** shelter, entertainment
6   **at** of
7   **would or no** i.e. would offer the harbour
or not (making his behaviour the more
callous)
    got me up either got up to leave, or
forced my way upstairs
8   **spurned** kicked
10   **them** the widow and tapster. B&T points

out that Shakebag may well therefore be
carrying bags of body parts to dispose of
in the river, as is the case in the domestic
plot of the 1601 play by Robert
Yarrington, *Two Lamentable Tragedies*,
based on a 1594 crime. There, the murderer '*Puts on his cloake; taketh vp the
bag*', stating, 'I will returne when I haue
left my loade' (sig. F3ʳ).
12   **take sanctuary** claim immunity from
arrest, as a fugitive; see 3.46n. for this
function of Blackfriars. See 14.247–8 for
the widow's residence in Southwark,
hence Shakebag's need to cross the water.

Sc. 15] *Hugo;* ACT V. SCENE III. *Tyrrell;* ACT V. SCENE II *Delius*   0 SD *alone] (solus)*   1–2] *Delius
lines* days / stout, /   1 Chambley] *(Chambly)*   4–5] *Delius lines* harbour / wont, /   12 SD] *(Exit
Shakebag)*

[Sc. 16]   *Here enters the* MAYOR, [*and the* Watch,
            guarding] MOSBY, ALICE, FRANKLIN, MICHAEL
            and SUSAN. [ARDEN'S *body is discovered.*]

MAYOR

See, Mistress Arden, where your husband lies.
Confess this foul fault and be penitent.

ALICE

Arden, sweet husband, what shall I say?
The more I sound his name, the more he bleeds.
This blood condemns me, and in gushing forth   5
Speaks as it falls, and asks me why I did it.
Forgive me, Arden; I repent me now,
And, would my death save thine, thou shouldst not die.
Rise up, sweet Arden, and enjoy thy love,
And frown not on me when we meet in heaven –   10
In heaven I love thee, though on earth I did not.

MAYOR

Say, Mosby, what made thee murder him?

sc **16**.0.3   ARDEN'S . . . *discovered* The body
is '*discovered*', probably by pulling back
the curtain over the discovery space in
the wall at the back of the stage, perhaps
by an actor on entry, although B&T suggests that the Mayor might reveal it on
his first line. For other such 'discoveries'
see Dessen and Thomson, 69–70; the
method of discovery is often unclear, as
for example in *Doctor Faustus*, '*Hell is
discovered*' (Sc. 5). The intimacy of
Alice's address to Arden's corpse makes
the couple the focal point of the scene,
establishing her dignity in the closing
passages of the play. Wine, following
Hugo, has the SD '*leaning over the body*'
for Alice's speech, which, while rather
restrictive, does focus the address.

4–5 Corpses were popularly believed to
bleed in the presence of their murderer,
the test of cruentation (in which suspects
were brought before the body to see if it
bled to accuse them, see 14.263 and n.)
forming a part of the legal apparatus of
contemporary murder cases and having
credence for individuals of all status
groups; see *R3*, 1.2.55–8.

6   The idea of speaking blood has its roots in
the biblical story of Cain and Abel, where
the latter's blood cried out to God from
the ground for justice (Genesis, 4.9).

9   **Rise up** poetic fantasy of his return to
life, but also allusion to his journey to
heaven in the following line, where Alice
inexplicably thinks she'll meet him
despite committing his murder

sc. **16**] *Hugo*; ACT V. SCENE IV. *Tyrrell*; ACT V. SCENE III. *Delius*   0.1–2 *and . . . guarding*] *B&T*   0.3
ARDEN'S . . . *discovered*] *Wiggins*

FRANKLIN [*to Mosby*]

Study not for an answer; look not down.
His purse and girdle, found at thy bed's head,
Witness sufficiently thou didst the deed. 15
It bootless is to swear thou didst it not.

MOSBY

I hired Black Will and Shakebag, ruffians both,
And they and I have done this murderous deed.
But wherefore stay we? Come and bear me hence.

FRANKLIN

Those ruffians shall not escape. I will up to London 20
And get the Council's warrant to apprehend them.

Exeunt.

[**Sc. 17**] *Here enters* [BLACK] WILL.

BLACK WILL

Shakebag, I hear, hath taken sanctuary,
But I am so pursued with hues and cries

---

13 **Study** cast about; deliberate
14 In Holinshed's account, Mosby is found in bed at the Fleur-de-Lis, and condemned by the blood on his own purse and hose (see below, p. 301). With the alteration to his being taken in possession of Arden's purse and girdle, the playwright allies him with common thieves who steal men's purses.
16 **bootless** useless
19 **stay** halt, pause
21 **Council's** Privy Council's (of which the historical Sir Thomas Cheyne was a member); see also 14.371. They acted quickly at the time of the historical murder in arranging for the apprehension of conspirators and the punishment of those already captured (Hyde, 91–3), to ensure law and order in the town. The case was heard at the assizes (see 2.41n. on '*size*) on commission from the King. The Commission of Oyer and Terminer still exists, issued on 5 March 1551 to Sir Thomas Cheyne, the mayor Sir Thomas Moyle and others, with the royal seal on it and a tag saying 'upon the death of Arden' (Hyde, 112–13).

Sc 17 Will has already been hounded out of Sittingbourne, but his search for an *oyster boat* (5) suggests he is still near the north Kent coast.

2 **hues and cries** outcries calling for physical pursuit of criminals by all able-bodied men, who were legally required to pursue perpetrators once alerted by the shouting of a witness

13 SD] *B&T* 17–19] *Delius; Q1 lines (*Shakebagge, / *)* both, / deed. / we? / hence. / 18 murderous] (*murthrous)* 20–1] *Delius; Q1 lines* escape. / *(*warrand / *)* them. / **Sc. 17**] *Hugo;* ACT V. SCENE V. *Tyrrell;* ACT V. SCENE IV. *Delius*

282

For petty robberies that I have done
That I can come unto no sanctuary.
Therefore must I in some oyster boat   5
At last be fain to go aboard some hoy,
And so to Flushing – there is no staying here.
At Sittingbourne the watch was like to take me,
And had I not with my buckler covered my head
And run full blank at all adventures,   10
I am sure I had ne'er gone further than that place,
For the constable had twenty warrants to apprehend
    me;
Besides that, I robbed him and his man once at
    Gadshill.
Farewell, England; I'll to Flushing now.   *Exit.*

[**Sc. 18**]   *Here enters the* MAYOR, [*and the* Watch,
    guarding] MOSBY, ALICE, MICHAEL, SUSAN
    and BRADSHAW.

MAYOR [*to the Watch*]
  Come, make haste, and bring away the prisoners.

---

5   **oyster boat** boat used in oyster fishing; Wine quotes Jacob's 1774 *History of the Town and Port of Faversham*, which states that Faversham oysters were 'most regarded by the industrious Hollanders, who have had . . . a constant traffic here'.

6   **fain** glad under the circumstances
    hoy small boat for carrying passengers and goods short distances around the coast (word of Dutch origin)

7   **Flushing** major Netherlandish port, modern-day Vlissingen. Holinshed says Will was 'burnt on a scaffold at Flishing [Flushing] in Zeland' (see below, p. 302).

10   **full blank** A blank was a white spot in the centre of a target, so 'at full tilt'.

at all adventures whatever the consequences; whatever happened

13   **Gadshill** hill on the London road, just outside Rochester; scene of Falstaff's 'robbery' in *1H4*, 2.2

Sc. 18.0 SD Wine points out that the Wardmote book (local court records) indicates that they were sentenced in the 'Abbey Hall which the said Ardern purchased' (although Jackson ('Material') thought this inserted by a later hand); i.e. probably in the hall to Arden's gatehouse property, in the wing now demolished. The elevated language of the scene and the formal way in which the characters speak in turn suggest a legal context.

8 Sittingbourne] *(Sittinburgh)*   12 twenty] *(20)*   14 SD] *(Exit Will)*   **Sc. 18**] *Hugo;* ACT V. SCENE VI. *Tyrrell;* ACT V. SCENE V. *Delius*   0.1–2 *and . . . guarding*] *B&T*   1 SD] *B&T*

BRADSHAW

 Mistress Arden, you are now going to God,
 And I am by the law condemned to die
 About a letter I brought from Master Greene.
 I pray you, Mistress Arden, speak the truth: 5
 Was I ever privy to your intent or no?

ALICE

 What should I say? You brought me such a letter,
 But I dare swear thou knewest not the contents.
 Leave now to trouble me with worldly things,
 And let me meditate upon my saviour Christ,   10
 Whose blood must save me for the blood I shed.

MOSBY

 How long shall I live in this hell of grief?
 Convey me from the presence of that strumpet!

ALICE

 Ah, but for thee I had never been strumpet!
 What cannot oaths and protestations do   15
 When men have opportunity to woo?
 I was too young to sound thy villainies,
 But now I find it, and repent too late.

SUSAN [*to Mosby*]

 Ah, gentle brother, wherefore should I die?
 I knew not of it till the deed was done.   20

MOSBY

 For thee I mourn more than for myself.
 But let it suffice, I cannot save thee now.

---

4 **About** concerning, in reference to; on account of

9–11 Alice follows the advice of *Ars Moriendi* or 'art of dying' texts here, by focusing on spiritual rather than worldly matters.

11 echoes her line in Holinshed, 'Oh the bloud of God helpe, for this bloud haue I

shed' (see below, p. 301), the balance and control of the contrast giving her speech gravitas

13 **strumpet** unchaste woman, prostitute

17 **sound** measure the depth of

22 **suffice** be enough, presumably to satisfy her of his remorse

7] *Delius; Q1 lines* say? / letter. / 14 had never] neuer had *(conj. B&T (CRE))* 19 SD] *Wine (Hugo subst.)*

MICHAEL [*to Susan*]   An if your brother and my mistress
    had not promised me you in marriage, I had ne'er
    given consent to this foul deed.   25
MAYOR
    Leave to accuse each other now,
    And listen to the sentence I shall give:
    Bear Mosby and his sister to London straight,
    Where they in Smithfield must be executed;
    Bear Mistress Arden unto Canterbury,   30
    Where her sentence is she must be burned;
    Michael and Bradshaw in Faversham must suffer
      death.
ALICE
    Let my death make amends for all my sins.
MOSBY
    Fie upon women! – this shall be my song.
    But bear me hence, for I have lived too long.   35
SUSAN
    Seeing no hope on earth, in heaven is my hope.
MICHAEL
    Faith, I care not, seeing I die with Susan.
BRADSHAW
    My blood be on his head that gave the sentence!
MAYOR
    To speedy execution with them all!   *Exeunt.*

---

26   **Leave to** leave off, stop
29   **Smithfield** grassy area east of the Tower
of London, just outside the city walls,
used for a livestock market and as a regular place of execution. Mosby and
Susan's death there is recorded in Henry
Machyn's *Diary* (see pp. 2–3).
30   **Canterbury** Machyn records that Alice
was 'burnyd at Canturbery and her
sarvand [servant] hangyd ther' on 14

March 1551 (see p. 3); Canterbury
Chamberlain's accounts for 1550–1
show 43s paid 'for the charges of the
brennyng Mistress Arden and the
executyon of George Bredshawe'
(Hyde, 93).
31   **burned** at the stake, for petty treason:
the punishment for wives who murdered
their husbands
34   **Fie upon** expression of disgust

23–5] *Wiggins; Q1 lines* Mistres, / marriage, / deede. /   23 SD] *Wine (Hugo subst.)*   An] *(And)*   30
Mistress] *(M.)*

[**Epilogue**]   *Here enters* FRANKLIN.

FRANKLIN

Thus have you seen the truth of Arden's death.
As for the ruffians, Shakebag and Black Will,
The one took sanctuary and, being sent for out,
Was murdered in Southwark as he passed
To Greenwich, where the Lord Protector lay.   5
Black Will was burned in Flushing on a stage.
Greene was hanged at Ospringe in Kent.
The painter fled, and how he died we know not.

Epil. Franklin performs the summary of punishment that rounds off Holinshed's account of the murder, before moving on explicitly to explore the audience's response. Epilogues were common in plays of this period, partly informed by medieval tradition and partly by classical models designed to invite applause; for a list see Cioni. Franklin, the playwright's most significant invented role, therefore both opens and closes the play, bringing theatrical shape and moral closure to the historical events.

3   **sent for out** sent for to be brought out (*OED* sent 9b, this line being the earliest example). It may be that this describes a legal intervention, as sanctuary for serious crimes had been virtually abolished under Henry VIII.

4   **murdered** murderèd

5   **Greenwich** The town to the east of London was the site of a royal palace, Placentia, until 1660; Henry VIII and Elizabeth I were born and Edward VI died there, and Tudor monarchs spent a great deal of time in the palace, hence the Lord Protector's presence (see 1.2n.).

6   **stage** raised platform, scaffold for execution

7   **Ospringe** village adjacent to Faversham on Watling Street, the main route from London to the east Kent coast. The presence of a Maison Dieu, a thirteenth-century wayside hospital, originally offering prayer and shelter for sick or aged pilgrims, attests to its importance as a stopping-place on the road, and therefore as a site of punishment with a large audience. In 1550, ownership of the manor had passed to Sir Thomas Cheyne. 'Osbridge', the Q1 form, is rarely found as a place name. The Commission of Gaol Delivery specifies punishment in Faversham, but Stowe gives 'in the highe way agaynst Feuersham betwen Osprynge and Bowghten' (fol. 37r), which Holinshed repeats as 'Ospring & Boughton against Feuersham' (see below, p. 302). Jacob gives 'Ospringe'. Curiously, at a meeting of the Privy Council at Hampton Court on 19 November 1592 (i.e. shortly after the publication of Q1), the appearance of 'Mr Robert Stranson of Osbridge in the countie of Kent' is noted in precisely the Q1 spelling (*CSPD*, vol. 11 [95], p. 313, PC 2/20, fol. 130). Stranson, or Streynsham, at one stage secretary to the Earl of Pembroke, left the 'scyte or dwellinge howse of the late dissolved monastery of feuersham' to his daughter in his will of 1604 (KHLC 11/104/229, fol. 87).

Epilogue] *Hugo;* ACT V. SCENE VI *Delius*

But this, above the rest, is to be noted:
Arden lay murdered in that plot of ground   10
Which he by force and violence held from Reede.
And in the grass his body's print was seen
Two years and more after the deed was done.
Gentlemen, we hope you'll pardon this naked tragedy,
Wherein no filed points are foisted in   15
To make it gracious to the ear or eye;
For simple truth is gracious enough
And needs no other points of glozing stuff.   [*Exit.*]

FINIS

9   **above the rest** especially, above all else
10–13 Holinshed too ends his tale with a long paragraph on 'This one thing' that 'séemeth verie strange and notable', noting that 'the grasse did not grow where his bodie had touched: but betwéene his legs, betweene his armes, and about the hollownesse of his necke', and commenting that 'manie strangers came in that meane time, beside the townesmen, to see the print of his bodie there on the ground in that field' (see below, p. 303).
14   **Gentlemen** i.e. the audience, here flattered as members of the gentry
     naked unadorned; without rhetorical ornament
15   **filed** polished, neatly finished; adjective often applied to both tongues and phrases; filèd
     points parts, details, here of an argument; with *naked* and *filed* perhaps suggesting a weapon, as befits a tragedy
     foisted introduced surreptitiously in order to cheat or deceive
18   **glozing** veiled with specious comments; involving fair words or smooth, flattering language

18 SD] *W&P*

APPENDIX 1
Arden's story in Holinshed's Chronicles

The following account of Arden's murder (see pp. 7–10 for discussion of this text and its connections to the Stowe MS) is taken from the 1587 revised edition of the *Chronicles of England, Scotland, and Ireland*, ed. Raphael Holinshed et al. (STC 13569, pp. 1062–6).[1]

There are no differences material to the narrative between this and the earlier 1577 edition (STC 13568, pp. 1703–8), except for the addition of substantial marginal glosses in the 1587 text, which is reproduced here as the fuller of the two. There is, however, no conclusive proof as to which edition the playwright(s) consulted. Wine argued that the marginal notes 'arc revealing for the moral stress that they place on passages where Holinshed's tone is essentially dispassionate and for the way that they highlight dramatic possibilities inherent in the narrative' (xl). Bourus and Taylor, in contrast, argue that 'any playwright is likely to be looking for "dramatic possibilities", without needing the prompting of a marginal note; likewise, all Elizabethan playwrights tend to emphasize the moral implications of their tragic narratives' (2).

1 The texts of both the 1577 and 1587 editions are transcribed and rendered comparable by The Holinshed Project, http://www.cems.ox.ac.uk/holinshed/. This appendix is based on their transcription, checked against the EEBO images during lockdown in 2020. Line breaks and typography have been normalized; the position of marginal notes relative to the main text has been maintained as far as possible within the page format; apparent errors are emended and noted in the footnotes, although it has not been possible to consult the original directly.

1551 Anno Reg. 5.
Arden murthered.

About this time there was at Feuersham in Kent a gentleman named Arden, most cruellie murthered and slaine by the procurement of his owne wife. The which murther, for the horriblenesse thereof, although otherwise it may séeme to be but a priuate matter, and therefore as it were impertinent to this historie, I haue thought good to set it foorth somewhat at large, hauing the instructions deliuered to me by them, that haue vsed some diligence to gather the true vnderstanding of the circumstances. This Arden

Arden described.

was a man of a tall and comelie personage, and matched in marriage with a gentlewoman, yoong, tall, and well fauoured of shape and countenance,

Loue and lust.

who chancing to fall in familiaritie with one Mosbie a tailor by occupation, a blacke swart man, seruant to the lord North, it happened this Mosbie vpon some misliking to fall out with hir: but she being desirous to be in fauour with him

A paire of siluer dice worke much mischiefe.

againe, sent him a paire of siluer dice by one Adam Foule dwelling at the Floure de lice in Feuersham.

After which he resorted to hir againe, and oftentimes laie in Ardens house: in somuch that within two yeares after, he obteined such fauour at hir hands, that he laie with hir, or (as they terme it) kept hir, in abusing hir bodie. And although (as it was said) Arden perceiued right well their mutuall familiaritie to be much greater than their honestie, yet bicause he would not offend hir, and so loose the benefit which he hoped to gaine at some of hir fréends hands in bearing with hir lewdnesse, which he might haue lost if he should

Arden winketh at his wiues lewdnesse, & why!

haue fallen out with hir: he was contented to winke at hir filthie disorder, and both permitted, and also inuited Mosbie verie often to lodge in his house. And thus it continued a good space, before anie practise was begun by them against maister Arden. She at length inflamed in loue with Mosbie, and loathing hir husband, wished and after practised the meanes how to hasten his end.

Ardens wife attempteth means to make awaie hir husband.

There was a painter dwelling in Feuersham, who had skill of poisons, as was reported. She therefore demanded of him, whether it were true that he had such skill in that feat or not? And he denied not but that he had in déed. Yea (said she) but I would haue such a one made, as should haue most vehement and speedie operation to dispatch the eater thereof. That can I doo (quoth he) and forthwith made hir such a one, and willed hir to put it into the bottome of a porrenger, & then after to powre milke on it. Which circumstance she forgetting, did cleane contrarie, putting in the milke first; and afterward the poison. Now maister Arden purposing that daie to ride to Canturburie, his wife brought him his breakefast, which was woont to be milke and butter. He hauing receiued a spoonefull or two of the milke, misliked the tast and colour thereof, and said to his wife; Mistresse Ales what milke haue you giuen me here? Wherewithall she tilted it ouer with hir hand, saieng, I wéene nothing can please you. Then he tooke horsse and road towards Canturburie, and by the waie fell into extreme purging vpwards and downewards, and so escaped for that time.

Arden is poisoned by his wife but recouereth.

She deuiseth another waie to dispatch hir husband Arden.

After this, his wife fell in acquaintance with one Greene of Feuersham, seruant to sir Anthonie Ager, from which Greene maister Arden had wrested a péece of ground on the backeside of the abbeie of Feuersham, and there had blowes and great threats passed betwixt them about that matter. Therefore she knowing that Gréene hated hir husband, began to practise with him how to make him awaie; and concluded, that if he could get anie that would kill him, he should haue ten pounds for a reward. This Gréene hauing dooings for his master sir Anthonie Ager, had occasion to go vp to London, where his maister then laie, and hauing some charge vp with him, desired one Bradshaw a goldsmith of Feuersham that was his neighbor, to accompanie him to Grauesend, and he would content him for his pains. This

Bradshaw, being a verie honest man, was content, and road with him. And when they came to Rainham downe, they chanced to sée three or foure seruingmen that were comming from Léeds: and therewith Bradshaw espied comming vp the hill from Rochester, one blacke Will, a terrible cruell ruffian with a sword and a buckler, and another with a great staffe on his necke.

A notorious murthering ruffian.

Then said Bradshaw to Gréene; We are happie that here commeth some companie from Léeds, for here commeth vp against vs as murthering a knaue as anie is in England: if it were not for them we might chance hardlie to escape without losse of our monie and liues. Yea thought Gréene (as he after confessed) such a one is for my purpose, and therefore asked; Which is he? Yonder is he quoth Bradshaw, the same that hath the sword and buckler: his name is blacke Will. How know you that, said Gréene? Bradshaw answered, I knew him at Bullongne, where we both serued, he was a soldier, and I was sir Richard Cauendishes man, and there he committed manie robberies and heinous murthers on such as trauelled betwixt Bullongne and France.

Marke how the diuell will not let his organs or instruments let slip either occasiõ or opportunitie to conmitt most heinous wickednesse.

By this time the other companie of seruingmen came to them, and they going all togither, met with blacke Will and his fellow. The seruingmen knew blacke Will, & saluting him, demanded of him whither he went? He answered; By his bloud (for his vse was to sweare almost at euerie word) I know not, nor care not, but set vp my staffe, and euen as it falleth I go. If thou (quoth they) wilt go backe againe to Grauesend, we will giue thée thy supper. By his bloud (said he) I care not, I am content, haue with you: and so he returned againe with them. Then blacke Will tooke acquaintance of Bradshaw, saieng; Fellow Bradshaw how doost thou? Bradshaw vnwilling to renew acquitance, or to haue ought to doo with so shameles a ruffian, said; Why doo ye know me? Yea that I doo (quoth he) did not we serue in Bullongne togither? But ye must pardon me (quoth Bradshaw) for I haue forgotten you.

A desperat villaine.

An honest man is ashamed to renew old acquaintance with a knaue,

Then Greene talked with blacke Will, and said;
When ye haue supped, come to mine hosts house
at such a signe, and I will giue you the sacke and
sugar. By his bloud (said he) I thanke you, I will
come and take it I warrant you. According to his
promise he came, and there they made good
cheare. Then blacke Will & Greene went and
talked apart from Bradshaw, and there concluded

The match made to
murther Arden.

togither, that if he would kill master Arden, he
should haue ten pounds for his labor. Then he
answered, By his wounds that I will if I maie
know him. Marie to morrow in Poules I will shew
him thee, said Gréene. Then they left their talke,
& Gréene bad him go home to his hosts house.
Then Greene wrote a letter to mistresse Arden, &
among other things put in these words: We haue
got a man for our purpose, we maie thanke my

Simplicitie abused.

brother Bradshaw. Now Bradshaw not knowing
anie thing of this, tooke the letter of him, and in
the morning departed home againe, and deliuered
the letter to mistresse Arden, and Greene & blacke
Will went vp to London at the tide.

At the time appointed, Gréene shewed blacke Will
maister Arden walking in Poules. Then said
blacke Will, What is he that goeth after him?
Marie said Gréen, one of his men. By his bloud
(said blacke Will) I will kill them both. Naie (said
Greene) doo not so, for he is of counsell with vs

Blacke will maketh no
conscience of bloudshed
and murther.

in this matter. By his bloud (said he) I care not for
that, I will kill them both. Naie said Gréene in
anie wise doo not so. Then blacke Will thought to
haue killed maister Arden in Poules churchyard,
but there were so manie gentlemen that
accompanied him to dinner, that he missed of his
purpose. Gréene shewed all this talke to maister
Ardens man, whose name was Michaell, which
euer after stood in doubt of blacke Will, lest he
should kill him. The cause that this Michaell

Why Ardens man
conspired with the rest
to kill his maister.

conspired with the rest against his maister, was:
for that it was determined, that he should marrie a
kinswoman of Mosbies.

After this, maister Arden laie at a certeine parsonage which he held in London, and therefore his man Michaell and Gréene agréed, that blacke Will should come in the night to the parsonage, where he should find the doores left open, that he might come[2] in and murther maister Arden. This Michaell hauing his maister to bed, left open the doores according to the appointment. His maister then being in bed, asked him if he had shut fast the doores, and hée said yea: but yet afterwards, fearing least blacke Will would kill him as well as his maister, after he was in bed himselfe, he rose againe and shut the doores, bolting them fast. So that blacke Will comming thither, and finding the doores shut, departed, being disappointed at that time. The next daie blacke Will came to Gréene in a great chafe, swearing and staring bicause he was so deceiued, and with manie terrible oths threatened to kill maister Ardens man first, wheresoeuer he met him. No (said Gréene) doo not so, I will first know the cause of shutting the doores.

One murthering mind mistrusting another, doo hinder the action whereabout they agréed.

Then Greene met and talked with Ardens man, and asked of him, why he did not leaue open the doors, according to his promise? Marie (said Michaell) I will shew you the cause. My maister yesternight did that he neuer did before: for after I was in bed, hée rose vp and shut the doores, and in the morning rated me for leauing them vnshut. And herewith Gréene & blacke Will were pacified. Arden being redie to go homewards, his maid came to Gréene & said; This night will my maister go downe. Whervpon it was agréed that blacke Will should kill him on Reinam downe. When maister Arden came to Rochester, his man still fearing that blacke Will would kill him with his maister, pricked his horsse of purpose, and made him to halt, to the end he might protract the time, and tarie behind. His maister asked him

The fourth attempt to make Arden awaie disappointed.

2   come] como

whie his horsse halted, he said, I know not. Well (quoth his maister) when ye come at the smith here before (betwéene Rochester and the hill foot ouer against Cheetam) remooue his shoo, and search him, and then come after me. So maister Arden rode on: and yet[3] he came at the place where blacke Will laie in wait for him, there ouertooke him diuerse gentlemen of his acquaintance, who kept him companie: so that blacke Will mist here also of his purpose.

Blacke Will misseth his purpose.

After that maister Arden was come home, hee sent (as he vsuallie did) his man to Shepeie to sir Thomas Cheinie, then lord warden of the cinque ports, about certeine businesse, and at his comming awaie, he had a letter deliuered sent by sir Thomas Cheinie to his maister. When he came home, his mistresse[4] tooke the letter and kept it, willing hir man to tell his maister, that he had a letter deliuered him by sir Thomas Cheinie, and that he had lost it; adding that he thought it best that his maister should go the next morning to sir Thomas, bicause he knew not the matter: he said he would, and therefore he willed his man to be stirring betimes. In this meane while, blacke Will, and one George Shakebag his companion, were kept in a storehouse of sir Anthonie Agers at Preston, by Greenes appointment: and thither came mistresse Arden to sée him, bringing and sending him meat and drinke manie times. He therfore lurking there, and watching some opportunitie for his purpose, was willed in anie wise to be vp earlie in the morning, to lie in wait for maister Arden in a certeine broome close, betwixt Feuersham & the ferrie (which close he must néeds passe) there to doo his feat. Now blacke Will stirred in the morning betimes, but mist the waie, & taried in a wrong place.

Ardens wife visiteth, succoureth, emboldneth, and directeth black Will &c: how to accomplish his bloudie purpose.

3 yet] yer
4 mistresse] mist resse

Maister Arden & his man comming on their waie earlie in the morning towards Shornelan, where sir Thomas Cheinie laie: as they were almost come to the broome close, his man alwaies fearing that blacke Will would kill him with his maister, feined that he had lost his pursse; Why said his maister, thou foolish knaue, couldst thou not looke to thy pursse but loose it? What was in it? Thrée pounds said he. Why then go thy waies backe againe like a knaue (said his maister) and séeke it, for being so earlie as it is, there is no man stirring, and therefore thou maist be sure to find it, and then come and ouertake me at the ferrie. But neuerthelesse, by reason that blacke Will lost his way, maister Arden escaped yet once againe. At that time, blacke Will yet thought hée should haue beene sure to haue met him homewards: but whether that some of the lord wardens men accompanied him backe to Feuersham, or that being in doubt, for that it was late to go through the broome close, and therfore tooke another waie, blacke Will was disappointed then also.

Note here the force of feare and a troubled conscience.

Blacke Will yet againe disappointed.

But now saint Ualentines faire being at hand, the conspirators thought to dispatch their diuelish intention at that time. Mosbie minded to picke some quarrell to maister Arden at the faire to fight with him; for he said he could not find in his heart to murther a gentleman in that sort as his wife wished: although she had made a solemne promise to him, and he againe to hir, to be in all points as man and wife togither, and therevpon they both receiued the sacrament on a sundaie at London, openlie in a church there. But this deuise to fight with him would not serue, for maister Arden both then and at other times had beene greatlie prouoked by Mosbie to fight with him, but he would not. Now Mosbie had a sister that dwelt in a tenement of maister Ardens néere to his house in Feuersham: and on the faire éeuen, blacke Will was sent for to come thither, and Gréene bringing him thither, met there with

A prepensed quarel against Arden by the conspirators.

Ardens wife, blacke Will, & the knot of vilans meet and conclude vpon their former prepensed mischiefe.

mistresse Arden, accompanied with Michaell hir man, and one of hir maids. There were also Mosbie and George Shakebag, and there they deuised to haue killed him in maner as afterwards he was. But yet Mosbie at the first would not agree to that cowardlie murthering of him, but in a furie floong awaie, and went vp the abbeie stréet toward the flower de lice, the house of the aforenamed Adam Foule, where he did often host. But before he came thither now at this time, a messenger ouertooke him, that was sent from mistres Arden, desiring him of all loues to come backe againe to helpe to accomplish the mater he knew of. Herevpon he returned to hir againe, and at his comming backe, she fell downe vpon hir knées to him, and besought him to go through with the matter, as if he loued hir he would be content to doo, sith as shee had diuerse times told him, he néeded not to doubt, for there was not anie that would care for his death, nor make anie great inquirie for them that should dispatch him.

O importunate & bloudie minded strumpet!

Thus she being earnest with him, at length hee was contented to agree vnto that horrible deuise, and therevpon they conueied blacke Will into maister Ardens house, putting him into a closet at the end of his parlour. Before this, they had sent out of the house all the seruants, those excepted which were priuie to the deuised murther. Then went Mosbie to the doore, and there stood in a night gowne of silke girded about him, and this was betwixt six and seuen of the clocke at night. Master Arden hauing béene at a neighbors house of his, named Dumpkin, & hauing cleared certeine reckonings betwixt them, came home: and finding Mosbie standing at the doore, asked him if it were supper time? I thinke not (quoth Mosbie) it is not yet readie. Then let vs go and plaie a game at the tables in the meane season, said maister Arden. And so they went streight into the parlor: and as they came by through the hall, his wife was walking there, and maister Arden said; How now

The practise to kill Arden is now set abroch.

297

Here the confederats
ioine their practises

mistresse Ales? But she made small answer to him.
In the meane time one cheined the wicket doore of
the entrie. When they came into the parlor, Mosbie
sat downe on the bench, hauing his face toward the
place where blacke Will stood. Then Michaell
maister Ardens man stood at his masters backe,
holding a candle in his hand, to shadow blacke
Will, that Arden might by no meanes perceiue him
comming foorth. In their plaie Mosbie said thus
(which séemed to be the watchword for blacke
Wils comming foorth) Now maie I take you sir if I
will. Take me (quoth maister Arden) which waie?
With that blacke Will stept foorth, and cast a
towell about his necke, so to stop his breath and
strangle him. Then Mosbie hauing at his girdle a
pressing iron of fourtéene pounds weight, stroke
him on the hed with the same, so that he fell
downe, and gaue a great grone, insomuch that they
thought he had béene killed.

The watchword to the
principall murtherer.

Then they bare him awaie, to laie him in the
counting house, & as they were about to laie him
downe, the pangs of death comming on him, he
gaue a great grone, and stretched himselfe, and
then blacke Will gaue him a great gash in the face,
and so killed him out of hand, laid him along,
tooke the monie out of his pursse, and the rings
from his fingers, and then comming out of the
counting house, said; Now the feat is doone, giue
me my monie. So mistres Arden gaue him ten
pounds: and he comming to Gréene, had a horsse
of him, and so rode his waies. After that blacke
Will was gone, mistresse Arden came into the
counting house, and with a knife gaue him seuen
or eight picks into the brest. Then they made
cleene the parlor, tooke a clout, and wiped where it
was bloudie, and strewed againe the rushes that
were shuffled with strugling, and cast the clout
with which they wiped the bloud, and the knife
that was bloudie, wherewith she had wounded hir
husband, into a tub by the wels side; where
afterwards both the same clout and knife were

Arden slaine outright.

Blacke will receiueth
ten pounds for his
reward of Ardens wife,
for murdering hir
husband.

found. Thus this wicked woman, with hir complices, most shamefullie murdered hir owne husband, who most entirelie loued hir all his life time. Then she sent for two Londoners to supper, the one named Prune, and the other Cole, that were grosers, which before the murder was committed, were bidden to supper. When they came, she said: I maruell where maister Arden is; we will not tarie for him, come ye and sit downe, for he will not be long. Then Mosbies sister was sent for, she came and sat downe, and so they were merie.

Marke what a countenance of innocencie and ignorance she bore after the murdering of hir husband.

After supper, mistres Arden caused hir daughter to plaie on the virginals, and they dansed, and she with them, and so séemed to protract time as it were; till maister Arden should come, and she said, I maruell where he is so long; well, he will come anon I am sure, I praie you in the meane while let vs plaie a game at the tables. But the Londoners said, they must go to their hosts house, or else they should be shut out at doores, and so taking their leaue, departed. When they were gone, the seruants that were not priuie to the murder, were sent abroad into the towne; some to séeke their maister, and some of other errands, all sauing Michaell and a maid, Mosbies sister, and one of mistres Ardens owne daughters. Then they tooke the dead bodie, and caried it out, to laie it in a field next to the church-yard, and ioining to his garden wall, through the which he went to the church. In the meane time it began to snow, and when they came to the garden gate, they remembred that they had forgotten the kaie, and one went in for it, and finding it, at length brought it, opened the gate, and caried the corps into the same field, as it were ten pases from the garden gate, and laid him downe on his backe streight in his night gowne, with his slippers on: and betwéene one of his slippers and his foot, a long rush or two remained. When they had thus laid him downe, they returned the same way they came through the garden into the house.

The workers of this mischiefe carie out Arden slaine into the field.

299

This she did to colour hir wickednesse which by no meanes was excuseseable.

They being returned thus backe againe into the house, the doores were opened, and the seruants returned home that had béene sent abroad: and being now verie late, she sent foorth hir folks againe to make inquirie for him in diuerse places; namelie, among the best in the towne where he was woont to be, who made answer, that they could tell nothing of him. Then she began to make an outcrie, and said; Neuer woman had such neighbors as I haue, and herewith wept: in somuch that hir neighbors came in, and found hir making great lamentation, pretending to maruell what was become of hir husband. Wherevpon, the maior and others came to make search for him.

Arden a couetous man and preferrer of his priuat profit before common gaine.

The faire was woont to be kept partlie in the towne, and partlie in the abbeie; but Arden for his owne priuat lucre & couetous gaine had this present yeare procured it to be wholie kept within the abbeie ground which he had purchased; & so reaping all the gaines to himselfe, and bereauing the towne of that portion which was woont to come to the inhabitants, got manie a bitter cursse. The maior going about the faire in this search, at length came to the ground where Arden laie: and

Ardens dead bodie is descried by one of his acquaintance.

as it happened, Prune the groser getting sight of him, first said; Staie, for me thinke I sée one lie here. And so they looking and beholding the bodie, found that it was maister Arden, lieng there throughlie dead, and viewing diligentlie the maner of his bodie & hurts, found the rushes sticking in his slippers, and marking further, espied certeine footsteps, by reason of the snow, betwixt the place where he laie, and the garden doore.

Footsteps all alongst from the dead bodie of Arden to his dwelling house.

Then the maior commanded euerie man to staie, and herewith appointed some to go about, & to come in at the inner side of the house through the garden as the waie laie, to the place where maister Ardens dead bodie did lie; who all the waie as they came, perceiued footings still before them in the snow: and so it appeared plainlie that he was brought along that waie from the house through the garden, and so into the field where he laie. Then the maior and his companie that were with him went into the house, and knowing hir euill demeanor in times past, examined hir of the matter: but she defied them and said, I would you should know I am no such woman. Then they examined hir seruants, and in the examination, by reason of a péece of his heare any bloud found néere to the house in the waie, by the which they caried him foorth, and likewise by the knife with which she had thrust him into the brest, and the clout wherewith they wiped the bloud awaie which they found in the tub, into the which the same were throwen; they all confessed the matter, and hir selfe beholding hir husbands bloud, said; Oh the bloud of God helpe, for this bloud haue I shed.

A péece of Ardens heare and bloud spilt in the house espied, as also a bloudie knife and a clout found.

Then were they all attached, and committed to prison, and the maior with others went presentlie to the flower de lice, where they found Mosbie in bed: and as they came towards him, they espied his hose and pursse stained with some of maister Ardens bloud. And when he asked what they meant by their comming in such sort, they said; Sée, here ye may vnderstand wherefore, by these tokens, shewing him the bloud on his hose and pursse. Then he confessed the déed, and so he and all the other that had conspired the murder, were apprehended and laid in prison, except Gréene, blacke Will, and the painter, which painter and George Shakebag, that was also fled before, were neuer heard of. Shortlie were the sessions kept at Feuersham, where all the prisoners were arreigned and condemned. And therevpon being examined whither they had anie other complices, mistres Arden accused Bradshaw, vpon occasion of the letter sent by Gréene from Graues end, (as before ye haue heard) which words had none other meaning, but onelie by Bradshaws describing of blacke Wils qualities; Gréene iudged him a méete instrument for the execution of their pretended murder. Whereto notwithstanding (as Gréene

Some of Ardens bloud vpon Mosbies pursse.

The principals of this murder fled awaie.

Bradshaw as vniustlie accused, as his simplicitie was shamefullie abused.

confessed at his death certeine yeares after) this Bradshaw was neuer made priuie; howbeit, he was vppon this accusation of mistres Arden, immediatlie sent for to the sessions, and indicted, and declaration made against him, as a procurer of blacke Will to kill maister Arden, which procéeded wholie by misvnderstanding of the words conteined in the letter which he brought from Greene.

Then he desired to talke with the persons condemned, and his request was granted. He therefore demanded of them if they knew him, or euer had anie conuersation with him, & they all said no. Then the letter being shewed and read, he

Innocencie no barre against execution.

declared the verie truth of the matter, and vpon what occasion he told Gréene of blacke Will: neuerthelesse, he was condemned, and suffered. These condemned persons were diuerslie executed in sundrie places, for Michaell maister Ardens man was hanged in chaines at Feuersham, and one

Note how these malefactors suffered punishment.

of the maids was burnt there, pitifullie bewailing hir case, and cried out on hir mistres that had brought hir to this end, for the which she would neuer forgiue hir. Mosbie & his sister were hanged in Smithfield at London; mistres Arden was burned at Canturburie the foure and twentith of March. Gréene came againe certeine yeares

Blacke Will burnt at Flishing.

after, was apprehended, condemned, & hanged in chaines in the high waie betwixt Ospring & Boughton against Feuersham; blacke Will was burnt on a scaffold at Flishing in Zeland. Adam Foule that dwelt at the floure de lice in Feuersham was brought into trouble about this matter, and caried vp to London, with his legs bound vnder the horsse bellie, and committed to prison in the Marshalseie: for that Mosbie was heard to saie; Had it not béene for Adam Foule, I had not come to this trouble: meaning that the bringing of the siluer dice for a token to him from mistresse Arden, as ye haue heard, occasioned him to renew familiaritie with hir againe. But when the matter was throughlie ripped vp, & that Mosbie had cléered him, protesting that he was neuer of knowledge in anie behalfe to the murder, the mans innocencie preserued him.

A wonder touching the print of Ardens dead bodie two yeares after he was slaine.

This one thing séemeth verie strange and notable, touching maister Arden, that in the place where he was laid, being dead, all the proportion of his bodie might be séene two yeares after and more, so plaine as could be, for the grasse did not grow where his bodie had touched: but betwéene his legs, betweene his armes, and about the hollownesse of his necke, and round about his bodie, and where his legs, armes, head, or anie other part of his bodie had touched, no grasse growed at all of all that time. So that manie strangers came in that meane time, beside the townesmen, to see the print of his bodie there on the ground in that field. Which field he had (as some haue reported) most cruellie taken from a woman, that had beene a widow to one Cooke, and after maried to one Richard Read a mariner, to the great hinderance of hir and hir husband the said Read: for they had long inioied it by a lease, which they had of it for manie yeares, not then expired: neuerthelesse, he got it from

God heareth the teares of the oppressed and taketh vengeance: note an example in Arden.

them. For the which, the said Reads wife not onelie exclaimed against him, in sheading manie a salt téere, but also curssed him most bitterlie euen to his face, wishing manie a vengeance to light vpon him, and that all the world might woonder on him. Which was thought then to come to passe, when he was thus murdered, and laie in that field from midnight till the morning: and so all that daie, being the faire daie till night, all the which daie there were manie hundreds of people came woondering about him. And thus far touching this horrible and heinous murder of maister Arden.

APPENDIX 2
Doubling of parts

The company that originally performed *Arden of Faversham* is unknown. The players would almost certainly all have been male. In the following chart, it is assumed that they belonged to an adult company in which the roles of women and boys were played by boy actors, though the possibility that the company was made up entirely of boy actors cannot be excluded. In either case, it would be usual to economize on the number of actors by doubling the roles that they played.

Many roles appear recurrently and cannot be doubled with each other: Arden, Bradshaw, Black Will, Franklin, Greene, Michael, Mosby, Shakebag, Alice and Susan. Of these, the actors playing Bradshaw and Susan have plenty of capacity to take on minor roles, and Greene's role ends in time for the actor to reappear as the Mayor, a significant role restricted to the final scenes. Although the turn-around is tight, the stage business is significant enough to be prolonged as needed. There is some flexibility in the distribution of minor roles. As the chart demonstrates, all the minor speaking roles can be played by the actors of the ten most recurrent roles as identified in the left-hand column: eight adults and two boys.

Non-speaking roles have not been included. These are the 'press' or crowd in Sc.3, Lord Cheyne's men in Sc. 9 and the Watch in Scs 14, 16 and 18.

The roles are identified in the chart with the following abbreviations:

AD	Adam	GR	Greene
AL	Alice	MA	Mayor
AR	Arden	MI	Michael
BR	Bradshaw	MO	Mosby
BW	Black Will	PR	Prentice
CH	Lord Cheyne	RE	Reede
CL	Clarke	SA	Sailor
FE	Ferryman	SH	Shakebag
FR	Franklin	SU	Susan

Adult actors

Sc.	1	2	3	4	5	6	7	8	9	10	11	12	13	14	15	16	17	18	Ep.
AR	AR		AR	AR		AR			AR	AR	AR		AR	AR		[AR]			
BR		BR						BR	CH		FE	FE	RE	BR				BR	
BW	AD	BW	BW		BW		BW		BW			BW	BW	BW AD			BW		
FR	FR		FR	FR		FR			FR	FR	FR		FR	FR		FR			FR
GR	GR	GR	GR		GR		GR		GR	GR		GR	SA	GR MA		MA		MA	
MI	MI		MI	MI		MI	MI		MI	MI			MI	MI		MI		MI	
MO	MO							MO		MO		MO	MO	MO		MO		MO	
SH		SH CL	SH		SH		SH		SH	CL		SH	SH	SH	SH				

Boy actors

Sc.	1	2	3	4	5	6	7	8	9	10	11	12	13	14	15	16	17	18	Ep.
AL	AL							AL		AL		AL	AL	AL		AL	AL	AL	
SU	SU		PR											SU		SU	SU	SU	

APPENDIX 3

Press variants

The following table records all known textual stop-press variants between the three surviving copies of Q1, as identified more fully on p. 94: Dyce (D, lacking leaves I4-K2), Malone (M), Huntington (H). Corrections are found on a single forme of each of six sheets: A Inner (DM>H), D Inner (M>DH), F Outer (M>DH), H Outer (H>MD), I Inner (H>MD), K Inner (M>H). The table is primarily based on readings identified by Wine. The signatures of readings absent from the Dyce copy are marked with an asterisk. The Malone copy is reproduced in *EEBO*, and the Huntington in the Hathi Trust Digital Library at https://babel.hathitrust.org/cgi/pt?id=inu.32000000997785&view=1up&seq=1.

Signature	Line reference	Uncorrected	Corrected
A2r	head title	*Feueshame*	*Feuershame*
D4r	sig. below 4.36	E. 4.	D. 4.
F1r	8.104	copesmate	copsemate
F1r	8.136	flght	flight
F3r	9.74	fact.	fact,
F3r	9.78	He	Her
F3r	9.100	Shepny	Sheppy
F4v	10.31	de rer	dearer
F4v	10.44	whether	weather
F4v	10.44	you lyes,	you, lyes
F4v	10.45	to	too
H1r	13.113	neitheir	neither
H1r	13.124	peirct	peirst
H1r	13.129	seete	sweet
I2r	14.298	some,	some
I2r	14.305	Ales	ailes
I3v	14.396	qustiones	questions
I3v	14.399	see.	see,
I3v	14.401	chambor	chamber
*I4r	15.10	ehe	the
*I4r	16.5	guishing	gushing
*K1v	18.37	not	not,

ABBREVIATIONS AND REFERENCES

Quotations and references relating to *Arden of Faversham* are keyed to this edition. Works of Shakespeare are cited from the most recent Arden Shakespeare editions. *OED* references are to *OED²*. Biblical citations are from the Bishops' Bible (see Bible). Place of publication is London unless otherwise noted. References to Wiggins followed by a number without punctuation (e.g. Wiggins 653) are to the catalogue number in Wiggins as listed in *Other works cited.*

ABBREVIATIONS

ABBREVIATIONS USED IN NOTES

*	precedes commentary notes involving readings altered from the base text
conj.	conjectured
d	penny, pence
fol.	folio
MS	manuscript
n.	commentary note
n.d.	no date
n.p.	no page numbers
n.s.	new series
pub.	published
rev.	revised
rpt.	reprinted
s	shilling(s)
SD	stage direction
SP	speech prefix
subst.	substantially
this edn	reading adopted or proposed for the first time in this edition
t.n.	textual note

WORKS BY AND PARTLY BY SHAKESPEARE

AC	*Antony and Cleopatra*
1H4	*King Henry IV, part 1*
2H4	*King Henry IV, part 2*
2H6	*King Henry VI, part 2*
Ham	*Hamlet*
Luc	*The Rape of Lucrece*
MA	*Much Ado About Nothing*
Mac	*Macbeth*
MND	*A Midsummer Night's Dream*
MW	*The Merry Wives of Windsor*
Oth	*Othello*
Poems	*Poems*
R2	*King Richard II*
R3	*King Richard III*
RJ	*Romeo and Juliet*
Son	*Sonnets*
TGV	*The Two Gentlemen of Verona*
Tit	*Titus Andronicus*
TN	*Twelfth Night*
TS	*The Taming of the Shrew*
VA	*Venus and Adonis*

OTHER ABBREVIATIONS

AEMD	Arden Early Modern Drama
BL	British Library
CRE	see B&T, in Editions
CSPD	*Calendar of State Papers (Domestic)*
DEEP	Database of Early English Playbooks
EEBO-TCP	Early English Books Online Text Creation Partnership
ELR	*English Literary Renaissance*
EMLS	*Early Modern Literary Studies*
ET	*Early Theatre*
JEMS	*Journal of Early Modern Literary Studies*
KHLC	Kent History and Library Centre, Maidstone, housing the county archives collection of inventories
Lib	*The Library*
MCE	see B&T
MRDE	*Medieval and Renaissance Drama in England*
NQ	*Notes and Queries*
ODNB	*Oxford Dictionary of National Biography Online*, www.oxforddnb.com

OED	*Oxford English Dictionary Online*, www.oed.com
PRO	Public Records Office
RADA	Royal Academy of Dramatic Art
RD	*Renaissance Drama*
RES	*Review of English Studies*
RSC	Royal Shakespeare Company
SAA	Shakespeare Association of America
SB	*Shakespeare Bulletin*
SEL	*Studies in English Literature, 1500–1900*
Sha	*Shakespeare*
SQ	*Shakespeare Quarterly*
STC	Short Title Catalogue
TLS	*Times Literary Supplement*
TNA	The National Archives (see *Material and visual sources*)
TNA STAC	The National Archives, Records of the Star Chamber and other courts
V&A	Victoria and Albert Museum (see *Material and visual sources*)

REFERENCES

EDITIONS OF *ARDEN OF FAVERSHAM* COLLATED

B&T	*Arden of Faversham*, ed. Terri Bourus and Gary Taylor, in *The New Oxford Shakespeare: The Complete Works*, gen. eds Gary Taylor, John Jowett, Terri Bourus and Gabriel Egan: *Modern Critical Edition* (*MCE*) (Oxford, 2016) and *Critical Reference Edition* (*CRE*), 2 vols (Oxford, 2017), vol. 1. All references are to *MCE* unless otherwise stated.
Bayne	*Arden of Feversham*, ed. R. Bayne, Temple Dramatists (1897)
BH&N	*Elizabethan and Stuart Plays*, ed. C. R. Bakervill, V. B. Heltzel and A. H. Nethercot (1934)
Brooke	C. F. Tucker Brooke, *The Shakespeare Apocrypha* (1908)
Bullen	*Arden of Feversham, a Tragedy*, ed. A. H. Bullen (1887)
Carrère	*Arden de Faversham*, Editions Montaigne, Collection bilingue des classiques étrangers, trans. Félix Carrère (Paris, 1950)

Craik   *Minor Elizabethan Tragedies*, ed. T. W. Craik (1974)

Delius   *Arden of Feversham*, in *Pseudo-Shakspere'sche Dramen*, ed. Nicolaus Delius, vol. 2 (Elberfeld, 1955)

Gide   *Arden de Faversham*, trans. André Gide (Paris, 1933)

Hopkinson   *Arden of Feversham*, in *Shakespeare's Doubtful Plays*, ed. A. F. Hopkinson (1898)

Hopkinson[2]   *Arden of Feversham*, in *Shakespeare's Doubtful Plays*, ed. A. F. Hopkinson, rev. edn (1907)

Hugo   *La Lamentable et vraie tragédie de M. Arden de Feversham, dans le Kent*, in *Oeuvres complètes de William Shakespeare, Vol XVII: Les Apocryphes*, trans. and ed. François-Victor Hugo (1867)

Jacob   *The Lamentable and True Tragedie of M. Arden of Feversham in Kent*, ed. E. Jacob (Faversham, 1770)

Malone   *Arden of Feversham 1592*, ed. H. Macdonald and D. Nicholl Smith, Malone Society Reprints (Oxford, 1947)

McIlwraith   *Five Elizabethan Tragedies*, ed. A. K. McIlwraith, World's Classics (1938)

Oliphant   *Shakespeare and His Fellow Dramatists*, ed. E. H. C. Oliphant (1929)

Q1   *The Lamentable and True Tragedy of Master Arden of Feversham in Kent*, STC 733 (Edward Allde for Edward White, 1592)

Q1a   Q1, Bodleian Library copy

Q1b   Q1, Huntington Library copy

Q2   *The Lamentable and True Tragedy of Master Arden of Feversham in Kent*, STC 734 (James Roberts for Edward White, 1599)

Q3   *The Lamentable and True Tragedy of Master Arden of Feversham in Kent*, STC 735 (Elizabeth Allde, 1633)

Schelling   *Typical Elizabethan Plays*, ed. F. E. Schelling (New York, 1926)

SMS   Southouse manuscript, anon., MS copy of *Arden of Faversham* with extracts from historical material including *Monasticon Favershamiense* (*c.* 1717), Huntington Library HM 1341

Sturgess   *Three Elizabethan Domestic Tragedies*, ed. Keith Sturgess (Harmondsworth, 1969)

Tieck	*Shakspeare's Vorschule*, vol. 1, ed. L. Tieck (Leipzig, 1823)
Tyrrell	*The Doubtful Plays of Shakespere*, ed. H. Tyrrell (1851)
W&P	*Arden of Feversham*, in *Pseudo-Shakespearian Plays*, vol. 5, ed. K. Warnke and L. Proescholdt (Halle, 1888)
White	*Arden of Faversham*, ed. Martin White, New Mermaids (1990)
Wiggins	*Arden of Faversham*, in *A Woman Killed with Kindness and Other Domestic Plays*, ed. Martin Wiggins, Oxford World's Classics (Oxford, 2008)
Wine	*Arden of Faversham*, ed. M. L. Wine, Revels Plays (1973)

MATERIAL AND VISUAL SOURCES

British Museum Collections: https://www.britishmuseum.org/collection/
English Broadside Ballad Archive: https://ebba.english.ucsb.edu/
Jamestown Rediscovery Collections: https://historicjamestowne.org/collections/artifacts/
Map of Early Modern London: https://mapoflondon.uvic.ca/
Mary Rose Collections: https://maryrose.org/the-artefacts/1/
Metropolitan Museum of Art, New York: https://www.metmuseum.org/art/collection/
Museum of London: https://www.museumoflondon.org.uk/collections/
National Trust Collections: http://www.nationaltrustcollections.org.uk/
Portable Antiquities Scheme (archaeological finds by members of the public): www.finds.org.uk/
Shakespeare Birthplace Trust Collections: http://collections.shakespeare.org.uk/
The National Archives: https://discovery.nationalarchives.gov.uk/
Victoria and Albert Museum: https://collections.vam.ac.uk/

OTHER WORKS CITED

Abbott	Edwin Abbott, *A Shakespearean Grammar* (1869, 1972).
Arnold	Janet Arnold (with Santina M. Levey and Jenny Tiramani), *The Cut and Construction of Linen Shirts, Smocks, Neckwear, Headwear and Accessories for Men and Women c. 1540–1660*, Patterns of Fashion 4 (2008)
Artaud	Antonin Artaud, *Manifeste du théâtre de la cruauté* (1932), reprinted as 'The Theatre of

	Cruelty (First Manifesto)', in *The Theatre and Its Double*, trans. M. C. Richards (New York, 1958)
Astington	John H. Astington, 'Visual texts: Thomas Middleton and prints', in *Middleton Companion*, 226–46
Attwell	David Attwell, 'Property, status, and the subject in a middle-class tragedy: *Arden of Faversham*', *ELR*, 21.3 (1991), 328–48
Bale	John Bale, *Three Laws* (1548), STC 1287
Bandello	Matteo Bandello, *Certain Tragical Discourses*, trans. Geoffrey Fenton (1567), STC 1356.1
Barry and Brooks	Jonathan Barry and Christopher Brooks (eds), *The Middling Sort of People: Culture, Society and Politics in England 1550–1800* (Basingstoke, 1994)
BCP	*Book of Common Prayer* (1559), STC 16293
Belsey	Catherine Belsey, 'Alice Arden's crime', *RD*, n.s., 13 (1982), 83–102
Bennett and Polito	Susan Bennett and Mary Polito (eds), *Performing Environments: Site-Specificity in Medieval and Early Modern English Drama* (Basingstoke, 2014)
Bentley	Gerald Eades Bentley, *The Profession of Dramatist in Shakespeare's Time, 1590–1642* (Princeton, N.J., 1971)
Bible	Bishops' Bible (1568), STC 2099
Bishai	Nadia Bishai, '"At the signe of the gunne": *Titus Andronicus*, the London book trade and the literature of crime 1590–1615', in Liberty Stanavage and Paxton Hehmeyer (eds), *Titus Out of Joint: Reading the Fragmented Titus Andronicus* (Cambridge, 2012), 7–48
Blayney	Peter Blayney, *The Stationers' Company and the Printers of London 1501–1557* (Cambridge, 2013)
Bloom	Gina Bloom, '"My feet see better than my eyes": spatial mastery and the game of masculinity in *Arden of Faversham*'s amphitheatre', *Theatre Survey*, 53.1, April 2012, 5–28: https://doi.org/10.1017/S0040557411000743
Bourus and Taylor	Gary Taylor and Terri Bourus, 'Introduction' to *Arden of Faversham*, in B&T (*CRE*), 1–18
Boorde	Andrew Boorde, *The Breviary of Health* (1547), STC 3373.5

Bourne	William Bourne, *The Art of Shooting in Great Ordnance* (1587), 2nd edn (1578), STC 3240
Bourus	Terri Bourus, 'Staging *Arden of Feversham*', paper for seminar on *Arden of Faversham* at the 44th Annual Meeting of the SAA, New Orleans, 23–6 April 2016
Breviat	*The Breviat Chronicle* (Canterbury, 1552), STC 9968
Butler	Samuel Butler, *Hudibras in three parts* (1684)
Cambises	Thomas Preston, *A Lamentable Tragedy Mixed Full of Pleasant Mirth, Containing the Life of Cambises* (1569/70), STC 20287
Campaspe	John Lyly, *A Most Excellent Comedy of Alexander, Campaspe, and Diogenes* (1584), STC 17048
Chaste Maid	Thomas Middleton, *A Chaste Maid in Cheapside*, ed. Linda Woodbridge, in Gary Taylor and John Lavagnino (eds), *Thomas Middleton: The Collected Works* (Oxford, 2007)
Chatterley	Albert Chatterley, 'Watson, Thomas', *ODNB* (2004)
Christensen	Ann Christensen, *Separation Scenes: Domestic Drama in Early Modern England* (Lincoln, Nebr., 2017)
Churchyard, *Challenge*	Thomas Churchyard, *Churchyard's Challenge* (1593), STC 5220
Churchyard, *Charge*	Thomas Churchyard, *Churchyard's Charge* (1580), STC 5240
Churchyard, *Worthiness*	Thomas Churchyard, *The Worthiness of Wales* (1587), STC 5261
Cioni	Fernando Cioni, 'Refashioning Italian theatrical and dramatic conventions: prologues, epilogues and inductions in early modern English drama', *Early Modern Culture Online*, 4.1 (March 2018), doi:10.15845/emco.v4i1.1508 (Appendix)
Collyer	Henry Collyer, '*A Short Account of Lord* Cheyne, *Lord* Shorland, *and Mr.* Thomas Arden' (Canterbury, 1739)
Cooper	Thomas Cooper, *The Mystery of Witchcraft* (1617), STC 5701
Copland	Robert Copland, *The Seven Sorrows That Women Have When Their Husbands Be Dead* (1565), STC 5734

Cornelia	Robert Garnier, *Cornelia*, trans. Thomas Kyd (1594), STC 11622
Cotgrave	Randle Cotgrave, *A Dictionary of the French and English Tongues* (1611), STC 5830
Craig and Kinney	Hugh Craig and Arthur F. Kinney (eds), *Shakespeare, Computers and the Mystery of Authorship* (Cambridge, 2009)
Cust	Lionel Cust, 'Arden of Feversham', *Archaeologia Cantiana*, xxxiv (1920), 101–38
Damon and Pythias	Richard Edwards, *Damon and Pythias* (1571), STC 7514
Davidson	Diane Davidson, *Feversham. A Story of Murder and Satanic Love* (New York, 1969)
Day	Angel Day, *The English Secretary* (1586), STC 6401
Dekker	Thomas Dekker, *The Shoemaker's Holiday* (*c.* 1599), ed. Jonathan Gil Harris, New Mermaids (2008)
Dent	R. W. Dent, *Shakespeare's Proverbial Language: An Index* (Berkeley and Los Angeles, Calif., 1981)
Dessen and Thomson	Alan Dessen and Leslie Thomson, *A Dictionary of Stage Directions in English Drama 1580–1642* (Cambridge, 2001)
Di Ponio	Amanda Di Ponio, *The Early Modern Theatre of Cruelty and its Doubles: Artaud and Influence* (Cham, Switzerland, 2018)
Dolan	Frances Dolan, *Dangerous Familiars: Representations of Domestic Crime in England, 1550–1700* (Ithaca, NY, 1994)
Edward II	Christopher Marlowe, *The Troublesome Reign and Lamentable Death of Edward the Second* (1594), STC 17437
Egan	Gabriel Egan, *The Struggle for Shakespeare's Text: Twentieth-Century Editorial Theory and Practice* (Cambridge, 2010)
Elegies	Christopher Marlowe, *The Complete Poems and Translations*, ed. Stephen Orgel (Harmondsworth, 2007)
Elliott and Greatley-Hirsch	Jack Elliott and Brett Greatley-Hirsch, 'Arden of Faversham, Shakespearean authorship, and "the print of many"', in Taylor and Egan, 139–81
Elvetham	anon., *The Honourable Entertainment* ... *at Elvetham* (1591), STC 7583

Endymion	John Lyly, *Endymion*, ed. David Bevington, Revels Plays (Manchester, 1996)
Erne	Lukas Erne, 'Introduction', in *Soliman and Perseda*
Esslin	Martin Esslin, *Antonin Artaud* (Auckland, 1977)
Everyman	anon., *Everyman* (1535), STC 1606.5
Fair Em	anon., *Fair Em the Miller's Daughter* (1591), STC 7675
Farmer and Lesser	Alan B. Farmer and Zachary Lesser, 'The popularity of playbooks revisited', *SQ*, 56.1 (2005), 1–32
Fenne	Thomas Fenne, 'Hecubae's Mishaps', in *Fennes Fruits* (1590), STC 10763
Fennor	William Fennor, *Cornucopiae* (1612), STC 10782.5
Fliotos and Vierow	Anne Fliotos and Wendy Vierow, *American Women Stage Directors of the Twentieth Century* (Champaign, Ill., 2008)
Foakes	R. A. Foakes (ed.), *Henslowe's Diary*, 2nd edn (Cambridge, 2002)
Folger MS	William Cook, 'Miscellaneous material chiefly relating to Thomas Arden and his murder, including a manuscript copy of the play' (*c.* 1750–70), Folger D.a.6
Foxe	John Foxe, *Christ Jesus Triumphant* (1579), STC 11231
FQ	Edmund Spenser, *The Faerie Queene* (1590), STC 23081
Freebury Jones	Darren Freebury Jones, 'The diminution of Thomas Kyd', *JEMS*, 8 (2019), 251–77
Freeman	Janet Ing Freeman, 'Mitchell [Mychell], John', *ODNB* (2004)
Gascoigne	George Gascoigne, *The Poesies of George Gascoigne Esquire* (1575), STC 11637
Gibson	James M. Gibson, *Kent*, 2 vols, Records of Early English Drama (Toronto, 2002)
Gilchrist	Kim Gilchrist, 'Mucedorus; the last ludic playbook, the first stage Arcadia', *Sha*, 15.1 (2019), 1–20
Gorboduc	Thomas Norton and Thomas Sackville, *The Tragedy of Gorboduc*, Q3 (1590), STC 17029
Gowing	Laura Gowing, *Domestic Dangers* (Oxford, 1996)

319

di Grassi	Giacomo di Grassi, *The True Art of Defence* (1594), STC 12190
Great Herbal	anon., *The Great Herbal* (1526), STC 13176
Hamling	Tara Hamling, *Decorating the Godly Household* (New Haven, Conn., 2010)
Hamling and Richardson	Tara Hamling and Catherine Richardson, *A Day at Home in Early Modern England: Material Culture and Domestic Life, 1500–1700* (New Haven, Conn., 2017)
Hart	Alfred Hart, *Stolne and Surreptitious Copies: A Comparative Study of Shakespeare's Bad Quartos* (Melbourne, 1942)
Hayward	Maria Hayward, *Rich Apparel: Clothing and the Law in Henry VIII's England*, (Ashgate, 2009)
Headlam	W. Headlam, '*Arden of Feversham*: "pathaires"', *Athenaeum*, 3974, 26 December 1903
Helgerson	Richard Helgerson, 'Murder in Faversham: Holinshed's impertinent history', in Donald R. Kelley and David Harris Sacks (eds), *The Historical Imagination in Early Modern Britain* (Cambridge, 1997), 133–58
Hercules	*Hercules Furens*, trans. Jasper Heywood, in *Seneca*
Hindle, 'Peace'	Steve Hindle, 'The keeping of the public peace', in P. Griffiths, A. Fox and S. Hindle (eds), *The Experience of Authority in Early Modern England* (1996)
Hindle, *State*	Steve Hindle, *The State and Social Change in Early Modern England* (Basingstoke, 2000)
Hirrel	Michael J. Hirrel, 'Thomas Watson, playwright: origins of modern English drama', in David McInnis and Matthew Steggle (eds), *Lost Plays in Shakespeare's England* (New York, 2014), 187–207
Holinshed	Raphael Holinshed et al., *Chronicles of England, Scotland, and Ireland*, 2nd edn (1587, STC 13569), vol. 1; see also 1st edn (1577, STC 13568), vol. 1
Honigmann and Brock	E. A. J. Honigmann and Susan Brock (eds), *Playhouse Wills, 1558–1642: An Edition of Wills by Shakespeare and His Contemporaries in the London Theatre* (Manchester, 1993)

Hyde	Patricia Hyde, *Thomas Arden in Faversham* (Faversham, 1996)
Ingram	Martin Ingram, *Church Courts, Sex and Marriage in England 1570–1640* (Cambridge, 1990)
Jackson, *Determining*	MacDonald P. Jackson, *Determining the Shakespeare Canon: 'Arden of Faversham' and 'A Lover's Complaint'* (Oxford, 2014)
Jackson, '*Lover's*'	MacDonald P. Jackson, 'Shakespeare, *Arden of Faversham*, and *A Lover's Complaint*', in Taylor and Egan, 123–35
Jackson, 'Material'	MacDonald P. Jackson, 'Material for an edition of *Arden of Feversham*', unpub. B.Litt thesis (Oxford, 1963)
Jackson, 'Quarrel'	MacDonald P. Jackson, 'Shakespeare and the quarrel scene in *Arden of Faversham*', *SQ*, 57 (2006), 249–93
Jansohn	Christa Jansohn, 'From private to public evil', *Actes des congrès de la Société française Shakespeare*, 15 (1997)
Jew of Malta	Christopher Marlowe, *The Jew of Malta*, ed. William H. Sherman and Chloe Preedy, AEMD (2021)
Jowett	John Jowett, 'Shakespeare supplemented', in Douglas A. Brooks (ed.), *The Shakespeare Apocrypha* (Lampeter, 2007), 39–73
Kenilworth	Robert Laneham, *The Entertainment unto the Queen's Majesty at Killingworth [Kenilworth] Castle* (1575), STC 15190.5
Kerrigan	John Kerrigan, *Shakespeare's Binding Language* (Oxford, 2016)
Kesson, 'Comedy'	Andy Kesson, 'Was comedy a genre in English early modern drama?', *British Journal of Aesthetics*, 54.2 (2014), 213–25
Kesson, 'Woman'	Andy Kesson, '"It is a pity you are not a woman": John Lyly and the creation of woman', *SB*, 33.1 (2015), 33–47
Kinney	Arthur F. Kinney, 'Authoring *Arden of Faversham*', in Craig and Kinney, 78–99
Kirwan	Peter Kirwan, *Shakespeare and the Idea of Apocrypha* (Cambridge, 2015)
Knutson	Roslyn Knutson, 'Shakespeare's repertory', in David Scott Kastan (ed.), *A Companion to Shakespeare* (Oxford, 1999), 346–61

Lambarde   William Lambarde, *A Perambulation of Kent* (1576), STC 15175

'Lamentation'   anon., 'The complaint and lamentation of Mistresse Arden of Feversham in Kent' (n.d.), STC 732

Levin   Richard Levin, '*Titus Andronicus* and "The ballad thereof"', *NQ*, 47.1 (2000), 63–8

Like Will   Ulpian Fulwell, *Like Will to Like* (1568, repr. 1587), STC 11473.5, 11474

Lillo   George Lillo, *Arden of Feversham: A Historical Tragedy* (1762)

Lockwood   Tom Lockwood, 'Introduction', *Arden of Faversham*, ed. Martin White (1990; rev. ed. 2007)

Lodge and Greene   Thomas Lodge and Robert Greene, *A Looking Glass for London and England* (1594)

Loughnane   Rory Loughnane, 'Shakespeare and the idea of early authorship', in Loughnane and Power, 21–53

Loughnane and Power   Rory Loughnane and Andrew Power (eds), *Early Shakespeare, 1588–1594* (Cambridge, 2020)

Machyn   *The Diary of Henry Machyn, Citizen and Merchant-Taylor of London, 1550–1563*, ed. J. G. Nichols (1848), *British History Online*: http://www.british-history.ac.uk/camden-record-soc/vol42

Maguire   Laurie Maguire, *Shakespearean Suspect Texts: The 'Bad' Quartos and Their Contexts* (Cambridge, 1996)

Mankind   anon., *Mankind* (c. 1470), Macro Manuscript Folger V.a.354

Marino   James J. Marino, 'Lost in the Huntington: or, *Arden of Faversham* for Jacobites', *Studies in Philology*, 116.1 (2019), 54–72

Marrapodi   Michele Marrapodi (ed.), *Italian Culture in the Drama of Shakespeare and His Contemporaries* (Aldershot, 2007)

Martin   Randall Martin, '"Arden winketh at his wife's lewdness, & why!": a patrilineal crisis in *Arden of Faversham*', *ET*, 4.1 (2001), 13–33

Mascall   Leonard Mascall, *The First Book of Cattle* (1587), STC 17580

McCormick   John McCormick, *The Victorian Marionette Theatre* (Iowa, 2004)

McKerrow	R. B. McKerrow, 'Edward Allde as a typical trade printer', *Lib*, 4.10 (1929), 121–62
McKerrow and Ferguson	R. B. McKerrow and F. S. Ferguson, *Title-Page Borders Used in England and Scotland 1485–1640* (1932)
McLuskie	Kate McLuskie, *Plays on Women* (Manchester, 1999)
Medea	*The Seventh Tragedy of Seneca, Entitled Medea*, trans. John Studley (1566), STC 22224
Meres	Francis Meres, *Palladis Tamia* (1598), STC 17834
Merry Riddles	anon., *The Book of Merry Riddles* (1617)
Mexia	Pedro Mexia, *The Treasury of Ancient and Modern Times* (1613), STC 17936
Middleton Companion	Gary Taylor and John Lavagnino (eds), *Thomas Middleton and Early Modern Textual Culture: A Companion to the Collected Works* (Oxford, 2013)
Middling Culture	https://middlingculture.com
Mirror	anon., *The Mirror for Magistrates* (1587)
Mortimer	Ian Mortimer, PAPER No. 021, Kent Archaeological Society, 'A directory of medical personnel qualified and practising in the Diocese of Canterbury, circa 1560–1730'; https://kentarchaeology.org.uk/sites/default/files/publications/021.pdf
Mulcaster	Richard Mulcaster, *Positions* (1581), STC 18253
Muldrew	Craig Muldrew, *The Economy of Obligation: The Culture of Credit and Social Relations in Early Modern England* (Basingstoke, 1998)
Munro	Lucy Munro, *Archaic Style in English Literature 1590–1674* (Cambridge, 2013)
Nashe	Thomas Nashe, *Pierce Penniless* (1592)
Neill	Michael Neill, '"This gentle gentleman": social change and the language of status in *Arden of Faversham*', *MRDE*, 10 (1998), 73–97
Nicholls	John Nicholls, *John Niccols Pilgrimage* (1581), STC 18534
Nigro	Don Nigro, *Ardy Fafirsin* (New York, 1993)
Northbrooke	John Northbrooke, *Spiritus Est Vicarius Christi* (1557)
Nosworthy	J. M. Nosworthy, 'The Southouse text of *Arden of Feversham*', *Lib*, 5th series, 5 (1950), 113–29

Oliphant, *Dramatists*   E. H. C. Oliphant (ed.), *Elizabethan Dramatists Other than Shakespeare* (New York, 1931)

Oliphant, 'Hand'   E. H. C. Oliphant, 'Marlowe's hand in *Arden of Faversham*', *New Criterion*, 4 (1926), 76–93

Orlin, *Locating*   Lena Orlin, *Locating Privacy in Tudor London* (Oxford, 2008)

Orlin, *Private*   Lena Orlin, *Private Matters and Public Culture in Post-Reformation England* (Ithaca, NY, 1994)

Osborne   Francis Osborne, *Traditional Memoirs of the Reigns of Q. Elizabeth and King James I* (1658), repr. in Walter Scott, *Secret History of James I* (Edinburgh, 1811)

Painter   William Painter, *The Palace of Pleasure* (1566), STC 19121

Palmer   Stuart Palmer, 'Book printing and Protestant reform in Reformation Canterbury, 1532–1556', in Claire Bartram (ed.), *Kentish Book Culture, Writers, Archives, Libraries and Sociability 1400–1660* (Oxford, 2020), 157–84

Pickering   John Pickering, *Horestes* (1567), STC 19917

Pincombe   Mike Pincombe, 'English Renaissance tragedy: theories and antecedents', in Smith and Sullivan, 3–16

Poel   William Poel, *Lilies that Fester, and Love's Constancy* (New York, 1906)

Power   Andrew J. Power, 'Roles and requirements for *Arden of Faversham*', in B&T (*CRE*), 19–20

Psalms   Thomas Sternhold and John Hopkins, *The Whole Book of Psalms* (1578), STC 2450.5

Puttenham   George Puttenham, *The Art of English Poesie* (1589), STC 20519

Quarles   Francis Quarles, *Job Militant* (1624), STC 20550

Rainolds   John Rainolds, *A Defence of the Judgement of the Reformed Churches* (1609), STC 20607

Rare Triumphs   anon., *The Rare Triumphs of Love and Fortune* (1589), STC 24286

Rasmussen and Bate   Eric Rasmussen and Jonathan Bate, *William Shakespeare and Others: Collaborative Plays*, RSC Shakespeare (Basingstoke, 2013)

Raven   James Raven, 'St. Paul's precinct and the book trade to 1800', in Derek Keene, Arthur Burns and Andrew Saint (eds), *St. Paul's: The Cathedral Church of London, 604–2004* (New Haven, Conn., 2004)

Rich   Barnabe Rich, *A Right Excellent and Pleasant Dialogue Between Mercury and an English Soldier* (1574), STC 20998

Richardson, *Domestic*   Catherine Richardson, *Domestic Life and Domestic Tragedy* (Manchester, 2006)

Richardson, 'Properties'   Catherine Richardson, 'Properties of domestic life: the table in Heywood's *A Woman Killed With Kindness*', in Natasha Korda and Jonathan Gil Harris (eds), *Staged Properties* (Cambridge, 2002)

Richardson, 'Scene'   Catherine Richardson, '"Scene of the murder": *Arden of Faversham* and local performance cultures', *EMLS*, special issue 28 (2019): https:// extra.shu.ac.uk/emls/journal/index.php/emls/ article/view/448

Rolland   John Rolland, *Thrie Tailes of the Thrie Priests of Peblis* (Edinburgh, 1603), STC 19528

Rosenfeld   Sybil Rosenfeld, *Strolling Players & Drama in the Provinces, 1660–1765* (Cambridge, 1939)

RSC 1970   Royal Shakespeare Company, *Arden of Faversham*, production records (1970 production), RSC/SM/2/1970/20: prompt book, RSC/ SM/1/1970/ARD1; stage manager's script, RSC/ SM/1/1970/ARD2; costume designs, RSC/ DE/1/1970/ARD1

RSC 1982/3   Royal Shakespeare Company, *Arden of Faversham* production records (1982/3 production): prompt book, RSC/SM/1/1982/ARD1; production files, RSC/OP/2/1/24, RSC/OP/1/1/11; rehearsal notes and prop list, RSC/SM/2/1982/91; stage manager's script, RSC/SM/2/1982/94; reports, RSC/ SM/2/1982/92; scene breakdown, RSC/ SM/2/1982/93

RSC 2014   Royal Shakespeare Company, *Arden of Faversham*, Swan Theatre (2014 production), production records, prompt book, RSC/ SM/1/2014/ARD1

Sapho   John Lyly, *Sapho and Phao* (1584), STC 17086

Schafer   Elizabeth Schafer, 'Troublesome histories', in T. Hoenselaars (ed.), *The Cambridge Companion to Shakespeare and Contemporary Dramatists* (Cambridge, 2012), 244–68

Schoch   Richard Schoch, *Writing the History of the British Stage, 1660–1900* (Cambridge, 2016)

Schutzman   Julie Schutzman, 'Alice Arden's freedom and the
                           suspended moment of *Arden of Faversham*', *SEL*,
                           36.2 (1996), 289–314
Seneca   *Seneca His Ten Tragedies, Translated Into English*
                           (1581), STC 22221
Sheeha   Iman Sheeha, *Household Servants in Early
                           Modern Domestic Tragedy* (Abingdon, 2020)
Shoemaker's Holiday   Thomas Dekker, *The Shoemaker's Holiday*, ed.
                           Jonathan Gil Harris, New Mermaids, 3rd edn
                           (2008)
Sidney   Philip Sidney, *A Defence of Poetry*, ed. Jan Van
                           Dorsten (1966)
Smith   Henry Smith, *A Preparative to Marriage* (1591),
                           STC 22687
Smith and Sullivan   Emma Smith and Garrett A. Sullivan, Jr (eds), *The
                           Cambridge Companion to English Renaissance
                           Tragedy* (Cambridge, 2010)
Soliman and Perseda   Thomas Kyd, *Soliman and Perseda*, ed. Lukas
                           Erne, Malone Society Reprints (Manchester,
                           2014)
Southouse   Thomas Southouse, *Monasticon Favershamiense
                           in Agro Cantiano* (1671)
Southouse MS   see SMS (*Editions . . . collated*)
Spanish Tragedy   Thomas Kyd, *The Spanish Tragedy*, ed. Clara
                           Calvo and Jesús Tronch, AEMD (2013)
Speaight   George Speaight, *The History of the English
                           Puppet Theatre* (1955)
Spurr   John Spurr, 'A profane history of early modern
                           oaths', *Transactions of the Royal Historical
                           Society*, 11 (2001), 37–63
Stationers' Register   Stationers' Register Online: https://stationersregister.
                           online/
Stern   Tiffany Stern, *Documents of Performance in Early
                           Modern England* (Cambridge, 2009)
Stowe   John Stowe, 'The history of a moste horrible
                           murder commytyd at Fevershame in Kent' (n.d.),
                           BL Harl MS 542, fols 34^r–37^v
Stubbes, *Anatomy*   Philip Stubbes, *The Anatomy of Abuses* (1583),
                           STC 23376
Stubbes, *2 Anatomy*   Philip Stubbes, *The Second Part of the Anatomy of
                           Abuses* (1583), STC 23380
Stubbes, *Motive*   Philip Stubbes, *A Motive to Good Works* (1593),
                           STC 23397

Sullivan, 'Arden' Garrett A. Sullivan, Jr, '"Arden lay murdered in that plot of ground": surveying, land, and *Arden of Faversham*', *ELH*, 61.2 (1994), 231–48

Sullivan, 'Tragic' Garrett A. Sullivan, Jr, 'Tragic subjectivities', in Smith and Sullivan, 73–85

Syme Holger Syme, 'A bit of theatre history: Shakespeare, female characters, and big leads': http://www.dispositio.net/archives/2495, accessed 12.3.2018

1, 2 Tamburlaine Christopher Marlowe, *Tamburlaine the Great . . . Divided into Two Tragical Discourses*, parts 1 and 2 (1590), STC 17425

Tarlinskaja, 'Additions' Marina Tarlinskaja, 'Shakespeare in *Arden of Faversham* and the additions to *The Spanish Tragedy*: versification analysis', *JEMS*, 5 (2016), 175–200

Tarlinskaja, *Versification* Marina Tarlinskaja, *Shakespeare and the Versification of English Drama, 1561–1642* (Farnham, Hants, 2014)

Taylor, Gary Gary Taylor, 'Shakespeare, *Arden of Faversham*, and four forgotten playwrights', *RES*, 71.302 (2020), 867–95

Taylor, John John Taylor, *The Carriers' Cosmography* (1637), STC 23740

Taylor and Egan Gary Taylor and Gabriel Egan (eds), *The New Oxford Shakespeare: Authorship Companion* (Oxford, 2017)

Taylor and Loughnane Gary Taylor and Rory Loughnane, 'Canon and chronology', in Taylor and Egan, 417–602

Temple Robert Temple, *A Sermon Teaching Discretion in Matters of Religion* (1592), STC 23869

Treswell Ralph Treswell, *London Surveys*, ed. John Schofield (1987)

Tusser Thomas Tusser, *A Hundred Good Points of Husbandry* (1570), STC 24373

Verney Frances Parthenope, Lady Verney, *Peasant Properties, and Other Selected Essays* (1885)

Vickers, 'Authorship' Brian Vickers, 'Authorship candidates for *Arden of Faversham*: Kyd, Shakespeare and Thomas Watson', *Studies in Philology*, 118.2 (spring 2021), 308–41

Vickers, 'Kyd' Brian Vickers, 'Thomas Kyd: secret sharer', *TLS*, 18 April 2008, 13–15

Vincent	Arthur Vincent, *Twelve Bad Women: Illustrations and Reviews of Feminine Turpitude Set Forth by Impartial Hands* (1897)
Wells	Stanley Wells, 'Introduction' to *Two Gentlemen of Verona*, in William Shakespeare, *The Complete Works*, ed. John Jowett, William Montgomery, Gary Taylor and Stanley Wells (Oxford, 1986)
West	Richard West, *The Court of Conscience or Dick Whippers Sessions* (1607), STC 25263
Whigham	Frank Whigham, *Seizures of the Will* (Cambridge, 1996)
Whipday	Emma Whipday, '"Marrow prying neighbours": staging domestic space and neighbourhood surveillance in *Arden of Faversham*', *Cahiers Élisabéthains*, 88.1 (2015), 95–110
Wiggins	(see note at head of *Abbreviations and references*) Martin Wiggins (in association with Catherine Richardson for electronic edition), *British Drama 1533–1642: A Catalogue*, 11 vols (Oxford, 2011–)
Wiggins, *Journeymen*	Martin Wiggins, *Journeymen in Murder: The Assassin in English Renaissance Drama* (Oxford, 1991)
Williams	Gordon Williams, *A Dictionary of Sexual Language and Imagery in Shakespearean and Stuart Literature*, 3 vols, continuously numbered (1994)
Williamson	Elizabeth Williamson, 'The uses and abuses of prayer book properties in *Hamlet, Richard III*, and *Arden of Faversham*', *ELR*, 39.2 (2009), 371–95
Withals	John Withals, *A Short Dictionary for Young Beginners* (1553), STC 25874
Women's Sharp	anon., *Women's Sharp Revenge* (1640), STC 23706

MODERN PRODUCTIONS CITED

1897	Elizabethan Stage Society, St George's Hall, London, *Lilies That Fester* (one-act version of *Arden of Faversham*), dir. William Poel
1925	Renaissance Theatre at the Scala, Charlotte Street, London, dir. William Poel
1952	Davington Priory, Davington, near Faversham, 700th anniversary of town charter celebrations, produced by John Spalding

1955	Theatre Workshop, Theatre Royal, Angel Lane, Stratford East, dir. Joan Littlewood
1967	Hamburg State Opera, Hamburg, Germany, *Arden muss Sterben*, music by Alexander Goehr and libretto by Erich Fried, dir. Egon Monk, cond. Charles Mackerras
1970	La MaMa Experimental Theatre Club, New York, dir. Andrei Serban
1970	RSC, The Roundhouse, London, dir. Buzz Goodbody
1975	RADA, Vanburgh Theatre, London, and Queen Elizabeth's School, Faversham, dir. Geoff Bullen
1982	RSC, The Other Place, Stratford-upon-Avon, dir. Terry Hands
1983	RSC, The Pit, London, dir. Terry Hands
1986	Arden's House, Faversham, amateur production, dir. Les Shaw
1990	Classics on a Shoestring, Old Red Lion Theatre, Islington, dir. Katie Mitchell
1992	Arden's House, Faversham, amateur production, produced by Alan Pope for 400th anniversary of the play
2000	Arden's House, Faversham, amateur production, dir. Ian Garner
2014	RSC, Swan Theatre, Royal Shakespeare Company, dir. Polly Findlay
2016	Hoosier Bard Theatre Company, Indianapolis University-Purdue University, Indianapolis, dir. Terri Bourus

INDEX